T0332304

Pedagogy, Presence, and Motivation in Online Education

Aaron Michael Perez
GOAL Academy, USA

Şenol Orakcı
Aksaray University, Turkey

IGI Global
PUBLISHER of TIMELY KNOWLEDGE

A volume in the Advances in Mobile and Distance Learning (AMDL) Book Series

Published in the United States of America by
  IGI Global
  Information Science Reference (an imprint of IGI Global)
  701 E. Chocolate Avenue
  Hershey PA, USA 17033
  Tel: 717-533-8845
  Fax: 717-533-8661
  E-mail: cust@igi-global.com
  Web site: http://www.igi-global.com

Library of Congress Cataloging-in-Publication Data

Names: Perez, Aaron, 1976- editor. | Orakcı, Şenol, 1983- editor.
Title: Pedagogy, presence, and motivation in online education / Aaron Perez
  and Senol Orakci, Editor.
Description: Hershey, PA : Information Science Reference, [2022] | Includes
  bibliographical references and index. | Summary: "The objective of this
  edited book is to provide real-world solutions to online and hybrid
  educators with the aim of training educators to develop online culture,
  healthy and inclusive communication, and how to use the online classroom
  environment in parallel or stand-alone with a face-to-face classroom"--
  Provided by publisher.
Identifiers: LCCN 2021027682 (print) | LCCN 2021027683 (ebook) | ISBN
  9781799880776 (hardcover) | ISBN 9781799880783 (paperback) | ISBN
  9781799880790 (ebook)
Subjects: LCSH: Web-based instruction. | Critical pedagogy. | Motivation in
  education. | Classroom environment.
Classification: LCC LB1044.87 .P44 2022 (print) | LCC LB1044.87 (ebook) |
  DDC 371.33/44678--dc23
LC record available at https://lccn.loc.gov/2021027682
LC ebook record available at https://lccn.loc.gov/2021027683

This book is published in the IGI Global book series Advances in Mobile and Distance Learning (AMDL) (ISSN: 2327-1892; eISSN: 2327-1906)

British Cataloguing in Publication Data
A Cataloguing in Publication record for this book is available from the British Library.

All work contributed to this book is new, previously-unpublished material.
The views expressed in this book are those of the authors, but not necessarily of the publisher.

For electronic access to this publication, please contact: eresources@igi-global.com.

Advances in Mobile and Distance Learning (AMDL) Book Series

ISSN:2327-1892
EISSN:2327-1906

Editor-in-Chief: Patricia Ordóñez de Pablos Universidad de Oviedo, Spain

MISSION

Private and public institutions have made great strides in the fields of mobile and distance learning in recent years, providing greater learning opportunities outside of a traditional classroom setting. While the online learning revolution has allowed for greater learning opportunities, it has also presented numerous challenges for students and educators alike. As research advances, online educational settings can continue to develop and advance the technologies available for learners of all ages.

The **Advances in Mobile and Distance Learning** (AMDL) Book Series publishes research encompassing a variety of topics related to all facets of mobile and distance learning. This series aims to be an essential resource for the timeliest research to help advance the development of new educational technologies and pedagogy for use in online classrooms.

COVERAGE

- Mobile Learning
- Technology Platforms and System Development
- Managing Sustainable Learning
- Administration and Organization
- Lifelong Learning
- Globalization
- Course Design
- Online Collaborative Learning
- Online Class Management
- Student-Teacher Interaction

IGI Global is currently accepting manuscripts for publication within this series. To submit a proposal for a volume in this series, please contact our Acquisition Editors at Acquisitions@igi-global.com or visit: http://www.igi-global.com/publish/.

Titles in this Series

For a list of additional titles in this series, please visit:
www.igi-global.com/book-series/advances-mobile-distance-learning/37162

Cases on Innovative and Successful Uses of Digital Resources for Online Larning
Pamela Sullivan (James Madison University, USA) Brian Sullivan (James Madison University, USA) and Jessica Lantz (James Madison University, USA)
Information Science Reference • © 2022 • 396pp • H/C (ISBN: 9781799890041) • US $195.00

Online Distance Learning Course Design and Multimedia in E-Learning
Ana Paula Lopes (Polytechnic of Porto, Portugal) and Filomena Soares (Polytechnic of Porto, Portugal)
Information Science Reference • © 2022 • 302pp • H/C (ISBN: 9781799897064) • US $195.00

Measurement Methodologies to Assess the Effectiveness of Global Online Learning
Pedro Isaias (University of New South Wales, Australia) Tomayess Issa (Curtin University, Australia) and Piet Kommers (UNESCO, The Netherlands)
Information Science Reference • © 2022 • 366pp • H/C (ISBN: 9781799886617) • US $195.00

Transferring Language Learning and Teaching From Face-to-Face to Online Settings
Christina Nicole Giannikas (Cyprus University of Technology, Cyprus)
Information Science Reference • © 2022 • 382pp • H/C (ISBN: 9781799887171) • US $195.00

Handbook of Research on Managing and Designing Online Courses in Synchronous and Asynchronous Environments
Gürhan Durak (Balıkesir University, Turkey) and Serkan Çankaya (İzmir Democracy University, Turkey)
Information Science Reference • © 2022 • 731pp • H/C (ISBN: 9781799887010) • US $245.00

For an entire list of titles in this series, please visit:
www.igi-global.com/book-series/advances-mobile-distance-learning/37162

701 East Chocolate Avenue, Hershey, PA 17033, USA
Tel: 717-533-8845 x100 • Fax: 717-533-8661
E-Mail: cust@igi-global.com • www.igi-global.com

Table of Contents

Detailed Table of Contents

Şenol Orakcı, Aksaray University, Turkey
Savaş Karagöz, Aksaray University, Turkey

The aim of this chapter is to examine and assess distance education, purpose and requirements of distance education, basic principles in the effective use of distance education, the role of teacher and student in distance education, material in distance education, and measurement and evaluation in distance education. It also aims at determining learning theories in distance education technology such as behavioral learning theory, cognitive learning theory, constructivist learning theory, adult education theory, theory of independent study, autonomy theory, theory of industrialization of teaching, connectivism learning theory, and interaction and communication theory. In the last part of the chapter, technology-supported education methods such as interactive video, teleconferencing systems, cloud technology, virtual reality, and web-based (online) training were explained in detail.

Prasad G., Dayananda Sagar University, India

Higher education in the modern era is gradually changing. Students from lecture rooms are rapidly volunteering into the digital world of the internet, embracing technologies like the distant learning with unique pedagogy. Education, to educate future citizens to operate in the field of resource sharing, will need to undergo further adaptive changes. Flexibility of location and time, personalization of the offer, collaboration, and adaptability are all trends of techniques and tools. This research work has been carried as a contribution towards the goals of National Education Policy 2020 framework proposed by Government of India. To equip citizens to engage in and benefit from the increasingly connected virtual and physical worlds, together with the rising need for information alongside limited time resources, higher education will be dynamic.

Chapter 3

Digital AVC (which stands for accessibility, voice, and consistency) is a three-tiered system that helps teachers develop a digital presence in their online or hybrid classrooms. Online educators need to be able to utilize the technology available to them to intentionally create an online presence that is both appealing and inviting to students so that students are more interested in interacting with their online class and learning materials. This chapter explains how educators can create an online presence that makes students feel connected, valued, and interested in engaging in the classroom material through a more intentional focus on their own digital accessibility, digital voice, and digital consistency.

Chapter 4

The mission of this chapter is to provide principals and teachers with an understanding of how to create a positive learning culture within an online classroom through utilization of the engagement triangle: students, teachers/school staff, and outside community members. The chapter introduces student agency through online instructional strategies and techniques for teachers to increase student motivation. Further, assessment practices are addressed in ways that can add to a positive classroom culture. At the end of the chapter, case study scenarios and reflective questions will be shared for practicing P-12 teachers to consider when designing learning opportunities in their online courses.

Chapter 5

Education systems and methods are shaped according to the needs of societies and technology. Today, technological possibilities bring about deep and radical changes in every field. With the educational environments becoming computer-aided and online, the measurement and evaluation of student achievement had to be computer-assisted and online. The purpose of this chapter is to provide the basic logic of computer-based measurement and evaluation and to explain the methods. Computer-based assessment and evaluation have many benefits for students, teachers, and institutions. While the advantages include continuous monitoring of students, low cost, and rapid and equal access to many students at the same time, it is seen as a disadvantage that students have the opportunity to cheat and get outside help.

Chapter 6

    Devery J. Rodgers, California State University, Long Beach, USA
    Alvaro Brito, Boise State University, USA

Virtual hybrid education is challenging for the average educator and less known with the additional stresses of emergency remote education. In most cases, educators rely on trial-and-error to determine what works best in online and hybrid instruction. Through this applied research, two education technology specialists engage in a duoethnography of their support over the 2020-2021 pandemic year. Having assisted hundreds of educators in an urban K12 school district with online and hybrid engagement practices, this study answers the question, "How can technology help facilitate student engagement in online and hybrid environments?" This chapter is built from narrative analysis and provides research-based and practitioner-focused promising practice techniques and real-world solutions to educators in building and maintaining a positive digital culture.

Chapter 7

    Juliana M. Namada, United State International University Africa, Kenya

Asynchronous e-learning has been popularized by the onset and rapid spread of the COVID-19 pandemic. This is because this approach of e-learning speaks to social distancing which is a key element in controlling the spread of the coronavirus. This chapter starts by defining asynchronous e-learning and contrasting it with the synchronous approach. It progresses into identifying and discussing different digital tools used in asynchronous e-learning among them threaded discussion forums, recorded live events, documented cases, emails, blogs, wikis, and reflective journals. The chapter describes interactive, mediated, active, and collaborative learning as some of the key strategies used in asynchronous e-learning. It proceeds to explain the principles used in the development of asynchronous content together with highlighting best practice in effective asynchronous teaching. The chapter ends by identifying some of the key challenges associated with asynchronous e-learning and suggests mitigation strategies for dealing with the challenges.

Chapter 8

Şenol Orakcı, Aksaray University, Turkey
Mehmet Durnali, Bülent Ecevit University, Turkey

Online education is one of the most dynamic and enriched forms of learning available today. The aim of the present study is to reveal the self-regulated learning levels of pre-service teacher and to determine whether these levels change in terms of their gender and class. The sample of the study consists of Aksaray University Educational Sciences Department students who received online education due to the COVID-19 global epidemic in the 2020-2021 academic year. The data of the study were collected with the "Self-Regulation in Self-Paced Open and Distance Learning Environments Scale." The first result of the study revealed that the self-regulated learning levels of the participants were close to medium. The self-regulation scores of male students receiving online education at university were also found to be significantly higher than the scores of female students. The final result obtained from the research is the existence of a significant difference between grade level and self-regulated learning skills.

Chapter 9

Marina Apaydin, American University of Cairo, Egypt
John D. Branch, University of Michigan, USA
Amy Gillett, University of Michigan, USA

Virtual exchanges are an emerging form of learning in which students from different countries are connected via technology. The authors created a virtual exchange, Business & Culture, to connect students at institutions in the USA, Egypt, Lebanon, and Libya. The focus of the Business & Culture virtual exchange was on teaching cultural competence, a key skill in today's increasingly globalized workplace. In this chapter, they explore the design and implementation of Business & Culture. They enumerate the challenges of incorporating the needs and resources of four different institutions. They discuss the benefits of the Business & Cultural virtual exchange to both students and instructors. And they outline the evaluation of the Business & Cultural virtual exchange, which allowed them to both gauge its effectiveness and improve its design and implementation.

Chapter 10

Aaron M. Perez, GOAL Academy, USA

Principal leadership is a role that revolves around quickly changing tasks. In a broad sense, the ability of a principal leader to communicate clearly, build culture, and empower others has positive benefits that lead to school progress. Along with these skills, another skill to consider mastering is plan development and follow-through. Besides skill-related tasks, taking time to meet with staff to connect on a personal level and empowering staff to continue their professional development is a great method for building work culture, just as the leader would expect staff to connect with students. This is one technique for modeling how one would like his or her staff to interact with students. Lastly, this chapter will focus on some lessons learned from the pandemic, specifically revolved around leading through unknown territory, being comfortable with being uncomfortable, and focusing on the fundamentals of the organization.

Chapter 11

The purpose of this chapter is to explain multi-tiered systems of support (MTSS), the process required to implement school change efforts, and how MTSS differs in the virtual environment. The chapter includes a history of legislation leading to the development of MTSS framework and recent legislative changes surrounding school improvement. The components and responsibilities within each level of education related to MTSS are examined through a hierarchy with a discussion of barriers and aspects specific to virtual schools. The chapter also incorporates necessary actions within each stage of implementation and examples of programs that have been used to improve student outcomes at each school level.

Chapter 12

The purpose of this study was to determine the perceptions of the sport sciences students on distance education in terms of the advantages, disadvantages, difficulties, concerns, and suggestions during the COVID-19 period. The mixed method was used in the study. Participants were 312 volunteer university students. A questionnaire and an open-ended question were used. Results indicated that male students considered the advantages of distance education more important. In addition, students studying in the departments of Coaching Education and Physical Education and Sport Teaching considered the disadvantages of distance education more important. Female students considered the difficulties of distance education less important, and students who prefer distance education had more concerns about distance education. In conclusion, students suggested extending the duration of the lesson, strengthening the technology and internet infrastructure, conducting the lessons interactively, teaching the lessons more efficiently by the teachers, and standardizing the lesson practices.

Preface

Pedagogy, Presence, and Motivation in Online Education was born out of a time of uncertainty within the field of education. Teachers and School leaders were struggling to find answers to solve their educational issues. Educators were struggling to mimic their authentic classroom experiences so as to ensure students were still learning, growing, and developing.

This book is intended for K-12 school leaders, teachers, college instructors, university professors, and faculty in teacher preparation programs.

When writing this book, Dr. Aaron Perez is a Principal for an online/hybrid high school in Colorado, United States. He earned his doctorate from Regent University in Education. The program is a blended/online program, and he completed this program utilizing online resources first-hand as an end user. What one must understand about online programs is that they are more difficult than brick-and-mortar schools in so many ways, and that is why brick-and-mortar educators were having difficulty with provide high quality online education to their students.

Dr. Senol Orakci is an Associate Professor in the Department of Curriculum & Instruction at Askray University in Turkey. His work focuses on teacher education, curriculum studies, and education technology.

This book employs research from online and online/hybrid high schools and online university programs around the world to understand best practices in online education. Topics such as digital presence, culture, student assessment, principal leadership, MTSS and distance education and sports sciences will be covered. This book has been an exciting journey as we discuss the hardships of navigating online education and how we have overcome these struggles with positive results.

Chapter 1 opens with an examination and critical assessment of distance education. First, an overview of distance education (purpose and requirements) and some of the basic recommended principles of how distance education can be utilized. Various learning theories will be discussed for the reader to examine how these learning theories can be implemented in distance education. Additionally, a detailed discussion on "technology supported education methods". Though it is not the role of education to keep up with technology, the author discusses how technology will promote educational progress.

Building on this idea, Chapter 2 is a research study aimed at developing a smart classroom management system. This system is based on the Internet of Things. Specific examples are provided as well as research on how other companies have addressed this phenomenon. According to the author, smart class best practices begin with developing a student friendly environment. This is accomplished by ensuring that access to education is equitable and of high quality. Practical examples of how one can accomplish this are provided.

In Chapter 3, there is a focus on digital presence: how teachers appear to, interact with, and present themselves to students within an online classroom setting. A three-tiered system is described: digital accessibility, digital voice, and digital consistency. The discussion on digital presence begins with how it relates to online teaching. Fundamentally, as the author notes, great teaching starts with quality relationships between the educator and student. Next, there is a practical discussion about how to build an online course in such a way that continually engages students. Then, there is pragmatic analysis of Digital Accessibility, Voice, and Consistency in the scope of an online environment.

The next chapter continues the discussion of online school culture development by an in-depth discussion of specific instruction, assessment and engagement strategies for online education. The foundation of the discussion is focused on the foundation of school structure. According to the author, it is important to build intentional and authentic opportunities for students and staff to interact. Students cannot feel as if they are alone or isolated from a conducive online learning environment. Another key component of online education is student agency. It is critical for students to feel empowered to learn. There is a practical discussion on how agency is fostered and the role of motivation in student empowerment. Finally, a discussion on how to utilize assessments to foster positive culture. This last concept ties back to the first, in that authentic and intentional opportunities can promote positive student/ teacher relationships.

Assessments can be challenging in an online and hybrid learning environment, especially those that promote student reflection and improvement. In Chapter 5, various online assessment tools are examined and provided in a practical way that helps educators understand how to utilize them efficiently. For example, just as students are expected to learn about the three branches of government in their history class, it is also important for students to learn how they will be assessed and ask for students' feedback around the assessment process. Though students may not have other teachers that do this, doing things with consistency and intentionality will build a positive culture in your classroom by empowering student agency. Formative and summative assessments are discussed in a virtual learning environment and when each type of assessment can be utilized to enhance student learning.

Chapter 6 is an investigation of online and hybrid student engagement. There are many more challenges in an online or hybrid environment in comparison to those in a face-to-face or brick-and-mortar environment. This study aims to answer the following question: how can technology help facilitate student engagement in online and hybrid environments? Other sub-questions are answered as well to understand the interplay of technology and student engagement. The research provided in this chapter discusses the importance of student engagement in online and hybrid education. In a general sense, teachers (and other school educators) that were used to face-to-face instruction were likely not trained (nor potentially had previous experience) teaching or leading in an online or hybrid environment. There is a plethora of recommendations from this research study to engage students in various ways.

Teaching asynchronous courses is quite challenging. From designing the course content to utilizing different learning strategies, asynchronous learning can be very time consuming when attempting to troubleshoot how to best instruct students. Chapter 7 is a great resource for various learning strategies and course content design. Additionally, the author describes 10 best practice solutions for effective asynchronous teaching that support student engagement. The author then cautions educators about some of the key challenges for online learning. For example, in online group projects, it is more difficult to know if a student is "joyriding in group assignments". However, the teacher can utilize anonymous team evaluations to provide peer feedback.

Chapter 8 examines how pre-service teachers learning levels are affected. Online self-regulated learning is a key attribute to online learning. These skills are personal skills in which students are actively involved in their learning and can observe how they are moving through the process and can take the skills learned and apply them to future learning. As explained by the author, "this research was conducted to reveal the self-regulated learning levels of pre-service teacher and to determine whether these levels change in terms of some variables". The findings revel a gender difference in self-regulated learning levels. Further, there were significant differences between learning levels of pre-service teachers self-regulated learning levels. As a result of these results, suggestions are provided to promote self-regulation in a university setting.

The focus of Chapter 9 is on the exploration of a business and culture virtual exchange and the value of business and culture in education. The need for this study is because of an interconnected economy and providing a face-to-face opportunity to understand others cultures and to gain a deeper understanding of their own. Additionally, there is a gap in the curriculum to provide an international exchange for student competencies in business. This chapter discusses the development of this course, as well as its intended impacts.

The focus of Chapter 10 is on principal leadership in an online environment. The lessons learned and seven tips provided in this chapter are key elements for leadership in an online or hybrid environment. In addition to these practical examples, is how to lead a professional learning community or PLC and how to conduct ongoing PLC's and learning and development for teachers and staff.

The next chapter is centered on multi-tiered systems of support or MTSS. MTSS is a method for providing support to low performing students. The students may be low performing for various reasons. The chapter begins with a background on MTSs and various factors related to MTSS implementation. Later, a discussion on barriers to MTSS implementation and then an in-depth discussion on how MTSS can be implemented in a virtual learning environment. For example, the issues with behavior are quite different in virtual environment. In many virtual schools, truancy is one prevalent example that requires intervention. At the end of the day, the intent is the same as brick-and-mortar, to improve student achievement. However, the best practices and issues are different.

The final chapter is to determine how faculty perceive sports science students. The study aimed to answer the advantages and disadvantages of distance education, and the difficulties of distance education. Further, students were also asked about their education preference and suggestions around distance education. One advantage of distance education was that students can listen to recoded lessons more than once. On the other hand, one disadvantage was that immediate feedback is not available. One difficulty was that students were unable to concentrate in the lessons. This research study provides recommendations of distance education that are relevant for how educators develop and implement effective distance education methods.

In conclusion, this book aims to provide practical knowledge and guidance on how to successfully implement teaching, enhance learning, and/or provide appropriate interventions for improving student learning. Additionally, there is a discussion on how to develop a multi-country college course and how to provide K-12 leadership in a virtual learning environment. Though the topics vary, there is a deep analysis and practical use of each chapter to ensure that each topic is fully covered. In closing, we hope you enjoy this resource as much as we have enjoyed writing it!

Chapter 1
The Pedagogy of Distance Education

Şenol Orakcı

(iD) https://orcid.org/0000-0003-1534-1310
Aksaray University, Turkey

Savaş Karagöz
Aksaray University, Turkey

ABSTRACT

The aim of this chapter is to examine and assess distance education, purpose and requirements of distance education, basic principles in the effective use of distance education, the role of teacher and student in distance education, material in distance education, and measurement and evaluation in distance education. It also aims at determining learning theories in distance education technology such as behavioral learning theory, cognitive learning theory, constructivist learning theory, adult education theory, theory of independent study, autonomy theory, theory of industrialization of teaching, connectivism learning theory, and interaction and communication theory. In the last part of the chapter, technology-supported education methods such as interactive video, teleconferencing systems, cloud technology, virtual reality, and web-based (online) training were explained in detail.

INTRODUCTION

Although distance education remains current as a new phenomenon, it dates back to a very long history, almost three centuries ago. Distance education has been tried in different ways at different times. The reasons such as the inability to bring education

DOI: 10.4018/978-1-7998-8077-6.ch001

to all parts of the country or regions, and the disadvantages of time and space can be cited for this situation. As for the definition of distance education, there are several widely accepted definitions of distance education. For example, according to Keegan (1986), distance education is a learning process where learners and teachers are not usually in the same place, under an institutional structure, electronic environments and technologies are used to establish two-way communication, and mostly individual learning takes place. On the other hand, UNESCO (2002) defined distance learning as approaches that focus on opening (facilitating) access to education and training opportunities, freeing learners from the limitations of time and space, and providing individuals with flexible learning opportunities. The most widely accepted definition in recent years is that learners are separate from each other; learners, resources and teachers connect with interactive telecommunication technologies and that it is institution-based, structured (formal) education (Simonson, Smaldino, Albright, & Zvacek, 2006).

Purpose and Requirements of Distance Education

The most basic purpose of distance education is to get rid of the time and space limitations in the education-teaching process. Education is a process. Distance education, on the other hand, has taken an active role in not interrupting this process. Distance education is used not only in the educational process but also in meetings, symposiums, conferences and seminars.

With the development of technology day by day, the distance education process is also being restructured. As a result of this change and development, distance education has become a necessity with the globalization of the world. Distance education requirements can be listed as follows (Altun & Ateş, 2008; Anderson, 2003; Benson, & Samarawickrema, 2009; Demirel, 2010; İşman, 2011; Uşun, 2006):

- Every individual has the right to education
- Time and place constitutes an obstacle in the education process in some cases
- The differentiation of the demands of the society with the increase in the use of technology
- Elimination of financial expenses such as transportation and accommodation
- Providing access to larger audiences at the same time
- It can be used at every stage of education in different disciplines
- Being able to access/repeat the source/message repeatedly with offline education
- Distance education has become a necessity thanks to its benefits such as enabling individuals to act more independently in the learning process.

Basic Principles in the Effective Use of Distance Education

Every training that is done and intended must be within a certain plan and in line with the principles. There must also be certain principles in distance education. According to Uşun (2006), these principles are listed below:

1. Distance education should not be seen as an option of face-to-face education, but rather as a complement to face-to-face education processes.
2. The preparation of the contents should be carried out by commissions formed by members from different disciplines.
3. Written and printed materials to be used in distance education should be prepared in accordance with the principles of material preparation and delivered to students through regular channels.
4. Video recordings should be used instead of live broadcasts. Because live or recorded broadcasts are made at certain times and this timing is not suitable for every individual.

These principles in the distance education process will develop with the increase of its use and feedback. The principles to be considered in distance education can be expanded as follows:

- Since the time spent in front of the screen will increase, the planning should be done accordingly.
- Motivation can disperse more quickly in distance education. Therefore, it is important to keep the motivation high while preparing the educational contents.
- Information flow and time management in distance education should be planned within itself rather than face-to-face education.

The Role of Teacher and Student in Distance Education

Teachers have a great role in the distance education process. These roles can be stated in detail. For example, in distance education, besides teaching, the teacher should be able to intervene as a technical support officer in solving the problems that may arise. He/She should know how to use different programs and should be able to include them in the process in the lessons. During the course, he/she should be able to attract the curiosity and interest of the student on the subject to be learned and motivate the students sufficiently (Garrison, 2003; Liyanagunawardena, Adams, & Williams, 2013). On the other hand, Karadağ and Şen (2014) emphasized the role of the teacher in distance education as a technology specialist, manager, editor, psychologist, instructor, designer, socialization specialist, consultant, researcher, leader, assessment and evaluation specialist, content designer, and a project manager. In short, the teacher should be able to be involved in all aspects of the distance education process.

The concept of student is a broad concept and the age range it addresses is also wide. Today, a teacher takes on the role of a teacher when teaching his/her class. In educational activities such as in-service courses, he/she assumes the role of a student. In face-to-face education, the student has certain responsibilities and roles. In distance education, these responsibilities and roles continue, although they differ. Schrum and Hong (2002) addressed student roles in distance education as follows:

- Having access to the necessary tools for learning
- The ability to use technology effectively
- The ability to implement the aims and objectives of learning
- Having personal traits and character themes
- Being responsible for his/her task
- Having self-learning
- The ability to direct their consultants in terms of access methods
- The ability to communicate effectively in trainings as in face-to-face training.
- The ability to self-assess
- The ability to self-isolate himself/herself from prejudices that cause communication barriers.

Material in Distance Education

The use of materials in the distance education process differs compared to face-to-face education. One of the main reasons for this is that distance education takes the education process out of the classroom environment. In distance education conducted over technological devices, materials are generally selected from virtual environments and obtained by using computer programs. One of the biggest advantages of this is instant access to countless information on the internet with screen sharing. Instructors can deal with the subject from different sources, and ensure the reinforcement of learning with different examples. Distance education has many advantages as well as some disadvantages. In this process, since the students are in front of the screen, they stay away from three-dimensional objects and cannot touch the object. At the same time, they cannot interact with peer groups and exchange ideas on the material. While a material is used by the whole class or school in face-to-face education, it is not possible for a material to circulate from hand to hand in distance education. In the future, these deficiencies can be eliminated with different studies on this subject (Moore, & Kearsley, 2012).

Measurement and Evaluation in Distance Education

In traditional education, measurement and evaluation system fulfills the same task in distance education, as it gives the most reliable information such as giving feedback on student achievements, determining how effective the program is, and determining whether the materials serve the purpose or not.

In distance education, traditional measurement tools are used together with technology. The most common of these is computer and communication technologies. Distance education provides some advantages in terms of providing students with the opportunity to take the exam when they feel ready and facilitating exam evaluations in addition to the use of computer and communication technologies in the measurement and evaluation process, reducing the number of personnel to take part in the exam, and decreasing the expenses of consumables (Freeman, 1997).

In distance education, as in face-to-face education, measurement and evaluation must be done completely in order to increase the effectiveness of education and training and to manage the process in a healthy way.

Learning Theories in Distance Education Technology

With distance education, educational institutions turn into virtual schools, the age of learning becomes unlimited and the roles of teachers change depending on all these. This change caused by new technologies requires considering different perspectives as well as existing theories in the field of learning. As traditional educational environments are replaced by electronic environments, student and teacher characteristics and other components need to be redefined (Ally, 2008).

1. Behavioral Learning Theory

Behavioral learning theory supporters argue that learning is understood only as a result of observable behavior change. Principles of behavioral learning theory are as follows:

- It is essential that the student learns in learning by doing. Because the student learns by what he/she does.
- Reinforcement is important in learning. Giving stimulants that increase the frequency of repetition of behaviors is effective in learning.
- Repetition is important in learning. Repetition is useful as long as it improves learning.

In this context, the achievements that students will reach at the end of the course should be clearly stated in distance education. Various alternatives such as level determination and self-evaluation can be offered to students (Ally, 2008). Quick and detailed feedback with appropriate methods can be given to students in order to monitor their own learning processes. The content of educational materials should be structured logically from simple to complex, from existing knowledge to newly learned, from knowledge to practice.

2. Cognitive Learning Theory

Cognitive theory deals with cognitive processes such as perceiving stimuli, encoding, comparing new information with old ones, storing and remembering, and explains the learning process in this way. The principles of cognitive learning theory are listed below.

- Learning takes place thanks to the interaction of the teacher and the student.
- New learnings are helpful as they offer the opportunity to expand on previous knowledge.
- Learning is an effort to impose meaning.

Cognitive theory accepts learning as an internal process and in this process, prior knowledge, information processing process and how information is coded are emphasized. Various strategies can be tried to facilitate perception and attract attention. In e-learning environments, it is primarily important whether the student is cognitively ready to receive the information. The presented information should be presented in a way that will make the learning process effective, by dividing it into meaningful parts. All strategies that enable students to internalize knowledge by applying, analyzing, synthesizing, interpreting and evaluating can be used. Students can be offered a choice of activities that are suitable for different learning styles and that they can choose according to their learning preferences. Content should be presented taking into account individual differences. It would be appropriate to use strategies to motivate students both internally and externally in the e-learning process. Students should be encouraged to use their cognitive skills and activities should be designed in a way that supports this idea. In order to increase the permanence of learning, activities that can be adapted to different environments and real life should be used. In short, concepts such as recognition, recall, generalization, modification, repetition, and reconstruction are taught with cognitive theory in online learning. Within this context, the main purpose of education is to enable students to produce more adequate, more comprehensive, stronger and more accurate "meanings" (Newmann, 1994).

3. Constructivist Learning Theory

It occurs as a person's perception of the environment based on his/her own interpretation, and the student is active in the process. Adaptation of this theory in distance education environments can be realized in line with the following suggestions (Ally, 2008).

- In the distance education process, applications in which students will take an active role should be made and activities should be arranged accordingly.
- In order for meaningful learning to occur, it is important that all dimensions of the content contain high-level interaction as much as possible.
- Collaborative and cooperative activities can be designed to guide constructivist learning. Students should be able to control their own learning processes.
- Applications and environments where students can reflect the knowledge they have learned should be prepared.
- The content should be structured in a way that makes the information meaningful.
- Students should be able to live a life where they can feel that they are socially involved in the process.

4. Adult education theory

Discussed by Knowles (1990), this theory suggests that effective adult education can only be successful with an approach designed in line with the characteristics of adults. In this context, there are various suggestions regarding the assumptions that form the cornerstones of adult education theory (Knowles, 1996) and what can be done in the distance education process for each of them.

- Creation of a learning environment suitable for adults
- Creating a participatory organizational structure
- Examination of felt and required adult needs
- Guidance
- Development of designs for activities
- Planning for targets

5. Theory of Independent Study

Wedemeyer developed the theory of independent study. Wedemeyer states that it is a learning and teaching activity in which teachers and students perform their duties and responsibilities separately from each other and communicate in different ways. Wedemeyer states that independent study should allow learners freedom in the choice of goals, individualized learning, and learners should learn at their own pace. From this point of view, in the theory of independent study, it is understood that it is essential for students and teachers to be in separate places, for learners to be responsible for their own learning, for the choice of courses, the format of the course and the method of the course, and for students to learn at their own pace, whenever and wherever they want. Wedemeyer's introduction of the theory of independent study contributed to the formation of consensus among educators and contributed to the emergence of new theories (Keegan, 1996).

6. Autonomy theory

Autonomy theory was developed by Moore, influenced by Wedemeyer's theory of independent study. With Wedemeyer's theory of independent study, Moore highlighted the autonomy dimension as well as the individual's self-learning. In several of his works, Moore wrote on the autonomy of independent learners. In particular, he observed that students were very dependent on teachers in matters such as explanations, guidance, asking questions, and taking action. Moore states that such an approach leaves the decision-making process to more teachers and this is not suitable for adult education (Keegan, 1996). From this point of view, Moore (1973) emphasized that distance education, unlike face-to-face education, is an education system where the learner is separate and autonomous from the teacher in terms of time and place. Moore's analyzes revealed that learner autonomy, which is stated as a theoretical component of distance education, is necessary in distance education. Moore states that autonomous students are individuals who have the ability to self-stimulate, know the ways they will use to achieve goals, and assess their success (Keegan, 1996; Moore, 1973; Moore, 1990).

7. Theory of Industrialization of Teaching

Peters (1988) developed an industrial approach to the distance education process. While conducting analytical and comparative studies on distance education institutions, Peters discovered that there are similarities between the industrial production process and the teaching-learning process of distance education and developed a theoretical structure related to the field. According to Peters, distance education is the industrialized form of education. In other words, Peters states that the production of teaching materials in distance education is an industrial process. From this point of view, he compared the distance education process and the industrial production process and explained it under headings. These are: "Rationalization", "Division of Labor", "Mechanization", "Assembly line", "Mass production", "Preparatory work", "Planning", "Organization", "Scientific control methods", "Formalization", "Change of function", "Objectification", and "Concentration and centralization" (Keegan, 1996). Besides, while working on Peters theory, he found similarities between distance education and industrial production process and continued to explain them. This theory of Peters was not seen as a theory for learning in distance education, and this theory was misunderstood by many scholars. The basis of this is its focus on the production of teaching materials and the explanation of this production as an industrial process. However, Peters responded to every misunderstanding by emphasizing that there are similarities between the industrial production process and the teaching-learning process of distance education (Peters, 2010).

8.   Connectivism learning theory

The power of networks is increasing with new technologies and the idea of network society emerges as a new concept in distance education. With these developments, we have entered a period where access to information is more important than the information itself (Bozkurt, 2014).

Connectivism Learning Theory, which explains learning on networks in today's distance education, has been one of the most important issues. In order to catch up with the technological developments and the requirements of the information age, a new theory called "Connectivism" has been put forward, which better explains the learning-teaching processes (Downes, 2005; Siemens, 2008).

Siemens (2005) states that learning takes place through the process of connecting information resources and private networks, and that the development of connections to facilitate learning and the maintenance of these connections are the basic principles of the connectivist approach. In addition, Siemens states that the learning capacity of individuals is more important than what is currently known in the connectivist approach, and draws attention to the necessity of individuals' ability to see the connection between fields, ideas and concepts, and states that this is the basis of the connectivist approach.

Siemens states that such methods or tools "Wiki", "Blog", "E-mail", "Chat", "Social bookmarking", "Web Conferencing", "Podcasting" and "Forum" can be used in the implementation of the principles of the connectivist approach. Downes (2011) states that an online course that will use the principles of the connectivist approach can have autonomy, diversity, openness, connectedness and interactivity.

In short, "Connectivism Learning Theory" is a theory that tries to explain how both individuals and organizations learn. Accessing accurate and up-to-date information is one of the most important points emphasized by the theory. Decision making is part of the learning process. Learning is seen as a knowledge construction process and it is emphasized that it is very important to support this process with learning tools and design approaches. The rules of this theory are listed as follows (Siemens, 2008).

- Learning and knowledge are hidden in differences of opinion.
- Learning is a process that takes place with the connection of different sources of information.
- Learning can take place with technological tools and equipment.
- Learning capacity is more important than existing knowledge.
- Establishing and expanding links is necessary to support continuing education.
- Seeing the relationships between ideas, fields and concepts is the most basic skill.
- Access to adequate and up-to-date information should be at the core of all learning activities.
- Decision making is part of the learning process. It is very important to decide what to learn and to criticize the information encountered, because information that is true today may change tomorrow and this may affect decisions.

9. Interaction and Communication Theory

Baath, Holmberg, Daniel, Sewart, and Smith carried out extensive and important studies on communication and interaction theory. Baath focused on two-way interaction and communication, Holberg studied on guided didactic speech, and Daniel, Sewart, and Smith, on the other hand, focused on the management of distance education systems. Baath is seen as the pioneer of two-way interaction and communication and has contributed to the establishment of this idea in today's distance education systems with important theoretical and empirical studies (Keegan, 1996).

Baath emphasizes solid learning teaching materials for specific objectives in distance education and he states that flexible learning models for specific goals make simultaneous communication between students and teachers more desirable (Batth 1972, cited in Keegan, 1996). In this respect, Baath states that while preparing educational materials, it is possible to provide two-way communication with exercises, questions or control tests in the material. In addition, he emphasizes that the instructor has an important role in especially distance education students' starting to work, providing motivation and meeting their needs.

Holmberg states that there are important elements in individual learning such as "management", "counseling", "teaching", "group work", "enrolment" and "evaluation", and defines these elements as a support organization. He defines the relationship between the support organization (teacher/management) and the student as guided didactic conversation and states that students' participation in this communication has positive effects on learning. In this respect, the communication between the teacher and the student forms the basis of learning (Horzum, 2007; Karataş, 2005; Keegan, 1996). He also states that the basis of this communication are factors such as providing interaction, enjoying learning, motivation, facilitating learning and transferring what has been learned, and states that learning will become easier if these factors trigger each other (Keegan, 1996).

Daniel sees distance education systems as activities in which the student studies alone and interacts with other individuals. Daniel states that socialization and feedback are the main functions of interactive activities and that courses should not be prepared independently. Daniel emphasizes that the success of distance education systems can only be achieved by adjusting the balance between the student's independent study activities and interactive activities (Keegan, 1996).

10. Technology Supported Education Methods

Today, expectations on the effective use of technology are also increasing with the rapid development and widespread use of technology in education and training institutions (Kağızmanlı, 2014). Technology is one of the most important factors that will promote progress in education. In the light of these developments, teachers should follow the innovations in the field of technology and be able to use them in the areas where they are successful academically. However, in order to be effective in these studies, they must keep up with every change in technology with many aspects (Akkoyunlu, 2002).

Since generation Z, which constitutes today's students, was born into technology, the education to be given to them must be technology supported education and the rapid change in this technology has to be followed. In the light of this rapidly changing and developing technology, teachers should have the competence to develop the necessary tools and equipment as well as using technology while giving information about the subject to the students.

According to Noe (2009), there are many benefits of getting help from technology in education and training methods. Some of those are as follows;

- Individuals who receive training have the chance to decide on the place and time of the training.
- Individuals who receive training can obtain the information they desire and can get help from the system that will mentor them when they need it.
- Individuals receiving education can see and feel the learning space just like a workspace, thanks to the help of virtual reality and cloud technology.
- The desired media for use in the education system can be determined and selected by the individuals receiving education.
- Electronic media can be used in accessing the resources from which education is provided, in the measurement and evaluation phase of the learned information, and in the enrolment phase of a system, thus saving both time and reducing correspondence for administrative affairs.

In sum, technology supported education methods are as follows:

a) **Interactive video:** It is the type of instruction where the student not only watches the video to get information, but also provides an effective communication. Learning with the interactive video method is carried out by giving information and guidance in the environment established through educational presentations, remarkable videos or internet networks. Interactive video training provides individual learning opportunities and the opportunity to learn in fields determined by individuals in line with their own abilities and curiosity. Students are provided with the opportunity to watch different methods and lectures over and over again. The interactive video methods aimed to reveal and improve individual abilities (Noe, 2009).

In the past, any information was stored on a video disc or CD-ROM, but nowadays, interactive videos of the information we obtain through web-based technologies can be accessed. In the current version of interactive video trainings, when you do not understand the visual you watched for information, it can be replayed and watched, it can be stopped and postponed without time problems, and it is possible to switch to a different section to learn another interesting information that arouse curiosity (Hammoud, 2006).

b) **Teleconferencing systems:** It is a technology-based training material that is connected to the telecommunication system, and that the video images created by the audio and video used in education are located in different places at the same time, allowing the number of participants to be very large (Noe, 2009). These voice-enabled systems provide the opportunity to interact through technological tools that differ between individuals or participants in different places of education (Özmen, 2010). Learners can receive education from teachers in various geographies and can communicate effectively with the teacher through various communication tools (Noe, 2009).

The education method provided by teleconferencing allows the students who receive education and the people who instruct to communicate each other without transportation problems. In addition, it provides the opportunity for many students residing in different regions to receive education given in the same time period from the teacher.

c) **Cloud technology:** Today, information technologies, which are found in all areas of our lives, have gained an undeniable importance with the benefits of making a contribution to education as well as our daily work. Rapid developments in information technology have made information easily accessible. By using Cloud Technology, it can be provided to make learning more effective and efficient by providing effective solutions to mobile learning issues. Cloud Technology, which is one of the innovative technologies offers innovative benefits in accessing information (Michael et al., 2010).

According to the "cloud computing model" expressed by John McCarthy in 1960, it is stated that producing and sharing information will occur through new networks established throughout the country in the following years (Sevli, 2011).

d) **Virtual reality:** Noe (2009) expressed virtual reality as information technology that creates a perception of reality in the minds of the learners with the help of information tools. Virtual reality is based on graphics and images in information technologies to provide a different representation of a real situation (Bayram, 1999). Virtual reality recreates the information available in real life in a different environment (Noe, 2009). According to Stone (1991), virtual reality is a multimedia that appeals to human senses, developed to increase communication between human and machine.

e) **Web-based (online) training:** This method, which is provided over the internet, is expressed as the delivery of training to students with the help of computers with developing internet technologies (Noe, 2009). The internet, which is used to meet many needs today, has a significant place in education and training applications in terms of using it to provide new and rich learning experiences for students. The internet has taken on the role of mentor in situations such as creating information, using it in common and gaining difference by being renewed in the places where education is given, and (Karaman, Özen, Yıldırım, & Kaban, 2009).

Web-based training provides an opportunity for students in different and distance education environments to share their knowledge and thoughts, work together, find different solutions and develop personal learning methods. It also brings the distance closer and allows individuals from different cultures to share their knowledge about any subject. On the other hand, the participation of the individuals who receive education or teach from the places where they live, leads to a decrease in the costs of education in today's schools (Kurubacak, 2000). The benefits of web-based training can be listed as follows (Erdoğan, Bayram, & Deniz, 2007);

a) Communication problems between the learner and the trainer in the educational environment can be resolved.

b) It allows the educational environment to be enriched in terms of resources and equipment.

c) It allows the learner to go out of his/her inner world and communicate with other people.

d) It provides a free environment in terms of time and space in the realization of education.

e) It facilitates the determination, correction and delivery of the information to be given in education.

f) It ensures that education takes place at less cost.

g) It provides training opportunities with continuous and up-to-date information.

Using a computer and being online are not enough for web-based training to produce a beneficial result. If the supplementary books, notebooks, planning of the lesson and other education and training methods, which are needed for the realization of the education in the classroom environments where traditional education is applied, should be applied together, there is a need for supplementary education environments that should also be applied in web-based training. Online forums, wikis, personal blogs, social media sites and learning management systems are the most used in environments where they are needed.

○ **Online forums:** In our time, information technologies are used more and more in almost every moment of the learning process. Thanks to the discovery and evaluation of knowledge, the importance of explaining the associations in social communication in the environment where learning takes place is increasing over time (Haşlaman, Demiraslan, Mumcu, Dönmez, & Aşkar, 2008). Online learning environments have played an important role in sharing information on the Internet, communicating with each other and strengthening this interaction. Enabling this interaction is done by sending a message to a message box. In online education forums, a discussion environment is created by sending a message to the message box, under the guidance of the teacher. Özçınar and Öztürk (2008) stated that online forums allow students to share their individual knowledge with the freedom of time and space, with other students and experts in the field, to discuss and examine different ideas, and to produce meaningful information by taking into account the criticisms. Özçınar and Öztürk (2008), in their study, also concluded that the individuals receiving education learned the information and thoughts of the students who think contrary to themselves in online forums, they supported that they wanted to create the discussions with large masses for reasons such as getting faster answers to their messages, and that when the number of users increased, the learning individuals had difficulty in following the discussion.

○ **Wikis:** Doğan, Duman, and Seferoğlu (2011) defines Wiki as a software that allows users to create new pages, make edits and link these pages. It is an environment where individuals who want to receive education on the subject they want to improve themselves are allowed to upload documents on the subject, make arrangements on these documents, and work together in a virtual environment over a computer network. Wikis allow eductional activities to be gathered under certain topics. Thus, a collective discussion environment is created where learners can do research and share their thoughts.

The use of wikis gives the opportunity to create content that cannot be created on classical websites (Aytekin, 2011). The fact that students and teachers share the knowledge they have obtained by working together and provide quality information increases the importance of wikis in the educational program. The co-educational environment provided for use also makes a difference in terms of mutual interaction between learners (Deperlioğlu & Köse, 2010). The individual who receives education on the Internet realizes that his/her shares are followed as he/she reaches the information shared on the wiki about the subject he/she is working on, and his/her confidence in the collective discussion environment increases with this awareness (Doğan, Duman, & Seferoğlu, 2011). At the same time, it is an important method in terms of obtaining a collaborative learning environment, with individuals who receive education expressing themselves not only as readers but also as writers in the process of continuing education (Altun, 2008).

○ **Blogs (Weblog):** Blogs, which are web-based information access networks, are websites used for other users to access individual entries via machines (Deperlioğlu & Köse, 2010). Thanks to the blogs that can be defined as online diaries, pictures, videos and different information can be shared (Doğan, Duman, & Seferoğlu, 2011). Individuals using blogs can access and interpret mutually shared information. Thus, they can exchange ideas with each other.

Thanks to blogs on the Internet, the creation of a blog community consisting of educators and individuals receiving education, enabling individuals to determine the subjects they are interested in, commenting on the shared information and expanding it with additional information, and the planning of the learning process by the individual himself/herself can increase the self-confidence of the learner (Deperlioğlu & Köse, 2010). Karaman, Kaban, and Yıldırım (2010), in their research, concluded that blog studies increase the interest in the subjects they receive education, and students share their thoughts about the course by providing them with extracurricular interaction and communication among themselves. Individuals who receive education can continue to interact with teachers and other individuals receiving education thanks to blog diaries (Doğan, Duman, & Seferoğlu, 2011). Atıcı and Özmen (2011) found that students who used blogs had a higher sense of classroom community compared to students who are trained in a school environment in the study of individuals who have blogs outside of classes. Thanks to the web literacy that emerges through internet diaries, interaction can occur between the blogger and the readers and allows individuals to share their thoughts with each other (Karaman, Kaban, & Yıldırım, 2010).

- **Social Networking Sites**: The advantages of this educational method are that these sites, which are created by people interacting with each other over the internet for a certain purpose, are easy to use, not high in cost, and can be accessed anytime from all places where there is a computer network (Doğan, Duman, & Seferoğlu, 2011). Thus, it provides convenience for individuals to interact with each other, share information and receive feedback in online environments. Social networking sites appeal to many users with functional interfaces and privacy features (Gülbahar, Kalelioğlu, & Madran, 2010).

Today, Facebook is one of the social networks where groups can be formed, visual, audio and text-based tools and materials can be shared, discussion platforms can be created, and many individuals participate in communication at the same time or in different time periods. Individuals who receive online education can make friends with participants and trainers and they can share products and ideas (Doğan, Duman, & Seferoğlu, 2011). On Twitter, another social networking site, they can write short messages called "Tweet" and share them with other users. At the same time, information about an article can be exchanged and its address can be published on the Internet. Individuals who are well-versed in their subject can be followed and information sharing about their expertise on the subject can be reached. (Gülbahar, Kalelioğlu, & Madran, 2010).

- **Learning management systems**: Noe (2009) has accepted learning management systems as a field of technology (technology) thought that can be used for the management, development and self-realization of educational syllabuses. Elmas, Doğan, Biroğul, and Mehmet (2008), on the other hand, defined learning management system as a management tool that allows the individuals receiving education in different timed or mixed education to determine the courses to be chosen, to access the content of them, to criticize the information at the beginning and end of the education, and to monitor the educational data.

CONCLUSION

The present chapter aims to examine and assess distance education, purpose and requirements of distance education, basic principles in the effective use of distance education, the role of teacher and student in distance education, material in distance education, measurement and evaluation in distance education. In addition, learning theories in distance education technology such as behavioral learning theory, cognitive learning theory, constructivist learning theory, adult education theory, theory of independent study, autonomy theory, theory of industrialization of teaching, connectivism learning theory, and interaction and communication theory were presented clearly. In the last part of the present chapter, technology supported education methods such as interactive video, teleconferencing systems, cloud technology, virtual reality and web-based (online) training were explained in detail.

REFERENCES

Akkoyunlu, B. (2002). Educational technology in Turkey: Past, present and future. *Educational Media International, 39*(2), 165–174. doi:10.1080/09523980210155352

Ally, M. (2004). *Foundations of educational theory for online learning.* AU Press.

Ally, M. (2008). Foundations of educational theory for online learning. In *The Theory and Practice of Online Learning* (2nd ed., pp. 15–44). Athabasca University Press.

Altun, A. (2008, May). Yapılandırmacı öğretim sürecinde viki kullanımı. *International Educational Technology Conference (IETC)'da sunulan bildiri.*

Anderson, J. (2020). *Brave New World The coronavirus pandemic is reshaping education.* Retrieved from https://qz.com/1826369/how-coronavirus-is-changing-education/

Anderson, T. (2003). Getting the Mix Right Again: An updated and theoretical rationale for interaction. *International Review of Research in Open and Distance Learning, 4*(2), 1–14.

Ateş, A., & Altun, E. (2008). Bilgisayar öğretmeni adaylarının uzaktan eğitime yönelik tutumlarının çeşitli değişkenler açısından incelenmesi. *Gazi Eğitim Fakültesi Dergisi, 28*(3), 125–145.

Atıcı, B., & Özmen, B. (2011). *Blog kullanımının sınıf topluluğu duygusuna etkisi.* Uluslararası Eğitim Teknolojileri Sempozyumu'nda sunulan bildiri.

Aytekin, Ç. (2011). Wiki uygulamalarına iletişimsel yaklaşım ile bir model önerisi. *Online Academic Journal of Information Technology, 2*(5), 7–17.

Bayram, S. (1999). *Bilgisayar destekli öğretim teknolojileri.* Marmara Üniversitesi Yayınevi Kitap Koleksiyonu.

Benson, R., & Samarawickrema, G. (2009). Addressing the context of e-learning: Using transactional distance theory to inform design. *Distance Education, 30*(1), 5–21. doi:10.1080/01587910902845972

Bozkurt, A. (2014). *Ağ toplumu ve öğrenme: Bağlantıcılık. In Akademik Bilişim 2014 (pp. 601-606).* Mersin Üniversitesi.

Demirel, Ö. (Ed.). (2010). *Eğitimde Yeni Yönelimler.* Apegem Akademi.

Deperlioğlu, Ö., & Köse, U. (2010). *Web 2.0 Teknolojilerinin eğitim üzerindeki etkileri ve örnek bir öğrenme yaşantısı. In XII. Akademik Bilişim Konferans Bildirileri.* Muğla Üniversitesi.

Doğan, D., Duman, D., & Seferoğlu, S. S. (2011). E-öğrenme ortamlarında toplumsal buradalığın arttırılması için kullanılabilecek iletişim araçları. *Akademik Bilişim,* 2-4.

Downes, S. (2005). *An Introduction to Connective Knowledge.* https://www.downes.ca/post/33034

Downes, S. (2011). *"Connectivism" and connective knowledge.* https://www.huffingtonpost.com/stephendownes/connectivismandconnecti_b_804653.html

Elmas, Ç., Doğan, N., Biroğul, S., & Mehmet, K. O. Ç. (2008). Moodle eğitim yönetim sistemi ile örnek bir dersin uzaktan eğitim uygulaması. *Bilişim Teknolojileri Dergisi, 1*(2).

Erdoğan, Y., Bayram, S., & Deniz, L. (2007). Web tabanlı öğretim tutum ölçeği: Açıklayıcı ve doğrulayıcı faktör analizi çalışması. *Uluslararası İnsan Bilimleri Dergisi, 4*(2), 1–14.

Freeman, R. (1997). *Managing open systems*. Kogan Page.

Garrison, D. R. (2003). Self-directed Learning and Distance Education. In M. G. Moore & W. G. Anderson (Eds.), *Handbook of Distance Education*. Lawrence Erlbaum Associates.

Gülbahar, Y., Kalelioğlu, F., & Madran, O. (2010). Sosyal ağların eğitim amaçlı kullanımı. In XV. Türkiye'de İnternet Konferansı. İstanbul Teknik Üniversitesi.

Hammoud, R. I. (2006). *Interactive Video Algorithm and Technologies*. Springer. doi:10.1007/978-3-540-33215-2

Haşlaman, T., Demiraslan, Y., Mumcu, F. K., Dönmez, O., & Aşkar, P. (2008). Çevrimiçi ortamda yapılan grup tartışmasındaki iletişim örüntülerinin söylem çözümlemesi yoluyla incelenmesi. *Hacettepe Üniversitesi Eğitim Fakültesi Dergisi*, *35*(35), 162–174.

İşman, A. (2011). *Uzaktan Eğitim*. Pegem Akademi.

Kağızmanlı, T. B., Tatar, E., & Zengin, Y. (2014). Öğretmen adaylarının matematik öğretiminde teknoloji kullanımına ilişkin algılarının incelenmesi. *Ahi Evran Üniversitesi Kırşehir Eğitim Fakültesi Dergisi*, *14*(2), 349–370.

Karadağ, A., & Şen, Y. A. (2014). *Uzaktan Eğitimde Rol Alan Kişiler ve Öğretmen Öğrenci Rolleri*. Anadolu Üniversitesi.

Karaman, S., Kaban, A., & Yıldırım, S. (2010). Sınıf blogu ile grup bloglarının öğrenci katılımı ve görüşleri açısından karşılaştırılması. *Eğitim Teknolojileri Araştırmaları Dergisi*, *1*(2), 1–12.

Karaman, S., Özen, Ü., Yıldırım, S., & Kaban, A. (2009). Açık kaynak kodlu öğretim yönetim sistemi üzerinden internet destekli (harmanlanmış) öğrenim deneyimi. *Akademik Bilişim Konferansı*, 11-13.

Karataş, S. (2005). *Deneyim Eşitliğine Dayalı İnternet Temelli ve Yüz yüze Öğrenme Sistemlerinin Öğrenci Başarı ve Deneyimi Açısından Karşılaştırılması*. Doktora Tezi, Ankara Üniversitesi, Eğitim Bilimleri Enstitüsü.

Keegan, D. (1986). *The foundations of distance education*. Croom Helm.

Keegan, D. (1996). *Foundations of Distance Education*. Routledge.

Knowles, M. (1996). Adult learning. In R. L. Craig (Ed.), *ASTD training & development handbook: A guide to human resource development* (4th ed., pp. 253–265). McGraw Hill.

Knowles, M. S. (1990). *The Adult Learner: A Neglected Species*. Gulf Publishing Co.

Kurubacak, G. (2000). *Online learning: A study of students' attitudes towards Web-based instruction* (WBI) (Doctoral dissertation). University of Cincinnati.

Liyanagunawardena, T. R., Adams, A. A., & Williams, S. A. (2013). MOOCs: A systematic study of the published literature 2008-2012. *International Review of Research in Open and Distance Learning*, *14*(3), 202–227. doi:10.19173/irrodl. v14i3.1455

Michael, A., Armando, F., Rean, G., Anthony, D. J., Randy, K., Andy, K., ... Matei, Z. (2010). Bulut bilişimin görüntüsü. *ACM'nin İletişimi*, *53*(4), 50–58.

Moore. M. (1973). Toward a theory of independent learning and teaching. *Journal of Higher Education*, *44*, 661-679.

Moore, M. (1990). *Background and overview of contemporary American distance education*. Pergamon.

Moore, M. G., & Kearsley, I. G. (2012). *Distance education: A systems view of online learning* (3rd ed.). Wadsworth Publishing.

Newman, B. (1994). *The Marketing of the President: Political Marketing as Campaign Strategy*. Sage.

Noe, R. A. (2009). *İnsan Kaynaklarının Eğitimi ve Geliştirilmesi*. Beta Basım A. Ş.

Özçınar, H., & Öztürk, E. (2008). Student opinions about case discussions in online environments. *Yuzuncu Yıl University Journal of Educational Faculty*, *5*(2), 154–178.

Özmen, Z. M. (2010). Bir lisansüstü öğrencisinin telekonferans ve uzaktan eğitim uygulamaları dersindeki deneyimleri. *Turkish Journal of Computer and Mathematics Education (Turcomat)*, *1*(2), 217–232.

Peters, O. (1988). Distance teaching and industrial production: A comparative interpretation in ouline. In D. Sewart, D. Keegan, & B. Holmberg (Eds.), *Distance education: International perspectives* (pp. 95–113). Routledge.

Peters, O. (2010). *Distance Education in Transition* (5th ed.). BIS-Verlag der Carl von Ossietzky Universität Oldenburg.

Schrum, L., & Hong, S. (2002). From the field: Characteristics of successful tertiary online students and strategies of experienced online. *Education and Information Technologies*, *7*(1), 5–16. doi:10.1023/A:1015354423055

Sevli, O. (2011). *Bulut bilişim ve eğitim alanında örnek bir uygulama* (Unpublished master's thesis). Süleyman Demirel Üniversitesi, Isparta.

Siemens, G. (2005). Connectivism: A learning theory for the digital age. *International Journal of Instructional Technology & Distance Learning, 2*(1), 1–8.

Siemens, G. (2008). *About: Description of connectivism. Connectivism: A learning theory for today's learner.* http://www.connectivism.ca/about.html

Simonson, M., Smaldino, S., Albright, M., & Zvacek, S. (2006). *Teaching and learning at a distance: Foundations of distance education* (3rd ed.). Prentice Hall.

Stone, R. J. (1991). Virtual Reality and Cyberspace: From Science Fiction To Science Fact. *Information Services & Use, 11*(5-6), 283–300. doi:10.3233/ISU-1991-115-603

UNESCO. (2002). *Open and Distance Learning. Trends, Policy and Strategy Considerations.* UNESCO.

Uşun, S. (2006). Uzaktan Eğitim. Ankara: Nobel Yayınları.

KEY TERMS AND DEFINITIONS

Distance Education: It is a form of education based on the use of various communication tools without being face-to-face between the student and the teacher.

Distance Learning Theories: They are the theories that show how to carry out distance education, how to teach and learn in distance education.

Teaching Principles and Methods in Distance Education: Principles regarding the establishment of educational activities within the framework of a specific plan and program.

Technology-Supported Education Methods: The methods benefited from the use of technology in the field of education.

Web-Based Instruction: It is an instruction system in which teachers and learners can operate together independently of time, place, and distance.

Chapter 2
Online Education in Industry 5.0

Prasad G.
Dayananda Sagar University, India

ABSTRACT

Higher education in the modern era is gradually changing. Students from lecture rooms are rapidly volunteering into the digital world of the internet, embracing technologies like the distant learning with unique pedagogy. Education, to educate future citizens to operate in the field of resource sharing, will need to undergo further adaptive changes. Flexibility of location and time, personalization of the offer, collaboration, and adaptability are all trends of techniques and tools. This research work has been carried as a contribution towards the goals of National Education Policy 2020 framework proposed by Government of India. To equip citizens to engage in and benefit from the increasingly connected virtual and physical worlds, together with the rising need for information alongside limited time resources, higher education will be dynamic.

INTRODUCTION

Thanks to many advantages and opportunities online education offers, it is indispensable in the education of today's world (Karagöz, 2021; Karagöz, & Rüzgar, 2021). Teaching and Technology are blended in the new era of education. If an Education Institution is emerging, the opportunity of the employment around the surrounding peoples are created. Campus management has gotten a lot of attention as the number and size of education institution has grown. This study creates a smart classroom management system based on the Internet of Things in order to

DOI: 10.4018/978-1-7998-8077-6.ch002

monitor the classroom environment and analyse the classroom environment and usage purpose of skill development, Innovation and Entrepreneurship development. As for the user interface, that's the Internet of Things.

Ally et al. (2014) studied the influence of teachers for a mobile world, to improve access to education. Alrasheedi and Capretz (2015) identified the Critical Success Factors Affecting Mobile Learning in his work. Crompton (2013) discussed the benefits and challenges of Mobile Learning for the purpose of Learning & Leading with Technology. Du and Lin (2012) studied on System Design and Security Management for Campus Mobile Learning. Evans-Cowley (2010) proposed the future of Mobile Technology in education. Handal, Ritter, and Marcovitz (2014) implemented large scale Mobile Learning education institution Programs in his research. The objective is to disseminate the latest technology in education for the future generation smart classrooms.

Digital Energy audit in educational institute is the need of the hour. Lighting, fans, and air conditioners are frequently left on while students leave the classroom. However, while not in use, the equipment room's computers and switches utilise a significant amount of vitality. Even yet, in order to implement automatic control, several characteristics must be evaluated, such as whether or not the classroom is in use and whether or not the lights should be turned off for the energy management in campus. The indoor environment, on the other hand, has a direct bearing on people's health, well-being, and productivity. As the Internet of Things evolves, consumers will be able to get a better deal on their surroundings. In order to save dynamism and reduce emissions in education institution, lighting, air conditioners, projections, and other electrical equipment must be intelligently controlled for automatic detections. It is vital, however, to strike a balance that can save energy and reduce education institution operating costs while still meeting the everyday needs of instructors and students in order not to disrupt their learning and working environments. Solar panels and small wind turbines are the sustainable renewable energy that can be utilized in the educational intuitions. Students and teachers' activities, environmental changes in the room, and the use of electrical appliances need to be recorded and analysed afterwards to identify a balance point using classroom and office environmental data. However, the Internet of Things generates enormous amounts of data on its own. The typical relational database is no longer able to keep up with the growing demand. In the near future, there will be an urgent requirement for a new data storage method. Then classrooms and offices can be outfitted with gateways for uploading environmental data and accepting control commands for indoor equipment. Campus Internet of Things (IoT) solutions are also rising in number. Campus network can be joined wirelessly even in classes without a network cable. It's possible that as a device's IP address and source identification grow, storage issues will occur. A huge amount of data is also being generated on a daily basis by the Internet of

Things, and each classroom contributes a significant proportion of this. Relational databases which have traditionally served this purpose, have fallen short. To help education institution and universities better manage their environments, this article uses Internet of Things (IoT) technology, which combines relational databases with non-relational databases and a distributed file system. With this approach, the previous way's isolation and rationality are no longer a problem, and the benefits of global optimization and unified administration are now available to businesses. Abdel-Basset et al (2018) proposed Internet of Things (IoT) and its impact in future technologies. Ball, Stephen (2021) discussed the modern changes to be carried in his work "The education debate". Balakrishnan (2021) summarised the NEP 2020 policy in terms of excellence in education. Goyal et al. (2021) and Gupta (2021) studied the alternative structure of delivering management education in India. Haddad et al. (2021) carried a survey on internet of things security, requirements, challenges, and solutions. Loyalka et al. (2021) analysed the skill levels and gains in university STEM education in China, India, Russia and the United States. Disadvantages of IOT is lack of digital literacy, extra distractions for students, failing technology and health concerns.

INTERNET OF CLASSROOM (IOC)

College topic instruction is currently set up in such a way that application-oriented talent is severely out of step with the times' development requirements, making it difficult to meet the needs of the society for highly creative employees. The following are the root causes of the issue: In the first place, college topic curriculum stresses theory, law, and deductions instead of reflecting the current state of affairs and available knowledge. Secondly, the curriculum for college courses cannot match the needs of undergraduate talent training focused on application-oriented knowledge and skills training, etc. students have a low level of interest in the subject matter. The fourth issue is that the college curriculum does not adequately meet the needs of professionals as well as students, and the teaching style is not suitable for cultivating students' engineering practise ability as well as their innovation ability. Reforming college courses instruction based on the premise of "Internet + education" is of internet.

The Internet of Things is an extension of the Internet itself. In order to achieve information transmission, mobile communication technology is used, together with cloud computing technology for data analysis and processing. Smart cities, smart homes, and smart campuses have all emerged in the growth of the Internet of Things. In order to store and manage large amounts of data efficiently, it can be utilised in place of standard relational databases. Additionally, it fits the IoT data storage requirements for scalability, flexibility and dependability. It's been recommended to use a storage approach that combines the advantages of relational and non-relational databases to fulfil the simplicity of routine queries while also accommodating enormous amounts of data. However, blocks are excellent data storage for backups because they boost data fault tolerance and availability.

Figure 1. Internet of Education

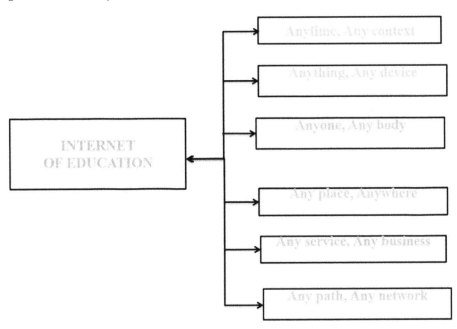

Figure 1 illustrates the significance of Internet of Education in modern world. Three important outcomes will be produced of this research work:

1) To investigate the influence of online learning initiatives on learning and teaching at universities, an uniform model is needed.
2) Comprehensive assessment of pilot studies and other projects, including the methods used to evaluate them, across a wide range of fields.
3) Special education students can take an online learning assessment. Insights into emerging mobile technologies, the objective assessment of mobile learning efforts, and the prioritisation of proposed investments in education within different learning settings are all included here.

Figure 2. Smart Classrooms

SMART CLASSES

Creating a student friendly environment is one of the main objectives as an eminent teacher. Every classroom should have access to the Internet as a useful and affordable learning resource. Using the internet in your classes can be done in a number of ways.

1.   Video tutorials to your advantage.
2.   Send out an invitation to distant speakers.
3.   Create teams for collaboration.
4.   Public files and papers can be shared with anyone.
5.   Increase the visual appeal of your teaching.

Figure 2 shows Smart Classrooms facilities by Dayananda Sagar University, Bangalore, India. No matter what subject students study, videos are an excellent method to make learning more enjoyable and innovate the additional information. Because there are many expert in each field, when they teach the latest research in the course can be gained with additional knowledge. Additionally, no longer need to reserve a separate room for video classes because software now allows you to project movies from your phone or tablet directly into the classroom screen. The fact that you can quickly locate many free instructional channels on YouTube is also a significant advantage. After all, most of these videos are brief, amusing, and visually stimulating, so subscribing to a few in your subject area could save you a lot time when preparing for your next session. A win-win situation for both kids and teachers, without a doubt. The section when you start thinking about showing this article to your teacher if you happen to be a student. You must pick the most liberal lecturer, that's all.

Ismail et al. (2013) and Lampe et al. (2011) studied on student use of Facebook for organizing collaborative classroom activities. Park (2011) discussed pedagogical Framework for M-learning: Categorizing Educational Applications of Mobile Technologies. Rose (2013) made his work in BYOD: An Examination of Bring Your Own Device in education. Sharples (2013) studied on Mobile learning: research, practice and challenges in future. If you're teaching the younger students, you might use a remote version of the "who I want to be when I grow up" lesson, where representatives from various professions participate remotely rather than physically. In order to interest older kids, consider inviting subject matter experts – your contacts will play a large role in this activity. Furthermore, there is a huge selection of apps to pick from. Skype, Viber, and WhatsApp all free to use, and all you need is a screen and an Internet connection.

There are some projects where teamwork is critical. All of the above-mentioned messaging services allow users to create groups where project related issues can be discussed. It's also worth noting that slack, another similar tool, is widely utilised by a wide range of firms that employ teams. It's quite beneficial for many issues to create specialised chat/discussion groups that allow the entire team to work together towards a single goal. Student collaboration, brainstorming, and contributing their fair share of effort are all demonstrated in this example, which may be a lab report or a training marketing project. Another major benefit of these forums is that they help students become ready for the real-world workplace by emphasising the need of teamwork and, in turn, shortening the learning curve.

When it comes to collaborating, the Google suite has made things a whole lot easier. With Google Docs, you can share text documents, spreadsheets, and even entire folders with others using a single click of the mouse. Even while Apple's docs have the same features, it's doubtful that all of your pupils will be Mac/Apple users, hence the Apple product has limitations. Instead of using a desktop operating system, Google uses a web browser to access all of its files in the cloud, thus the user's operating system doesn't matter here. Google Docs may be used in a plethora of ways to boost productivity. The simplest method is to provide all of the new assignments to the entire class at the beginning of the semester. Students will be able to collaborate on documents, presentations, graphs, reports, and other materials with shared files, rather than just discussing projects online. Having access to other student papers from their class can even help them better their college essay writing. You may also add comments to documents in Google Docs, so you can choose a few examples of work and offer your thoughts on them by using this tool. You can teach pupils how to write by giving them particular examples of papers and commenting on what is right and wrong with each one.

Last but not least, the Internet offers teachers the opportunity to make all of their classes more visible. The most reliable method of achieving this goal is through the use of images and photographs. When it comes to visual materials, the options are virtually endless. You can use internet maps, for example, to transport your audience to faraway places when teaching geography. Teaching culture and history can also benefit from the use of maps (for example, an old photo of the location vs. a present-day street view). With this method, students will feel more connected to the material, increasing the likelihood of it sticking in their minds long after they have learned it. Use of slides in your courses is an additional notion, no matter how apparent it seems. Using slides in lectures is not a new idea; it has been around for a long time. However, you can give your old visuals a fresh look by uploading them on the internet. We don't necessarily mean photos and graphs when we say "visuals." Text snippets, quotations, and pretty much any other textual information you want to emphasise can be used as this.

The academic community has traditionally lagged behind in terms of innovation, especially in fields like computer science and engineering. Honestly, to say there's been a "little" is an understatement here. Teachers still refuse to accept technology and integrate it into the educational process, which is unquestionably a problem with municipal budgets because some education institution have horrendously outdated computers. Teachers nowadays must recognise that the millennial generation is steadily overtaking older workers in the labour market, and that millennial who are nearing graduation are unconcerned about the old traditions. For the new generation of education institution kids, who are now referred to as digital natives, the same is even more relevant today than it was before.

METHODOLOGY OF IOT IN EDUCATION

IOT Mode in Teaching First, the matching line will be taught via the IOT platform before class. When it comes to achieving college Subject talent training objectives, teachers must create online teaching resources, help students study, and conduct training tests ahead of time so that they can quickly assess students' understanding and know exactly what they need help with.

To that end, online and offline blended in class instruction is being considered. Instructional steps: coaching in class, participatory discussion in class and assessment in class. The following is a detailed description of the implementation procedure: Sub-project groups allow teachers to provide technical support while students serve as project group members. This encourages student team cooperation while also igniting their passion for taking on new responsibilities. Loey et al. (2021) worked on hybrid deep transfer learning model with machine learning methods for face mask detection in the era of the COVID-19 pandemic. Marley et al. (2021) discussed the extending an Ethic of Hospitality to the student feedback process. Mohan (2021) carried a research on Higher Education in India-Issues and Challenges. Muthuprasad et al. (2021) analysed the Students' perception and preference for online education in India during COVID-19 pandemic. Nimavat et al. (2021) carried the Online Medical Education in India Different Challenges and Probable Solutions in the Age of COVID-19. Pandit et al. (2021) discussed the Exploring challenges of online education in COVID times. Serneels and Dercon (2021) carried a research on Aspirations, Poverty, and Education.

And lastly, it's important to create after education institution clubs where students may learn both online and off campus. Calculus in college serves as a key foundational course that is tightly tied to the major, which in turn serves as a vital stepping stone to the professional track. education institution courses associations, combined with competitions, with corresponding task requirements set up, teachers' guidance throughout the entire process, excellent students as president ensure the enthusiasm and initiative of students' online and offline learning and exchange in this extracurricular interest group for core subject education.

Figure 3 picture shows Technology Enhanced Learning technique implemented in Dayananda Sagar University, Bangalore, India. There are several ways to conduct the assessment and evaluation, which includes both online and off-line methods. The findings of the online and offline assessments and evaluations will be combined according to a weighted percentage for the final assessment and evaluation. In order to ensure student motivation, the mix of online and offline assessment forms emphasises the manner of process evaluation. Additionally, it ensures that the instructor is in constant control of the teaching process as a whole, making it possible to monitor the entire thing. Online assessment is based on the learning of curriculum teaching resources (video, lesson plan, PPT, MOOC), online homework, testing, etc., whereas offline assessment is based on attendance, classroom performance, offline homework, stage quiz, final exam, etc., as the major evaluation indicator.

Figure 3. Technology Enhanced Learning

Technology Tools for Students

New educational approaches using technology to help students are becoming more popular. Two most popular Online education platforms are discussed below.

1. SWAYAM –NPTEL
    SWAYAM is a government-sponsored initiative aimed at achieving the three cardinal principles of education policy: access, equity, and quality. The goal of this initiative is to make the best teaching and learning tools available to everyone, especially the most disadvantaged. SWAYAM aims to close the digital divide for students who have been left behind by the digital revolution and are unable to participate fully in the knowledge economy. Learners can take SWAYAM courses for free, but if they want a SWAYAM certificate, they must register for the final proctored tests, which cost money, and take them in person at designated centres on specific days. The certificate's eligibility will be posted on the course website, and learners will only receive certificates if this condition is met. The marks/certificate achieved in these courses can be used for credit transfer by universities/colleges that approve credit transfer for these courses. SWAYAM's courses are divided into four sections: (1) video lectures, (2) specially prepared reading material that may be downloaded/printed, (3) self-assessment tests in the form of tests and quizzes, and (4)

an online discussion forum for clearing up any doubts. Efforts have been made to enhance the learning experience through the use of audio-video and multi-media, as well as cutting-edge pedagogy and technology.

2.   ISRO –IIRS

Information and communication technology, as well as better broadband internet connectivity, have expanded the scope of learning to include learning at any time and from any location, in addition to the traditional classroom setting. In 2004, the Indian Space Research Organisation and the Government of India built a specialised communication satellite called EDUSAT to assist distant learning. Tele-education, Tele-medicine, Village Resource Centers, mobile satellite services, emergency management support, and television programming training farmers for agriculture and other purposes are all common uses for the satellite. Tele-education at various levels (i.e. school level/UG/PG level) by various ministries/autonomous organizations/departments/institutions/universities in India has proven to be one of the most effective uses of the EDUSAT satellite. The main goal of IIRS was to use the EDUSAT satellite for distant learning, but the scope was expanded to include the internet, allowing users to connect to a huge number of institutions/universities/individuals at a low cost. Today, this programme is bringing together more professional and user departments and ministries from across the country to improve their knowledge of geospatial technologies and applications.

CONCLUSION

The impact of Industry 5.0 on Online Education and the overall economy is studied from an economic and productivity point of view, with the argument that Industry 5.0 will create more jobs in technology of Industry 5.0. There are more benefits than drawbacks to using the Internet to further your knowledge. Prepare for your lectures by thinking like your students and speaking their language. This is the finest method to captivate a maturing audience. With the concept of "Internet of education," this study investigates the mixed mode of teaching college subjects, first introducing the current situation and problems of university in classroom and then presenting the mixed mode of learning college courses and the concrete classroom implementation method in view of the above problems and finally expounding the benefits of technology in teaching mode. For college and education institution curriculum reform, fresh ideas and new thinking can be provided by organically integrating education with information technology and reforming all course teaching methods, teaching content, and evaluation methods.

ACKNOWLEDGMENT

The author is the SPOC for SWAYAM NPTEL Local chapter and Indian Space Research Organisation IIRS coordinator at Dayananda Sagar University, Bangalore, India. He would like to thank IIT Madras and ISRO for their online education contribution for the development of India Education.

REFERENCES

Abdel-Basset, M., Manogaran, G., & Mohamed, M. (2018). Internet of Things (IoT) and its impact on supply chain: A framework for building smart, secure and efficient systems. *Future Generation Computer Systems, 86*, 614–628. doi:10.1016/j.future.2018.04.051

Ally, M., Grimus, M., & Ebner, M. (2014). Preparing teachers for a mobile world, to improve access to education. *Prospects, 44*(1), 1–17. doi:10.100711125-014-9293-2

Alrasheedi, M., & Capretz, L. F. (2015). Determination of Critical Success Factors Affecting Mobile Learning: A Meta-Analysis Approach. *The Turkish Online Journal of Educational Technology, 14*(2), 41–51.

Balakrishnan, K. (2021). Empowering Emerging India through Excellence in Education-Reflections On NEP 2020. *Elementary Education Online, 20*(1), 3596–3602.

Ball, S. J. (2021). *The education debate*. Policy Press. doi:10.2307/j.ctv201xhz5

Crompton, H. (2013). The Benefits and Challenges of Mobile Learning. *Learning and Leading with Technology*, 38–39.

Du, S., & Lin, J. (2012). Research on System Design and Security Management for Campus Mobile Learning. *IEEE International Conference on Computer Science and Automation Engineering (CSAE)*. 10.1109/CSAE.2012.6273001

Evans-Cowley, J. (2010). Planning in the Real-Time City: The Future of Mobile Technology. *Journal of Planning Literature, 25*(2), 136–149. doi:10.1177/0885412210394100

Goyal, J. K., Daipuria, P., & Jain, S. (2021). An alternative structure of delivering management education in India. *Journal of Educational Technology Systems, 49*(3), 325–340. doi:10.1177/0047239520958612

Gupta, A. (2021). Teacher-entrepreneurialism: A case of teacher identity formation in neoliberalizing education space in contemporary India. *Critical Studies in Education*, *62*(4), 422–438. doi:10.1080/17508487.2019.1708765

HaddadPajouh, H., Dehghantanha, A., Parizi, R. M., Aledhari, M., & Karimipour, H. (2021). A survey on internet of things security: Requirements, challenges, and solutions. *Internet of Things*, *14*, 100129. doi:10.1016/j.iot.2019.100129

Handal, B., Ritter, R., & Marcovitz. (2014). *Implementing Large Scale Mobile Learning School Programs: To BYOD or not to BYOD*. In EdMedia, Tampere, Finland.

Hew, K. F., & Brush, T. (2007). Integrating Technology into K–12 Teaching and Learning: Current knowledge gaps and recommendations for future research. *Educational Technology Research and Development*, *55*(3), 223–252. doi:10.100711423-006-9022-5

Ismail, I., Azizan, S. N., & Azman, N. (2013). Mobile Phone as Pedagogical Tools: Are Teachers Ready? *International Education Studies*, *6*(3), 36–47. doi:10.5539/ies.v6n3p36

Karagöz, S. (2021). Evaluation of distance education: The sample of guidance and counseling students (Example of Aksaray University). *The Universal Academic Research Journal*, *3*(1), 18–25.

Karagöz, S., & Rüzgar, M. E. (2021). An investigation of the prospective teachers' viewpoints about distance education during the COVID-19 pandemic. *International Journal of Curriculum and Instruction*, *13*(3), 2611–2634.

Lampe, C., Wohn, D. Y., Vitak, J., Ellison, N. B., & Wash, R. (2011). Student use of Facebook for organizing collaborative classroom activities. *International Journal of Computer-Supported Collaborative Learning*, *6*(3), 329–347. doi:10.100711412-011-9115-y

Loey, M., Manogaran, G., Taha, M. H. N., & Khalifa, N. E. M. (2021). A hybrid deep transfer learning model with machine learning methods for face mask detection in the era of the COVID-19 pandemic. *Measurement*, *167*, 108288. doi:10.1016/j.measurement.2020.108288 PMID:32834324

Loyalka, P., Liu, O. L., Li, G., Kardanova, E., Chirikov, I., Hu, S., Yu, N., Ma, L., Guo, F., Beteille, T., Tognatta, N., Gu, L., Ling, G., Federiakin, D., Wang, H., Khanna, S., Bhuradia, A., Shi, Z., & Li, Y. (2021). Skill levels and gains in university STEM education in China, India, Russia and the United States. *Nature Human Behaviour*, *5*(7), 892–904. doi:10.103841562-021-01062-3 PMID:33649462

Marley, C., Faye, A. D., Hurst, E., Moeller, J., & Pinkerton, A. (2021). Moving Beyond 'You Said, We Did': Extending an Ethic of Hospitality to The Student Feedback Process. In *Online Postgraduate Education in a Postdigital World* (pp. 1–19). Springer. doi:10.1007/978-3-030-77673-2_1

Mohan, G. V. M. (2021). Higher Education in India-Issues and Challenges. Assessment, Accreditation and Ranking Methods for Higher Education Institutes in India. *Current Findings and Future Challenges*, 134.

Muthuprasad, T., Aiswarya, S., Aditya, K. S., & Jha, G. K. (2021). Students' perception and preference for online education in India during COVID-19 pandemic. *Social Sciences & Humanities Open*, *3*(1), 100101. doi:10.1016/j.ssaho.2020.100101 PMID:34173507

Nimavat, N., Singh, S., Fichadiya, N., Sharma, P., Patel, N., Kumar, M., Chauhan, G., & Pandit, N. (2021). Online Medical Education in India–Different Challenges and Probable Solutions in the Age of COVID-19. *Advances in Medical Education and Practice*, *12*, 237–243. doi:10.2147/AMEP.S295728 PMID:33692645

Pandit, D., & Swati, A. (2021). *Exploring challenges of online education in COVID times*. FIIB Business Review. doi:10.1177/2319714520986254

Park, Y. (2011). A Pedagogical Framework for M-learning: Categorizing Educational Applications of Mobile Technologies into Four Types. *International Review of Research in Open and Distance Learning*, *12*(2), 78–102. doi:10.19173/irrodl.v12i2.791

Rose, C. (2013). BYOD: An Examination of Bring Your Own Device In Business. *Review of Business Information Systems*, *17*(2), 65–70. doi:10.19030/rbis.v17i2.7846

Serneels, P., & Dercon, S. (2021). Aspirations, Poverty, and Education. Evidence from India. *The Journal of Development Studies*, *57*(1), 163–183. doi:10.1080/00220388.2020.1806242

Sharples, M. (2013). Mobile learning: Research, practice and challenges. *Distance Education in China*, *3*(5), 5–11.

KEY TERMS AND DEFINITIONS

EDUSAT: Educational Satellite belongs to Indian Institute of Remote Sensing, Indian Space Research Organisation (https://www.iirs.gov.in/EDUSAT-News).

IoT: Internet of things is the emerging technologies with information and communication.

MOOC: Massive open online courses for online education.

NEP 2020: National Education Policy 2020 implemented by Government of India (https://www.education.gov.in/sites/upload_files/mhrd/files/NEP_Final_English_0.pdf).

NPTEL: National Programme on Technology Enhanced Learning proposed by IITs (https://nptel.ac.in/).

SWAYAM: Study Webs of Active Learning for Young Aspiring Minds (https://swayam.gov.in/).

Technology: It is the application of scientific knowledge to create different resources and tools for the welfare of human beings.

Chapter 3
Developing Digital Presence for the Online Learning Environment:
A Focus on Digital AVC

Jennifer Ashley Bowens
ⒾⒹ https://orcid.org/0000-0002-6224-6992
GOAL High School, USA

ABSTRACT

Digital AVC (which stands for accessibility, voice, and consistency) is a three-tiered system that helps teachers develop a digital presence in their online or hybrid classrooms. Online educators need to be able to utilize the technology available to them to intentionally create an online presence that is both appealing and inviting to students so that students are more interested in interacting with their online class and learning materials. This chapter explains how educators can create an online presence that makes students feel connected, valued, and interested in engaging in the classroom material through a more intentional focus on their own digital accessibility, digital voice, and digital consistency.

THE GROWING NEED FOR A DIFFERENT KIND OF TEACHER

In the more traditional education classroom setting, teachers have from the time the bell signals the beginning of the class until the time that bell rings again to release students to complete their learning objectives. Within each class period, teachers should teach, scaffold instruction, differentiate, interact, model, encourage, re-teach,

DOI: 10.4018/978-1-7998-8077-6.ch003

and explain the assigned homework set for the next class within a given class period. However, distance learning, or the education of students who are not physically present at school by using online/virtual work assignments, is on the rise. In the 2017-2018 school year, about 21% of public schools in the 2017-2018 school year offered some or all courses entirely online while 30% of all charter schools had online course options. ("Distance Learning", n.d.). Online teachers need to complete all the same tasks as those in traditional teaching roles and be able to manage this with a distance learning setting.

While there are many similarities between the traditional and online classroom settings, they also have unique challenges. Despite the growing popularity of distance learning opportunities, Christopher Pappas of eLearning Industry shares a list of barriers that online learners struggle with. Among the list, he notes that many online learners often face boredom. Finding ways to successfully teach to all different types of learners within the confines of an online course is challenging. Learners who are not getting all their needs met in their online courses can easily find themselves disengaged and uninterested in the materials. Furthermore, it is difficult for online learners to be self-motivated and often uncertain of how to be successful in an online environment. (Pappas, 2016). Online students in primary and secondary grades can still find success in online classes if they have teachers with a working knowledge of how to differentiate instruction to fit the online models.

So, then, how do teachers evolve to meet the needs of today's 21 Century learners and make their (partial or fully) virtual classes both relevant and engaging? Some schools allow for a hybrid teaching model where there is instruction completed both in person and online so that students can experience both learning models. However, the online classroom still needs to be managed in a way that supports student learning and growth. The key to this task is for the teacher to immerse themselves in the class and develop a digital presence within that online learning environment. By creating an accessible, personalized, consistent experience for students, and by modeling these behaviors for students, an online classroom can be just as engaging and successful as the more traditional face-to-face classrooms.

Online educators need to be able to utilize the technology available to them to intentionally create an online presence that is both appealing and inviting to students so that students are more interested in interacting with their online class and learning materials. Educators can create an online presence that makes students feel connected, valued, and interested in engaging in the classroom material; this can be done through a more intentional focus on their own digital accessibility, digital voice, and digital consistency (otherwise known in this chapter as a teacher's Digital AVC).

The Purpose of Digital Presence

Regardless of whether an online instructor is consciously building their digital presence or not, they do, in fact, have a digital presence; the question is whether their digital presence is having a positive or negative impact on their students' learning. Educators that are not conscious of their digital presence within online/ hybrid classrooms are almost certainly the ones with a negative digital presence and are likely lacking in student engagement (and ultimately student success) as a result.

How, then, is digital presence defined? According to Goran Paun of Forbes.com, digital presence consists of:

an active and consistent social media presence [that] allows you to stay relevant to your audience and connect on a more personal level. ... It can give your brand the opportunity to boost engagement with your target audience, build your credibility and maintain your reputation. (Paun, 2020, para. 4).

While the term "digital presence" originated as a marketing term, it can still apply to the online presence that teachers create. Teachers need to be mindful of the digital presence they are creating within their virtual classrooms and ensuring this level of digital intentionality for all their students, who, in many ways, are the consumers of education.

How Digital Presence Relates to Online Teaching

A big part of developing one's own digital presence is to "stay relevant to your audience and connecting on a more personal level." (Goran, 2020, para. 7). Teachers that do not take the opportunity to connect on a personal level and build a quality relationship with their students - in either the traditional or online classroom - decrease the chances that their students will remain engaged with the course or their teacher. In 2019, Education Week reported that teachers who built strong relationships with their students saw an increase in student outcomes including attendance, engagement, and grades. They also saw a decrease in poor classroom behaviors and dropout rates" (Sparks, 2019). Truly effective teachers will build their classes on a foundation of strong, intentional, professional relationships with their students. Teachers who choose not to build quality relationships with their students decrease the chances that those students will be motivated to invest themselves in the class.

In terms of digital presence, online educators must consistently ensure they "boost engagement with [their] target audience, build credibility, and maintain [their] reputation" (Goran, 2020, para. 7). First, boosting engagement efforts with online students requires teachers to develop creative ways that lead to the class being more interesting for students; online learning should be fun. Second, building credibility within an online course requires teachers to built trust and confidence in their students so that everyone knows what to expect from the teacher and the course. This makes their experience more predictable and worthwhile. Finally, maintaining one's reputation as an online teacher is done by maintaining consistency in interactions and expectations throughout a course. When students, as the consumers of learning, come to see that they can rely on a teacher to be engaging, trustworthy, and consistent, then students will be more interested in returning for more online learning experiences.

DIGITAL ACCESSIBILITY, VOICE, CONSISTENCY (DIGITAL AVC)

Digital AVC consists of a three-tiered system created to assist online educators in the development of their own digital presence within online or hybrid classrooms. It is considered a tiered system because each piece builds on the one before. The development of one's digital presence takes time, practice, and intentionality. The Digital AVC system provides tools for teachers to work on over time as they work to develop a strong, positive digital presence.

Digital Accessibility

The first step in the Digital AVC tiers is: Digital Accessibility. Digital Accessibility is the idea that the teacher has setup the online experience to be user-friendly: the class and materials are all easy to find, easy to use, and easy to follow/ understand. Classroom setup traditionally comes before any learning begins. The setup of any class often speaks volumes to a student about the teacher's personality and expectations. Within an online classroom, the layout and chosen aesthetics are often the first introduction a student gets of their teacher, and much thought and care should be taken to ensure a good first impression for students. As actor Will Rogers once said, "You never get a second chance to make a first impression." Online teachers, likewise, should take care to ensure their classroom setup gives their students the best first impression of themselves and their class as possible.

Since much of the learning within online and hybrid schools happens in an asynchronous or individual capacity, students must be able to easily navigate course content when the teacher is not around; depending on the school, the amount of time in which a teacher is not actively present in their online class could range from not often to very often. If students are expected or allowed to complete work when the teacher is not immediately available, the course and assignments need to allow students to move from one task to another more-or-less effortlessly.

Easy for Students to Find

Students need a course that is easy to find. Course materials should be in a location and format that are simple to locate and access. The first barrier to this may simply come down to the usernames and passwords required for their online course platform(s). Teachers need to plan for this issue and make sure to provide the login information in a format that is very easy to find and read. Emailing logins to school accounts is probably not going to fix this issue because students will then need to figure out how to log into their school email to access it. One solution to this would be to directly text individual students the link to their course home page and their login info to sign in with. This method ensures that students have those first steps at their fingertips-and that they have the phone number to their teachers before they even start working in the class.

Another important note to support the ease of students accessing their course content is to ensure all materials and tools are all located in the same place. With so many wonderful apps, tech tools, and programs that support student learning and allow for more engaging lessons, it can also be very cumbersome and frustrating if students are constantly redirected to new pages or platforms to complete their assignments. Finding ways to minimize the number of redirects that students require to complete their lessons can make their experience in an online class much easier to manage. Utilizing a learning management system (LMS) that allows for items to be directly imbedded into the class is one way to help minimize this issue.

One final note on making online course materials easy for students to find is for teachers to make a conscious effort to organize their content and sections clearly. As students are navigating their course materials, it can be easy to get lost if there is a lack of clarity in what they see on the screen. Students need to be able to follow the thought process of the teacher, especially when they are engaged in asynchronous work. Teachers must be able to leave very clear directions and have their course materials free of obscurities so that students are clear of what their next steps are as they work through their online course.

Easy for Students to Use

Today's students have grown up in the modern digital age and spend an average of seven hours and 44 minutes a day on technology (Jacobo, 2019). However, their technology-based experiences do not make them naturally good at navigating the online platforms that classroom content and assignments are housed in (Jacobo, 2019). In fact, during a 2017 interview-style discussion with multiple college students, many stated they still had not mastered even the more commonly used programs such as Microsoft Word, Microsoft Power Point, or Google Docs. (Abamu, 2017). Even if students are highly experienced with technology, able to use a variety of apps, or are an up-and-coming YouTube star, it does not automatically mean that they are going to be able to navigate their online courses without support or training. Recognizing that students are coming into their online courses with a variety of technological proficiencies is imperative for online educators as they plan for and develop course content that is truly user-friendly. Some ways to support students with lower levels of technological proficiency include:

- imbed video tutorials of the course.
- use short videos or screen snapshots to demonstrate how students can navigate their way to/through new digital content.
- be willing to restate the steps students need to use when accessing their course content.

Just as teachers assess the background knowledge of their students before introducing new academic content, it is also important for online educators to assess the background knowledge that their students have regarding technology. This can be done through questionnaires, skills-assessments, or even short interviews with students at the beginning of a school year. Ensuring that all content - both academic and technological - is appropriately scaffolded to meet the learning needs of each individual student is a highly important tasks for all online educators.

Easy for Students to Follow or Understand

While there are some smaller steps teachers can take to make their online course user friendly, teachers also need to be mindful of the educational limitations of their students and plan for differentiation within their online content. All students have different learning needs. Research even shows that the way people learn is as unique as their fingerprints (Loder, 2020). Online educators are not off the hook when it comes to providing differentiations and choice within their curriculum. Diversifying online course content and planning for diverse learners helps ensure that the assignments themselves do not become a learning barrier for students.

Not all students learn the same way and many students today also struggle with reading. In fact, according to the Ascend Learning Center (2021), 66% of American students are not reading at a proficient level. Therefore, it is important to be mindful of student limitations and work with them to find ways to support them when they are stuck or uncertain of how to proceed.

Planning for Diverse Learners Online. Teachers must always plan for diverse learners in their class; online classrooms are not the exception to the rule. There are many best practices for supporting diverse learners in the traditional classroom and many of those practices also work for online students (even if the implementation looks a little different). Online teachers do sometimes have to be a little extra creative when developing or diversifying their lessons and assignments to meet the differentiated needs of their students. However, planning to support diverse learners in an online course is still an imperative part of making sure the class is accessible to all students.

While the focus of this chapter is online presence, it is important to make note of some of the ways in which online teachers can implement their skills of digital accessibility to support diverse learners in their course. Consider, for example, an online class that has students with multiple learning styles, stages of language development, and reading levels. An online teacher with just these three differentiated needs in their class could incorporate the following tactics to improve online accessibility:

- provide students with more than one choice of how to complete an assignment.
- present content to students in both written and recorded (video) form so they can both listen to and read the information.
- introduce new or important vocabulary before a new unit.
- allow students to move through the class at their own pace.

Besides supporting the diverse learning needs of students, these online supports also allow for student autonomy and choice as they navigate through their course. Students will have the ability to learn at a pace appropriate for their individual needs as well as engage in lessons that support their own format preferences.

Additionally, readers at all levels need to be given clear instructions at every step, have repetition of important pieces of learning sprinkled throughout lessons, and be given frequent checks for understanding throughout the course. Online instructors need to be mindful of these needs and ensure that these learning supports are also integrated into their class and the resulting data utilized to improve student outcomes (Universal Design for Learning, 2018).

Content Display and Layouts. Being mindful of how information is displayed within the online classroom is also an important part of ensuring online courses are easy to follow/understand. For example, many readers are intimidated by large blocks of text. Sometimes referred to as text walls, large blocks of text with no break in them can be daunting or off-putting. This is especially true for lower-level readers or readers with difficulty in reading comprehension. One formatting method that could be used to minimize the use of text walls is chunking, which is the process of dividing information into clearly related groups of content (Moran, 2016).

Chunking also allows readers to scan text for information more easily and this can support readers as it becomes easier to preview their lessons or take notes before, during, or after their reading. Previewing and taking notes are both important steps of reading process, particularly when comprehension and overall understanding of the material is the goal. Lower-level readers and those who are not yet proficient in English often need to take in information a slower pace as their fluency and/or comprehension skills are often lacking. Chunking gives students the information in more easy-to-chew pieces.

Some minor ways to display information on the digital pages of an online course to support students as they aim to identify key information include:

- highlight key words or vocabulary words.
- utlize numbered or bulleted lists to avoid large text blocks.
- choos fonts and colors that are not difficult to see.
- insert visuals, short videos, or conicise summaries to aid comprehension.

Mindful presentation of the curriculum on the digital page can support students in their quest to internalize their subject matter. Intentional layouts can minimize confusion and allow students to feel more confident as they move on with their asynchronous learning adventures.

Online Teachers as Customer Service Reps. One very important part of Digital Accessibility is that the teacher is made available to students who find themselves needing extra support, needing answers to unresolved questions, or facing technical difficulties. If students could teach themselves, they would. Even though the internet allows them access to the answers of nearly every question imaginable, students simply do not always know what it is that they still do not know. In other words, students still need teacher assistance to truly grow in their understanding of subject matter and find success. For online educators and students, the customer service piece of answering questions about both academic content and online platforms/technology is integral to student success.

The interactions and support students receive from their teacher are highly important to their success in the class. A survey among 61 educators from a primarily online school in Colorado (GOAL High School) showed that students often give up and stop engaging in a class if they cannot understand an assignment or at least easily access their teacher for support when a question arises. The question posed to this group was, "based on your experiences, how many times will a student try something on their own before they give up?"

Those surveyed had varying levels of experience working in both education and within the hybrid format of GOAL High School. More than 78% of staff who were surveyed shared that, in their experience, students would not try more than two times to figure something out before failing to persist. The reality exposed here is that if students cannot easily access their teacher or they cannot understand the content, they will give up. In a traditional brick and mortar class, this would be the equivalent of a student choosing to ditch class because they are not satisfied with the support that they are getting in class, or they have determined that their teacher is unreliable and/or does not care to support their individual needs. Students need their teachers to be good customer service representatives. Students need someone who is supportive, show they care, and are digitally accessible for support and encouragement.

Digital Voice

The next step in the AVC tier system is Digital Voice. In literature, once's voice refers to the emotions, attitude, tone, and point of view of the author. Both writers and teachers can infuse their voice into a work through intentional and meaningful use of word choice and writing style (Voice, n.d.). Online teachers double as authors as they write and create online materials for their students to learn from and interact with. Teachers need to be mindful of the tone they are setting within the contexts of their online course.

In a traditional classroom, the voice of the teacher can set a tone for the class. For example, teachers can speak in a loud or soft tone, a slow or hurried tone, and even in an enthusiastic or disinterested tone. Students may interpret these tones in different ways and the tone a teacher uses can just as easily inspire learning as it can intimidate or frustrate them. While online teachers may not get to utilize their voice in the same way as classroom teachers do, they do use their voice just as often. Some ways that voice can be demonstrated within an online course:

- the use of text that does/does not match the reading level of the students.
- how often words of encouragement may/may not be used.
- have lessons and directions are/are not formatted in user-friendly ways.
- if inclusive language is/is not present.

Since digital communications do not always allow the use of non-verbal cues, it is even more important for online educators to choose words and phrases that promote their true intentions. However, it is possible to be engaging and inviting when operating in a primarily online environment. One way this has been proven true is through the success of social media; blogs, pod casts, YouTube, TikTok, and so many more online platforms have demonstrated ways that voice and tone can be effectively shared with audiences of all backgrounds. Likewise, teachers should be mindful to use words and phrases (in both verbal and text-based communications) that help to convey their own interest in the lessons they create and conversations they participate in. Creating a patient and supportive online environment can be possible when teachers are intentional about the digital voice they use.

The Role of Non-Verbal Communication

Non-Verbal communications include all the things that contribute to the meaning of a conversation, outside of the actual words and sounds associated with speech. Speakers constantly give clues and signals to the listener - be it intentional or not intentional - of that conversation from which they can interpret as important to the overall meaning. Some examples of non-verbal communication include posture, eye contact, and facial expressions. Other subtleties, such as tone and inflection also add to the listener's overall understanding of what the speaker is telling them.

Communication is much more than just the words we speak (or type). The Mehrabian Theory, developed by Albert Mehrabian, Professor of Psychology, asserts that a mere seven percent of communication is comprised of the words we use (Mehrabian, 1971). Another 38% of our communication is comprised of the tone of the words we use (Mehrabian, 1971). Tone in this instance refers to the sounds and speed of speech. That leaves 55% of our communications to be wrapped up in non-verbal communications (Mehrabian, 1971). Meaning that over half of what a listener takes away from a conversation has nothing to do with what is even being said.

For educators working in primarily online settings, which are not setup to allow for constant sharing or decoding of non-verbal communications, having clear communications can be quite a challenge. In online communications, more than half of all content that makes up communication is likely to get left out entirely (Mehrabian, 1971).

Online educators are at a disadvantage because many of the modes of communication used in an online education setting do not allow for the sharing of non-verbal cues and therefore the overall meaning of conversations can easily be misinterpreted. Lost in Translation author, Kristen Betts (2009), confirms that body language is effectively non-existent in online courses and that teachers need to find ways to compensate for the loss of this traditional communication tool. While the online classroom setting allows students more freedom to work anywhere, practicing intentionality in how communications are shared is highly important to ensure that students are able to clearly understand the expectations and intentions behind all teacher communications.

If students cannot see a teacher speaking and cannot hear them speak, then most of the cues listeners typically rely on to deduce the meaning of a conversation are null and void. So, whenever possible, online educators need to plan to minimize miscommunications within their platforms. Physician Alex Lickerman (2010) asserted that textual communications, such as through text or email, are more likely to lead to misunderstandings by the reader than verbal communications. This is due to the lack of non-verbal communications which make it much more likely for the recipients of those texts or emails to incorrectly decode the meanings or intentions behind the communication - they are, in effect, lacking context and clarity.

There are some best practices that online educators can utilize to minimize the possibility of miscommunications within their interactions with students when using text-based communications. These best practices include:

- Utilize step-by-step instructions.
- Use visuals (pictures, videos, screen shots, etc.) often.
- Reduce the use of idioms.
- Re-read messages for clarity.

Teachers are human and therefore can not remove all possibility of miscommunications. There are many different reasons that miscommunications might happen even when one is being careful with their communications. Some miscommunications are the result of a difference in backgrounds. Sometimes it is due to a lack of careful listening/reading on behalf of the other participant. It might also be due to a lack of relational capacity built between two parties and therefore they are not able to make appropriate inferences about the other's intentions. (Spoelma, 2018). Despite these (and other) natural hazards of communication, teachers can still find success in digital communication formats and ensure that miscommunications are minimized when interacting with online students.

Modes of Communication

Digital voice is also about being intentional with the mode of communication chosen for a given situation. Constantly assessing student interactions to find the best mode of communication to effectively solve an issue is a best practice for virtual teachers to get in the habit of doing. Sharing lengthy texts or visual examples is not always the best way to teach a subject or answer a question. Online instructors should always be looking for ways to minimize confusion and frustration among their students. To that end, educators also need to be willing and able to:

- create/share videos in place of the traditional mini lesson.

- initiate a phone call or video call with a student to help provide clarity or answer questions in a one-on-one or small group setting.
- share screenshots or visual examples that more clearly convey what the teacher is expecting from the student.

Students have a lot of responsibilities as learners; they should attend class, behave, be ready and willing to learn, complete all assignments, give every assignment 100% of effort, grow their knowledge, grow as a person…and do each of these things for every teacher/subject. Students need to be allowed to focus on learning and growing; teachers need to focus on breaking down barriers to student learning and ensuring they each are capable of being successful. For both parties to be successful in these endeavors, online communications need to be constantly being assessed for accuracy and usefulness.

Digital Consistency

Finally, teachers need to focus on Digital Consistency in their online classrooms. Digital Consistency is the idea that teachers are consistently active within their online classrooms and easily noticeable to their students. Students need to see the evidence of teacher activity throughout their classrooms. Some examples include weekly updates posted in the class, teacher engagement in online discussions, and frequent feedback notes on student assignments. Since online classrooms often do not require daily face-to-face instruction, students need to have constant evidence that the teacher is present and active within the class. This consistency helps to develop course structures, enforce expectations, and even foster relationships between students and teachers since they are both being active participants in the learning environment.

Consistency of Course Structures

Humans are creatures of habit; they like having routines and to know what to expect from a typical day. All good teachers implement norms, routines, and tradition into their classes to help ease transitions and allow students to feel more comfortable. Within an online course this can - and should - still be done, although it may look a little different from the implementations seen in more traditional classrooms. Some examples of utilizing consistency in course structures may include: using the same formats in lesson delivery, having students complete similar assignment types across different units, and even having similarities in the types of reminders and updates shared throughout the week. When students learn how to be successful and the teacher chooses to use similar assignments and systems in the future, then students will be able to recall the previous experiences and employ the same or similar tactics to find success again. Allowing students to see and interact with similar assignments and systems over time also reduces the number of questions from students, limits the amount of clarification needed, and helps students repeat their successes with fewer struggles as time goes on.

Communication methods can also be an example of course structures in an online setting. Being clear about the formats in which students and teachers will be communicating and collaborating on assignments allows students to be confident about how and when feedback can be sought or given. Furthermore, teachers can create consistency by having a standard timeframe for answering student questions or when giving assignment feedback. Turn-around times on student support and feedback enforce structure within a course and help the teacher to prove they are more than just a robot. When students know how to reach their teacher and where to look for feedback, they are then empowered to take on a more active role in their own learning.

Online educators should also build consistency around the types of technology tools used within their class. There are many apps and digital tools at the disposal of the 21st Century teacher. While variety can be fun, it can quickly become cumbersome for students to have to navigate the nuances or intricacies of different tools. By being intentional and consistent with the systems used within a particular class, students can find some comfort in the routines found throughout their class. Consistency can help minimizes how often students might get stuck or confused on assignments too. If students see consistency in the platforms they are being asked to navigate, then students will be able to alleviate some anxiety and allow for more focus on educational growth than seeking out technical support.

The Importance of Video Chats. One tool that all online educators need to establish early on as a consistent learning experience is video chats. For the purpose of creating consistency within classroom structures, it is important to ensure that video chats (or live video lessons) be established early on in the course and be used often. Students will have questions and, as discussed previously, not all questions can be effectively answered through textual communications. In a face-to-face setting, conversations can happen more fluidly and naturally. Students and teachers can also speak more candidly and not have to worry as much about the miscommunications that more easily happen in text-based interactions. For online/blended schools that do not offer physical locations for students and educators to work in together, video meeting platforms provide a great resource to utilize instead.

Along with establishing consistency through video chat sessions, teachers must also be intentional about creating a safe, welcoming, and collaborative environment for students so that they feel comfortable and encouraged to come back to that space. Not all students are accustomed to online live videos, and it is not uncommon for students to feel uncomfortable showing their video (or living space, for that matter) right away. It is often quite awkward to see oneself on video, but teachers should be both encouraging and patient with students while they get accustomed to a new way of learning and collaborating.

It can take time for students to get accustomed to any new class structures and feel confident enough to trust those systems. Teachers can ease those tensions by continuing to extend both patience and encouragement to their students throughout this process. It is important for teachers to champion online classroom expectations through modeling and repetition as well.

Consistency of Expectations. Every course should have a set of pre-determined expectations that drive the daily interactions of students and teachers. Typically, when a teacher outlines class expectations and holds students accountable to those expectations, it is referred to as classroom management. Classroom management techniques must be present in online classes just as they are within more traditional settings. Classroom expectations in a blended course should include clear responsibilities for both students and teachers.

A healthy class culture is predicated by a set of carefully determined classroom rules. All students need to know what behaviors and outcomes are expected of them. There should also be clear consequences - and rewards - for student behaviors. All students should know what the teacher expects and to feel secure in their standing on any given day.

Student interactions within blended classes vary depending on the school's setup and what the school's systems or policies allow. Depending on the type and frequency of student interactions in an online course, different rules of engagement may need to apply. Whatever the online classroom expectations may be, both clarity and consistency are imperative. Teachers should post the expectations within the course and remind students of those expectations regularly. Students who do not follow class rules should already know what the consequences will be because the teacher will have, by that point, made both expectations and consequences very clear.

Since students in blended courses are often working on content and assignments in an asynchronous capacity, the relationship between students and the course itself is an important dynamic for online educators to be aware of. While students need to be fully aware of the expectations for independent work, it is the teacher's responsibility to follow up with and ensure that students are following teacher expectations in their absence.

Constant monitoring of student interactions with the course can offer the teacher an opportunity to provide useful feedback to students regarding their academic progress. Making a point of providing regular feedback notes to students not only helps a teacher see who is doing well/ who needs extra support, but it also allows the teacher to be proactive in reaching out to students for praise, encouragement, and clarifications.

Setting clear expectations for academic progress is also helpful to students. For example, teachers should consider the following: how students are to turn in their assignments, how many assignments should students complete in a week, what is the process for redoing a particular assignment, and are students allowed to test out of a unit or section. The answers to these types of questions should be clearly communicated to students. When students know how to properly interact with their course and navigate a typical day or week, they will be set up for greater success when the teacher is not immediately available.

Consistency in Teacher Interactions. Interactions with the teacher is a typical part of any class. While different online schools may require a different amount of direct teacher-student interaction, there are still many opportunities for an online teacher to integrate themselves within their class. Students should be able to expect consistency in the way their teacher interacts with them throughout the course.

In the fall of 2020, a group of teachers from GOAL High School - an online public charter school that has been serving at-risk youth since 2010 - were surveyed. These teachers were asked about the most frequently used methods of interactions being utilized in their online courses. The teachers' answers included:

- weekly teacher updates posted.
- recorded video lessons imbedded.
- using GIFs/memes/emojis to break up the monotony.
- scheduled class times (for optional live lessons).
- engaging in intentional check-ins with students that were not academically based.

One of the teachers surveyed simply noted that, "some students like to see the teacher's face." There is a lot to be said about human interaction. All people need human interaction. In fact, human interaction is highly beneficial to one's overall health. Jane Brody (2017) of the New York Times surmised from research of several studies that people who had regular interaction with others had overall improved health and longer life span than those that did not have regular interactions with others. Holding face-to-face interactions in high regard is a best practice for any educator wanting to improve the social/emotional wellbeing of their students.

Another important note on consistency is that teachers should not shy away from letting their personality come through in lessons and interactions with students in their online courses. This allows students to feel even more connected to their teachers and class curriculum as well as to see each class as a new experience instead of a continuation of one mundane online class after another. That is why it is important to develop a digital presence for online learning environment – it leads to a richer and more meaningful learning experience and is highly likely to lead to more engagement and improved learning outcomes.

When teachers share a bit of themselves and allow their personalities to come through in their interactions with students, it allows for both parties to connect on more meaningful levels. This allows for relationships to form and trust to be built between students and teachers, which can improve student self-esteem and even encourage positive attitudes to develop towards opportunities to interact with peers and course materials (Andersen, 1981).

Student-teacher relationships are crucial to overall achievement. Students want to get positive feedback on course work, but they need to have positive and authentic interactions with teachers to strengthen their desires to be accepted and successful.

CLOSING: DEVELOPING A STRONG DIGITAL PRESENCE

The basic practices of Digital AVC apply to the online education of all student types. However, depending on the age or ability level of the students in a given class, it may be necessary for teachers to rely more heavily on one or another element of the AVC tiers. For example, online elementary students may require more relationship building opportunities with the teacher than older students. A group of teenage students that are not reading at grade level could benefit more greatly from video lessons that come with transcripts to follow along with. Furthermore, college-age students taking online courses can also benefit greatly from a professor that utilizes Digital AVC even though they may not need as many reminders of requirements and expectations throughout the class as younger students. All online students deserve to have a teacher that knows how to utilize the digital environment to improve the learning experience.

Schools that are either fully online or simply offer online and/or hybrid course options are on the rise. The 21st Century teacher needs to be aware of how to build a strong digital presence so that they are prepared to take on the challenge of teaching students in an online setting. Utilizing the three-tiered process of Digital AVC gives educators clear and actionable goals that help them to create a stronger digital presence within their own online classrooms. Online educators need to be showing their students that they are available, supportive, consistent, and personable. By developing a strong and positive digital presence in an online course, teachers can foster a culture where students are capable and eager to focus on their own learning and personal growth.

REFERENCES

Abamu, J. (2017). *Students Say They Are Not as Tech Savvy as Educators Assume.* EdSurge Inc. https://www.edsurge.com/news/2017-06-20-students-say-they-are-not-as-tech-savvy-as-educators-assume

Andersen, J. F., Norton, R. W., & Nussbaum, J. F. (1981). Three Investigations Exploring Relationships Between Perceived Teacher Communication Behaviors and Student Learning. *Communication Education, 30*(4), 377–392. doi:10.1080/03634528109378493

Betts, K. (2009). Lost in Translation: Importance of Effective Communication in Online Education. *Online Journal of Distance Learning Administration, 12*(2). https://www.westga.edu/~distance/ojdla/summer122/betts122.html

Brody, J. E. (2017). Social Interaction Is Critical for Mental and Behavioral Health. *New York Times.* https://www.nytimes.com/2017/06/12/well/live/having-friends-is-good-for-you.html

Distance Learning. (n.d.). *National Center for Education Statistics.* Retrieved from https://nces.ed.gov/fastfacts/display.asp?id=79

Gottfried, M. A. (2009). Excused Versus Unexcused: How Student Absences in Elementary School Affect Academic Achievement. *Educational Evaluation and Policy Analysis, 31*(4), 392–415. doi:10.3102/0162373709342467

How Many Students are Actually Reading Below Grade Level?! (2021). *ASCEND Learning Center.* https://www.ascendlearningcenter.com/blog-highlights/howmanystudents

Jacobo, J. (2019). *Teens spend more than 7 hours on screens for entertainment a day: Report.* ABC News. https://abcnews.go.com/US/teens-spend-hours-screens-entertainment-day-report/story?id=66607555#:~:text=Teens%20spend%20an%20average%20of,technology%20and%20media%20for%20children

Kamenetz, A. (2019). *It's A Smartphone Life: More Than Half of U.S. Children Now Have One.* NPR. https://www.npr.org/2019/10/31/774838891/its-a-smartphone-life-more-than-half-of-u-s-children-now-have-one

Lickerman, A. (2010). The Effect of Technology on Relationships. *Psychology Today.* https://www.psychologytoday.com/us/blog/happiness-in-world/201006/the-effect-technology-relationships

Loder, M. (2020). *The Fingerprints of your Classroom.* Arizona State University. https://teachonline.asu.edu/2020/05/universal-design-and-your-allyies-pedagogical-strategies/

Mehrabian, A. (1971). *Silent Messages.* Wadsworth Publishing.

Moran, K. (2016). *How Chunking Helps Processing.* Nielsen Norman Group. https://www.nngroup.com/articles/chunking/

Pappas, C. (2016). *Top 8 eLearning Barriers that Inhibit Online Learners Engagement with eLearning Content.* eLearning Industry. https://elearningindustry.com/top-elearning-barriers-that-inhibit-online-learners-engagement-elearning-content

Paun, G. (2020). Building A Brand: Why A Strong Digital Presence Matters. *Forbes.* https://www.forbes.com/sites/forbesagencycouncil/2020/07/02/building-a-brand-why-a-strong-digital-presence-matters/?sh=306ff1a849f2

Sparks, S. D. (2019). Why Teacher-Student Relationships Matter. *Education Week.* https://www.edweek.org/teaching-learning/why-teacher-student-relationships-matter/2019/03

Spoelma, J. (2018). *Communication Breakdown: How Misunderstandings Happen and What to Do About Them.* https://careerforesight.co/blog-feed/communication-breakdown-how-misunderstandings-happen-and-what-to-do-about-it

The UDL Guidelines. (n.d.). *CAST.* https://udlguidelines.cast.org

Voice. (n.d.). *Literary Terms.* https://literaryterms.net/voice/

KEY TERMS AND DEFINITIONS

Chunking: The process of dividing information into clearly related groups of content.

Digital Accessibility: The idea that the teacher has setup the online experience to be user-friendly; the class and materials are all easy to find, easy to use, and easy to follow and/or understand.

Digital AVC: A three-tiered system that supports online teachers in the construction of their own digital presence so that student engagement and success can flourish in an online setting.

Digital Consistency: This is the idea that teachers are consistently active within their online classrooms and easily noticeable to their online students.

Digital Presence: How teachers appear to interact with and present themselves to students within an online classroom setting.

Digital Voice: The idea that teachers are intentional with the tone and mode of communication chosen for a given situation within the online setting.

Distance Learning: The education of students who are not physically present at school by using online/virtual work assignments.

Hybrid: A teaching model where there is instruction completed both in person and online so that students can experience both learning models.

Text Walls: Large blocks of text with no break in them.

Chapter 4
Developing a Positive Culture in the Online Classroom

Kristen Carlson

https://orcid.org/0000-0002-4559-8531
Minnesota State University, Moorhead, USA

ABSTRACT

The mission of this chapter is to provide principals and teachers with an understanding of how to create a positive learning culture within an online classroom through utilization of the engagement triangle: students, teachers/school staff, and outside community members. The chapter introduces student agency through online instructional strategies and techniques for teachers to increase student motivation. Further, assessment practices are addressed in ways that can add to a positive classroom culture. At the end of the chapter, case study scenarios and reflective questions will be shared for practicing P-12 teachers to consider when designing learning opportunities in their online courses.

INTRODUCTION

School structure, such as the number of days of school attended, schedules, and class offerings, have changed only slightly in format since the early 19th century. Schools in the 19th century were not designed for the 21st and 22nd centuries, where technology has infiltrated our lives from smart TVs to Alexa-enabled outlets that answer questions one might ponder. While there has been an abundance of innovation, invention, and information advancement in the world since the 19th century, the structure of the classroom environment and the schooling system has not changed as drastically as life outside of the classroom has, until recently. Over the last decade,

DOI: 10.4018/978-1-7998-8077-6.ch004

technology-enhanced classrooms with an emphasis on creativity and problem-solving when designing lessons has started to enter education. This, joined with innovative educators, has allowed some schools to transform K-12 classrooms for tomorrow. Post-coronavirus pandemic, educators will have the opportunity to create and foster a new classroom culture, one of positivity for one another and towards their learning. This chapter will provide implementation strategies for how instruction, assessment, and other engagement strategies can be utilized to develop a positive learning culture for K-12 learners in distance learning environments.

BACKGROUND

Learning in our K-12 classrooms can be strengthened or weakened by our teachers and school structure. The procedures, policies, and classroom interactions all enhance or detract from the classroom and school culture. As you have likely experienced, in a face-to-face setting, the school culture can be seen and felt upon entering the school building. Sometimes, the classroom culture is more difficult to read immediately, but by spending time in the class, adults can often perceive how the students and teacher feel about one another and whether the learning culture is positive or negative. In an online classroom, there are additional barriers such as technology and course design that can also impact classroom culture, making it more difficult to immediately perceive and requiring intentional forethought to the community design of the online learning spaces.

There are several types of online learning environments that have existed over the last few years, if not decades, at the K-12 school level, ranging from fully asynchronous programs to completely synchronous. While doing school fully synchronous, the live video conferencing all day scenario can quickly burnout a teacher and the students in terms of screen time on the computer. However, it can often be easier to develop a sense of community within the synchronous classroom because students and the teacher can interact simultaneously and read one another's body language and/or tone of voice. In the asynchronous classroom, where students and the teacher work on their own times, not in a live setting via video streaming, the opportunity to connect can be more difficult if not built intentionally into the course delivery mechanisms. In the online classroom, "if a learner feels alone or isolated in the course, they will quickly disengage with the content and assessments. However, when a sense of community is present the learner feels more comfortable engaging with the content, asking deeper questions to the instructor, and discussing [learning material] with their classmates" (Carlson, 2021, p. 155). Purposeful teacher engagement and classroom community building activities need to be added to the online course. With the increase in collaboration tools found on the internet, this is easier than ever to do asynchronously if planned for in the course design.

STUDENT AGENCY

Student Engagement through Agency

Student choice and voice provides learners with the opportunity to feel empowered with the knowledge they are constructing. In an online course this can occur in a variety of means: opportunity for collaboration with other students, relevancy-based assessments, and problem-based content learning for example. The connectivism theory focuses on digital technology and social networking opportunities to facilitate and guide learning. This requires learners to be open to gaining new knowledge, sharing information with their network, and creating new content. Examples may include collaborative note-taking amongst students within the same class, video-conferencing opportunities for students to question experts related to the topic of study, and partnering with local businesses in the community on projects that align to the course. By asking students to be open to trying new strategies for learning within the course, students will experience "expression of self, control, and independence" (Smidt, et al., 2017, p. 2118). Likewise, connectivism can allow for learners to seek creative, diverse opinions and solutions by connecting with far-away learners or scholars. As more is being learned about connectivism, K-12 school staff are beginning to integrate key components of the approach into their classrooms. For example, in a high school Somali language classroom, the teacher may have students collaborating with one another to build language acquisition skills. From there, they may connect with local agencies or historical societies to apply their Somali language learning to create activities for visitors of the agencies, to volunteering at the agency, and more. This community engagement allows the learners to connect with classmates, the language teacher, and the external community members all working in unison to foster stronger Somali speaking, reading, or writing skills for the students in the course and to also, create a positive, supportive connection between school and community. When students are actively involved in utilizing the content knowledge from the course to help others, they become invested in their learning. In an online course, the same example might apply but the finished product may be different. The students may create a translated video to submit back to the local agency, they may have created a digital brochure or started a website for the agency. Based on the community organization's needs and the students' interests, a choice can be provided. By providing student empowerment in the classroom, "we might find that our students' contributions can raise the level of engagement and provide more depth and rigor to the curriculum" (November, 2010, p. 194).

In addition to collaboration opportunities, the inclusion of technology can empower students to become engaged. Sheskey (2010) noticed that when providing his face-to-face students with digital cameras during their science lab for the purpose of adding pictures to their lab reports, student motivation for writing lab reports significantly increased. Similarly, by showing other students' lab pictures to his class, Sheskey (2010) found that the students entered the peer-review process without his guidance. They were able to have deeper, meaningful discussions about the lab set-ups and results. Curiosity, engagement, and authentic connections between students and content were the result. Students made comments regarding the visual results on the screen and asked their classmates questions about how their procedures were able to get a result in that way. The teacher facilitated the discussion, impromptu, instead of summarizing each of the group's results as he had in previous years. To make authentic connections in the online classroom, these same techniques can be utilized to provide student agency. Teachers should work to facilitate relevancy-based assignments. When students can make a connection between their content learning, their life, and have control over the end result, they will have personal agency. Examples of relevancy-based assignments could include, at the elementary level, that students conduct an assessment that includes meal planning for a week, going into as much detail as appropriate for the grade level. This could include using the nutrition guidelines to select main entrees, sides, drinks and then budgeting the costs. At the secondary level, students may design book reviews or podcasts to critique a recent literature book for their peers or they may design a new playground or park in a mathematics class. By utilizing relevancy-based assignments, students will likely allow themselves to feel motivated, empowered, and in-control of their own learning. As students become comfortable with this method of learning, the classroom culture will move in the positive direction. Students will have the opportunity to ask question of one another and the teacher-facilitator. To begin establishing student agency for the purpose of improving classroom culture in the online environment, the next section will discuss specific instructional strategies for the teacher.

Online Instructional Strategies

Whether teaching content in a science course or an arts course, the basic structure of learning still exists - where students must understand the goals of the unit, how the goals will be measured for success, and the learning content must be delivered to students through a mechanism for learning. Instructional strategies are abundant and can fit many subject areas. In Gagné's (1965) Nine Events of Instruction, he provided instructional strategies that address the steps required for effective learning.

These steps include: i) Gain attention, ii) Provide a learning objective, iii) Stimulate recall of prior knowledge, iv) Present the material, v) Provide guidance for learning, vi) Elicit performance, vii) Provide feedback, viii) Assess performance, ix) Enhance retention and transfer (Clark, 2014).

Of those nine events, in online coursework, often step five, learning guidance and step six, elicit practice/performance are overlooked. In a face-to-face classroom, learning guidance is facilitated by the teacher based on live interaction with the students. A teacher may notice the class is struggling with a concept or are asking numerous questions around a key piece of information. If this happens, the teacher has the opportunity to facilitate this learning guidance by reframing a content lecture and by offering supplemental readings or videos. Then, in step six elicit practice, students have the opportunity to take notes or to interact with the learning content through small group work. These important instructional strategies are not managed in the online classroom by teachers in the same way as in the face-to-face setting described above. In the learning management system of the asynchronous course, there is not a teacher circling the room, monitoring students and providing immediate learning guidance (step five of Gagné's Nine Events of Instruction). However, the instructional support still needs to be provided. In the online course, teachers need to anticipate and develop learning guidance before the students need to access it. It could come in the form of pre-developed study guides, self-check quizzes, case studies and built-in models of examples and non-examples.

The second event that needs to be pre-designed for the online course that is often embedded into the face-to-face lesson plan is that of eliciting student performance (or practice), step six in Gagné's (1965) Nine Events of Instruction. Through discussions and debates, formative assessments, and projects, students have the opportunity to showcase their learning in a safe and often collaborative environment. During in-class worktime, in a face-to-face classroom, students can talk to one another which creates a close-knit community bond. They can also obtain feedback from one another and the teacher on their learning performance. This occurs during daily work time where often, a teacher will roam around the classroom checking in with students who might be practicing their learning on worksheets, with manipulatives, and /or discussing with peers. However, in an online classroom, students may be doing their coursework at very different times throughout the day or week causing impromptu check-ins to become difficult to manage for the teacher. This can cause isolation for students if purposeful community building and elicitation of performance is not built in. To support intrinsic motivation of the active learner processes for the students in an online course, the teacher must design and develop purposeful opportunities for eliciting performance and for feedback between students. One use of this is through problem-based learning scenarios at the end of a particular unit or lesson. A teacher could create case studies that relate to the unit where students have the opportunity to reflect and respond, debate, and /or think critically about a different story or scenario than previously discussed in class. A teacher could also allow students to work collaboratively in small groups to present information about the unit to showcase their learning. For example, a trio of students could design a brief, graphic novel retelling a historical event (social studies) or a story about geometry proofs (mathematics) or the life cycle (biology). Further, students could design interview scenarios where they write a script about an interview of historical person (in any content area) and then record the podcast with software such as Anchor.fm. These interviews can be shared within the asynchronous course using URLs and /or file shares between the teacher and the students.

In an effort to maintain student to student connection in an asynchronous, online course, teachers must think outside of the box when designing collaborative components. Peer review on assignments builds communication and engagement, but collaborative assessment creation helps students to feel empowered as well. In a study conducted by Smidt, et al. (2017), the connectivism approach was blended with problem-based learning to create a new theoretical approach for future implementation. The researchers set out to "operationalize the connectivism principles into an actionable framework with inclusion of problem-based learning and contextual learning" within a middle school setting (p. 2116). In their research, they describe the components of connectivism and how they relate to the STEM coursework, when infused with problem-based learning. Relevancy and connectivism in the classroom, whether online or in-person, can facilitate an increase in motivation for student learning. Connectivism provides opportunity for learners to grow in unprecedented ways by using an approach that "presents a model of learning that acknowledges the tectonic shifts in society where learning is no longer an internal, individual activity" (Siemens, 2004, p.4). Rather, learning becomes a collaborative process with peers to build upon our current knowledge. Teachers have the opportunity to facilitate the learning process by creating relevancy-based assignments and assuring students are moving in successful directions when investigating additional topics and applying their learning in the project- based setting. By embracing online instructional strategies that emphasize thoughtful implementation and student motivation techniques, teachers can support student agency while contributing to a positive classroom environment.

MOTIVATION IN ONLINE CLASSROOMS

Intrinsic and Extrinsic Motivation

Intrinsic motivation for an online learner often comes from an interest in the learning material and /or a student's connection with the teacher or other students within the course. Regular communication with students through weekly announcements, mini-lectures, and assignment feedback helps students maintain their own intrinsic motivation in the online setting. The teacher to student communication process and schedule for providing feedback regularly within the length of the course will also foster a stronger learning culture. By clearly outlining the communication expectations and processes for the course in the syllabus, the teacher can begin to build intrinsic motivation for the student by setting boundaries for feedback, questions, and assignments. If students know ahead of time how to communicate appropriately with the teacher and the other students, they will feel successful in their first few attempts to interact with everyone in the classroom. Demotivation occurs when communication processes seem unclear and /or are not followed.

Extrinsic motivation can be built into an online course through graded assignments, required activities and visual awards. In an online classroom, visual cues such as sticker images can act as an extrinsic motivator. In corporate professional development scenarios, the learners may call these badges but at the K-12 level and within the classroom, these are similar to sticker reward charts. Simply adding images and personalization to the grading feedback can be an extrinsic motivator to students. For example, an image of a star or Bitmoji thumbs-up provides extrinsic reward to young learners. At some age levels, the earning of one hundred percent or a high score creates extrinsic motivation. On a discussion board, the teacher may choose to add images of graphs or famous landmarks to support the relevant topic at hand. The inclusion of a second type of media, first audio recorded feedback, but then, the supporting visual image(s) provides motivation and further cements the learning within the students' brain.

When designing the online course, it has been successful to utilize video gaming techniques to provide extrinsic motivation. This has been referred to as gamification, which is the "integration of game elements like point systems, leaderboards, badges, or other elements related to games into 'conventional' learning activities in order to increase engagement and motivation" (Centre for Teaching Excellence, 2021, para. 3). Grades do not have to be the driving factor to motivate students. In fact, some students will become demotivated by grades. To promote extrinsic motivation, in a two-hundred level undergraduate course, content for the next unit was not visible to students until they successfully "leveled up" by interacting appropriately (either showing mastery of a learning outcome through an activity or engaging with the

Figure 1. A screenshot from the 200-level digital media online course
Note. *The course has been gamified to include Bitmoji characters to tell a story. In this example, the students are moving to the next world, or unit in typical education-speak. You can see a rather large easter egg, or fun exploration icon, at the end of the world introduction dialogue.*

So... you went from traveling in time backwards to some weird futuristic year... seriously, where are you? In this world, creativity is looked upon favorably unless you are trying to steal someone else's copywritten work or create fake news. Both of those will get you locked up! But what is creativity?

You'll need to explore your inner self and find your creativity within to survive this level!

content for a particular amount of time) with the content learning in the current unit. While this motivation is not grade related, it did excite students to frequently check their content area to see if new units, badges, and /or quests had appeared based on their work in the previous unit.

Examples of gamifying that might occur in an online elementary or secondary course could be very similar to that at the undergraduate level since the idea of gamification is based on board games. A teacher could create competition between themselves and the students whether academic or community building. Another idea would be to create role-playing opportunities where students work together to solve a case study, puzzle, and /or fix a problem. Finally, using real-world applications, such as Google Maps, Duolingo, or Geogebra, within the online course will add its own gamification from utilizing the app for the content exploration. For example, in Google Maps, students can explore Washington D.C. or the Egyptian pyramids using Street View. This activity can then be gamified by the teacher's design of the lesson, meaning, what the teacher asks the students to report back on can be gamified through the digital worksheet or slide creation.

Techniques for Teachers

There are several techniques that teachers can use to engage and motivate students in an online course such as welcoming students, following regular communication processes, providing quality feedback, and building relationships with their students. First, by sending a welcome message for the course from the teacher to the students, the students are better prepared for a successful start. This is similar to the first day of class in a face-to-face environment. A classroom teacher would not immediately approach the whiteboard and begin lecturing, he or she typically talks through the classroom expectations, syllabus, and classroom features. This should occur in an online course as well. The connection built and delivered in a welcome message shows the teacher's interest for the students and sets the extrinsic motivation level for the classroom culture. The students also have the opportunity to learn about course software processes, assignment expectations, and more. Through the detailed written message or video welcome, the student has the opportunity to get to know the teacher as well as have a better understanding of the course.

Examples of how this might be implemented in an online course include sending a welcome email about a week before the course begins. This email might include a personal, yet, professional biography of the teacher, a list of the course materials that each student should have before the first day, and how to access the course (whether it is a video conferencing link with a day and time or a URL to the learning management system with directions on how to enter the specific course). Then, in the asynchronous course itself, the instructor may choose to create a five to ten-minute video that is a walk-through of the class. This is helpful for students as sometimes each teacher may utilize different tools and organizes the learning material in different ways. A brief video provides students with the opportunity to hear directly from the teacher about how to navigate and expectations for use of each tool in the course. These two items, a welcome email and brief video, allows the students to be prepared for success within the course from the very first interaction. In turn, this teacher action sets each student up for success which leads to an increase in intrinsic motivation and the "can do" attitude.

Second, through communication processes, such as modeling and active engagement, from the teacher during each unit of the online course contributes to student motivation as well. The explicit responses from the teacher to students' posts on a discussion board signal to the students that the teacher is reading the posts and is engaged within the course. If students are asking similar questions or are struggling to complete particular assignments, a teacher may create a short video walk-through of the assignment or consider posting an example of a completed assignment with specific annotations on it of where assessment criterion were well done and /or could be improved. Likewise, if a teacher posts an exemplar discussion post prior to the required assignment due date, students have a better understanding of the end product for a unit. This motivates and encourages students without causing angst about what to do or how the finished product should look.

To maintain communication, one particularly quick way to check-in with all students within the course is to create short weekly videos. In these, no course content would be shared, but the teacher summarizes what he/she has been working on in the course (such as providing feedback) and shares the perceptions of the work seen. Also, the teacher might talk about what is upcoming in the course, if there are any upcoming deadlines, large projects or items to be aware of course or school wide. In my courses, these (less than) five-minute videos are posted every Monday in the announcement area of our learning management system. The placement of these videos is purposeful, it is the first section that students must see when they access our course in the learning management system. The Monday Minute is essentially a brief meeting between myself and the students about recapping last week and stating what everyone should be working on this week. At particular times within the course, I will remind students about upcoming school-wide events, such as course registration for the upcoming year and counseling or advising services.

The third technique teachers might try to encourage learning engagement and build motivation would be by providing feedback to students. Teachers should work to regularly compliment students on the skills they demonstrated and encourage them to develop those skills further. This is a strengths-based approach to providing feedback that can help to build students' intrinsic motivation over time. Feedback is most effective for learners when it is constructive, but also future-focused (Leibold & Schwarz, 2015). In their article, Leibold & Schwarz (2015), outline seven best practices for giving feedback in an online setting. These include: i) addressing the learner by name, ii) frequent feedback, iii) immediate feedback, iv) balanced feedback, v) specific feedback, vi) a positive tone, vii) and ask questions to promote thinking.

These best practices can be implemented in an online K-12 classroom via assignment feedback or discussion board replies. The feedback can be in different mediums, as discussed previously, and may include written text feedback, audio, or video-based feedback. Providing feedback may also happen during synchronous online sessions as well. For example, teachers may hold a regular class meeting time, similar to in a face-to-face setting. Immediate feedback while working through content learning together would align with Liebold & Schwarz's (2015) best practices. Likewise, teachers could provide one-on-one office hour appointments for specific assignment feedback or just regularly schedule online drop-in times to meet synchronously. The more engaged a teacher is in the feedback process and the more personality a teacher can inject within a course, the more the students will be engaged and motivated to persevere through the course.

The final technique addressed in this section would be to build purposeful interactions that foster relationships between teacher and students. This may occur anytime the teacher enters the online classroom, whether asynchronous or synchronously. During content knowledge delivery through recorded lectures, if the teacher uses his or her own webcam and voice, as opposed to found lectures published on YouTube, the students are more likely to be engaged and invested in the lecture material in a more meaningful way (Mayer, 2021). Similarly, utilizing personal cartoons and /or real photographs of the teacher within the course gives the content more depth and personal engagement opportunities for the student to build a connection with their teacher.

These pieces of personality might show through when grading assignments or when providing weekly or unit announcements as well. When grading, a teacher can typically provide multiple types of feedback on assignments, written, graphic, annotated on the assignment, audio recording, and /or video recording. Images and clipart can be used as a means of showing a sticker within the gradebook. On pass or fail assignments that likely do not require in-depth written or verbal feedback, a quick thumbs-up Bitmoji, or avatar smiley can build a connection with a student or at least allow the student to feel like a valuable member of the course. For lengthy written assignments, like essays or reflection papers, the teacher could add a more personal touch by providing a one-minute audio recording for feedback instead of typing out their statements. This method also does not take longer than the written feedback because in most cases, the teacher can record and read the document simultaneously within the learning management system, speaking as if the student is right before the teacher discussing the student work together. The modality principle states that "people learn more deeply from pictures and spoken words than from pictures and printed words" (Mayer, 2021, p. 281). Incorporating this principle into the feedback process allows the teacher to encourage students to remember the feedback for the future. This could include images along with a brief narration or even a screen recording of the teacher providing feedback on the students' works. Personality can also be injected into the regular announcements through video, but also the use of dialogue that might be different than when writing a lecture or course content. When designing announcements or unit introductions, write with an active voice. It can help to imagine talking with one of the students and to let the words flow seamlessly, revising after all of the information is written out. This dialogue creates the warmth and empathy can tend to be absent between teacher and students in an online course, simply due to distance in time and space from one another.

Finally, a teacher can design opportunity to allow students the time and space to provide feedback to one another fostering the student to student interaction and relationship building opportunities. The accountability of students to know the information and to teach each other increases their engagement. Students do not want to share incorrect information to their peers, so they work diligently to learn the content within the unit, especially if they know they will need to use it to assist their peers at the end of the unit. These collaborative opportunities for students to give content and /or skill-based feedback alongside of the teacher can occur through asynchronous activities such as discussion boards (written or video), online documents (such as Google Docs), and through synchronous opportunities if the school permits via video conferencing software (such as Google Meet or Zoom) or live text chat (such as Discord or Google Hangouts). Intrinsic and extrinsic motivation can be supported in the course design and through the teacher's implementation of several techniques such as clear communication, feedback best practices, and student to student opportunities. These techniques help to support the positive classroom environment in an online modality.

USING ASSESSMENTS TO FOSTER POSITIVE CULTURE

Online Formative Check-Ins

Often when the term *assessment* comes to mind, teachers and students immediately think of a traditional paper and pencil test. However, there are many formative learning opportunities that would also fall under the heading of assessment. In an online classroom, formative assessments can provide the student and teacher opportunity to connect relationally with one another as well as provide learning feedback. Through evidence of learning and feedback (without associated points or grades), students can be provided with a chance to feel engaged in the course, with the learning material, and with the teacher. Similarly, purposeful peer review can help a student feel empowered in their own knowledge to provide resources to another student but it also reinforces their own learning of the content, in addition to fostering student to student connection.

To conduct formative check-ins in an online environment, the feedback should remain student-focused, not work focused. Williams and Scalise (2021) explain that students should work to improve future products. Doing this will reduce the emotional reaction of the student; similarly, action-based feedback that is "more work for the recipient than for the giver" (para. 16) is not meant to penalize the student but provides opportunity for improvement. Feedback in itself is helpful regardless of if students are in a face-to-face or online classroom. However, in the online environment, relationships between the feedback giver (teacher or student) and receiver (student) will make or break the effectiveness of the feedback. Without a pre-existing relationship or community amongst the students in the class, feedback can be received in the wrong way because of the tone of the provided feedback. Liebold & Schwarz (2015) recommend including praise and encouragement to motivate the student towards improvement. In addition, including specific feedback will build a positive rapport amongst students. In the peer review process, students should have clear criteria to follow for providing feedback to their partners. For example, instead of accepting a comment that says "good job" coach students to provide more information, such as "good job with including the frame of reference on your answers" or "good job using proper in-text citations". These positive relationships exist because of purposeful design of a classroom community at the beginning and throughout the school year through collaborative activities and communication processes. When meeting synchronously with the class, in small groups, or individually, the use of screensharing and text chat to provide feedback will provide an increase in student engagement (Williams & Scalise, 2021).

Authentic Assessment Strategies

Whether teaching content in a science course, a world language course, or really, any content or age level, authentic assessments can promote a positive culture. Authentic assessments are typically summative in nature and allows the students to create content to showcase their learning (Wiggins, 2015). Opportunity to share their creative endeavors with the students in the class through peer review or formal presentations increases both student motivation to do the assessment well but also allows them to feel part of the community. This, then leads to fostering a positive culture. In an online course, teachers may feel they cannot create authentic opportunities but with a little creativity and stronger understanding of authentic assessments, K-12 students can be solving "realistic but fair complexities" (Wiggins, 2015, para.8) within their content area. Examples of authentic assessments in an online course might include the creation of a website that showcases the students curated knowledge. Students might create a podcast series to share with others about their learning over the course of a year or semester.

Key components to designing this type of assessment include a feedback loop, allowing for several formative check-ins, long term growth and reflections from the student, and an opportunity to share the created outcome with others – whether that be classmates, the school, or the outside community. In an online classroom, the check-ins with peers or the teacher can be held through discussion boards, Flipgrid videos, or live meetings such as Google Meets or Zoom sessions. The final product showcase might be held online via a website but depending on what the output is, perhaps it could be broadcast at the face-to-face affiliated school in the lunch or commons area, or even distributed via local businesses in the district's city. Overall, teachers and administrators should plan for authentic assessments and formative feedback opportunities when implementing online courses. The engagement and communication channel are most important when establishing a positive learning culture in the online classroom.

FUTURE RESEARCH DIRECTIONS

Following the conclusion of the COVID-19 pandemic, schools may choose to continue utilizing distance learning options to provide flexibility to students, especially, those at the secondary level. As distance education increases and continues to move towards mainstream, at least in hybrid form, in K-12 public school districts, students deserve to have top notch experiences. This cannot happen if our teachers are not prepared to teach using the online modality. Teacher preparation programs and educational researchers would serve the K-12 students well by continuing to research online learning best practices while integrating multimedia theories into their education sequences for preservice teachers. Further research to understand how teachers should best prepare to design, develop, and serve online students would be beneficial. For example, should teachers be receiving instructional design training or online development skills during preservice training and what type of in-service trainings do veteran teachers need to thrive in an online learning model? Finally, online teaching is still teaching, the modality does not change the purpose or end result for our students. Administrators, current teachers, and teacher educators must remain innovative and willing to try new techniques for the benefit of our future students.

CONCLUSION

Teachers and administrators have the opportunity to create engaging, rich, online communities in which courses are delivered. With the proper design and development of learning content and community building, the students will develop a positive learning culture within their online classroom. By increasing the student to student interaction and through utilization of motivational techniques, teachers will foster a strong learning environment where students can be themselves. Further, the use of authentic assessments instead of traditional exams will strengthen the learning culture for everyone involved in the learning process. Students will become engaged with the content and their peers while teachers will be able to make relevant connections in the content for students. As online learning continues to be an option for K-12 students, teachers and administrators should embrace the opportunity to develop meaningful connections with students through this modality.

Case Study

1. You are currently teaching an online advanced course in *{your subject area}*. Students in the course tend to be high achieving and self-motivated to do well. The online curriculum that you have designed relies on an introductory college

level textbook. Students read a chapter, answer questions on the discussion board, and complete an assessment that varies by unit. This format is repeated each week for the sixteen-week course. By week 9, students are starting to become less active and engaged. Discussion board posts are submitted last minute and student replies to one another are sometimes overlooked by the time the deadline arrives. How could you use non-graded, extrinsic motivation to encourage students to participate in the discussion boards in a timely manner, thus increasing student to student interaction within your online class?

2.   This is your first semester teaching in an online environment. The course curriculum and technologies were pre-designed for you, but you have the ability to modify it as needed. For the most part, you did not need to make too many changes to the course for it to fit your teaching style in regard to student to content and student to student interaction. You began the semester without any concerns about student engagement. It is now six weeks into the new online course. While you did respond to each student on the introductory discussion board and you have graded the first two assignments, you are beginning to notice that the visual cues you relied on in the physical classroom are lacking in the online environment. It almost seems like the course you were provided relied heavily on individual student emails, outside of the learning management system, for the teacher to student interactions. In your previous face-to-face courses, you enjoyed talking with students at the beginning and end of every class. This allowed you to build a relationship with students, take a temperature of how they were feeling about the course material, notice if there were any gaps in understanding, and any be up-to-date on any outside pressures that might be impacting your students' lives. Where would you start to now begin building a relationship with students, even though it is six weeks into the semester? How would you check-in with the students? And, how would you re-design the course in the future regarding teacher to student interactions to include that important formative check-in and relationship building components?

Reflective Questions

1.   How might you adjust your current grading and assessment practices to increase student motivation within your course?
2.   What strategies might you employ and what might you say to motivate a student who is struggling in your online course (for reasons unrelated to the content of the course)?
3.   What advice would you give to a student who is new to online learning?
4.   How might you re-design your online course to encourage student to student interaction?

REFERENCES

Carlson, K. (2021). Supporting Students Through Online Learning. In Handbook of Research on Inequities in Online Education During Global Crises (pp. 148-162). IGI Global. doi:10.4018/978-1-7998-6533-9.ch008

Centre for Teaching Excellence. (2021). *Gamification and game-based learning.* University of Waterloo. https://uwaterloo.ca/centre-for-teaching-excellence/teaching-resources/teaching-tips/educational-technologies/all/gamification-and-game-based-learning

Chickering, A. W., & Ehrmann, S. (1996). Implementing the seven principles: Technology as a lever. *AAHE Bulletin.*

Clark, D. (2014). Robert Gagné's Nine Steps of Instruction. *Big Dog & Little Dog's Performance Juxtaposition.* http://www.nwlink.com/~donclark/hrd/learning/id/nine_step_id.html

Finley, T. (2014). *Dipsticks: Efficient ways to check for understanding.* Edutopia. https://www.edutopia.org/blog/dipsticks-to-check-for-understanding-todd-finley

Gagné, R. (1985). *The Conditions of Learning and the Theory of Instruction* (4th ed.). Holt, Rinehart, and Winston.

Leibold, N., & Schwarz, L. M. (2015). The Art of Giving Online Feedback. *The Journal of Effective Teaching, 15*(1), 34–46. https://uncw.edu/jet/articles/vol15_1/leibold.html

Mayer, R. (2021). *Multimedia Learning* (3rd ed.). Cambridge University Press., doi:10.1017/9781316941355

November, A. (2010). Power Down or Power Up? In H. Jacobs Hayes (Ed.), *Curriculum 21: Essential education for a changing world.* ASCD.

Sheskey, T. (2010). Creating Learning Connections with Today's Tech-Savvy Student. In H. Jacobs Hayes (Ed.), *Curriculum 21: Essential education for a changing world.* ASCD.

Siemens, G. (2004). *Connectivism: A learning theory for the digital age.* http://www.elearnspace.org/Articles/connectivism.htm

Smidt, H., Thornton, M., & Abhari, K. (2017). The future of social learning: A novel approach to connectivism. *Proceedings of the 50th Hawaii International Conference on System Sciences.* 10.24251/HICSS.2017.256

Wiggins, G. (2015). 27 Characteristics of Authentic Assessment. *Teach Thought.* https://www.teachthought.com/pedagogy/27-characteristics-of-authentic-assessment/

William, D., & Scalise, K. (2021). Formative Assessment for Remote Teaching: Evidence and Feedback. *Respond & Reimagine: Academics in Uncertain Times*, (16), 9.

ADDITIONAL READING

Black, L. J., Wygonik, M. L., & Frey, B. A. (2011). Faculty-preferred strategies to promote a positive classroom environment. *Journal on Excellence in College Teaching*, 22(2), 109–134.

Boettcher, J. V., & Conrad, R.-M. (2016). *The online teaching survival guide: Simple and practical pedagogical tips* (2nd ed.). Jossey-Bass.

Clark, R., & Mayer, R. (2016). *E-Learning and the Science of Instruction.* Wiley. doi:10.1002/9781119239086

Conrad, R. M., & Donaldson, J. A. (2011). *Engaging the online learner: Activities and resources for creative instruction.* Jossey-Bass.

Darby, F., & Lang, J. M. (2019). *Small teaching online: Applying learning science in online classes.* Jossey-Bass.

Felten, P., & Lambert, L. M. (2020). *Relationship-Rich Education: How Human Connections Drive Success in College.* Johns Hopkins University Press.

Kosslyn, S. (2021). *Active Learning Online: Five Principles that Make Online Courses Come Alive.* Alinea Learning.

Nilson, L. B., & Goodson, L. A. (2018). *Online teaching at its best: Merging instructional design with teaching and learning research.* Jossey-Bass.

Pijanowski, L. (2018). *Architects of Deeper Learning: Intentional Design fr High-Impact Instruction.* International Center for Leadership in Education.

Stavredes, T., & Herder, T. (2014). *A Guide to Online Course Design: Strategies for Student Success.* Jossey-Bass.

Tokuhama-Espinosa, T. (2021). *Bringing the Neuroscience of Learning to Online Teaching: An Educator's Handbook.* Teachers College Press.

KEY TERMS AND DEFINITIONS

Authentic Assessment: Summative assessments where the students create or construct their learning for the teacher or other viewer. It often allows for creativity and shows relevance to the students' lives.

Connectivism: A learning theory expanded upon constructivism where students work collaboratively amongst themselves to create new knowledge and understanding.

Engagement: Students interact with course material and regularly communicate with the teacher and other classmates.

Extrinsic Motivation: An outside influence, often teacher-driven incentives, for a student to engage with the course learning material.

Intrinsic Motivation: A student's internal drive to engage in the course learning.

Learning Culture: The norms and expectations of community that are established between the students, teacher, and the school.

Learning Environment: A space, virtual or physical, in that the teacher and / or student has created for learning to occur.

Student Agency: The student has opportunity for shaping his/her own learning and is comfortable communicating and expressing himself/herself creatively to reflect on the learning process.

Student-to-Content Interaction: The student interacts with the course instructional materials, such as a video lecture, reading the textbook, or using adaptive learning materials.

Student-to-Student Interaction: Students interact with one another during a course via communication methods such as discussion boards, video messages, and collaborative class projects.

Teacher-to-Student Interaction: The teacher interacts with an individual, small group, or whole class of students to communicate information. This can be through video or text class announcements, discussion board posts, video lectures, or electronic communications.

Chapter 5
Assessing Student Learning in Online and Hybrid Classrooms

Gökhan Kayır
https://orcid.org/0000-0002-9830-0006
Ministry of National Education, Aarburg, Switzerland

ABSTRACT

Education systems and methods are shaped according to the needs of societies and technology. Today, technological possibilities bring about deep and radical changes in every field. With the educational environments becoming computer-aided and online, the measurement and evaluation of student achievement had to be computer-assisted and online. The purpose of this chapter is to provide the basic logic of computer-based measurement and evaluation and to explain the methods. Computer-based assessment and evaluation have many benefits for students, teachers, and institutions. While the advantages include continuous monitoring of students, low cost, and rapid and equal access to many students at the same time, it is seen as a disadvantage that students have the opportunity to cheat and get outside help.

INTRODUCTION

The industrial revolution that started in the 1800s is now followed by the information revolution. The Prussian education model, which follows a systematic and school-based education, is no longer able to serve the needs of our age, because the information is increasing at a rate that has never been before, and with the development of technology, people can access information from different sources. Although increasing information and technology is seen as a threat to the classical functions of the school, educational institutions now have to adapt themselves to the times.

DOI: 10.4018/978-1-7998-8077-6.ch005

New technologies allow the continuous delivery of educational services that would normally be interrupted by pandemics, natural disasters, or geographical conditions.

Today, hybrid, distance and online education methods provide teaching services to a wide audience, mainly in higher education and non-formal education. The purpose of this chapter is to explain what online and hybrid teaching is and to provide information on the evaluation of student success, especially in such educational settings. The integration of technology in classrooms has become crucial competency for teachers as it improves learning. Students pay more attention to the lessons if they are reinforced with technological and digital tools (Al-Mahdi, Al-Hattami & Fawzi, 2018).

While studies on technology-based assessment were directed towards the use of computer programs until the end of the 1990s. Since the 2000s, it has become internet-based. The spread of the Internet has made material distribution easier, reaching more people, and time-space independence (Reiss & Reips, 2016).

Has the Conventional Schools Place in the Future?

When we look at the development of the concept of school historically, it is seen that there is a need for an institutional school and an education system to train the human type needed with the industrial revolution. The education process, which could be carried out in a master-apprentice relationship in agricultural societies, had to reach wider masses due to the increase in production. Information produced more slowly than today could be transferred to students in this traditional school system. Today, it seems impossible to give the rapidly increasing information in teacher-student communication and in the form of the teacher being the source of information. Will this lead to the disappearance of schools? It is accepted by everyone that a technological and pedagogical transformation has begun and it will inevitably continue. However, we still need the school.

Berge (2000) states that teacher and student communication is provided through technology in synchronous online lessons. While these face-to-face lessons require many materials such as blackboard, chalk, books, notebooks and pencils, technology can eliminate most of them. Moreover, students can access the lessons later if they are registered. However, although there is an interaction, it is also a matter of debate whether it is of quality as in a normal classroom setting.

In a traditional classroom setting, the teacher instantly evaluates the students' situations from their behavior and other non-verbal cues. Thanks to these perceptions about whether his students are bored, whether he understands the subject or his current mental state, he can reach him more. It can improve the quality of teaching by completing the missing points. While the success of the student in the classroom environment depends on his characteristics, in online classes, the student must have a technological infrastructure and be sufficient to use technological tools (Bakerson, Trottier & Mansfield, 2015).

The fact that the transition process from face-to-face education to online education was faster than expected has made it challenging for teachers to design lessons or adapt their lesson plans in face-to-face education to online lessons. The most common difficulty was that the opportunities brought by interaction and cooperation in face-to-face lessons could not be realized in online education (Lock & Redmond, 2015).

What is a Computer Based/ an Online Classroom?

Online classrooms (also called virtual classrooms) are computer-mediated systems that offer a teaching and learning environment to their users. Like a school with different classrooms, they have "workspaces" in the software (Hiltz, 1997). Online classes offer unique and exciting opportunities for assessing student achievement (Clecker, 2007). It is possible to reach data about the student that cannot be obtained in a traditional classroom and to evaluate the student in a multidimensional way in online classrooms. The fact that teachers are competent to make such an assessment is the compelling point of such assessments.

In the past 20 years, online education has become more and more important in our lives. Although educators have difficulty in adapting to this type of education method because it requires learning new technologies, the quality of learning outcomes is at the expected level, which causes this field to attract more attention (Aly, 2013). It can be stated that online education is changing our approach to teaching and learning deeply day by day (Durnalı, Orakcı, & Aktan, 2019).

Shank and Sitze (2004) explain the high interest in online learning as; it provides more access and flexibility; standardization; improved control. It is good for faster delivery and cost savings. Also, it facilitates communication and collaboration.

Online classes can be of two types. The first of these are synchronous classrooms, which require simultaneous connection of students and teachers to a system, as in the real classroom. In these environments, participants can perform real-time training activities by connecting to a system independent of their physical environment. Such classes, which were carried out on television or cable TV in the early stages of online education, are now held over internet applications and one-way communication can now be carried out in two ways (Berge, 2000).

The other type of online lesson is an asynchronous course. These type of lessons are not live and students and the instructor does not simultaneously connect a software. Instead, lessons are recorded and students can reach these records whenever and wherever they want. These types of lessons let students think more reflectively and check their learning before going on to the next lesson (Hiltz, 1997).

The implementation of lessons in an online classroom is very similar to a classic classroom. The only difference here is the planning of the effective use of technological opportunities. Determining the learning objectives is a key issue that affects the success of the course at this stage, as in any environment. After determining what students need to learn, learning situations, tools and assessment methods will be designed accordingly (Bakerson, Trottier, Mansfield, 2015).

The Definition of the Hybrid Classroom

Hybrid classes are finding more and more applications today as a method that can overcome the inadequacy of classical classes and close the lack of face-to-face interaction in online classes. Providing students with the opportunity to realize their full potential, the use of technological tools and the provision of a flexible program increase the probability of success of this type of teaching. As in online education, it can enable groups that would be socio-economically disadvantaged in classical education to be more involved in education. It allows individuals with children and employees to experience the feeling of being a member of an academic community (Harrington, 2010).

Assessing Learning in Digitalized Classrooms

Assessment can be defined as the documentation of students' learning with measurable evidence. Students' knowledge, abilities and beliefs are evaluated according to educational levels. The aim here is to increase students' learning (Bakerson, Trottier & Mansfield, 2015).

The criteria to be used by the teacher in assessment and evaluation must be shared with the students at the beginning of the semester. They should have information about the expectations of the course and the teacher themselves by doing studies by these criteria beforehand (Lock & Redmond, 2015).

Today, accountability is among the top priorities in educational environments as it is in every environment. Teachers are also responsible to students, parents and administrators about the processes of their evaluations. Measures that increase accountability in face-to-face education cannot be expected to work in the same way in online environments (Bakerson, Trottier & Mansfield, 2015).

Joshi et. al (2020) summarize the advantages of online assessment for teachers, students, institutions and educational goals as such:

The use of technological tools at online classrooms makes assessment easier for the teachers. However, there are a lot of criteria to be followed. Palloff & Pratt (2003) lists the principles to be followed in the assessment process in a digitalized classroom as follows:

Table 1. Advantages of online assessment (Joshi et al. 2020).

Students	• Higher control, friendly interface • Higher flexibility • Fast and easy to use • Easy accessibility from remote areas • Receive immediate feedback • Increased motivation to enhance performance
Teachers	• Greater flexibility with any place and any time assessments • Better utilization of time through simplified and quicker examination procedures • Improved quality of feedback to students • Can track students' progress • Easy to analyze assessments • Reduced workload • More flexible and imaginative assessments are possible, with greater relevance for students, for example; by using simulations, audio and video clips
Institution	• Fast and accurate results • Reduced cost for the institution
Educational goals	• Supports higher-order thinking skills like critiquing, problem-solving, reflection on cognitive processes and facilitate group work projects • Provide accurate results by adaptive testing

1. Use learner-centered assessment tools that students can reflect on.
2. Develop rubrics that take into account the active role of students in the process.
3. Plan collaborative work where students can comment on each other's work and be share with different people.
4. Constantly provide students with feedback to motivate them, providing a model to frame them where necessary.
5. Plan activities that are simple, understandable, well-structured and applicable online.
6. In the first week of class, discuss with the students how the assessment should be done and get their opinion as well.

Accrording to the schema at Figure 1, which was developed by Barbossa and Garcia (2005), the content of a lesson should be readapted for the online course and the content should be turned into a form that is suitable for e-learning. The acquired knowledge should be assessed by the teacher via online tools. Teacher should evaluate the result for the students and for him/herself. Then the instructor continues with the new user profile and knowledge level at the next course or year.

Benson & Brack, 2010 (p.126) group the tools to be used in measurement and evaluation in digitalized environments under 4 subheadings. These are;

Figure 1. Assessment in the e-learning process (Barbossa & Garcia 2005; p. 1)

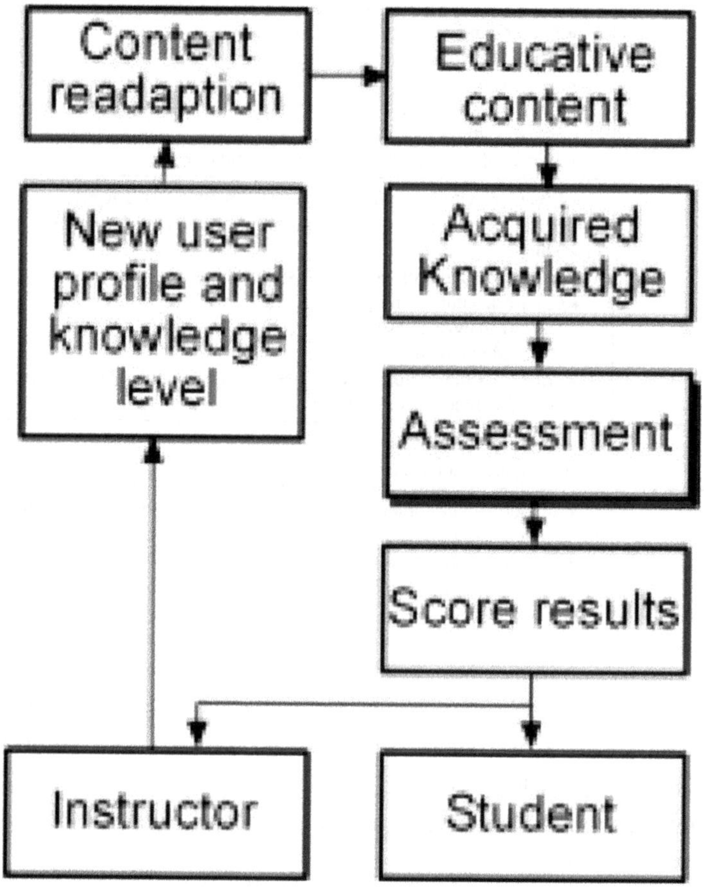

Studies uploaded to the system: discursive, descriptive and analytical articles; project reports; critical and analytical evaluations; visual materials of pictures, audio, video and presentations.

Automatic assessment: multiple-choice, matching, fill-in-the-blank, check-and-drop, true-false questions; multimedia with animation.

Online discussions: case studies and forums to discuss projects; role games; games with role cards

Webcast: e-portfolios; web pages such as blogs and wikis; shared documents.

One of the strong sides of computer-based assessment is that it enables the use of authentic assessment. The use of these tools in digitalized classroom environments is effective in achieving the purpose of measurement and assessment. Lock and Redmond (2015) list the common features of authentic assessment as follows.

a) The events themselves or the context of the event are realistic or relevant to the real world.

b) the task is performance-based, not very tightly structured, and allows for different answers.

c) Students collaborate with others to complete the task. They advocate and discuss their solutions.

d) Indicators showing that learning has taken place after the completion of the task are valid, reliable, and as told to the students beforehand.

Criteria for a Good Computer-Based/ Online Assessment

Numerous studies are listing the criteria of a good computer-based / online assessment. At one of the last and comprehensive studies, Westhuizen (2016) makes a comprehensive criteria list. The list is shown in Table 2.

Formative vs. Summative Assessment

In general, evaluation can be divided into two subgroups as formative and summative evaluation. Although measurement and evaluation are generally seen as a method of grading students' success and making a decision about it. For teachers, it also means diagnostic assessment, where they can check their students' learning and get information for their subsequent teaching. The type of assessment that teachers use for this descriptive assessment and their subsequent feedback is called formative assessment. From this point of view, it can be considered as the opposite of summative assessment (Boston, 2002).

The type of summative assessment shows a summative feature at the end of the training process and aims at a certification. It usually shows a passive feature and does not affect the learning-teaching process. However, it is a prerequisite for the student's further learning. From this point of view, the difference between formative and summative assessment is in terms of purpose and effect (Sadler, 1989).

Formative assessment leads to new educational experiences for the teachers and learners. It is like a pedagogical strategy for learning. With the formative assessment term, a critical change in the assessment and evaluation field happened. As it provides interactivity and formative feedback, Students have meaningful, multidimensional, and self-regulated learning (Gikandi, Morrow & Davis, 2021.)

Formative assessment with computer technology brought new concepts to education. One of them is "cyber coaching" a model of formative assessment without papers. This is a teaching approach in which teachers monitors, adjust their instruction and learn student needs via formative assessment tools (Chang & Petersen, 2006).

Table 2. Criteria for a good online assessment (Adapted from Westhuzen, 2016).

Criteria	Explanation
Longitudinal Reflection	Using formative assessment tools enables teachers to improve teaching practices and future learning tasks of the students.
Higher-Quality Feedback	The assessment process should be done with feedbacks that are designed timely, detailed, and constructively.
Readymade Tools	The student performance should be assessed with assessment standards and other standard forms like rubrics.
Authentic learning with Technology	Online assessment tasks should include real-life situations.
Student Collaboration	Tasks should require student collaboration and student discussion.
Rich Variety	There are a lot of online assessment tools present. A good teacher uses multiple tools to do a more accurate assessment.
Diversity	A good online assessment procedure takes into account student diversity such as socioeconomic status, racial-cultural differences. The students may not have technological means of devices or technological knowledge to use those devices.
Technology Readiness	The school should be ready to implement an online assessment procedure. To do this, teachers, IT staff and students should have enough IT knowledge.
Detecting students who are at risk	Teachers should monitor students' results and see the students who are behind the group and they should plan comprehensive catch-up programs for those children.

Table 3. Formative and Summative Assessment Compared (Adapted from Chanpet et al, 2018)

ASSESSMENT		
Type	**Formative**	**Summative**
Aim	Assessment for learning	Assessment of learning
When	During the course, by scaffolding	At the end of the course
What it is for	It is for improving learner knowledge,	Required for accreditation, diploma and validation
Can be done with ICT/ Internet	Yes, Easy to follow traces of activity	Visible and provable tools

Formative assessment methods serve better while grading according to individual differences. However, it is not easy to do them with online programs. The system must serve many learners at the same time and take into account their differences. If the system allows individual use and test adaptation, it will help to provide equality of opportunities (Ilgaz & Adanır, 2020).

Self – assessment

Feedback is an important part of formative assessment. It generally originates from the teacher. However, today it is widely accepted that students can assess their learning by doing self-assessment (Boston, 2002). For providing students to assess themselves, teachers can give them questionnaires, multiple-choice tests. Here one of the aims is to allow learners to promote their awareness about their learning. In this way, they will be aware of their needs (Booth, 2003).

The ability to manage self-assessment and peer assessment processes well is among the most basic skills for teachers. While the number of students is increasing at all education levels, online methods are also used more (Seifert & Feliks, 2018). In this case, it is important for the quality of assessment and evaluation that teachers have students do some of the assessment.

One of the areas where internet-based assessment is used most is self-assessment applications. Such applications can actively serve in the fields of career counseling, higher education, and health counseling (Reiss & Reips, 2016).

Peer Assessment

Peer assessment is another useful way to assess students in online or hybrid classrooms. In this way, students get comments about their works from their friends. As these comments were given by their friends who use the same language, It will cause more effect. Peer assessment is similar to collaborative learning as it may cause new knowledge and understanding. From this aspect, peer assessment is perfect if the teacher aims to do a formative assessment (Pol et al, 2008). Anonymity at the peer assessment process may lead to more honest and accurate reviews also the knowledge level of the group is important for assessment quality (Booth, 2003).

The use of peer assessment strategies by teachers improves classroom community development and allows students to learn by analyzing and criticizing the work of others. Rubrics are one of the tools used for peer assessment. The concrete setting of target performance criteria and the ability to reconstruct a normally large task in small parts makes this assessment tool advantageous. The peer-review process can be very effective especially in writing studies. Peer learning can be more effective in upper age group students who have reached a certain learning level (Kearns, 2012).

Mann (2006) lists benefits and limitations of peer assessment:

Table 4. Benefits and Limitations of peer assessment (Mann, 2006).

Benefits	Limitations
• The students learn how to think evaluatively. • They focus on the criteria related to their learning. • They get on their sense of assessment. • They set common criteria by working collaboratively. • It is good for understanding the system. • They take responsibility for marking • They have an opportunity to judge their work by comparing. • They develop self-awareness. • They become more motivated. • They can reflect on their learning. • They assess an analytic task.	• This kind of assessment requires a whole perspective on education. If the student-teacher and system definitions are too traditional, this assessment will most likely be useless. • Students may feel anxious while assessing their friends. They may feel incapable. • Students may not manage criticism if they are not educated so. They must be aware of the limits of social relations. • Students may not feel comfortable when they get negative feedback from their friends. • They may feel peer pressure. •

Assessment Tools for Digitalized Classrooms

Measurement and evaluation are some of the most important dimensions of education and training processes. It demonstrates the success of the program while providing concrete documentation of students' learning. The progress of students in certain subjects is also monitored through measurement and evaluation studies (Joshi et al, 2020).

Online assessment is not a new phenomenon for educators. Since the 1970s ways of using computers to deliver and analyze exams are studied. After the widespread use of the internet new methods are found. The independence from time and place is one of the causes of this kind of assessment (Graff, 2003).

Reeves (2000) states that the most important point to be considered in measurement and evaluation is the balancing of various elements of teaching. It is very important that the balance between course objectives, teaching methods, content, teacher and student competencies can be achieved while measuring and evaluating with technological tools.

Edublogs

Teachers must file assignments and tasks of the students during the formative assessment process. This is the most of the work and can be challenging for teachers, If they have many students. Blogs can be really helpful by helping teachers by filing the work online. Teachers of different subjects are using blogs for monitoring their students' learning. Especially language teachers have a growing interest in this kind of exercise because blogs support interactivity and content sharing (Ducate & Lomicka, 2008).

Considering that the courses are online, students can also be expected to provide online products. A website and online publications that students will develop individually or with a group of friends will help to involve peers or other different evaluators in the process (Booth, 2003).

Wong and Hew (2010) summarize the educational specialties of blogs as;

a.   Blogs enable students to publish their works immediately.
b.   The blog content does not need to include sophisticated technical knowledge.
c.   People can easily give feedback to the blog entries.
d.   The entries can be archived according to the entry date or the subject.
e.   The blog entries can be linked to other blogs and bloggers.
f.   Most of the blogs don't have spelling checkers as in word processors (Microsoft Word etc.) so the bloggers mostly rely on their spelling.
g.   When a blog is published, it is open to all internet users. However, most blog sites give the bloggers the chance to limit the entries.

Web-2 tools

While Web 1.0 technology is an environment where users are passive and use the produced information, with web 2.0 technology, it has been possible for users to contribute to the production of information and to make various opportunities with their inputs. Users can create content and interact with each other. Thus, the content on the Internet has increased very rapidly (Benson & Brack, 2010).

Like the other kinds of assessment tools, using web 2.0 activities for student assessment requires good planning. If the assessment process is properly done, students get a chance to learn more. If the teacher is not competent enough using web 2.0 tools, students may act prejudicial and do not participate in web 2.0 activities. Most of the Web 2.0 activities involve collaboration, negotiation of meaning, interacting with each other, so the assessment procedure should include the required steps proper use of these tools (Hung & Huang, 2016).

Gray and her colleagues (2009) summarize the criteria for a good assessment with Web-2 tools in seven items.

1.   Learning outcomes should be presented explicitly, the criteria should be clear and there should be statements for different learning levels.

2. There should be a close match between the assessment tasks and intended learning outcomes. Tasks should include the knowledge and skills that will determine the success of the work.
3. The tasks should be compatible with web 2.0 technology.
4. The grades should be just and make a direct link between the intended learning outcomes and students' actual performance on assessment tasks.
5. The grades of the tasks should be independent of the students' competencies for using web-2 tools.
6. The assessment tasks should include higher-order thinking skills and learning outcomes.
7. The tasks should be compatible with students' ages and proficiency levels.

Learning Management Systems

Learning management systems are the software used for managing online courses to train, educate or direct a group of students. Their aim is not the creation of content. These kinds of software are just for providing training materials and monitoring students' learning (Croitoru & Dinu, 2016).

There are a lot of tools available on the internet today and every day new ones come to the market. Although they have some differences, they are mainly for providing tools for course administration. Their pedagogical specialties differ for the aim and level of the learners. Coates, James & Baldwin (2005) lists functions of these types of software as;

- They provide asynchronous and synchronous communication (announcement board, e-mail platform, chat Windows, instant messaging and discussion rooms)
- They enable the users to develop content and deliver them to the other user both person-to-person and person-to-group.
- They enable the teachers to assess students both formatively and summatively. Students may submit their work or do multiple-choice tests. Also, they do collaborative projects. Teachers and other students can comment and give feedback to the others Works.
- Learning management systems has also an administrative use. The administrator can add students to the class, make timetables, manage student and teacher activities also electronic office hours.

Figure 2. Course design and the effect of feedback (Chang & Petersen, 2006, p115).

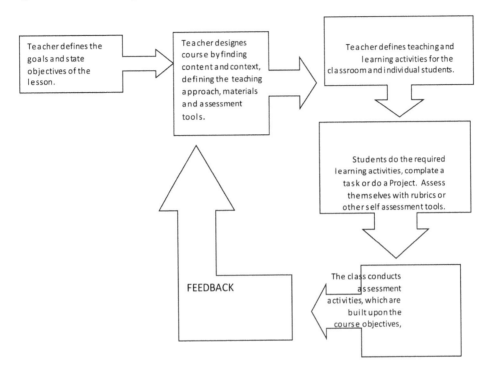

Student Feedback Tools

The difference between summative and formative assessment is feedback. It is defined by how successfully something is conducted or is being done (Sadler, 2009).

Chang and Petersen (2006) define the feedback process as a loop. The visualization of their scheme is below:

Rourke & Sawicki (2018) list three types of interaction in the online classroom as; student to student, student to instructor and instructor to student. The last one is about the content of the course generally. Student-to-student interaction helps students to learn from each other. Peer learning is one of the contributing factors to open-minded learning. Student to instructor interaction happens when a student asks a question to the instructor. Instructor-to-student interaction is about one-to-one feedback. Instructor-to-student interaction allows students to reflect on their learning (Rourke & Sawicki, 2018).

Classroom Response (Communication) Systems

Classroom response systems (CRS) have been used in classrooms widely since the 2000s. Generally, it is used for checking the attendance of the students to the lessons and summative assessment data, it is also useful when collecting data about students' previous knowledge of attitudes towards a subject. (Fies & Marshall, 2006).

Class response systems are often called also as classroom communication systems. These systems can be as simple as 2 buttons or can require an advanced computer system for each student. This network connects student units to the teacher's computer. A specially designed software controls the system and the whole system acts as a single unit. The teacher can send questions and all the answers are shown on his computer instantly with different statistics (Abrahamson, 1998). Today even with free apps teachers can use that technology. An internet connection and smartphone are enough today thanks to wireless technology.

Classroom response systems are especially useful in the classrooms where students are active, teaching occurs with discussion-centered techniques and learnings are co-constructed. Beatty (2004) summarizes the features of classroom response systems in these classrooms as;

-Teachers can immediately see the answers of the children in different statistical and visual ways.
  ◦ The students can see their own and their friends' answers on a big screen, so they can get a conclusion about their success.
  ◦ The system acts as a portfolio dossier as students log in with their passwords. The system collects personal data and can give individual results.
-Teacher sees the answers of the children individually and can give feedback to each.
  ◦ The system provides a map for the classroom. The students may see a lot of related information about their classroom and their learning. They can see the relation of the subject with other subjects.

Beatty (2004) offers a model to visualize the classroom response systems. The model has a cycle form and begins with developing sets of questions about the subjects. Then the system automatically selects the suitable ones. The teacher sends the questions to the students one by one or together. Students see the questions and then discuss them with small groups. They send their answers via the system. The system does the required analysis and draws tables and histograms. Lastly, the teacher and students discuss the answers cooperatively.

Figure 3. The question cycle - an effective model for classroom response/communication systems (Beatty, 2004, p.4)

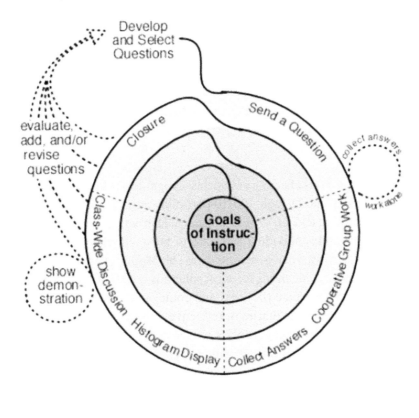

e- Rubrics

Rubrics are considered a useful tool in the evaluation of online studies. It provides clarity on expectations from student performance. Students' subjective studies become objective in this way (Paloff & Pratt, 2009).

A well-prepared rubric enables students to act more creatively, they can concentrate their topics more deeply and they can see and get interesting viewpoints. A good rubric also reduces gaps in the evaluations as it provides a scale for the teacher. Also, it minimizes the grading differences of the teachers or evaluators who grade the same subject with different students (Seifert & Feliks, 2018).

There are many different compelling factors in peer and self-assessment practices. It is important to prepare tasks that will entertain and motivate students while doing them. In the task that is first evaluated, the competence of the students in performing the task needs to be questioned. They deal with the problems related to their competence in the technological dimension of the assessment at the initial assessment stage. This also applies when they first encounter the rubric on the website. They may not be able to demonstrate their capacity in examining the rubric and performing accordingly. They can close this gap in the next missions. For this reason, the technical level of the students should be taken into account as well as the evaluation level in rubrics and other technological measurement tools. (Seifert & Feliks, 2018). The structure of a rubric can vary from a simple checklist to complicated task lists. Here the aim is to specify target performance criteria for the assignment. Developing a rubric simplifies the grading process. Typical criteria set can be used for online discussion (Kearns, 2012).

e-Portfolios

Portfolios are a purposeful collection of students' assignments (Apple & Shimo, 2004) According to Baturay and Daloğlu (2010) portfolios provide accurate information about students' learning and are seen as a practical alternative to standardized tests. They are by their nature individual and hard to be standardized. Thus, teachers generally act subjectively when assessing them (McMullan et al, 2002).

While performance evaluations focus on solutions, portfolios teachers describe the process it takes to evaluate the steps and complete the task. Students can do portfolio work with electronic diaries or reflective writings (Reeves, 2000).

One of the advantages of e-portfolios is that they can show both formal and informal learning. By structuring an online portfolio, students can present and document their learning and products. Teachers get a chance to assess their studies. When the portfolio system is flexible, it allows students to show both their academic learning and their learning outside the classroom. These kinds of portfolios become a tool for life-long learning (Goodwin-Jones, 2008).

According to Davis and Ponnamperuma (2005) state that portfolio assessment is a holistic process and made in five stages:

1. Teacher collects evidence about students' works.
2. Students reflect on their learning.
3. Teacher evaluates the evidence.
4. Students explain and present their works.
5. Teacher grades students' works.

Online Discussion

Learning occurs within the activity, context and culture in which students are involved. Information should be presented in authentic settings that require the use of that information. The realization of learning in real environments, in a way that is meaningful to the student, increases permanence. Social interaction is also a key factor in this regard. In online discussion groups, students make weekly discussion entries and other students contribute to these entries. These messages, sent at specific time intervals, are a necessary element of the app community. Online discussions require the student to prepare in class and perform pre-learning by doing specific readings to participate in this discussion. Discussion groups give students the chance to express their ideas and listen to the ideas of others. During discussions, students respect the opinions of others and contribute constructively (Kayler & Weller, 2007).

Teachers can use chatrooms, forums and other learning management systems for online discussions. Some sets of tasks for individuals and groups can be set. Both teachers and other class members can evaluate them (Booth, 2003).

In a traditional class, discussions are made face-to-face and teachers can intervene, comment or support a discussion immediately. However, in an online class, this may take time. On the other hand, It is easier to use graphics, videos and charts during an online discussion by just sharing the screen (Graff, 2003).

Computer-based Quizzes and Exams

Teachers want to systematically monitor students' work and motivation from the beginning of the semester and ensure the continuity of their studies. Continuous evaluation is useful for this purpose. Quizzes and multiple-choice quizzes are frequently used for this purpose. In this context, information and communication systems are useful and relevant. Because it can be applied to a large number of students continuously (Ardid et al, 2015).

Booth (2003) lists criteria to do an effective online test as such:

1. Start and stop times should be pre-defined, students should log in with their user ids and passwords.
2. Doing regular online quizzes before a final exam and making them a small component of final assessments will be useful and keep students motivated.
3. Quizzes are useful for introducing an online assessment environment to the students.
4. Multiple choice exams generally assess knowledge level information. However, the teacher can assess a broad range of topics.
5. Multiple choice exams can be delivered to large groups of learners. They can be accessible to the learners at any time and place.

There are two types of computer-based exams depending on the internet use of the computer. e-exams can be done without an internet connection while online exams are done on online platforms. Both of these have advantages ve disadvantages for students, teachers, and schools. They reduce the time, the tests become more secure, data can be restored easier, students get their results fast, they cost more cheaper as that requires no classroom or paper, can be subjected to statistical analyses easier (Ilgaz & Adanır, 2020).

Questions that will measure high-level thinking skills should be asked in the measurement processes carried out in measurement and evaluation environments where students are not under observation and made from different sources. Students should not find the answers to the questions directly in a source but should process the information. (Bakerson, Trottier & Mansfield, 2015).

Generally, it is thought that students cheat more at online exams, However that is not always the case (Harmon & Lambrinos, 2008). The cheating behaviors of students are generally the same in traditional testing environments and online testing. That behavior generally depends on the institutional culture of the school, policies enacted by the instructors and students' history and attitudes about academic integrity (King, Guyette & Piotrowski, 2009).

Assessment integrity is an important and challenging issue and it is harder in computerized tests because the procedure testing is away from the classroom setting. Many institutions use proctored testing methods to provide assessment integrity. For proctored testing, students may require to physically attend a testing session at a designed classroom at the institution or a partner institution. Some institutions rely on the honor system. Students may sign or electronically approve an agreement. Many institutions use online real-time proctor services. They use webcams and microphones and some special software that will not allow students to cheat. (Milone et al, 2017).

CONCLUSION

With the advancement of information and communication technologies, online education has become more applicable technologically, economically and operationally (Susam, Durnalı, & Orakcı, 2020). It is clear that computer-based and online methods are taking more and more place in all education levels and courses. Today, hybrid and completely distance education systems are in demand. For these systems to function properly, institutions and teachers should be equipped with computer-based assessment and evaluation. There are many benefits of computer-based assessment and evaluation systems in the process of supporting students' learning with self-assessment and peer assessment, evaluating them in a formative way, examining their success, seeing their deficiencies, and directing them to a higher education system. Computer-based measurement and evaluation systems, which have been used in various ways in the last 20 years, can be used in more areas by gaining new features and improving themselves.

REFERENCES

Abrahamson, A. L. (1998, June 3–6). *An Overview of Teaching and Learning Research with Classroom Communication Systems.* Paper presented at the International Conference of the Teaching of Mathematics, Village of Pythagorion, Samos, Greece.

Adanır, H., & Ilgaz, G. A. (2020). Providing online exams for online learners: Does it really matter for them? *Education and Information Technologies, 25*(2), 1255–1269. doi:10.100710639-019-10020-6

Aly, İ. (2013). Performance in an online introductory course in a hybrid classroom setting. *Canadian Journal of Higher Education, 43*(2), 85–99. doi:10.47678/cjhe.v43i2.2474

Ardid, M., Gómez-Tejedor, J. A., Meseguer-Dueñas, J. M., Riera, J., & Vidaurre, A. (2015). Online exams for blended assessment. Study of different application methodologies. *Computers & Education, 81*, 296–303. doi:10.1016/j.compedu.2014.10.010

Bakerson, M., Trottier, T., & Mansfield, M. (2015). The value of embedded formative assessment: An integral process in online learning environments implemented through advances in technology. In S. Koç, X. Liu, & P. Wachira (Eds.), *Assessment in Online and Blended Learning Environments.* Information Age Publishing, Inc.

Barbosa, H., & Garcia, F. (2005). Importance of Online Assessment in the E-learning Process. *6th International Conference on Information Technology Based Higher Education and Training*, F3B/1-F3B/6. 10.1109/ITHET.2005.1560287

Baturay, M. H., & Daloğlu, A. (2010). E-portfolio assessment in an online English language course. *Computer Assisted Language Learning, 23*(5), 413–428. doi:10.1080/09588221.2010.520671

Beatty, I. D. (2004, February 3). *Transforming Student Learning with Classroom Communication Systems.* Retrieved October 1, 2021, from http://www.utexas.edu/academic /cit/services/cps/ECARCRS.pdf

Benson, R., & Brack, C. (2010). *Online Learning and Assessment in Higher Education: A Planning Guide.* Chandos Publishing. doi:10.1533/9781780631653

Berge, Z. L. (2000). Components of the online classroom. *New Directions for Teaching and Learning, 84*(84), 23–28. doi:10.1002/tl.843

Bonanno, P. (2015). Assessing Technology-Enhanced Learning: A Process-Oriented Approach. In S. Koç, X. Liu, & P. Wachira (Eds.), *Assessment in Online and Blended Learning Environments.* Information Age Publishing, Inc.

Booth, R., & Berwyn, C. (2003). The development of quality online assessment in vocational education and training. *Australian Flexible Learning Framework*, *1*, 17–32.

Boston, C. (2002). The Concept of Formative Assessment. *Practical Assessment, Research & Evaluation*, *8*(9), 1–4.

Chang, N. & Petersen, N. (2005). Cybercoaching: An Emerging Model of Personalized Online Assessment. *Online Assessment, Measurement and Evaluation: Emerging Practices*, 110-130. . doi:10.4018/978-1-59140-747-8.ch008

Chanpet, P., Chomsuwan, K., & Murphy, E. (2020). Online project-based learning and formative assessment. Technology. *Knowledge and Learning*, *25*(1), 685–705. doi:10.100710758-018-9363-2

Coates, H., James, R., & Baldwin, G. (2005). A critical examination of the effects of learning management systems on university teaching and learning. *Tertiary Education and Management*, *11*(1), 19–36. doi:10.1080/13583883.2005.9967137

Croitoru, C. N. (2016). A Critical Analysis of Learning Management Systems in Higher Education. DINU. *Ecological Informatics*, *16*(1), 5–18.

Ducate, L. C. I, & Lomicka, L. (2008). Adventures in the blogosphere: From blog readers to blog writers. *Computer Assisted Language Learning*, *21*(1), 9–28. doi:10.1080/09588220701865474

Durnalı, M., Orakcı, Ş., & Aktan, O. (2019). The smart learning potential of Turkey's education system in the context of FATIH project. In A. Darshan Singh, S. Raghunathan, E. Robeck, & B. Sharma (Eds.), *Cases on Smart Learning Environments* (pp. 227–243). IGI Global. doi:10.4018/978-1-5225-6136-1.ch013

Fies, C., & Marshall, J. (2006). Classroom Response Systems: A Review of the Literature. *Journal of Science Education and Technology*, *15*(1), 101–109. doi:10.100710956-006-0360-1

Gikandi, J. W., Morrow, D., & Davis, N. E. (2011). Online formative assessment in higher education: A review of the literature. *Computers & Education*, *57*(4), 2333–2351. doi:10.1016/j.compedu.2011.06.004

Godwin-Jones, R. (2008). Emerging technologies. Web-writing 2.0: Enabling, documenting, and assessing writing online. *Language Learning & Technology*, *12*(2), 7–13.

Graff, M. (2003). Cognitive Style and Attitudes Towards Using Online Learning and Assessment Methods. *Electronic Journal of e-Learning, 1*(1), 21-28.

Gray, K., Thompson, C., Sheard, J., Clerehan, R., & Hamilton, M. (2010). Students as Web 2.0 authors: Implications for assessment design and conduct. *Australasian Journal of Educational Technology, 26*(1), 105–122. doi:10.14742/ajet.1105

Harmon, O. R., & Lambrinos, J. (2008). Are Online Exams an Invitation to Cheat? *The Journal of Economic Education, 39*(2), 116–125. doi:10.3200/JECE.39.2.116-125

Harrington, A. M. (2010). Problematizing the hybrid classroom for ESL/EFL students. *TESL-EJ, 14*(3), 1–13.

Hiltz, S. R. (1997). Impacts of college-level courses via asynchronous Learning Networks: Some Preliminary Results. *Journal of Asynchronous Learning Networks, 1*(2), 1–19.

Hung, S. T. A., & Huang, H. T. D. (2016). Blogs as a learning and assessment instrument for English-speaking performance. *Interactive Learning Environments, 24*(8), 1881–1894. doi:10.1080/10494820.2015.1057746

Joshi, A., Virk, A., Saiyad, S., Mahajan, R., & Singh, T. (2020). Online assessment: Concept and applications. *Journal of Research in Medical Education & Ethics, 10*(2), 49–59. doi:10.5958/2231-6728.2020.00015.3

Kayler, M., & Weller, K. (2007). Pedagogy, Self-Assessment, and Online Discussion Groups. *Journal of Educational Technology & Society, 10*(1), 136–147.

Kearns, L. R. (2012). Student Assessment in Online Learning: Challenges and Effective Practices. *Journal of Online Learning and Teaching, 8*(3), 198–208.

King, C., Guyette, R., & Piotrowski, C. (2009). Online exams and cheating: An empirical analysis of business students' views. *The Journal of Educators Online, 6*(1), 1–11. doi:10.9743/JEO.2009.1.5

Klecker, B. M. (2007). The impact of formative feedback on student learning in an online classroom. *Journal of Instructional Psychology, 34*(3), 161–165.

Lock, J. V., & Redmond, P. (2015). Empowering Learners to Engage in Authentic Online Assessment. In S. Koç, X. Liu, & P. Wachira (Eds.), *Assessment in Online and Blended Learning Environments*. Information Age Publishing, Inc.

Mann, B. L. (2006). Testing the Validity of the Post and Vote Model of Web-Based Peer Assessment. In Online Assessment, Measurement, and Evaluation: Emerging Practices. Hricko Science Publishing. doi:10.4018/978-1-59140-747-8.ch009

McMullan, M., Endacott, R., Gray, M., Jasper, M. A., Miller, C. M., Scholes, J., & Webb, J. (2003). Portfolios and assessment of competence: A review of the literature. *Journal of Advanced Nursing, 41*(3), 283–294. doi:10.1046/j.1365-2648.2003.02528.x PMID:12581116

Milone, A. S., Cortese, A. M., Balestrieri, R. L., & Pittenger, A. L. (2017). The impact of proctored online exams on the educational experience. *Currents in Pharmacy Teaching & Learning, 9*(1), 108–114. doi:10.1016/j.cptl.2016.08.037 PMID:29180142

Palloff, R. M., & Pratt, K. (2003). *The Virtual Student: A Profile and Guide.* Jossey - Bass.

Palloff, R. M., & Pratt, K. (2009). *Assessing the Online Learner: Resources and Strategies for the Faculty.* Jossey - Bass.

Ponnamperuma, G. G. (2005). Portfolio assessment. *Journal of Veterinary Medical Education, 32*(3), 279–284. doi:10.3138/jvme.32.3.279 PMID:16261482

Reeves, T.C. (2000). Alternative assessment approaches for online learning environments in higher education. *Educational Computing Research, 23*(1), 101-111.

Reiss, S., & Reips, U. D. (2016). Online-Assessment. In K. Schweizer & C. DiStefano (Eds.), *Principles and Methods of Test Construction.* Hogrefe.

Sadler, D. R. (1989). Formative assessment and the design of instructional systems. *Instructional Science, 18*(2), 119–144. doi:10.1007/BF00117714

Seifert, T., & Feliks, O. (2018). Online self-assessment and peerassessment as a tool to enhance student-teachers' assessment skills. *Assessment & Evaluation in Higher Education, 44*(2), 169–185. doi:10.1080/02602938.2018.1487023

Shank, P., & Sitze, A. (2004). *Making Sense of Online Learning A Guide for Beginners and the Truly Skeptical.* John Wiley & Sons, Inc.

Susam, T., Durnalı, M., & Orakcı, Ş. (2020). Administering education and training through a web-based system: E-curriculum. In M. Durnalı (Ed.), *Utilizing Technology, Knowledge, and Smart Systems in Educational Administration and Leadership.* IGI Global. doi:10.4018/978-1-7998-1408-5.ch002

Van der Pol, J., Van den Berg, B. A. M., Admiraal, W. F., & Simons, P. R. J. (2008). The nature, reception, and use of online peer feedback in higher education. *Computers & Education, 51*, 1804–1817. doi: .06.001 doi:10.1016/j.compedu.2008

Westhuizen, D. (2016). Guidelines for Online Assessment for Educators. Commonwealth of Learning.

Wong, R. M. F., & Hew, K. F. (2010). The Impact of Blogging and Scaffolding on Primary School Pupils' Narrative Writing: A Case Study. *International Journal of Web-Based Learning and Teaching Technologies*, 5(2), 1–17. doi:10.4018/jwltt.2010040101

Chapter 6
Online and Hybrid Student Engagement:
A Duoethnography With EdTech

Devery J. Rodgers
https://orcid.org/0000-0002-7376-7216
California State University, Long Beach, USA

Alvaro Brito
https://orcid.org/0000-0002-3650-9517
Boise State University, USA

ABSTRACT

Virtual hybrid education is challenging for the average educator and less known with the additional stresses of emergency remote education. In most cases, educators rely on trial-and-error to determine what works best in online and hybrid instruction. Through this applied research, two education technology specialists engage in a duoethnography of their support over the 2020-2021 pandemic year. Having assisted hundreds of educators in an urban K12 school district with online and hybrid engagement practices, this study answers the question, "How can technology help facilitate student engagement in online and hybrid environments?" This chapter is built from narrative analysis and provides research-based and practitioner-focused promising practice techniques and real-world solutions to educators in building and maintaining a positive digital culture.

DOI: 10.4018/978-1-7998-8077-6.ch006

INTRODUCTION

Over 15 months of the COVID-19 pandemic (March 2020-June 2021), Education Technology (EdTech) Specialists in America's K12 school districts culled information from online resources and one another to help support the extreme and rapid changes in emergency remote education (ERE). From crisis instruction and maintaining continued learning, to hyperfocused provisions for student engagement, EdTech Specialists provided promising practices with digital tools through supporting K12 school districts across America. While reports (Joy, 2021; Liberman, 2020; Office of Civil Rights, 2021; Richards, 2020) still focus on the lack of virtual and hybrid learning environments, pedagogical practices with technology have shown exponential growth over the pandemic year. Despite this growth, students' engagement has waned (Khlaif et al., 2021).

This chapter focuses on digital leadership for online and hybrid student engagement, as supported by Education Technology (EdTech) Specialists. Through a duoethnography of two sitting EdTech Specialists, it aims to answer the research question, "How can technology help facilitate student engagement in online and hybrid environments?" It will also answer these four subquestions:

- What resources were provided to educators to help pivot to online and hybrid teaching?
- What type of leadership was needed to help educators re-engage their school populations in online and hybrid environments?
- What strategies assisted most with student engagement?
- Which digital tools assisted most in online and hybrid student engagement?

BACKGROUND

Distance learning and online education has been embraced by school systems for years, but emergency remote education (ERE) came with the pandemic school shutdowns of 2020. The chapter first discusses this phenomenon and how it created a pandemic pedagogy. During ERE, student engagement was found waning--no matter how it was measured. After this discussion, it is then necessary to introduce the Technology Acceptance Model as a conceptual frame for which tools and strategies were used to catapult engagement. Finally, a discussion of crisis leadership ensues, leading to the management of professional development. This literature review will lend to a foundation for duoethnography, to study how technology helps facilitate student engagement in online and hybrid environments.

Emergency Remote Education and Pandemic Pedagogy

A pandemic pedagogy includes practices educators have undertaken in response to COVID-19. Pedagogies, during these times, have been referred to as emergency remote education (ERE). Hodges, et al. (2020) define ERE as a temporary shift of instructional delivery to an alternate delivery mode due to crisis circumstances, in contrast to distance learning experiences that are planned from the beginning and designed to be online. They continue by describing ERE as "the use of fully remote teaching solutions for instruction that would otherwise be delivered face-to-face or blended, and that will return to that format once the crisis or emergency has abated" (Hodges, et al., 2020, sec. 3).

Student Engagement

During ERE, student engagement was decreasing. There is very little research that focuses on attendance or engagement in K–12 online settings (Chambers, et al., 2020). The field initially tried to measure engagement via attendance, but found this method to be ineffective, as three million students had not yet checked into class within seven months in a sum of American school districts (Korman, 2020). Carminucci, et al. (2021) found that attendance rates dropped compared with previous school years, "with lower attendance rates in districts that were not providing primarily in-person instruction, as well as high-poverty districts and districts serving mostly students of color" (p. 1). As there is no established definition of "attendance" in an online environment (Chambers, et al., 2020; Sawchuk, 2021), this had to be established per district within school communities.

Some school districts measured engagement by the participation equivalent of online "instances." However, there was scant consistency to establish a firm baseline. Khlaif, et al. (2021) posit that the major factors that influence student engagement are teachers' presence and quality of content, in addition to external factors of parental concerns, norms, and traditions. Kurt, et al. (2020) found four themes associated with the factors affecting student engagement: instructional and student-related factors, along with those related to the learning environment and policies. Studies on engagement also uncovered that while students may be physically present and appear to be actively involved in using the technology tools, in reality, they might still be cognitively disengaged from the learning goals (Linnenbrink & Pintrich, 2003). Engagement should create an environment of active time-on-task learning, engaged in thinking, reflecting, and effortful mental activity (Wartella, 2015, as cited in D'Angelo, 2018). Studies have supported the idea that overall student engagement in learning is enhanced by the implementation of instructional technology (Mo, 2011; Schindler, et al., 2017).

Crisis Leadership

There is research which focuses on crisis management, but hardly any that focuses on crisis leadership. Klann (2003) differentiates the two by saying that crisis management relates mainly to operational issues, while crisis leadership principally deals with how leaders handle the human responses to a crisis. Senge, et al. (2008) described how leadership in these complex and challenging times is about creating capacity for adults to shape the future they desire, individually and collectively. From organizational and institutional theory, Shaked (2021) firmly situates buffering and bridging as part of crisis leadership. Buffering is defined as school leaders responding to external influences and needs by trying to insulate themselves, versus bridging referring to attempts to tailor organizational activities according to external demands and expectations (Kim and Kim, 2016). Crisis leadership is adaptive, demanding communication, clarity of vision and values, moving on actionable intelligence, and forging caring relationships.

Teaming

Edmonson (2018) defines teaming as empowering to work for a common goal collaboratively, instead of working for a leader. In teaming, a leader overcomes a basic human challenge of knowing everything and relies on collaboration with one another as a team as the best method to spark curiosity and solve challenging problems. Flowers, et al. (2000) concluded that in teaming, the team size, amount of common planning time, and length of time together as a team influence classroom instruction. Flowers, et al. (2000) continue, for teaming to be effective, teacher choice, curriculum-driven design, and administrative support are necessary. These factors must be taken into consideration when looking at teacher leadership during ERE.

Professional Development

A study conducted by Guskey (1988) suggested that the majority of teacher professional development programs fail because they do not take into account two crucial factors: (1) what motivates teachers to engage in professional learning, and (2) the process by which change in teachers typically occurs. Lam, et al. (2010) found that autonomous motivation (intrinsic and identified) was highly and positively connected with positive attitudes towards persistence in innovative teaching; while the relationship with negative attitudes was high and negative. Using autonomous motivation can further the advancement of educators to try new innovations such as blended learning in the classroom.

MAIN FOCUS OF THE CHAPTER

The school organization studied is an urban K12 school district with approximately 24,000 students (85% Latino and 15% African-American), more than 80% of which elected to continue with emergency remote instruction during the 2020-21 school year. With assistance from district partners and sponsors, the district employed a 1:1 device initiative, addressing the technology hardware equity gap during crisis instruction. The knowledge gap between teachers and technology integration might have widened the support gap for students. This study addresses stop-gap measures as noted by the school district's Education Technology (EdTech) Specialists.

Methods for the study include a duoethnography between two K12 EdTech Specialists of their districtwide support over the pandemic school year. Specialists are personnel who have deep knowledge of a discipline and are able to support others in that knowledge. EdTech Specialists at the K12 level were chosen researchers, as their special teaming relationships during ERE allowed heightened perspectives on professional development, instructional engagement and crisis leadership during the pandemic. Having assisted hundreds of stakeholders with online and hybrid engagement practices, this study answers the question, "How can technology help facilitate student engagement in online and hybrid environments?" These methods support the discovery of practitioner-focused promising practices in building and maintaining a positive digital culture.

Issues, Controversies, and Problems

With engagement as the manifested behavior of being motivated, a few technology integration models were considered, due to their attention to behavioral attitudes in technology usage. Davis' (1989) Technology Acceptance Model (TAM) decodes how users come to accept and use technology. The model suggests that when users are presented with new technology, two major factors influence their decision about how and when they will use it, perceived usefulness and perceived ease-of-use. There have been two modifications to this model. The first modification (Davis, Bogozzi, and Warshaw, 1989) allows for users' intent to match actual use. The second modification (Venkatesh & Davis, 1996) as shown in Figure 1, found that external variables (i.e., the multiplicity of variables from pandemic life) affect both perceived usefulness (i.e., "Can this help re-engage my learners?") and perceived ease of use (e.g., "On top of every other pandemic balance, can I learn and maintain this systems use?") and were found to have a direct influence on behavior intention (i.e., engagement), thus improving upon the first modification of TAM and eliminating the need for the attitude construct.

Figure 1. TAM, second modification
Notes: The second modification of the Technology Acceptance Model (Venkatesh & Davis, 1996) considers the pandemic as external variables, with perceived usefulness and ease of use contributing to engagement as a behavioral intention. Actual system use will be revealed in the study's results.

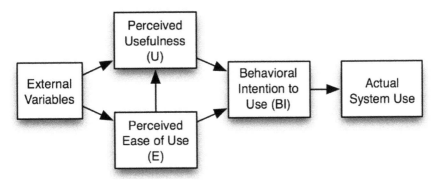

Rather than framing the study within normative and oppressive discourses, the two EdTech Specialists engaged in a contextual collaboration (Lei, et al., 2004) of their support for student engagement during ERE. During a duoethnography, abilities, knowledge, and experiences are recalled and explored in conversation with another (Sawyer & Norris, 2012). The foundational principles of this method are its polyvocal nature, the examination of life history as curriculum, and the intent not to profess but rather to learn from differences (Sawyer & Norris, 2015).

Having supported hundreds of educators over this pandemic year, their first-hand perspectives created a phenomenological ethnography. While borrowing from other qualitative methods, duoethnography is distinctive in its emphasis on the researchers and the interacting narratives as the site of the research (Brerault, 2016). The data was collected and analyzed for four months through an inductive process. Specialists met bi-weekly over Zoom for one-hour recorded conversations, in response to written narratives they responded to the week prior. The researchers started by answering the research questions themselves, from their expert knowledge. They then responded to one another on a collaborative document, using the 4 As Protocol (National School Reform Faculty, 2015), where they noted assumptions, agreements, arguments, and aspirations with their partner's text. As four recursive recorded discussions and written accounts evolved, a narrative analysis was used to ascertain where information converged or diverged.

SOLUTIONS AND RECOMMENDATIONS

Discussion of results surfaced themes that revealed strategies and digital tools adopted for online student engagement. Through dialogic engagement, we discovered answers to the research question, "How can technology help facilitate student engagement in online and hybrid environments?" We also answered four subquestions:

- What resources were provided to educators to help pivot to online and hybrid teaching?
- What type of leadership was needed to help educators re-engage their school populations in online and hybrid environments?
- What strategies assisted most with student engagement?
- Which digital tools assisted most in online and hybrid student engagement?

RQ1: How Can Technology Help Facilitate Student Engagement in Online and Hybrid Environments?

Our literature review supports students' engagement through technology behaviorally, emotionally, and cognitively. During our study, we found two ways in which technology assists with virtual student engagement, organizationally through collection and access to data points to drive decisions, and instructionally through the adaptation of tools or learning tasks through the integration of technology. Organizationally, technology helps educators collect, access, and analyze data for decision-making leading to greater engagement. Instructionally speaking, the two major areas in which technology can help facilitate student engagement in online and hybrid environments speak to generational engagement practices and alleviating pandemic disengagement.

Alleviating Pandemic Disengagement

During ERE with online and virtual hybrid environments, it was essential to understand digital engagement with students, as just being supplied with the technologies did not impact engagement. Some students were supplied with devices and did not log into class. Many students who logged into class did not turn their cameras on in videoconference. Some students who may have turned their cameras on did not show their faces. Students who showed their faces did not necessarily speak. Some students who did speak had to be cajoled. "In addition to knowing the research, having led thousands of PD sessions in my career--hundreds online, I had experiential knowledge of student engagement," (personal communication, Researcher 1, May 14, 2021). "One of the biggest challenges was getting students to actively participate during synchronous time either on Google Meet or Zoom. As I did my observations...I noticed students were being called upon during instruction but were not present or refused to participate by turning on their cameras during the attendance roll call" (personal communication, Researcher 2, May 20, 2021).

Influencing TAM's perceived usefulness (Davis, 1989), as practitioner-researchers, we helped teachers determine which technologies would be the most engaging, and how best to use those technologies for student engagement. We advised how traditional lectures could be videotaped with embedded questions; classroom discussions could be moved to a text-response thread application or video discussion platform; teachers were also assisted on how to manage a digital workflow through a learning management system. Educators were also supported with assessment tools to conduct formative and summative assessments virtually.

Generational Engagement Practices

K12 schools presently serve Generation Alpha and Generation Z (Jha, 2020), students who have never known a life without information technology. We learned from the research that students' brains in this generation have been rewired to a media-enhanced neomillennial learning style (Rodgers, 2012). This tells us that technology is not only what engages this population, but it is ubiquitous to their learning. Suggestions to support student engagement with media-rich programs were made throughout ERE. Creating breakout sessions on Zoom or Google Meet to emulate a blended learning environment, students worked in breakout rooms to complete various tasks and worked on specific media-rich assignments. Using videos from YouTube or self-made videos using Screencastify, teachers were encouraged to assign video lessons using EdPuzzle to ensure accountability and gather data on student performance. Teachers were also trained on how to use programs such as Flipgrid, where filters can be applied to student videos and can be used to mimic popular social media tools like TikTok or Snapchat. Just because technology is used, however, does not mean the students are engaged (Bergdahl, et al., 2019).

Data-driven Decisions

There were many tools already purchased by the District which led to teacher collection and use of data. During the pandemic, educators were encouraged to use data-rich programs such as Formative and Nearpod. These programs helped teachers by leveraging data-driven technology with teacher instruction/support. With the accessibility of personalized learning and engagement data through these apps, professional development sessions were created to continue to support teachers through their use. Unfortunately, many of these programs did not connect with the teacher's Learning Management System, so they found the interpretation of data to be cumbersome. The perceived usefulness of such programs quickly diminished and educators looked to alternatives for formative/summative data. As advocates of tools purchased by the District, the education technology department focused on particular tools in lieu of other tools that educators might have perceived as more useful or easier to use.

Recommendations: Continue Promising Practices with Technology

As shared in our literature review, engagement should create an environment of active time-on-task learning, engaged in thinking, reflecting, and effortful mental activity (Wartella, 2015, as cited in D'Angelo, 2018). We recommend that educators continue the use of technology to facilitate student engagement, ensure that they are gathering actionable data points through the technological choices made; be tailored to the generational group; and bolster student engagement by leveraging technology to meet students' needs, interests, and curiosity.

RQ2: What Resources were Provided to Educators to Help Pivot to Online and Hybrid Teaching?

We found three major areas in which educators were provided resource services to pivot to online and hybrid teaching: district structural support, hardware, and professional learning. EdTech Specialists became pedagogical and methodological experts in shaping ERE. EdTech needed to support not only the physical structures of ERE, but professional learning as well. From the provision of distance learning websites, to the establishment of technology education platforms and professional learning plans, EdTech specialists were part of the K12 build for pandemic pedagogy.

District Structural Support

From the provision of distance learning websites to the establishment of technology education platforms and professional learning plans, EdTech specialists were part of the K12 build for pandemic pedagogy. Besides the moral support, educators were guided by a comprehensive ERE website built by the EdTech Specialists, including FAQ sections for parents, guides for students, and step-by-step pacing-aligned lessons for classroom teachers. An internal survey found that parents, teachers, and students extensively used the website resources.

Hardware

The district provided computers, speakers, interactive touch panels, and education technology programs to help educators pivot to online and hybrid teaching. School site administrators were tasked with providing teachers with devices needed to support distance learning. Certain school sites equipped teachers with a second monitor, speakers for their devices, webcams, and microphones to walk around their hybrid classes.

To prepare for hybrid instruction, the district also purchased and provided each classroom teacher with an interactive touch panel. These interactive panels were 60-inch television monitors with computer capabilities. Some of the panels were mounted in classrooms, and others were mounted on carts for more classroom mobility. Educators were then untethered from their desks with Zoom, and able to teach from the interactive panel and share their screen in order for students in the classroom and at home to see/hear the instruction. Feedback gathered from the Education Technology Team during office hours revealed that while a few teachers appreciated the interactive touch screens, most did not incorporate it into their instructional practices. We conclude that this is because the rollout was done hastily, the trainers were not properly trained, and no one was consulted about the purchase before rollout for planning. Teachers were already overwhelmed with creating digital content and shifting to remote teaching and this innovation was met with frustration.

Professional Learning

EdTech needed to support not only the physical structures of ERE, but professional learning as well. There was a need to offer just-in-time PD during ERE to support the aim of professional development, as well as support instructional systems during virtual remote instruction. Cavanaugh and Dewese (2020) offer an analysis of hundreds of thousands of search terms during the crisis instruction months of the pandemic, and discovered a large shift in search terms from the year prior, suggesting that educators felt the need for support in their new digital learning environments. UNESCO (2020) found that "teachers were not equipped to organize, deliver and assess distance learning. They lack[ed] digital skills and readiness for employing distance learning pedagogies." For these reasons, teacher training was provided throughout the 2020-2021 pandemic school year.

EdTech Specialists exclusively offered professional development to all 2000 teachers each day, for four hours a day, over the first three months, then one session a day for the remainder of the school year. This was in addition to office hours, supporting general questions in Zoom, and individual questions and concerns through calendared appointments. Professional development was targeted to the supported online tools and pedagogies for ERE, some of which were in place prior to the pandemic. EdTech Specialists focused the professional development offerings on the educational technology tools and curriculum resources selected and purchased by the district (i.e., Nearpod, Flocabulary, Formative, Discovery Education) in order to support the existing blended learning initiatives. These tools were transitioned to support online/hybrid learning.

There was obvious influence from the Education Technology Department on a teacher's perceived ease-of-use, even though teachers' direct feedback revealed the technology's perceived usefulness. Remembering that a multiplicity of external variables (i.e., pandemic life) affected both perceived usefulness and perceived ease of use (Venkatesh & Davis, 1996), there was a direct influence on behavior intention (i.e., engagement).

Recommendations: Social-Emotional Learning and District Collaboration

Before transitioning from crisis instruction to ERE, there was a surfaced need to support students with social-emotional learning (SEL). Initially, there were no curated SEL resources available to educators (i.e., HeadSpace, Calm, etc.). By Fall 2020, some resources were being shared amongst school districts, and eventually posted on states' websites. We recommend that schools and districts take advantage of these resources to support students and educators as we return from the pandemic stay-at-home orders.

While the district came together to produce a united front and comprehensive services, internally there was little interdepartmental collaboration. Different departments tried to support, according to their specialty, in silos; interdisciplinary collaboration was nonexistent. The schism resulted in work being doubled. We recommend that learning organizations disseminate the vision and mission to the whole group before individual departments work on a collective assignment.

RQ3: What Type of Leadership was Needed to Help Educators Re-Engage their School Populations in Online and Hybrid Environments?

The goal for educational technology leaders during COVID-19 was to ensure students were learning using remote instruction. Banathy and Jenlink (2004) argued, "accepting the responsibility for creating new systems of education means committing ourselves to systems inquiry and design and dedicating ourselves to the betterment of education." The researchers found three types of leadership that helped educators re-engage their school populations in online and hybrid environments: Crisis Leadership, Teaming/Teacher Leadership, and Adaptive Leadership.

Crisis Leadership

Upon pandemic school closure, district leadership needed to act quickly to adapt structures for instruction and guide educators to remote teaching. Communication was key. Quick action was done through the creation of a comprehensive website for all stakeholder groups to access. Within the teacher portion of the site, there were a myriad of digital resources to guide curriculum planning, instructional pedagogy, and assessment strategies. Within the student portion of the site, students were able to log into their appropriate learning management system and learn from the specialized online guides for accessing their instructional material. Within the parent portion of the site, families were able to get pertinent information regarding resources, technology tutorials, and ways to support their students at home. Communication tools such as Parent Square and Aeries Parent Portal were also used to communicate with parents during ERE. Site administrators were provided with small group sessions to lead their stakeholders through the website of resources.

Teaming

Teaming was essential for the Educational Technology Department to quickly create remote teaching assets, protocols, procedures, and professional development. District leadership was looking for expertise in digital learning and leaning towards our department for support. Edmonson (2012) describes teaming as when part of a fast-moving work environment, the people who have the skills and flexibility successfully act collaboratively when and where challenges arise. Teaming was essential for EdTech Specialists to create resources quickly and effectively to support stakeholders during ERE. Using each Specialist's strengths to come up with solutions of support was essential. This was made possible through the act of teaming.

Specialists also teamed with classroom teachers. Working alongside teacher leaders during ERE was indispensable in supporting each other. Teachers shared what was useful and easy to use in terms of technology (both hardware and applications). Other instructional District specialists sought out teacher leaders to create digital content that supported the curriculum. Teaming helped solidify tool and strategy selection due to their perceived usefulness and ease of use in the classroom.

Adaptive Leadership

According to Northouse (2019), six leadership behaviors play a pivotal role in the process of adaptive leadership: get on the balcony, identify the adaptive challenge, regulate distress, maintain disciplined attention, give the work back to the people, and protect leadership voices from below. Our district employed these six strategies as such:

- get on the balcony: big picture view of the impact of the COVID-19 at the school district discussed with the school board, local education agency, and local and state levels
- adaptive challenge: meeting the needs for remote support with previously-adopted tools that were quick to implement
- regulating the distress: providing professional development, digital curriculum, information, and resources to stakeholders
- maintaining disciplined attention: provided weeks of lessons and ongoing professional development for educators
- give work back to the people: encouraged teachers to lead professional development efforts by sharing their promising practices
- protect leadership voices from below: teachers and administrators were encouraged to share, whole group, what was working at their site

Recommendations: Immediate and Constant Communications, Digital Citizenship Practices

While the impacts of COVID-19 on the learning organization were discussed internally among management, during the first month of lockdown, other stakeholder groups were left in a lurch. Site administrators were communicated with daily, as their assignments were to stay on their sites to field community response. Teachers called our helplines to understand what to access and how, because there was no clear communication to this stakeholder group for weeks. While district leadership may cite negotiations with the union, this still did nothing to mitigate the lack of communication with an essential stakeholder group. Within a month, needs surveys for technology and internet access were solicited from parents. Community partners reached out with help they could afford (e.g., laptops, funding for wifi, platforms for virtual instruction, etc.), and we eventually found space for their support within our ERE plans. Going forward, team leads need to over-communicate during a crisis, not under-communicate.

There was also missed opportunity with digital citizenship. By not strategically embedding digital citizenship into the online curriculum, we missed the chance to lay foundational digital attitudes and practices. The year held instances of negative online behaviors which could have benefitted from setting up norms and procedures for proper digital citizenship.

We also feel that teachers' mental well-being was neglected. Before transitioning from crisis instruction to ERE, there was a surfaced need to support students with social-emotional learning; as ERE progressed, the need became greater. However, there was no social-emotional support offered for educators experiencing the same trauma. In and out of crisis, we know the value of Maslow's Hierarchy of Needs. Focusing on the mental safety of your staff would also provide for the social-emotional stability of your students.

RQ4: What Strategies Assisted Most with Student Engagement?

There were multi-tiered systems of support to engage students. The researchers found five thematic areas in their narrative analysis, addressing the strategies found to assist most with student engagement: the effectiveness of the educator; whether the educator used collaborative activities; effective planning; providing social-emotional connections; and engaging in project-based learning.

Effective Educator

Research confirms that the most important school-related factor that influences student outcomes is the quality of teaching (Aaronson et al, 2007; Clotfelter, et al., 2007, Khlaif et al., 2021). We noticed effective virtual remote education being done by educators who previously had well-structured classrooms, with strategies for student engagement. If they did not find themselves digitally-astute, effective teachers sought out knowledge--on their own, or from us as Specialists--to supplement their digital instruction, versus their content instruction. These tips helped them determine perceived usefulness and ease of use. Appreciating the autonomy pandemic pedagogies brought, these effective teachers used open educational resources, as well as those provided by the District, to meet students' needs. They were soon implementing educational technology tools to engage their students during distance learning, mimicking some of the effective practices they would implement in their classrooms.

Collaborative Activities

There was a stark difference in the classrooms of teachers who used collaborative activities versus those who did not. Teachers who taught without collaborative activities essentially had no student accountabilities during ERE. Monitoring via videoconference instruction looked different than how it might be applied in a physical classroom. The digital and phytigal environments required use of collaborative platforms to understand which students were working, and how they were understanding content, as videoconferencing breakout rooms did not allow a teacher to monitor their students. Perceived usefulness was soon seen in classroom accountability tools such as the Google Suite, Jamboard, and Whiteboard.fi, which were used to monitor students' progress and ensure they were on task during classroom instruction both synchronously and asynchronously. Effective collaboration was seen throughout the district during ERE by those educators who leveraged tools for collaboration. Teachers who did not use such collaborative tools reverted to a more teacher-centered approach.

Effective Planning

Hundreds of support calls from teachers helped us understand that ERE took hours longer to plan for, than did traditional classroom instruction. Teachers now had to adapt their instruction for virtual remote engagement, and plan for connection activities within their chosen videoconferencing system. They had to plan for whole group engagement in a virtual environment; breakout room collaborations with immediate accountabilities; differentiating for students whose virtual engagement was challenged; and managing digital platforms. Teachers needed to align their lesson activities with digital tools that not only enhanced the lesson, but that they perceived as easy to use. Teachers who did not do this planning relied solely on the District'd weekly digital curriculum, aligning the text's pacing with specific educational technology tools for engagement.

SEL Connections

Those educators who opted to focus upon connections before curriculum fared better with their student engagement practices. One of our teachers expressed, "I just let the kids get on and talk for 10 minutes a day. They missed one another so much, and everything in their world was no more; they needed to connect," (personal communication, October 7, 2020). That teacher saw an average of 90% of his students online everyday through the pandemic year. Other teachers chose tools to celebrate their students' grades (e.g., ConfettiCanon), sense of being (e.g., Student of the Week acknowledgements), and planned online games for students to participate in and build connections.

Project-Based Learning

Prior to the pandemic, some teachers had already engaged in Project-Based Learning (PBL). Teachers who adopted Project-Based Learning during ERE also found creative ways to engage students with impactful projects that solved real-world problems. Educators had students collaborate as they explored real-world problems and modeled solutions through digital tools. From Minecraft Education worlds addressing climate change, Scratch projects addressing racial healing, and a variety of other tools to capitalize on the time, students addressed these challenges through digital solutions. Sometimes students were supported by their teachers, sometimes by the EdTech Specialists, and sometimes through industry partners. These projects let the students create and showcase their projects for wider digital audiences. Educators saw this perceived usefulness and supported their students to more PBL during the pandemic year.

Recommendations: Master Teacher Lecturer and Roll-Carrying Teacher as Learning Facilitator

As was adopted in another school district in which we connected for resources, an idea that might have had a greater positive impact on our students was to employ a Master Teacher the first few weeks of crisis instruction. This Master Teacher would be the subject/grade level representative for the school/district. Core lesson concepts would be given via webinar, then the roster-carrying-teacher would follow up with the digitally-supported lessons. This might have helped all teachers onboard into this digital world, without the projected learning loss students received from weeks of adjusted instruction. As Klan (2003) and Senge, et al. (2008) posit about crisis leadership, designating Master Educators to lead the change would help the bulk of your stakeholders to adjust appropriately, so that their actions might be stronger as situations progress.

RQ5: Which Digital Tools Assisted Most in Online and Hybrid Student Engagement?

The researchers found three categories of digital tools which assisted in online and hybrid student engagement, those within the District context, and tools of engagement for students and staff. Educators who utilized such tools reported greater satisfaction in supporting their stakeholders in the online and hybrid environments. After receiving professional development or watching a video tutorial, the educator assessed the tool on whether it is easy to use and would it be useful during ERE.

After the determination was made, the educators would ask for additional support in attempting to use the tool or successfully implement it during classroom instruction.

District Context

The two most important tools used during ERE were our online content management systems, Google Classroom and Seesaw. Our district is a Google-District, but not all educators had adopted its use. When the realization of ERE was upon us, educators had to adopt a content management platform that would be supported by district instructional services. Google Classroom, as a free robust platform, was chosen to complement the District's heavy use of Google tools. Seesaw was favored by teachers of early learners.

The next essential set of tools that helped support all stakeholders were the videoconferencing systems. The EdTech Department opted to support Zoom, as the most robust tool in the market at the time, and Google Meet, as the productivity suite companion. Both videoconferencing systems helped onboard and sustain stakeholders' engagement during ERE. Serving as the virtual classroom, both platforms got more robust during the school year, and teachers began to take advantage of the online whiteboards, virtual backgrounds, breakout rooms, and polls.

The next set of engagement tools was the adopted productivity suite. While most of our business offices preferred the Microsoft Office Suite, all instructional departments defaulted to the Google Suite. The ease of collaboration and the ample professional development provided in Google Suite resulted in the "ease of use" by educators throughout the district. The district also invested heavily in Chromebooks, which as a Google product, work seamlessly with Google Suite.

The district had already adopted certain digital tools before the pandemic. These tools were chosen for purchase due to their alignment with District goals towards blended learning. Teachers used educational technology tools such as Nearpod, Formative, and Flipgrid. As employees of the District, part of our jobs were to use the tools purchased. Thus, we supported teachers using Nearpod for interactive lectures, formative assessment, and student engagement, then to use the real-time data to pivot instruction. We also supported teachers in the use of Formative to auto-grade assessments/activities, provide instant feedback and provide the educator with accurate data for student learning. Educators were able to view data as students responded to each question; advanced use also allowed chat with students using Formative's premium features. Flipgrid training was focused to support educators in providing digital discussion and provide students with a platform to socialize via video submissions. Students and teachers were able to respond to each other's videos and comment, much like the popular social networks being used outside the classroom.

Due to District adoption, we had already published online guides and videos to support educators' knowledge for use. Additionally, coaching and professional development sessions were planned daily the first few months, to support stakeholders' ongoing knowledge of these tools during ERE. EdTech Specialists helped users see the perceived usefulness of each adopted platform.

Tools of Engagement for Students

Students used whatever their teachers designated for them to use. Mainly, students used the videoconferencing platform, the Google Suite, adopted applications from the District, then any OER their teachers were either guided to or adopted on their own. The videoconferencing platform and productivity suites were foundational to instruction, and the levels of engagement depended on the designed use by the teacher. Adopted applications will be discussed in terms of student engagement. OER will be discussed in terms of perceived usefulness, or ease of use.

Adopted applications were meant to engage students in blended learning environments even before the pandemic. Programs such as Nearpod can engage students through creating activities for participation during live instruction of a presentation. Flipgrid allows students to have video discussions or text responses, creating student agency and fueling creation in the classroom. In addition, Flipgrid can be used as an engagement tool, to bring out students' creativity through recordings and filters, mimicking a TikTok or Snapchat video. Formative can engage students through getting instant feedback on assignments and assessments.

Open education resources are vast. We will discuss those we saw widely adopted, and their observed effects on student engagement. Gamified formative assessments like Kahoot, Quizzlet, Blooket and Gimkit provide educators with a gamified alternative for vocabulary and content review. Tools like EdPuzzle gave educators ways to transform videos into instructional videos with built-in assessment questions.

Tools of Engagement for Staff

Educators adopted instructional engagement tools based on their perceived usefulness and ease of use. Three sets of tools were ubiquitous to virtual remote instruction, so their perceived usefulness was direct: videoconferencing platforms, content management systems, and productivity suites. The videoconferencing platform and productivity suites were foundational to instruction, so directly matched perceived usefulness. The depth to which Google Meet or Zoom were used for engagement was dependent on the teacher. Most teachers just learned the basic use to get on and instruct using more familiar means. Some teachers learned the advanced features of these programs to engage their students with polls, the online whiteboard, shared videos, and more. Similarly, Google Classroom and Seesaw were foundational to content management, but offered no further engagement; they directly matched perceived usefulness. Lastly, productivity suites such as Google Docs, Sheets, Forms, etc. helped teachers manage their online content and distribute and receive digital copies from their students. Adopted applications will be discussed in terms of student engagement. OER will be discussed in terms of perceived usefulness, or ease of use.

District-adopted applications which helped teachers engage students were the interactive television panel, GoGuardian, and the Google Suite. The Clear Touch Interactive panel assisted educators by connecting online students with the students in the classroom for hybrid instruction. It provided the means to facilitate discussion and engagement between students in the classroom and students at home. Educators were able to teach from the Clear Touch and share the screen in order for students in the classroom and at home could see/hear the instruction. Teachers could stand up, move around and teach from the front of the classroom instead of just being behind a desk interacting mostly with students online. The programs built in the Clear Touch such as Snowflake-Canvas and Easinote provided tools for the educator to annotate the screen, provide a digital whiteboard, and digital tools for instruction. GoGuardian was a later acquisition that was beta tested at the end of the school year. GoGuardian allows teachers to ensure students are on task on their Chromebook and redirect students to specific websites. Teachers also have the ability to block and direct students to specific websites during any given class session. The Google Suite fostered collaboration and accountability tools for students throughout ERE.

Open educational resources, referenced in Table 1, helped teachers engage students in digital ERE. Observed from online drop-ins, helpdesk conversations, coaching sessions, and Q&A during professional development sessions, these tools helped to engage students with one another, the teacher, and the content.

Recommendations: Open Educational Resources

Providing professional development and support for OER is a key recommendation. Open educational resources have been accessible for years, and only heavily used by education systems with low fiscal resources. However, there are many OER which can provide best for student's needs--if they are in compliance with privacy laws. "Teachers who have utilized such tools have reported a greater satisfaction in supporting their students in a hybrid learning work environment" (personal communication, Researcher 2, May 20, 2021). Filtering many of the OER for educators will be an aid to educators and their students going forward.

Table 1. Open Educational Resources of Engagement

Name of Application	Description of Tool and impact of Engagement
Wheel of Names	A digital name randomizer where you can copy and paste students' names and spin the wheel to randomly call on students. Party music is attached to the spin to engage the audience
Confetti Cannon	A web application, tied to a browser, which allows the user to click it, and the users in the shared videoconference will see confetti fly across the screen. We saw this app used to celebrate students for correct answers, participation, and sometimes just for being
Bitmoji Classroom	A digital alternative to a black board configurator, where a teacher can post a digital character of themselves by using the Bitmoji application and hyperlink resources using a Google Slide, Google Drawing, and/or Google Doc
ClassroomScreen.com	A web based digital screen that provides educators with widgets that are commonly used in the classroom (e.g., digital timer, clock, whiteboard, random name tool, and draw tool)
Screencasting (Google extension, iorad, Screencastify…)	Web extensions that provide educators with the ability to video record their screens, annotate/provide voice over as they record, then be shared via a link

FUTURE RESEARCH DIRECTIONS

Upon reflection from the data, we have nine questions to ask the academe for further research:

1. From pandemic pedagogy, how can school systems be reworked to adapt and consider the complexities of remote and hybrid learning?
2. As some educators were better equipped than others to perform effectively during ERE, what "stickiness factor" (Gladwell, 2002) prepares teachers for 21st-century teaching and learning?
3. How can collaboration within school departments be strengthened (e.g., the educational technology department collaborates with the educational services department) to create a systematic approach of support?
4. How was teachers' mental well-being and overall wellness a factor for adopting new technology tools for support?
5. To what extent can a strong digital citizenship curriculum and implementation plan support educators and students with ERE?
6. To what extent can a shift in pedagogy result from an increase in technical skills from educators in order to provide students with on-demand learning and support?
7. What differentiated approaches for teacher professional development are a direct result of ERE?

8. The pandemic exacerbated the digital divide, with a belief that the divide solely belongs to hardware access. How do we address the widening divide in technological knowledge and skills?
9. How can digital learning stemming from equity, inclusion, and diversity be incorporated into a systematic approach of engagement for all students?

CONCLUSION

This research-based and practitioner-focused chapter provides promising practice techniques and real-world solutions to educators in building and maintaining a positive digital culture. By examining student engagement in the emergency remote education environment, we address crisis leadership through teaming. Teaming helped support digital leadership for online and hybrid student engagement.

Through our duoethnography, we found that technology could help facilitate student engagement in online and hybrid environments through generational engagement practices and facilitating data-based decision-making. We also found that district support was the most helpful resource provided to educators to help pivot to online and hybrid teaching. Effective practices such as collaborative activities, effective planning, and SEL connections were strategies that assisted most with student engagement. Effective engagement practices develop from educators who are also experienced designers. Having someone model practice while others learn is a promising practice to revisit. Davis' TAM Model (1989) helped us understand why District-adopted tools, as well as open educational resources, assisted most in online and hybrid student engagement.

Our recommendations at the end of each section are towards implications for practice and policy. With any crisis, there should be an overcommunication, versus risking a lack of communication. Collaboration rather than working in isolation. Instead of anticipating things going "back to normal," create a "new normal" of embracing technology to facilitate student engagement to the generational group. We posit that learning organizations should collaborate interdepartmentally, and use technological tools to help gather actionable data. As learning organizations adopt technologies and allow for open educational resources, develop a sustainable digital citizenship plan. We further recommend that school leadership stay cognizant of stakeholder mental and physical health needs. Finally, acknowledge and address inequities as they come.

ACKNOWLEDGMENT

This research received no specific grant from any funding agency in the public, commercial, or not-for-profit sectors.

REFERENCES

Aaronson, D., Barrow, L., & Sander, W. (2002). *Teachers and student achievement in the Chicago public high schools.* Working Paper Series WP-02-28, Federal Reserve Bank of Chicago. doi:10.1086/508733

Banathy, B. H., & Jenlink, P. M. (2004). Systems inquiry and its application in education. In D. Jonassen (Ed.), *Handbook of research for educational communications and technology* (2nd ed., pp. 37–58). Lawrence Erlbaum Associates.

Breault, R. (2016). Emerging issues in duoethnography. *International Journal of Qualitative Studies in Education: QSE, 29*(6), 777–794. doi:10.1080/09518398.2016.1162866

Carminucci, J., Hodgman, S., Rickles, J. & Garet, M. (2021). *Student attendance and enrollment loss in 2020-21.* American Institutes for Research. https://www.air.org/sites/default/files/2021-07/research-brief-covid-survey-student-attendance-june-2021_0.pdf

Chambers, D., Scala, J., & English, D. (2020). *Promising practices brief: Improving student engagement and attendance during COVID-19 school closures.* U.S. Department of Education. https://insightpolicyresearch.com/wp-content/uploads/2020/08/NSAES_COVID19_Whitepaper_Final_508.pdf

Clotfelter, C., Ladd, H., & Vigdor, J. (2007). *How and why do teacher credentials matter for student achievement?* NBER Working Paper. doi:10.3386/w12828

D'Angelo, C. (2018). The impact of technology: Student engagement and success. *Technology and the Curriculum.* https://techandcurriculum.pressbooks.com/chapter/engagement-and-success/

Davis, F. (1989). Perceived Usefulness, Perceived Ease of Use, and User Acceptance of Information Technology. *Management Information Systems Quarterly, 13*(3), 319–340. doi:10.2307/249008

Davis, F. D., Bogozzi, R., & Warshaw, P. R. (1989). User acceptance of computer technology: A comparison of two theoretical models. *Management Science, 35*(8), 982–1003. doi:10.1287/mnsc.35.8.982

Edmondson, A. (2018, June 14). *How to turn a group of strangers into a team.* YouTube. https://youtu.be/3boKz0Exros

Edmondson, A. C. (2012). *Teaming: How organizations learn, innovate, and compete in the knowledge economy.* Jossey-Bass.

Fabre, P. (2019, June 3). A duoethnography study: How people's life histories shape their current academic beliefs. *Espacios, 40*(8), http://www.revistaespacios.com/a19v40n08/a19v40n08p29.pdf

Flowers, N., Mertens, S. B., & Mulhall, P. F. (2000). How teaming influences classroom practices. *Middle School Journal, 32*(2), 52–59. doi:10.1080/0094077 1.2000.11495267

Gladwell, M. (2002). *The tipping point.* Back Bay Books.

Guskey, T. R. (1988). Teacher efficacy, self-concept, and attitudes toward the implementation of instructional innovation. *Teaching and Teacher Education, 4*(1), 63–69. doi:10.1016/0742-051X(88)90025-X

Hodges, C., Moore, S., Lockee, B., Trust, T., & Bond, A. (2020, March 27). The difference between emergency remote teaching and online learning. *EduCause Review.* https://er.educause.edu/articles/2020/3/the-difference-between-emergency-remote-teaching-and-online-learning

Joy, S. (2021, July 13). Students lag in learning as Covid-19 pandemic widens digital gap. *Deccan Herald.* https://www.deccanherald.com/national/students-lag-in-learning-as-covid-19-pandemic-widens-digital-gap-1008227.html

Khlaif, Z. N., Salha, S., & Kouraichi, B. (2021). Emergency remote learning during COVID-19 crisis: Students' engagement. *Education and Information Technologies, 26*(6), 7033–7055. Advance online publication. doi:10.100710639-021-10566-4 PMID:33935578

Kim, S., & Kim, J. N. (2016). Bridge or buffer: Two ideas of effective corporate governance and public engagement. *Journal of Public Affairs, 16*(2), 118–127. doi:10.1002/pa.1555

Klann, G. (2003). *Crisis leadership: Using military lessons, organizational experiences, and the power of influence to lessen the impact of chaos on the people you lead.* Center for Creative Leadership.

Korman, H. T. N., O'Keefe, B., & Repka, F. (2020). *Missing in the margins: Estimating the scale of the COVID-19 attendance crisis.* Bellwether Education Partners. https://bellwethereducation.org/publication/missing-margins-estimating-scale-covid-19-attendance-crisis#How%20did%20you%20estimate%201-3%20million%20missing%20students?

Kurt, G., Atay, D., & Ozturk, H. A. (2020, June 16). Student engagement in K12 online education during the pandemic: The case of Turkey. *Journal of Research on Technology in Education.* Advance online publication. doi:10.1080/15391523.2021.1920518

Lam, S., Cheng, R. W., & Choy, H. C. (2010). School support and teacher motivation to implement project-based learning. *Learning and Instruction, 20*(6), 487–497. doi:10.1016/j.learninstruc.2009.07.003

Lei, H. (2004). Contextual collaboration: Platform and applications. IEEE International Conference on Services Computing. (SCC 2004). *Proceedings., 2004*(2004), 197–206. doi:10.1109/SCC.2004.1358007

Liberman, M. (2020, Nov 11). How hybrid learning is (and is not) working during COVID-19: 6 case studies. *Education Week.* https://www.edweek.org/leadership/how-hybrid-learning-is-and-is-not-working-during-covid-19-6-case-studies/2020/11

Linnenbrink, E. A., & Pintrich, P. R. (2003). The role of self-efficacy beliefs in student engagement and learning in the classroom. *Reading & Writing Quarterly, 19*(2), 119–137. doi:10.1080/10573560308223

Maslow, A. (1943). A theory of human motivation. *Psychological Review, 50*(4), 370–396. doi:10.1037/h0054346

Mo, S. (2011). Evidence on instructional technology and student engagement in an auditing course. *Academy of Educational Leadership Journal, 15*(4). http://citeseerx.ist.psu.edu/viewdoc/download?doi=10.1.1.727.5418&rep=rep1&type=pdf#page=157

Murata, R. (2002). What does team teaching mean? A case study of interdisciplinary teaming. *The Journal of Educational Research, 96*(2), 67–77. doi:10.1080/00220670209598794

Northouse, P. G. (2019). *Leadership: theory and practice* (8th ed.). SAGE Publications, Inc.

Office of Civil Rights. (2021). *Education in a pandemic: The disparate impacts of COVID-19 on America's students.* United States Department of Education. https://www2.ed.gov/about/offices/list/ocr/docs/20210608-impacts-of-covid19.pdf

Richards, E. (2020, Dec 12). Students are falling behind in online school. Where's the COVID-19 'disaster plan' to catch them up? *USA Today.* https://www.usatoday.com/in-depth/news/education/2020/12/13/covid-online-school-tutoring-plan/6334907002/

Rodgers, D. (2012). *The social media dilemma in education: Policy design, implementation and effects.* University of Southern California Dissertations and Theses, USC Digital Library. https://digitallibrary.usc.edu/CS.aspx?VP3=DamView&VBID=2A3BXZ88RGS9&SMLS=1&RW=1241&RH=591&FR_=1&W=1736&H=898

Sawchuk, S. (2021, July 14). Extreme chronic absenteeism? Pandemic school attendance data is bleak, but incomplete. *Education Week.* https://www.edweek.org/technology/extreme-chronic-absenteeism-pandemic-school-attendance-data-is-bleak-but-incomplete/2021/07

Sawyer, R., & Norris, J. (2015). Spr). Duoethnography: A retrospective 10 years after. *International Review of Qualitative Research, 8*(1), 1–4. doi:10.1525/irqr.2015.8.1.1

Sawyer, R.D., & Norris, J. (2012). *Understanding qualitative research: Duoethnography.* Oxford University Press. doi:10.1093/acprof:osobl/9780199757404.001.0001

Schindler, L. A., Burkholder, G. J., Morad, O. A., & Marsh, C. (2017). Computer-based technology and student engagement: A critical review of the literature. *International Journal of Education Technology in Higher Education, 14*(25), 25. Advance online publication. doi:10.118641239-017-0063-0

Senge, P., Smith, B., Kruschwitz, N., Laur, J., & Schley, S. (2008). *The necessary revolution: How individuals and organizations are working together to create a sustainable world.* Doubleday.

Shaked, H. (2021, May). Instructional leadership in times of crises and the goal of schooling. In J. Glanz (Ed.), *Crisis and Pandemic Leadership: Implications for Meeting the Needs of Students, Teachers, and Parents* (p. 71). Rowman & Littlefield.

Venkatesh, V., & Davis, F. D. (2000). A theoretical extension of the technology acceptance model: Four longitudinal field studies. *Management Science, 46*(2), 186–204. doi:10.1287/mnsc.46.2.186.11926

ADDITIONAL READING

Antes, A., & Schuelke, M. (2011). Leveraging technology to develop creative leadership capacity. *Advances in Developing Human Resources, 13*(3), 318–365. doi:10.1177/1523422311424710

Bergdahl, N., Nouri, J., & Fors, U. (2020). Disengagement, engagement and digital skills in technology-enhanced learning. *Education and Information Technologies, 25*(2), 957–983. doi:10.100710639-019-09998-w

Cavanaugh, C., & DeWeese, A. (2020). Understanding the professional learning and support needs of educators during the initial weeks of pandemic school closures through search terms and content use. *Journal of Technology and Teacher Education, 28*(2), 233–238. https://www.learntechlib.org/primary/p/216073

Chen, C., Calinger, M., Howard, B. C., & Oskorus, A. L. (2008). Design principles for 21st-century educational technology: Connecting theory and practice. *International Journal of Information and Communication Technology Education, 4*(4), 19–30. doi:10.4018/jicte.2008100103

Clark, R. E. (1994). Media will never influence learning. *Educational Technology Research and Development, 42*(2), 21–29. doi:10.1007/BF02299088

Clarke, G. Sr, & Zagarell, J. (2012). Technology in the classroom: Teachers and technology—a technological divide. *Childhood Education, 88*(2), 136–139. doi:10.1080/00094056.2012.662140

Jha, A. K. (2020, June 20). Understanding generation alpha. doi:10.31219/osf.io/d2e8gosf.io/d2e8g

Nicolaides, A., & McCallum, D. C. (2013). Inquiry in action for leadership in turbulent times: Exploring the connections between transformative learning and adaptive leadership. *Journal of Transformative Education, 11*, 246–260. doi:10.1177/1541344614540333

KEY TERMS AND DEFINITIONS

Blended Learning: Combining traditional teaching methods with technology to support student learning.

Digital Engagement: Using a variety of media and technologies to increase student participation and learning.

Duoethnography: The relation of autobiographical experiences between two persons which fosters new meaning of context.

Emergency Remote Education (ERE): A temporary shift of instructional delivery to an alternate delivery mode due to crisis circumstances.

Hybrid Instruction: Similar to blended learning, combines in-class instruction with online activities.

Pandemic Pedagogy: Speaks to the approaches employed in instructional environments to foster learning in the context of a serious health crisis.

Teaming: A group of individuals empowered to work collaboratively towards a common goal.

Chapter 7
Effective Methods of Teaching Asynchronous Classes

Juliana M. Namada
United State International University Africa, Kenya

ABSTRACT

Asynchronous e-learning has been popularized by the onset and rapid spread of the COVID-19 pandemic. This is because this approach of e-learning speaks to social distancing which is a key element in controlling the spread of the coronavirus. This chapter starts by defining asynchronous e-learning and contrasting it with the synchronous approach. It progresses into identifying and discussing different digital tools used in asynchronous e-learning among them threaded discussion forums, recorded live events, documented cases, emails, blogs, wikis, and reflective journals. The chapter describes interactive, mediated, active, and collaborative learning as some of the key strategies used in asynchronous e-learning. It proceeds to explain the principles used in the development of asynchronous content together with highlighting best practice in effective asynchronous teaching. The chapter ends by identifying some of the key challenges associated with asynchronous e-learning and suggests mitigation strategies for dealing with the challenges.

INTRODUCTION

The fact that developing information technologies have become an indispensable part of economic and social life has made it a necessity for educational institutions to focus on e-learning (Durnalı, Orakcı, & Aktan, 2019; Orakcı, 2020). Asynchronous learning is a type of e-learning approach which is now becoming commonly used. E-learning refers to all forms of electronically supported instruction. E-learning

DOI: 10.4018/978-1-7998-8077-6.ch007

has become an integral component of teaching due to COVID-19 pandemic which has been characterized by extensive lockdowns to reduce the spread of the virus in addition to that the pandemic has enabled the institutions to develop various educational policies (Orakcı, & Gelişli, 2021). Asynchronous e-learning has many benefits because it accommodates multiple learning styles. It fosters increased access to education, is cost-effectiveness, and fosters high level of interactivity. Mayadas (1997) noted that asynchronous learning is an interactive learning approach which is not limited by time, place, or the constraints of a classroom. Learning events are independently experienced by students and learning is not synchronized in time or space. Some of the digital tools commonly used in asynchronous e-learning are emails, blogs, wikis, and discussion boards, with the instructor playing a larger role as facilitator between the students.

Asynchronous instruction occurs in delayed time and does not require the simultaneous participation of teacher and students (Sabau, 2005). It describes the process of teaching and learning in a technology-mediated environment that does not require the teacher and the student to interact at the same time but rather happen in delayed time (Johnson, 2006; Rovy et al., 2001). It is thus a key component of flexible e-learning. This type of learning style is specifically beneficial to students who need more time to respond to situations. They benefit immensely from this type of e-learning as it provides enough reflective time. It also fits into the tight work schedules of mid-level career professionals and millennials who are mostly time constrained. Key amongst the benefits provided by asynchronous e-learning is flexibility. Asynchronous courses provide learners with a flexible environment that is self-paced with learners accessing course content using a variety of tools such as CD-ROMs, streamed prerecorded audio/video web recordings, and audio podcasts. Communication and collaboration are enhanced via asynchronous discussions (Skylar, 2005).

Synchronous learning on the other hand is real e-learning time instruction directed online where all participants are logged on at the same time. Synchronous approach creates a real physical touch with the students especially when they use the video functionality to see all the participants including the facilitator. During these sessions, the lecturer uses voice mediated tools like audio to virtually teach different modules, assess student performance and explain all aspects of the course. This allows the students to share and interact directly with the lecturer in a virtual classroom. Synchronous e-learning uses real time zoom sessions, Microsoft teams, video conferencing, twitter, Facebook, or blogs among others to facilitate information sharing which capture a large audience and gain the value of sharing knowledge with the community. It creates real time knowledge sharing and learning interactions. When video is used, both the instructor and the students can see each other. These tools facilitate learning through real-time information access, sharing and engagement. According to Skylar (2005), synchronous courses provide online learning environments that are very interactive and use web conferencing products such as Elluminate Live, Interwise, Wimba Live Classroom, Adobe Acrobat Connect Professional, and Saba Centra. Advantages of using a synchronous learning environment include real time sharing of knowledge and learning and immediate access to the instructor to ask questions and receive answers.

Asynchronous e-learning is more helpful when reflecting on complex issues which require more time and it is also favoured when synchronous meetings cannot function well because of work schedules, family commitments and other conflicting personal engagements. It provides more reflective time for students which is a near equivalent of a takeaway assignment which could be done through discussion boards, emails, blogs, recorded lectures, or recorded YouTube video lessons. Garrison (2004) noted that in asynchronous e-learning environment students are required to become proficient in the mediated tools required for the course, use improved communication methods for interaction, and strengthen dependency through interaction with peers and facilitators. In asynchronous e-learning students are the drivers of learning as they learn how to manage time for all the learning activities including work and family life.

Asynchronous e-learning prides from time lapse and geographic disparity. It is a learning model where learning occurs intermittently with time delay through recorded class videos and discussion forums. In this mode of e-learning, instructors can use recorded lecture approach, case studies, journal articles together with pre-recorded video series. This combination of teaching capture students who are both visual and audial. Digital tools used include discussion forums, wikis, blogs, among others. This approach of teaching embraces the "doing" part of learning which makes the learning experiences practical and compensates on time differences where the students are not able to log in at the same time. Asynchronous discussion groups form the heart of many virtual learning environment by providing the means for students to engage in collaborative exchange of knowledge (Britain & Liber, 2004).

The main differences between synchronous learning and asynchronous e-learning as noted by Bouhnik, Giat, and Sanderovitch (2009) is that asynchronous e-learning takes place real time through direct interaction using audio lectures, video conferences, online chats, instant messaging, and live web casting. Asynchronous e-learning on the other hand takes place in a time lagged scenario through threaded discussion forums, direct email communications, pre-recorded audio lectures, podcasting and recorded YouTube videos. Synchronous e-learning is beneficial because of real time interaction which is motivating to students and enables the instructor to keep the class connection through real-time teaching. Conversely, asynchronous e-learning affords the students the flexibility to learn at their own pace and time together with offering the students longer response time on tasks. The flip side of synchronous teaching is that it breeds rigidity by virtue of being time constrained. Asynchronous by its very nature has been criticized for creating a disconnection between the student and the instructor. This disconnection creates delayed feedback to the students and could cause anxiety which increases dropout rates. Asynchronous lecture notes on CD-ROMs with asynchronous lecture notes on WebCT, Skylar et al. (2005) found that both conditions were effective in delivering instruction.

Online education is a system that supports individual teaching and requires the learners to be responsible for their own learning process (Karagöz, 2021; Karagöz, & Rüzgar, 2021). The purpose of this chapter is to discuss asynchronous methods of online teaching and learning. To achieve the purpose the chapter starts by defining both asynchronous and synchronous online teaching and then moves to comparing and contrasting synchronous and asynchronous methods of online teaching to lay a candid foundation of the chapter before proceeding to discuss the key elements of asynchronous teaching.

LITERATURE REVIEW

Asynchronous e-Learning

Historically, asynchronous interaction is made up by what is ordinarily referred to as distance education. It has its roots in early forms of distance education such as correspondence courses (Keegan, 1996). Asynchronous interaction has been the traditional method for engaging students in their distance education courses. This mode of instruction is both flexible and student centred. Due to its flexibility the success rates are much higher than the real time interactive one which is limited by time. This is because students engage with the learning materials at their own time when their absorption rates are at the peak. Markel (2001) also emphasized that the instructor's responsiveness is one of the critical factors' contributing to successful online asynchronous teaching. The timing component make a significant component of asynchronous teaching.

Asynchronous e- learning happens both during the day and at night making it flexible for the learners. It takes care of time zone differences across the globe. Students spend more time refining their contributions, which in essence enriches their output and in essence improves performance. The authors argue that asynchronous learning thrives on constructivism which suggests that teaching and learning occurs when students are actively involved in the process of understanding the knowledge they acquire (Reed, 2008; Taber, 2011). Most of the learning activities are interactive as the approach holds strong to the fact that students learn better by doing. Asynchronous learning networks permit the kinds of interaction, feedback, and facilitation that have been difficult with traditional forms of correspondence distance learning. The primary benefit of asynchronous teaching is the flexibility it provides for anytime anywhere student preferences (Hrastinski, 2008; Stein, Wanstreet, & Calvin, 2009). Asynchronous e-learning taps into globalization and integration making cultural exchange live and real. Discussion forums form an important element of asynchronous learning.

Branon and Essex (2001) noted that asynchronous online discussions encourage thoughtful discussions, in depth critical thinking and it allows students enough time to respond to tasks and assignments. Students take time to consider their thoughts, engage with the content more deeply, feel a part of the learning community, and post more reflective comments in discussion boards (Hrastinski, 2008; Stein et al., 2009). Through asynchronous learning students can contemplate on the content and the questions before responding to discussion boards. Therefore, this type of asynchronous engagement increases cognitive engagement with the content, especially when the content is difficult to comprehend. Stein et al. (2009) in a study reported that when participants took ample time to reflect on their own ideas their interactions were deep and comprehensive. Asynchronous approach to e-learning borrows heavily from cognitive model.

According to the cognitive model, asynchronous communication increases a person's ability to process information and provides a better understanding of the content. Hrastinski (2008) asserted that in the asynchronous discussion it is easier to find more quality facts by referring to books, journals and periodicals. He also noted that being able to contemplate on the content before responding to discussion boards increased cognitive engagement and enabled the student to synthesize and internalize difficult content. Stein et al. (2009) study revealed that students believed that taking the time to reflect on ideas as well as those of their peers allowed them to interact more deeply and, in the process, form a community of engaged scholars.

Many adult students take online courses because of their asynchronous nature; not being bound by time, location, and space due to the demands of work and family life. Due to the heterogeneous nature of students in any one given class asynchronous approach is mostly favored because it encourages each of the student to work according to their own plan and liking. Based on a survey of student preferences, Dede, and Kremer (1999) concluded that asynchronous discussion provided richer and more inclusive type of interchange among fellow students and with the instructor. It should be noted that asynchronous e-learning favors independent learning because a big percentage of the learning depends on the student. Asynchronous courses allow the instructors to create a learning environment that enables greater choice for students, which in turn combines variety of learning styles. It gives students independence and self-initiative which are key components in e-learning. Hrastinski (2008) noted that the asynchronous approach allows students to log in at any time that fits their schedules to download documents, send messages to peers or instructors, or submit assignments. This flexibility allows students to spend more time refining their contributions, which is generally considered more thoughtful on submission. Several digital tools are used to effectively deliver asynchronous teaching.

ASYNCHRNOUS DIGITAL TOOLS USED IN TEACHING

There are a variety of digital tools which are used in asynchronous e-learning which include threaded discussion forums, recorded live videos and lectures, documented cases, emails, blogs, wikis, and reflective journals. The digital tools facilitate time lagged content transmission between the instructor and the students. They also have a historical framework of archiving documents which is a critical feature in a synchronous e-learning. This section discusses these tools showing how they facilitate asynchronous e-learning.

Threaded Discussion Forums

Discussion forums are digital online tools that facilitate threaded posts and responses. The online discussion forum allows students to work together on projects in small groups, participate in on-going discussions focused on course content, and present group projects to the rest of the class members. Postings in the discussion forums institutionalizes and legitimizes the discussions within the course making them part and parcel of the engagements in a class. Weekly discussion topics are coordinated and assigned readings for each week posted on the teaching platform. Students are asked to post their response to the assignment and then later, respond to the posts from the rest of the class members. Markel (2001) noted that threaded discussion forums which require students to respond to at least three other student postings initiates a round of insights and views among the participants. It creates a sense of connection and collegiality among the students. Each student's posting is listed in the forum under the weekly topic and is accessible to all other members in a class.

Threaded discussion forums are public and are accessible to the class. This means that all the students and the instructors listed under the course can access and read the discussions to enhance the course content. An advantage of discussion forums is that they are automatically archived so that they can be re-viewed as needed and readily accessible to all participants. This therefore means that all the threaded discussions can be accessed at a later stage for reference or for evaluation purposes. This written record constitutes a body of knowledge collectively written by participants in the course. In essence this is how new knowledge is generated and stored. As Hopperton (1998) noted, participation in online discussion forums provides opportunities for responsibility and active learning through the expectation of regular participation online. They construct knowledge through shared experiences that each participant brings to the collaborative discussions. This particular use of the discussion forum enables the students to negotiate and construct knowledge.

In a synchronous e-learning style some students engage with course content in discussion forums while others engage in generative processing of information posted in the forums. Generative processing of information results from activating appropriate mental models and using them to interpret new information, assimilating new knowledge into those models, re-organizing the models of the newly interpreted information, and then using models to explain, interpret, or infer new knowledge (Jonassen, 1998). Students draw upon their own experiences and interpretations and share different points of views in the group discussions. They draw on their own experiences to relate to the course content. They read other student responses and interpretations and compare these with their own thoughts. This involves the processes of reflection, construction, and re-construction of domains of knowledge to discern meaning.

Asynchronous e-learning favors students who have a reflective style of learning that does not lend itself to quick, off the hip questions or comments; they now have time to contribute their well thought out responses. Connections that few have time to make in the stream of classroom discourse now stand out in a discussion forum flow of asynchronous discussion. Those students who migrate to the back of classrooms suddenly find that in the virtual environment their voice is not only solicited, but it is required, and they discover that they can interact with the content of the course and their peers. This further enhances the learning process and fosters a better understanding of the content.

Discussion forums facilitate development of online identity as well as providing a voice as the students tell their stories and mutually construct understanding around the course content. This is of particular interest to online instructors and administrators as one of the goals in using an online discussion forum is to establish a virtual community of students and a sense of identity of a group. Online discussions enable students to read other students' answers and comments, while having time to reflect prior to reacting and responding (Mory, Gambill & Browning, 1998). The discussion forum is a public place for discussion that allows time for reflection. A discussion can be revisited and commented on as long as the forum is open.

Recorded Live Videos and Lectures

Recorded live events are contiguous audio-visual recording excerpts which are used in asynchronous online teaching. They include recorded lectures, YouTube videos, role play recorded events or document important societal and national happenings.

Videos on current life events enable students to interpret real life situations. Video clips from the websites of business news channels and periodicals can be more effective in that they tend to be shorter, more current, and thus give the instructors time to dissect the clip and show the significance to the topic at hand. The instructor can supplement the lesson with a video clip that explores concepts and specific theories. Video clips should not be used in isolation as a standalone teaching tool but as a complementary tool with other teaching resources. In addition, prerecorded videos allow students to view media at their own time is a beneficial component of asynchronous interaction (Griffiths & Graham, 2010).

Videos are used to integrate an idea into the course content. Videos establish a relationship among image, interactivity, and integration. To this extent the main advantage of using video as a learning tool is its ability to present images and animation. They are used as interactive and integrated instructional media. Videos in slides, discussion boards, chats, resource links are used to complement textbooks, as integral to a dynamic and meaningful learning environment. There are six characteristics that define meaningful learning which are related to the video clips. They are active, constructive, collaborative, contextual, emotional, and motivational. Videos have been known to fulfil most of the learning characteristics. In asynchronous engagements, students must be actively involved and, in this case, watch the recorded video clip or the lectures in the absence of the instructor. After the exposure to the videos, they then get to the mental and intellectual construction stage where they discern meaning from the clips and relate it to the content. The collaborative feature in this video learning is the fact that students are allowed to work in teams to share and compare ideas and interpretations of different members. The videos are emotionally involving as the students become part and parcel of the clip being watched.

Online video clips are termed as effective because they break the monotony of reading documented content throughout the class session. Stephen (2015) noted that the pedagogical effectiveness of using online video clips is dependent on the choice of appropriate video clips that are current and connect directly to course lessons. He further argued that the preparation undertaken to use video clips as other teaching resources by tying it to a specific learning outcome, previewing the video clips before showing it in the classroom is important. The instructor needs to include specific questions about the video clips on assignments and exams so that they can measure whether the desired student learning outcomes are being achieved by the videos. When rightly used videos become a useful component of class engagement which could easily attract and keep student attention.

Video clips enable instructors to present models and concepts covered in course content. They are used to cover and illustrate both current concepts to keep the students updated and show his past events to enable them to understand the historical developments of concepts. They offer a good starting point to familiarize students with terminology, before delving deeper into specifics about the diverse theories (Burbank & Cooper 2010). Video games offer students the opportunity to discuss more contested concepts such as that of societal collapse. Video games that incorporate the past as part of their narrative, theme or setting provide a great opportunity for experiential learning. Their inherently interactive character allows for an immersive experience and through this both a deeper and wider understanding of the played past.

Documented Cases

Cases are analysis of specific organizational happenings outlining the why, what, how, and who is involved in the management and daily operations. Case-based learning is an example of a deep structure in learning because it teaches students to imagine themselves as professionals, engaging with real-life scenarios and possibilities. Case studies hold great potential for engaging students in disciplinary content. Case-based learning comprises the use of authentic complex situations which prompt students' deep analysis of problems, principles and models for resolution and reflection on the problem-solving process (Ertmer & Koehler, 2014). Case-based learning helps educators to bridge the cognitive gap between theory and practice by inviting them to consider real-world problems (Mitchem, Koury, Fitzgerald, Hollingshead, Miller, Tsai & Zha, 2009). In other words, case-based learning provides students the opportunity to apply their knowledge to problems that mirror the real-world in a low-stakes environment. With e-learning, students review the case and then discuss it through discussion forums.

Real life cases offer problem-based approaches to learning. Research in post-secondary settings has demonstrated multiple advantages of problems pedagogies over traditional methods of instruction, including increased student learning and motivation. Problem-centered approaches result in deeper comprehension of content and more successful application of skills among secondary students (Pease & Kuhn, 2011). The most prominent of these affordances include engagement with real-world problems, interaction with diverse perspectives, and vicarious participation in professional realities. Specifically, in instructional design, these affordances provide students with an opportunity to simultaneously learn content and/or concepts, as well as problem-solving skills (Dabbagh et al. 2000).

On the other hand, Capon and Kuhn (2004) study revealed that interacting with real-world problems helps post-secondary students to make connections among personal experiences, course content, and new situations. Findings from a national survey verified faculty's agreement with these conclusions. Students who used case-based instruction approaches agreed that it enhances connections and a better understanding across content areas. Since cases facilitate an actual demonstration of success and failure of real companies they serve as an integration between theory and practice and facilitate informed decision making and critical thinking.

Emails, Blogs, Wikis and Reflective Journals

Emails, Blogs, Wikis and Reflective Journals are widely used as digital tools in asynchronous e-learning. Email is a short form for Electronic Mail. It is one of the most widely used features of the internet. Through email one can send and receive messages to and from anyone with an email address anywhere in the world. Emails are useful in asynchronous teaching because they enable the users to transmit information from one person to another. An instructor can compile an email list of all the students which makes it easy for transmitting class information. A mailing list is a collection of names and addresses used to send information to multiple recipients. The advantage of an email list is that an instructor can send a whole group message in one go rather than sending individual messages. It also ensures that there is uniformity in the messages sent to a set of recipients because it does not allow distortion.

Emails can be used for setting up flexible consultation sessions outside the set times. Students who may want to communicate with the instructor confidentially without involving the rest of the students can comfortably do it through email. Students could also use email to inform the instructor about confidential challenges they may be facing at individual levels in the classroom. Email is useful for answering the more mundane sorts of questions that arise about readings, assignments. An email can be used to send a message to a whole group of students in a particular class. In turn, the students can use instructor email to send their completed assignments for evaluation and grading.

Blogs are websites or web pages created for informal conversations between individuals and small groups. Blogs are used in asynchronous learning environment to facilitate collaborative project engagements among teams of students. Students post their contributions through blogs and get responses through the same blog. Blogs are useful in keeping the students up to date with the current news which they can use to illustrate the points. The advantage of a blog is its huge customization capacity. As an assessment tool, blogs can be used like discussion platform in which students can respond to prompts, pose their own questions, and summarize reading assignments. Blogs are used to write book recommendations, discuss current affairs issues or comment on other postings. Blogs can also be used as reflection journals to obtain feedback from the students on different topics. Through blogs, additional information can be generated by the student community to enhance learning. Blogs can also form a landing base for students so that they do not feel the isolation and loneliness associated with asynchronous online teaching and learning.

Another important digital tool is podcast. A podcast is a digital audio file transmitted through the internet. They are mostly found on iTunes, Spotify or google podcasts. It is a recording of an audio discussion on topics like business, travel, mining, and farming. Podcasting started as an independent way for individuals to get their message out there and build a community of people with similar interests. A podcast is essentially a talk series produced periodically on demand. This means that listeners don't need to turn up and tune in live but can listen any time making it a good tool for asynchronous teaching. In asynchronous teaching instructors can create podcasts as an additional teaching tool and post content to illustrate textbook concepts and theories. A podcast can guide a student through a process, allowing them to practice and understand the concept at their own pace and time. Williams (2014) noted that podcasts can replace time intensive contact with tutors or instructors and allows students to develop skills at their own pace.

Reflective journals offer important feedback to the instructors and course developers. They are personal records of students' learning experiences done on a weekly basis. Students record learning-related incidents during the learning process and transmit them to the instructor more often just after they occur. This helps the instructor to take precautionary measures or address such scenarios in the proceeding classes to avoid disruptions. Journals and learning logs are then submitted to the instructor for feedback. Both paper-based and online journals or logs can be turned in before or after each class period or at any other designated time. Reflective journals serve as formative evaluation tools of course instruction as the instructor gets to understand the success, relevance of course content the challenges and issues which the students may be struggling with through the course. The instructor can use the reflective journal information to modify the course to benefit all the students. All the digital tools used in asynchronous teaching are anchored different strategies as discussed in the following section.

STRATEGIES USED IN ASYNCHRONOUS E-LEARNING

Interactive Learning

Interactivity is a regular engagement between teacher and students, among students, and between students and the learning environment. Specifically, interactivity may be practiced in several ways; simple strategies such as having students introduce themselves to their classmates can reduce the anonymity of the course environment. Students can use it to make posts and make responses to other posts made by other members of the class. The principle of interactivity arises out of the fear that asynchronous learning reduces human interaction. Courses should be developed so that they encourage regular interaction between teacher and students, among students, and between students within the learning environment. The role of interaction between students and students has been known to bear fruit in a synchronous environment. This approach sets stage for interaction among the students.

Learning is an essentially social process that requires interaction for the purpose of ex- pression, validation, and the development of the human person. Instructors need to take the earliest opportunity to connect with the students and participants and take advantage of all the opportunities for interaction including provision of feedback, chat rooms and online office hours. Before commencement of each course. Registered students should receive a welcome note from the instructor, a course outline, and an encouragement to start navigating through the course. This provides an opportunity to contact the instructor in case of any concerns or questions related to the course. The students are also asked to send an email message to the instructor for the student to start the journey of familiarity with the instructor.

When the course begins, the students are given tasks which involve connecting with instructor and fellow students. They may be asked to introduce themselves, explain their family and academic background, mention where they are logged from, their hobbies and something notable about them. The students are then asked to respond/comment on other introductions. The course instructor creates a web of interaction between the students who are normally miles apart. Interaction between students and the instructor also occur after the submission of each assignment or exam. The instructor reads the exam, embed comments into the text, and return the assignment or exam to the student as part of e-mail communication.

Mediated Learning

In conventional classes, the instructors situate reading materials, ideas, and concepts within a theoretical framework through a lecture. However, in asynchronous learning, there is no physical lecture therefore the instructor needs to develop an alternative mediation strategy. This is because mediation serves as an intervention between the student and the subject matter. This enhances interaction between student, content, and the instructor. Mediation is an important engagement between the student and content. The instructor needs to be ready to fill int this gap so that it does not provide a chance for anxiety or unanswered questions on the students. Mediated learning occurs when students are guided through the process of learning by the instructor.

The key features of mediated learning are reciprocity, intent, meaning and transcendence. Reciprocity establishes a responsive connection between the student and the instructor. The student and the instructor both share their cultures by integrating values, ideas, feelings, and expectations. They also set rules and regulations to govern the engagement. Essentially, reciprocity allows the instructor and the student to form a working relationship based on trust, acceptance and understanding to foster openness in the learning process. Intent is the explicit goal that evolves between the instructor and the student. The instructor who acts as the mediator prepares intent ahead of time and determines how to catch and hold the student's attention. The intent may change according to the needs of the student. Meaning is the personal relevance of the learning experience. The mediator ensures that the children share in developing meaning about the activities. Finally, transcendence is the expansion of understanding beyond specific activities. Through transcendence students develop skills of coming up with learning strategies. The emphasis is on the process of learning how to learn. Transcendence emphasizes transferring knowledge and strategies from one situation to another (King, 1994; King, Staffieri, & Adelgais, 1998; McCombs 2001)

Mediation in a synchronous environment can be done through posting questions on the learning management system which is being used, student discussion forums or at the time of evaluation. Posting questions in weekly assignments requires students to apply the knowledge which was covered during the week and serves as a reminder to respond to the weekly content. Discussions facilitate mediated learning because they enables students to contribute to questions and synthesize the contributions made by fellow students by pointing out the areas of convergencies and divergencies. Development of an evaluation assignment enable students to evaluate a particular claim based on several sources of information which are normally provided for reference purposes. Students share variety of responses which stimulate further debate on the subject creating new knowledge on the subject. The mediator who in this case is the instructor deliberately controls the learning process in the background as a facilitator.

Active Learning

Active learning refers to a broad range of teaching strategies which are generally described as student centred. Students work together during class on projects and assignments. These teaching approaches range from short, simple activities like journal writing, problem solving and paired discussions or pedagogical frameworks like case studies, role plays, and structured team-based learning. The notion of active learning requires that students must learn by doing. They also must engage and participate in activities and tasks that enhance learning. One of the things students can do in active learning is by writing. Writing translates ideas into written prose and produces a clearer and more systematic understanding of the mater.

Active learning encourages students to solve problems, answer questions, formulate questions of their own, discuss, explain, debate, or brainstorm during class sessions. This encourages students to participate in hands on learning activities, providing them with an opportunity to practice application of the skills garnered in the class, helps them to become independent and above all it fosters collaborative engagements between the students. Active learning involves actively engaging students with the course material through discussions, problem solving, case studies, role plays and other methods. It places greater degree of responsibility on the student than passive approaches such as lectures, but instructor guidance is still crucial in the active learning classroom. Active learning activities may range in length from a couple of minutes to whole class sessions or may take place over multiple class sessions. Several scholars advocate for a writing-to- learn pedagogy (Coker and Scarboro 1990; Moore 1992).

Collaborative Learning

Collaborative learning occurs when groups of students work together to complete assigned academic tasks (Brindley, Blaschke & Walti, 2009). In collaborative learning, students establish and maintain active interaction with one another. In collaborative engagements, emphasis is placed on teamwork. The students work as a team and are accountable to one another in the team. In situations where a team member does not complete the assigned tasks, members of the team reprimand and ensure compliance to the set rules. Members become responsible to group tasks and bear responsibility to the group since they must collectively deliver on assigned tasks. Collaborative approach to learning fosters effective learning of content as a team where cognitive skills like problem solving and critical thinking are cultivated to all the members of the team. Development of social skills are collective, and each team sets rules to govern all the team members. The team works together respecting peers, naturing one another and developing friendship across board.

Collaborative learning means that both teachers and students are active participants in the learning process. In the process at emerges from active dialogue among those who seek to understand and apply concepts. Participants in a class interact and engage in the requisite dialogue by sharing ideas that produces new knowledge. Collaborative learning is enhanced with the design and use of the discussion forums. These forums are designed to allow work group to share and exchange thoughts and ideas on a variety of topics and questions. All members of the class could submit a new item for discussion, respond to an item already submitted, or comment on a response by other members of the class. Collaboration happens through constant and ongoing class discussions that revolved around a question posed to the students weekly.

Best practice in collaborative learning need to adopt the following procedures. Collaborative teams need to start with small and simple tasks to build trust among the group members. The groups need to be kept small between 5 to 7 members for effective management and cultivation of common values, norms, and social connection. The groups need to be heterogenous with diversity in terms of age, gender, culture, nationality, ethnicity, race, and religion. Team diversity serves several roles among them: fostering creativity, innovation, integrating different experiences and appreciating the group different and harnessing them for synergy. At the formation stage, teams need to be constituted with a mix of students who are high performers and low performers to leverage peer tutoring among the team members. As instructors prepare asynchronous content, they should be guided by the following principles and best practices which heavily depend on the established standards in online teaching. The principles and best practices enhance effectiveness of online teaching and need to be observed to the latter.

PRINCIPLES OF DESIGNING ASYNCHRONOUS CONTENT

1. Consider Student Capabilities and Existing Knowledge Base.

Student capabilities of the target audience is an important consideration in content preparation. The instructor needs to consider experiences, attitudes, and preferences of the student regarding e-learning. Such an understanding enables the instructor to design content according to the level and characteristics of the students. The baseline knowledge level of the students enables the instructor to pitch content correctly. Assuming that students are privy to some basic knowledge could become a disadvantage to some of the students who may not have background information on the subject. On the other hand, if the students have some basic information, they should not be bored on explanations of the basics. An instructor needs to strike a balance between what the students know and what they do not know to establish a good starting point.

2. Choose the Appropriate Tools and Resources for Developing Class Content.

Since asynchronous learning happens online, the instructor needs to choose an appropriate LMS platform and the digital tools to be used. A discussion forum is one important tool in asynchronous learning e-learning. It can be done using different approaches, one approach is the standard way where students post information regarding a task or question, the other approach is where students are required to make an initial post without seeing messages from fellow students to avoid bias then afterwards make comments, observations or provide additional information in form of links, references, or quotations to what other students have posted. On the other hand, an understanding of computer software, programing resources, educational pedagogies, multimedia functionalities, resource associated with the learning outcomes are important considerations. Resources for instruction development should be linked to the level of the programme. This alignment makes it easy for both the teacher and the student so that they are not receiving either too much or too little. The level of the course determines the amount of detail, breath, and complexity of the content.

3. Provide Learning Guidance Prior and during the Instruction Period.

Asynchronous e-learning resources do not have the benefit of real time instructor support and guidance. Therefore, the learning materials must be self-explanatory and easy to understand to avoid time wastage and unnecessary anxiety on the part of the student. The instructor needs to provide preliminary information before the beginning of the course. A tutorial orientation video which explains how students will access the reading resources, the technical support, and explanation of the expectations, learning outcomes and all the assignments are necessary. During the instruction period, the instructor needs to provide sufficient support especially when new concepts and skills are first introduced, followed by a gradual withdrawal of support as the student progresses and begins to assume an increasingly independent role. Such support could be in the form of definitions, descriptions and provision of sufficient examples and illustrations. The students should also be guided on how the tasks and the assignments feed into specific learning outcomes so that they do not see assignments as a burden.

4. Link Learning Outcomes with Content.

The course learning outcomes should be the starting point of content preparation. The learning outcomes should situate the learning content within a broader curriculum and allow the student to link current knowledge with what they set out to learn. Using learning outcomes to clearly outline the expectations, purpose, and rationale for the learning experience provides the student with the opportunity to develop their confidence as they learn new material. The students need to be guided on why a variety of learning resources like cases, videos, recorded lecture, and discussion forums must be used in different lessons. For example, if the learning outcome is creation of an alignment between theory and practice, the instructor needs to start by explaining the theoretical perspectives of the content using concepts, variables, and models, on the practical side cases of live companies which have exemplified the concepts, models and the constructs need to be used so that the students can understand the link between theory and practice.

5. Conceptualize and Create Meaningful and Engaging Content.

Conceptualization is an important starting point as it enables the instructor to apply appropriate content in detail, depth, and breadth at different levels of the courses. In conceptualization, complex constructs are broken down into simple and measurable concepts to create a common understanding among the users. Use of Bloom's taxonomy is helpful because it provides guidance to the complexity, detail, and quantity of the content. Lower-level courses need to focus on lower-level aspects of recall, comprehension and to a small extent simple direct application. Higher level courses need to focus on applications, analysis, evaluation and creation of models and cases. The Bloom's taxonomy is particularly useful here as this model helps the instructor to make informed instructional design decisions that move students from the most basic which is about providing knowledge to the highest which is evaluation. For content to be engaging, students must be able to remember and apply the content in real life situations well after completing the course.

6. Present the Stimulus Material at the Right Time.

A stimulus is an action which accelerates activity. A stimulus material in teaching refer to an aspect within the content which accelerates the learning process and reduces boredom amongst the students. There are a variety of stimulus teaching including discussions, projects, games, demonstrations and, role plays. Stimulus removes boredom and sustains student attention in class. To break the monotony during e-learning, the instructor need to vary the mode of presenting the content. New stimulus material must be directly aligned with the achievement of learning outcomes and serve to illustrate essential aspects of the content. The use of well-styled headings will allow larger and smaller text to remain relatively sized even if the student increases or decreases the font size to their comfort level. The default font sizes should be within accepted ranges and be tested across all major platforms, devices, and browsers for better visibility. Areas of emphasis need to be bolded or singled out conspicuously. Bolded, italized or enlarged words form an emphasis point in explanations.

7. Deliberate Attempt to Capture and Maintain the Student's Attention.

Students differ in their ability to learn due to individual differences. Studies show that students retain 10% of what they read, 20% of what they hear, 30% of what they see, 50% of what they hear and see, 70% of what they say while 90% of what they say and do. For these reasons, the instructor needs to use variety of methods to capture all the students and ensure that learning takes place among the different students. Animation, humor and demonstration of an unexpected event should be creatively used to facilitate engagement of the students. Use of exciting approaches which catch and keep student attention are highly encouraged. It could be in the form of a brief video from a prominent authority figure, a talk show, or a recorded documentary. They are effective tools in gaining student attention. Concentration span is normally small and generally decreases within adults. The span of concentration explains why an instructor must consider keenly how to capture and maintain the students' attention.

8. Design Objective Performance Assessments and Plan to Offer Timely Feedback.

Assessment should be effective and frequently undertaken throughout the e-learning program using variety of questions, tasks, and assignments to assess the students' achievement of the learning outcomes throughout the programme. Timely feedback on the other hand, allows the students to gauge their performance. It also reinforces learning, corrects misconceptions, and inspires confidence among the students. Feedback must be clear, specific, and meaningful to facilitate further learning and probing from the student perspective. Frequent feedback to the students also makes the students to realize that they are not alone but with the course instructor.

9. Incorporate Elements to Enhance Retention, Transfer, and Behavior Change.

The instructor should understand the absorption and retention rates of students by reattempting the e-learning resources at spaced intervals within the program. The e-learning program needs to focus on skill development or behavior change. The instructor needs to plan on how to eliminate or discourage external variables, such as negative attitudes, perceived social pressures, and behavioral vices to facilitate learning.

10. Conduct Peer Review of Content before the Start of the Module.

Peers should evaluate the teaching resources after completion of the assessment by the instructional designer. This serves as quality check and to check the logical flow and organization of the material. Since peers are the content experts, their evaluation enhances quality and provides corrective indicators for future reference.

BEST PRACTICE IN EFFECTIVE ASYNCHRONOUS TEACHING

1. Prepare students to work asynchronously in terms of the mindset, technology, and readiness to collaborate with fellow class members. Make them understand that there is no real time engagement. Information technology support must be maintained throughout the day and night. Before class begins the instructor should send to the students an introductory letter welcoming them to the programme and explain the asynchronous nature of the course. Explain to them the technological requirements in terms of the equipment with good reception and fast internet connectivity. Clarify the fact that collaboration with fellow students is part of the engagement not only to enhance understanding but also to build a community of scholars.

2. Prepare oneself regarding content, interactions, and time commitment. This commitment of time and effort to ensures that the collaboration between students goes smoothly. As the instructor you need to reorganize your diary so that you have lots of time available for the students. Asynchronous teaching is time demanding in terms of providing timely feedback to students, online consultation, and preparation of programme content.

3. Build a sense of community across members of the class and administrative support team. Make the students understand that each one of them is an important part of the significant whole. A sense of community is built using asynchronous discussion forum activities which enable the students to connect through class activities and assignments. Students working on practical projects together, critique one another, support one another and at the end build lasting community of scholars. Infuse into the class activities assignments which connect students together like role play where the students dramatize case scenarios of the concepts taught in class.

4. Nature the student expectations of the class to be that of self-initiative, collaboration, and teamwork. This is because asynchronous e-learning is student centred and the students have a bigger role to play in the learning process. Self-initiative plays a key role because the students have the discretion to choose

when to read the course content, when to attend to the assignments, when to carry out research and when to hold group discussions. The ability to work in a team is one of the core values because teamwork builds on each other's strengths while minimizing the weaknesses. An example is during presentation of work the orators can present while those good and writing skills compile the work to take advantage of the synergies in the team. Team spirit fosters diverse ways of thinking which leads to creativity and innovation in addressing specific learning outcomes.

5. Enhance communication by spending lots of your time online and develop students into thinking independently and contributing to the knowledge base of others. Give credit by praising the excellent performers as a way of motivating others. Frequent communication by the instructor is an assurance to the online students that the instructor is with them and at the same time encourages participation. In terms of contributing to the knowledge base, the students need to be encouraged to make comments to the asynchronous posts made by other students by providing additional references, relevant links and illustrative videos that provide more information.

6. Be a guide to facilitate learning, not dictate it so that you can tap into the experiences of the students to enhance the knowledge shared in class. One must be flexible enough to accommodate all the experiential knowledge gained by the members of the class. Most of the time, online students are working people who have a variety of practical experiences from the jobs they do. For example, a management class will benefit from the students who are holding managerial positions because they will share practical management experiences of concepts like planning organizing, motivating, budgeting, among others.

7. Be prepared in the approach you use in teaching and be ready to swing to either side as instructor, facilitator and sometimes collaborator as the situation demands. Flexibility enables course instructors to read the mood of the student and change to the student demands. Flexibility is a virtue in asynchronous e-learning. Flexibility will enable the instructor to withhold introduction of a complex content if it is discovered that students require more time to digest the preliminary content. Flexibility enables the instructor to meet the varied needs and requirements of the student because all students are unique in their own aspects. It leads to better performance of the students.

8. Offer students an opportunity to share their work and daily experiences so that they can clearly see the practicability of the course content in real life. Encourage the students to apply the content learned in their work lives to see the relevance of the course. Asynchronous e-learning benefits from weekly journals. The experiences could be in the form of most relevant content of the week, what they may have struggled with when reviewing the weekly resources

or recommendations of learning resources which could enhance the modules. The sharing serves two main roles; it informs the instructor of the progress of the course through indicators of success acts as a corrective tool to the course.

9. Evaluate the quality of online learning programs and familiarize yourself with the ethical and legal issues associated with online education. Quality standards need to be established and met by all the online courses. This can be done through benchmarking with similar courses in other institutions or establishing the standards and upholding to them so that one is not offering courses whose standards fall below the expectation. Understand the legal framework associated with all the videos, diagrams and cases used in the programme. This is important so that the content is used in online class does not become a subject of law suites by patent holders. Where online content is protected by property rights, then it is wise to seek permission from the copyright holders.

10. Provide timely and meaningful feedback to keep students interested and motivated throughout the course. Providing timely feedback is a way of assuring students that they are not alone, and they have a supporting backup. Feedback which is time bared could become irrelevant and confusing to the students. Timely feedback also means that the instructor need to spend a lot of time online. For feedback to be meaningful, the instructor keenly and thoroughly interrogate student posts and then establish areas of convergencies and divergencies to decern meaning.

CHALLENGES OF ASYNCHRONOUS E-LEARNING

Asynchronous e-learning has a few challenges which the instructor and the student need to be aware of and mitigate. It lacks an instant mechanism of providing feedback to the students. This is because the feedback in asynchronous learning is normally received after some time lapse. Timely feedback in e-learning is essential because it helps both the student and instructor to address issues and misunderstandings related to the online training course material. The quicker the feedback is received the better for the learning process. Since the asynchronous e-learning courses are not live, the students waste valuable time waiting for their questions to be answered by their instructors or fellow class members.

It lacks personal real time interaction based on the time lapse involved. In asynchronous learning context, the impartial nature of the model creates a feeling of loneliness and isolation which sometimes make students to eventually drop the classes. Learning in isolation may work for some, but it certainly does not work for most people who need personal interaction to maintain or even increase their motivation levels. Lack of real time interaction with other students can lead to failure to achieve the learning goals and objectives. Therefore, to minimize loneliness students should seek to build an active online community through teamwork.

Asynchronous e-learning at responses depend on the students' own pace in action and also means waiting for others to respond, often for long periods of time. Due to the absence of real time discussions and live collaborations between students and the instructors, it creates a sense of disconnection and may affect the students negatively especially those who thrive well in an established communal set up. Lack of live interaction can disengage and demotivate students who may need encouragement and stimulation to log into the system, read the material, and complete the online course assignments on time. Procrastination is more likely to occur in an asynchronous learning environment than in any other online learning environment. This is because personal interaction helps students maintain their interest, whereas isolation rarely boosts motivation.

Asynchronous learning requires students who are focused, goal oriented, and have great time management skills. Success in an asynchronous learning environment requires of students to be committed and disciplined which is a disadvantage to those students who may not be highly self-motivated. In asynchronous e-learning, students are unable to ask questions directly from the instructors in areas which they have not understood. In situations where the students are not able to understand the content posted, they do not have an opportunity to ask for clarification from the instructor instantly. Queries are posted for the instructor to answer which takes time. On the student side they may also take time to log onto the platform and read the instructors answers to the questions raised.

The teacher must pre-record and upload beforehand teaching content which is tiresome and time consuming. All the content in asynchronous e-learning is prepared in advance and uploaded on the platform for the students to access at a later stage. This is a tiresome process which consumes lots of time. The demand of self-learning is put on the student. A class normally comprises of different students who have varied characteristics. Some of the students learn faster than others, while some students can easily adopt to the self-learning style, others may struggle. Therefore, in asynchronous engagement, some students who may not easily adopt to the self-learning and those who do not thrive in teams may struggle to adopt to this style of learning. In the process some of them may drop out and discontinue their studies due to such reasons. In such cases instructor presence is required to provide the necessary support to the students.

There is a possibility of some students joyriding in group assignments and tasks. Since the teacher is not physically present, some students may find it easy to joyride without being found out. Joyriding simply means that the students will get certification or credits which they do not deserve because they did not work for them. When such students get employment based on merit, they will always perform below the expectation causing credibility issues regarding the online certificates presented at the time of recruitment. Anonymous evaluation of team members by the peers provides objective analysis of the participation of each member of the team. This approach minimizes joyriding of students in teams.

CONCLUSION

Asynchronous e-learning favors majority of the students who register for online classes by its very nature. Among the key benefits of this approach are flexibility, collaboration, building and naturing a community of scholars among the students and allowance of more response time to the students. This chapter contributes to the distance and e-Learning body of knowledge by validating asynchronous e-learning and suggesting the best practice while teaching online. Current research overwhelmingly shows that asynchronous learning benefits online students by allowing them to choose when and how to learn. Furthermore, it gives students more time to reflect on course content, which generally results in more substantive and quality work. Students should be made to understand that in asynchronous e-learning all interactions take place on-line, that course activities require a serious time commitment and decorum, and that participation and engagement are central features of asynchronous e-learning.

REFERENCES

Beyth-Marom, R., Saporta, K., & Caspi, A. (2005). Synchronous vs. asynchronous tutorials: Factors affecting students' preferences and choices. *Journal of Research on Technology in Education*, *37*(3), 245–262. doi:10.1080/15391523.2005.10782436

Bouhnik, D., Giat, Y., & Sanderovitch, Y. (2009). Asynchronous learning sources in a high-tech organization. *Journal of Workplace Learning*, *21*(5), 416–430. doi:10.1108/13665620910966811

Brindley, J. E., Blaschke, L. M., & Walti, C. (2009). Creating effective collaborative learning groups in an online environment. *International Review of Research in Open and Distributed Learning*, *10*(3). Advance online publication. doi:10.19173/irrodl.v10i3.675

Britain, S., & Liber, O. (1999). A Framework for Pedagogical Evaluation of Virtual Learning Environments. Academic Press.

Britain, S., & Liber, O. (2004). *A framework for pedagogical evaluation of virtual learning environments*. Academic Press.

Burbank, J., & Cooper, F. (2010). *Empires in World History: Power and the Politics of Difference*. Princeton University Press.

Capon, N., & Kuhn, D. (2004). What's so good about problem-based learning? *Cognition and Instruction*, *22*(1), 61–79. doi:10.12071532690Xci2201_3

Clouse, S. F., & Evans, G. E. (2003). Graduate business students performance with synchronous and asynchronous interaction e-learning methods. *Decision Sciences Journal of Innovative Education*, *1*(2), 181–202. doi:10.1111/j.1540-4609.2003.00017.x

Coker, F. H., & Scarboro, A. (1990). Writing to Learn in Upper-Division Sociology Courses: Two Case Studies. *Teaching Sociology*, *18*(2), 218–222. doi:10.2307/1318494

Dabbagh, N. H., Jonassen, D. H., Yueh, H.-P., & Sanouiloua, M. (2000). Assessing a problem-based learning approach to an introductory instructional design course: A case study. *Performance Improvement Quarterly*, *13*(3), 60–83. doi:10.1111/j.1937-8327.2000.tb00176.x

Dede, C., & Kremer, A. (1999). Increasing students' participation via multiple interactive media. *Invention: Creative Thinking About Learning and Teaching*, *1*(1), 7.

Durnalı, M., Orakcı, Ş., & Aktan, O. (2019). The smart learning potential of Turkey's education system in the context of FATIH project. In A. Darshan Singh, S. Raghunathan, E. Robeck, & B. Sharma (Eds.), *Cases on Smart Learning Environments* (pp. 227–243). IGI Global. doi:10.4018/978-1-5225-6136-1.ch013

Ertmer, P., & Koehler, A. A. (2014). Online case-based discussions: Examining coverage of The afforded problem space. *Educational Technology Research and Development*, *62*(5), 617–636. doi:10.100711423-014-9350-9

Hadullo, K., Oboko, R., & Omwenga, E. (2018). Factors affecting asynchronous e-learning quality in developing countries university settings. *International Journal of Education and Development Using ICT*, *14*(1), 152-163.

Hopperton, L. G. (1998). Computer conferencing and college education. *The College Quarterly*, *5*(2).

Hrastinski, S. (2007). The Potential of Synchronous Communication to Enhance Participation in Online Discussions, *International Conference on Information Systems*, 9–12.

Hrastinski, S. (2008). A study of asynchronous and synchronous e-learning methods discovered that each supports different purposes. *EDUCAUSE Quarterly, 4*, 51–55.

Hwang, W. Y., & Wang, C. Y. (2004). A study of learning time patterns in asynchronous learning environments. *Journal of Computer Assisted Learning, 20*(4), 292–304. doi:10.1111/j.1365-2729.2004.00088.x

Jaffee, D. (1997). Asynchronous learning: Technology and pedagogical strategy in a distance learning course. *Teaching Sociology, 25*(4), 262–277. doi:10.2307/1319295

Johnson, G. M. (2006). Synchronous and asynchronous text-based CMC in educational contexts: A review of recent research. *TechTrends, 50*(4), 46–53. doi:10.100711528-006-0046-9

Jonassen, D. H. (1994). Technology as cognitive tools: Students as designers. *IT Forum Paper, 1*, 67-80.

Karagöz, S. (2021). Evaluation of distance education: The sample of guidance and counseling students (Example of Aksaray University). *The Universal Academic Research Journal, 3*(1), 18–25.

Karagöz, S., & Rüzgar, M. E. (2021). An investigation of the prospective teachers' viewpoints about distance education during the COVID-19 pandemic. *International Journal of Curriculum and Instruction, 13*(3), 2611–2634.

Karppinen, P. (2005). Meaningful learning with digital and online videos: Theoretical perspectives. *Association for the Advancement of Computing In Education Journal, 13*(3), 233–250.

Kearsley, G., & Blomeyer, R. (2004). Preparing K—12 Teachers to Teach Online. *Educational Technology, 44*(1), 49–52.

Khine, M. S., & Lourdusamy, A. (2003). Blended learning approach in teacher education: Combining face-to-face instruction, multimedia viewing and online discussion. *British Journal of Educational Technology, 34*(5), 671–675. doi:10.1046/j.0007-1013.2003.00360.x

King, A. (1994). Guiding knowledge construction in the classroom: Effects of teaching children how to question and how to explain. *American Educational Research Journal, 31*(2), 338–368. doi:10.3102/00028312031002338

King, A., Staffieri, A., & Adelgais, A. (1998). Mutual peer tutoring: Effects of structuring tutorial interaction to scaffold peer learning. *Journal of Educational Psychology, 90*(1), 134–152. doi:10.1037/0022-0663.90.1.134

Kochtanek, T. R., & Hein, K. K. (2000). Creating and nurturing distributed asynchronous learning environments. *Online Information Review*, *24*(4), 280–293. doi:10.1108/14684520010350632

Markel, S. L., & Ecl, E. E. (2001). Technology and education online discussion forums. *Online Journal of Distance Learning Administration*, 4.

McCombs, B. L. (2001). What do we know about students and learning? The student centered framework: Bringing the educational system into balance. *Educational Horizons*, (Spring), 182–193.

Moore, J. L., & Marra, R. M. (2005). A comparative analysis of online discussion participation protocols. *Journal of Research on Technology in Education*, *38*(2), 191–212. doi:10.1080/15391523.2005.10782456

Moore, R. (1992). *Writing to Learn Biology*. Harcourt Brace Jovanovich.

Orakcı, Ş. (2020). The future of online learning and teaching in higher education. In Global Approaches to Sustainability Through Learning and Education. Hershey, PA: IGI Global. doi:10.4018/978-1-7998-0062-0.ch003

Orakcı, Ş., & Gelişli, Y. (2021). Educational policy actions in the times of Covid-19 and suggestions for future applications in Turkey. In L. Kyei-Blankson, J. Blankson, & E. Ntuli (Eds.), *Handbook of Research on Inequities in Online Education During Global Crises* (pp. 475–493). IGI Global. doi:10.4018/978-1-7998-6533-9.ch024

Pease, M. A., & Kuhn, D. (2011). Experimental analysis of the effective components of problem-based learning. *Science Education*, *95*(1), 57–86. doi:10.1002ce.20412

Sinclair, P. M., Levett-Jones, T., Morris, A., Carter, B., Bennett, P. N., & Kable, A. (2017). High engagement, high quality: A guiding framework for developing empirically informed asynchronous e-learning programs for health professional educators. *Nursing & Health Sciences*, *19*(1), 126–137. doi:10.1111/nhs.12322 PMID:28090732

Skylar, A., Higgins, K., Boone, R., Jones, P., Pierce, T., & Gelfer, J. (2005). Distance education: An exploration of alternative methods and types of instructional media in teacher education. *The Journal of Special Education*, *20*(3), 25–33.

Stephen, S. A. (2015). Enhancing the learning experience in finance using online video clips. *Journal of Financial Education*, 103-116.

Thornhill, S., Asensio, M., & Young, C. (2002). *Video Streaming. A guide for educational development*. JISC.

KEY TERMS AND DEFINITIONS

Active Learning: An approach to learning where the students are involved in doing a variety of activities to enhance the learning process.

Asynchronous: A type of e-learning is done after the event happens.

Collaborative Learning: Learning based on group synergy to solve problems.

Digital Tools: Computer based electronic devices used for transmitting and storing knowledge.

Discussion Forum: An online digital tool which facilitates threaded posts and responses.

E-Learning: A type of learning through computer system facilitated by internet connectivity.

Interactive Learning: Learning based on student engagement through social interactions.

Online: Done virtually through the internet.

Student: An individual who is engaged in is enrolled in a learning institution.

Teaching Strategies: Different ways of facilitating learning.

Chapter 8

An Investigation of Pre-Service Teachers' Self-Regulated Learning Levels in Terms of Various Variables

Şenol Orakcı

(iD) https://orcid.org/0000-0003-1534-1310
Aksaray University, Turkey

Mehmet Durnali

(iD) https://orcid.org/0000-0002-1318-9362
Bülent Ecevit University, Turkey

ABSTRACT

Online education is one of the most dynamic and enriched forms of learning available today. The aim of the present study is to reveal the self-regulated learning levels of pre-service teacher and to determine whether these levels change in terms of their gender and class. The sample of the study consists of Aksaray University Educational Sciences Department students who received online education due to the COVID-19 global epidemic in the 2020-2021 academic year. The data of the study were collected with the "Self-Regulation in Self-Paced Open and Distance Learning Environments Scale." The first result of the study revealed that the self-regulated learning levels of the participants were close to medium. The self-regulation scores of male students receiving online education at university were also found to be significantly higher than the scores of female students. The final result obtained from the research is the existence of a significant difference between grade level and self-regulated learning skills.

DOI: 10.4018/978-1-7998-8077-6.ch008

1. INTRODUCTION

With the impact of Covid 19 in the world, online education has begun to be seen as a necessity rather than a choice. In fact, the sector most affected by the Covid 19 epidemic was seen as the education sector after the health sector (Yamamoto & Altun, 2020). This influence has revealed the fact that online education is of vital importance in the realization of educational activities.

Online education is a system that supports individual teaching and requires the learners to be responsible for their own learning process. For this reason, students in online education system are expected to develop their learning to learn skills, plan and control their own learning process (Karagöz, 2021; Karagöz, & Rüzgar, 2021).

Since online education is one of the most dynamic and enriched forms of learning available today (Ergül, 2006), it draws attention as a preferable education method. The prevalence and increasing importance of online education makes researches on the effectiveness of online education more necessary than before. Therefore, while talking about the effectiveness of online education, the subject of self-regulation skills in the online education process is among the leading topics expected to be researched.

Self-regulation is the personal skills that students have to develop in order for their success to emerge, and these skills can be expressed as abilities that can be thought, learned and controlled (Çiltaş, 2011). Self-regulation skills are re-emerging as a factor that needs to be examined in online education, when viewed in terms of learning environment and learning style, unlike face-to-face education. Self-regulated learning requires students to regulate their emotions, thoughts and behaviors and systematically manage their own learning processes in order to reach their goals (Cabi, 2015). In this research, it is examined how possible it is for teacher candidates to develop self-regulation skills for themselves in terms of online education, which is a different learning environment from the face-to-face education environment.

1.1. Online self-regulation

Self-regulated students are individuals who determine the objective closest to them, meet the necessary criteria to achieve this goal, observe themselves in this process, and evaluate the whole process as a result of their performance, and can organize their future learning processes with regard to these results (Zimmerman, 2000). It was predicted that students with high self-regulation would be more successful in autonomous learning environments (Dabbagh & Kitsantas, 2004; Hartley & Bendixen, 2001). Barnard et al. (2009) argued that self-regulated learning skills are important for success in traditional or face-to-face learning environments, but these self-regulated learning skills may play a more important role in online learning environments. It has emerged with the literature review that self-regulation and self-regulated learning form the basis of online self-regulation. Below are the explanations of the concepts of self-regulation and self-regulated learning, respectively.

1.2. Self-regulation

Self-regulations is the planned and periodic formation of emotions, thoughts and actions of the individuals in order to achieve their own goals (Zimmerman, 2000). The concept of self-regulation has also been expressed with different concepts such as self-control and self-discipline. Self-regulation has been defined as the ability to dominate one's own learning process (Aydın & Atalay, 2015). This concept, which is considered important in terms of the learning process, has started to be used and taken into account more frequently in recent years in studies on education. Hrbackova and Safrankova (2016) sees self-regulation as a higher form of control of voluntary behavior and argues that it includes an unrealized (implicit) process based on the integration of processes and mechanisms that help to pursue the set goal. In addition, in the process of self-regulation, the person focuses on all his/her feelings, needs, emotions and looks for ways to move forward according to his/her related intentions.

In another definition, self-regulation is expressed as an active and follow-up process in which students determine their learning ideals, regulate their cognitive processes, motivational status, and accordingly their behaviors, and are limited and guided by goals and concrete observable features (Baysal & Özgenel, 2019; Pintrich, 2000).

1.3. Self-regulated learning

Studies on self-regulation in educational settings have emerged from various studies (Zimmerman & Schunk, 2011). Beginning in the 1970s, cognitive-behavioral researchers have explored how to improve students' self-control and therefore their academic learning. Cognitive-behavioral methods include the use of self-teaching and self-reinforcement. From this point of view, self-regulation includes ways of controlling the beginning and consequences of individuals' behaviors, as well as overt reactions such as feelings of anxiety (Thoresen & Mahoney, 1974). A group of researchers, on the other hand, approached self-regulation from a cognitive-developmental perspective. Young learners may show genetic differences in their behavioral control, but it is emphasized that language development has a significant impact on self-regulation. The most interesting research in this direction is Vygotsky's (1962) field of "zone of proximal development". According to this theory, the support of others is required in order to achieve a high level of performance. Language is internalized in the area of proximal development and takes the place of self-regulation.

Another developmental issue related to self-regulation is the "delay of gratification" (Zimmerman & Schunk, 2011).

With development, children may resist the temptation to win instantly by receiving larger rewards due to procrastination (Mischel, 1961). Postponing gratification is important for self-regulation because it allows them to deal with satisfying distractions and focus instead on learning tasks. Another group of researchers examined metacognitive and cognitive issues (Zimmerman & Schunk, 2011). These researchers have shown that students can be taught task strategies that improve their academic performance, but adaptation and continuity of strategies to new tasks is often very rare (Pressley & McCormick, 1995). Researchers have examined ways to encourage strategy use, such as informing students about the impact of strategies and showing how strategy use improves performance (Schunk & Rice, 1987). Social-cognitive researchers have studied the social and motivational effects on self-regulation. In Bandura's (1986) theory, "self-regulation" consists of three stages. These are: "self-observation", "self-judgment" and "self-reaction". During "self-observation", students monitor the characteristics of their performance; In "self-judgment", students compare their performance against standards, and "self-reaction" includes feelings of self-efficacy and emotional responses to their performance. Social-cognitive researchers have shown that teaching processes such as modeling convey information about students' learning progress, increase their self-efficacy and task motivation (Schunk, 2012).

Zimmerman (2002) re-examined the three-stage social-cognitive self-regulation processes together with learning on the question of how students should use certain learning processes by combining their self-awareness levels and motivational beliefs in order to be self-regulated. He revealed that self-regulation is not a mental ability or an academic performance, but a self-directed process by which students transform their mental abilities into academic ability. Zimmerman (2002) also explained the social-cognitive self-regulation processes in three stages as "forethought", "performance" and "self-reflection". In this statement, there are two main classes in the "common sense" process: "task analysis" and "self-motivation". "Task analysis" was also examined in two sub-categories as "goal setting" and "strategic planning". It is in this process that students set goals close to themselves and determine the strategies they will use while achieving these goals (Zimmerman, 2002). "Self-motivation" stems from beliefs about learning, such as student expectations about individual outcomes of learning and self-efficacy about individual ability. "Intrinsic interest" refers to the value of students' ability required for a task, and learning goal orientation refers to measuring the value of learning processes (Zimmerman, 2002). For example, students who find a subject in history interesting and enjoy increasing their knowledge about it are more motivated for self-regulated learning (Bandura, 1997).

The performance process of self-regulation has been examined under two sub-titles as "self-control" and "self-observation" (Zimmerman, 2002). "Self-control" is the use of strategies and methods determined at the forethought stage, where appropriate. The "self-control" process consists of "description", "self-teaching", "focus of attention", and "task strategies". A student who is learning a word describes this word in his/her mind, explains it to himself/herself, finds a quiet environment where he/she can focus his/her attention, and groups this word with similar words he/she has learned before. "Self-observation", on the other hand, is expressed by recording individual situations and making self-experiences to reveal the reasons for these situations (Zimmerman, 2002). For example, a student would need to record his/her own time usage so that he/she is aware of how much time he/she spends studying, or the student can find out by self-experimentation how studying together with a friend affects the speed of doing homework. Self-monitoring is the hidden form of self-observation. It is the monitoring of the individual's own cognitive functioning, such as the frequency of making spelling mistakes while writing an article (Zimmerman, 2002). The "self-reflection" process, on the other hand, consists of "self-judgment" and "self-reaction" elements. "Self-evaluation", which is one of the sub-items expressing "self-judgment", is the comparison of an individual's performance by "self-observation" with someone else's previous performance or with a set of standards. Another sub-item is the causal context, which expresses an individual's beliefs about the reasons for their mistakes or successes. Associating the student's score on a test with the use of wrong strategies instead of a talent deficiency will positively affect the student's next performance. Another form of "self-reaction" is the individual's positive feelings about "self-satisfaction" and "performance". The increase in "self-satisfaction" increases motivation but suppresses the effort to learn new things in the future (Schunk, 2001). "Self-reactions" are also shaped by adaptive or defensive inferences. A defensive response is when an individual avoids performance or learning opportunities, such as dropping out of a course or not taking an exam, in order to maintain their "self-esteem." On the contrary, it is the design of necessary arrangements to increase the effectiveness of learning methods, such as adaptive responses, changing or discarding ineffective learning strategies (Zimmerman, 2002). Zimmerman and Kitsantas (1999) found high correlations between the "forethought", "performance" and "self-reflection" phases of the "self-regulation" process. For example, it was found that students who set proximal goals observed their own performance more, approached their goals more, and were more "self-reflective" than students who did not set goals (Bandura & Schunk, 1981). In addition, many studies have proven that there is a high correlation between the quality and level of students' "self-regulation" and their academic achievement (McClelland & Cameron, 2011; Pekrun, Goetz, & Perry, 2002; Zimmerman & Martinez-Pons, 1986). Although Zimmerman's self-regulation studies were effective, his studies to measure self-regulated learning were generally qualitative studies (Schunk and Zimmerman 2012; Zimmerman and Martinez-Ponz, 1988; Zimmerman, 2002; Zimmerman & Schunk, 2001). Zimmerman's (2002) model is generally recognized by everyone and accepted as valid for face-to-face learning environments. In addition, Pintrich et al. focused on measurements based on experimental methods such as survey-based data collection (Pintrich, Smith, Garcia, & McKeachie, 1993). Pinritch et al. conducted an experimental study examining general motivational beliefs because motivation is related to student learning (Pintrich et al., 1993). The study focused on explaining how different motivational beliefs support, facilitate or sustain self-regulated learning. These motivational strategies were examined under three subheadings: a) self-efficacy beliefs b) task value beliefs c) goal orientation.

- **Self-efficacy beliefs:** Self-efficacy beliefs include the student's confidence in their own cognitive abilities to complete an academic study and learn. In many studies, highly positive relationships have been observed between the self-efficacy and self-regulated learning of both middle school and university students. It has been observed that students with high self-efficacy levels are more cognitively involved in situations where they learn by comparison than those with low self-efficacy levels. In addition, self-efficacy was found to be positively associated with self-regulation strategies such as planning, monitoring and regulation, and students' academic achievement (Pintrich, 1989; Pintrich & De Groot, 1990; Pintrich & Garcia, 1991).

- **Task value beliefs:** Three components of task value beliefs were introduced by Eccles (1983). These are the individual's perception of the importance of the task, the individual's interest in the task, the perception of the benefit of the task for its future goals. Task value beliefs are the individual's perception of the importance and salience of the task. Interest is expressed as the general attitude of the individual towards the task and his/her love for the task. The utility value is determined by individuals' perceptions of the utility of the task. For students, this may include their belief that the lesson will be momentarily beneficial to them in some way. Researchers have observed a positive relationship between belief in the value of the task and cognitive strategy, which includes repetition, elaboration, and organizational strategies. In addition, they found that students with high levels of interest and value use more strategies to organize their minds and monitor themselves (Pintrich, et al., 1993).

- **Goal orientation:** Goal orientation has been studied by concentrating on three general orientations (Wolters, Yu, & Pintrich, 1996). First, specialization goal orientation refers to an interest in learning and mastering the task using standards of self-development and self-adjustment. Second, extrinsic orientation involves focusing on getting good grades and pleasing people around, such as the teacher or family, as the main criterion for judging success. Finally, relative ability orientation refers to comparing an individual's ability or performance with that of others, performing a task well or doing better than others. Pintrich (1999) observed consistent relationships between different goals and self-regulation. Specialization goals are positively related to cognitive strategies as well as self-regulation strategies. Extrinsic goals, on the other hand, were found to be the only motivational variable negatively correlated with self-regulation strategies and performance. In addition, it has been determined that there is a positive relationship between relative goal orientation and self-regulation strategies and performance.

1.4. Purpose of the Research

This research was conducted to reveal the self-regulated learning levels of pre-service teacher and to determine whether these levels change in terms of some variables. In this context, answers to the following research questions were sought.

- What is the level of pre-service teachers' self-regulated learning?
- Do pre-service teachers' self-regulated learning levels change with regard to their gender and class?

2. METHOD

Research model

On the one hand, the present study is a descriptive study designed in the quantitative patterned survey model, since the first sub-objective of this research is to reveal the self-directed learning levels of pre-service teachers in the distance education process. The survey model is a research approach in which the views and attitudes of any group about a phenomenon or event are taken and in this way they are tried to be described (Büyüköztürk, Çakmak, Akgün, Karadeniz, & Demirel, 2016). On the other hand, the present study is a causal comparison study designed in the survey model since the second sub-objective is to reveal whether the self-directed learning levels of pre-service teachers differ with regard to their gender and class.

2.1. Universe and Sample of the study

The universe of the current research consists of all students studying at the Faculty of Education at Aksaray University in the 2020-2021 academic year. Convenient sampling, which is one of the non-random sampling types, was preferred. In this sample selection, the researcher collected data from the students studying in his department. In this case, the sample of the study consists of Aksaray University Educational Sciences Department students who received online education due to the Covid-19 global epidemic in the 2020-2021 academic year. For the research, 382 students were reached by sending online forms, but 327 students responded. As for the demographic characteristics of the study group of the research, 60% (197) of the students are females and 40% (130) are male students in terms of distribution of participants by gender. 34% (111) of the students attend 1st grade, 24% (78) 2nd grade, 25% (83) 3rd grade and 1% (55) 4th grade in terms of distribution of participants by class.

2.2. Data collection tool

The data of the study were collected with the "Self-Regulation in Self-Paced Open and Distance Learning Environments Scale" developed by Koçdar, Karadeniz, Bozkurt, and Büyük (2018). The scale, which has a five-point Likert type structure, consists of 30 items. "Cronbach Alpha" value of the scale. 937; "KMO" value is .953. The scale was "goal setting" (5 items); "goal setting, help seeking, self-study strategies, managing physical environment, and effort regulation" (9 items); "self-study strategies" (8 items); It consists of five factors under the headings of "managing the physical environment" (6 items) and " effort regulation" (2 items). Item factor loads. with 53. It ranges from 89. As a result of factor analysis, it was seen that 58.204% of the variance was explained. These values of the scale show that it is a reliable measurement tool. While analyzing the scale data, the "KMO" value at the reliability point was also calculated for this sample group and a high value of 910 was found. In this case, it was decided that the data set was suitable for analysis.

2.3. Analysis of data

The answers given by the participants to the scale were analyzed through the SPSS 21 package program. The level of significance was accepted as $\alpha=.05$ in the interpretation of the statistical procedures. Before the analyzes were performed, the "skewness" and "kurtosis coefficients" were divided by their standard errors to determine whether the data were in a normal distribution, and the value of ±1.96 was taken as basis. (Kalaycı, 2009) and the data were found to be in normal distribution. In order to determine the self-regulated learning levels of the participants on the basis of online courses, the descriptive statistics was used. For the purpose of determining whether these levels differ according to gender, "independent groups t test" was utilized and "One-way analysis of variance (ANOVA)" was used to reveal differences whether these levels differ according to classes. After it was understood that the variances were homogeneous (t=1.768), the Scheffe test, one of the post hoc tests, was preferred to interpret the difference between the groups.

3. FINDINGS

3.1. Findings Regarding Self-Regulated Learning Levels of Pre-service Teachers

The opinions of the participants about the self-regulation levels in the online environment were taken with a 30-item scale, and the mean and standard deviations for the relevant opinions on the basis of factors are given in Table 1.

When the table above was examined, it was determined that the students' self-regulation levels in online courses in general are a medium value as a result of near-negative opinions (X =2.91, sd=.715). When the item averages are examined on the basis of factors, it was determined that the self-regulation skills of the students were moderate [the factor of "goal setting" (X =2.87, sd=.793), the "help-seeking" factor (X=2.93, sd=.810), the "self-study strategies" factor (X =2.93, sd=.785). the "managing physical environment" factor (X=2.97, sd=.875) and the "effort regulation" factor (X =2.83, sd=.923)].

3.2. Findings Regarding whether the Self-Regulated Learning Levels of the Pre-Service Teachers Differ with Regard to their Gender

The second research question of the current study was to determine whether there was a significant difference between the self-regulated learning levels of students and their genders. Therefore, "independent groups t-test" was realized. The obtained results are presented in the Table 2 below.

When Table 2 is examined, it is seen that there is a significant difference between students' self-regulated learning levels (p=.023) by gender and this difference is in favor of male students. It was determined that male students (X=2.93) self-regulated learning levels in online learning environments were higher than female students (X= 2.81).

Table 1. Mean and Standard Deviation Values of Opinions of Pre-service Teachers

		Statements	Mean	SD
	1	I set my study goals daily.	2.860	.989
	2	I set goals for myself while studying.	2.907	1.056
	3	I study my lessons in a planned manner.	2.871	.981
	4	I set goals for myself to arrange my study hours for distance education lessons.	2.878	.945
	5	I do not compromise on the quality of what I do for my lessons.	2.759	.971
	6	I contact someone to discuss my understanding.	2.989	.976
	7	I participate in social media group discussions regarding study subjects.	3.021	1.042
	8	When I do not understand the distance education course material, I ask another student for help..	2.891	.910
	9	I contact other students, who I think are successful, on social media.	2.965	.975
	10	I determine what I will ask before receiving help.	3.073	.976
2 nd Factor -Help seeking	11	I find someone who has information about the course content to consult when I need help.	2.988	.988
	12	I share my questions about the lessons with other distance education students on the Internet.	3.910	1.089
	13	I try to talk face-to-face with my classmates in distance education if necessary.	2.871	.912
	14	I insist on receiving help from someone who has information about the course content on the Internet.	3.195	.971
	15	I think of questions on the subject while reading the material.	3.029	.993
	16	I draw up a draft of reading material to be able to organize my thoughts.	2.089	1.059
	17	I practice by repeating the contents of the material.	2.989	.919
3rd Factor -Self-study strategies	18	I review my reading materials and notes and try to find the most important opinions.	2.093	.945
	19	I create simple schemes, diagrams or tables to organize my study materials.	3.088	.936
	20	While studying my distance education lessons, I review my lesson notes and draw up a draft of the important subjects.	3.080	.978
	21	I summarize the subjects to understand what I have learned from the lessons.	2.869	.912
	22	I evaluate what I understand by pausing at regular intervals while studying.	2.895	.997
	23	I prefer studying in places where I can concentrate.	2.991	.912
	24	I choose a comfortable place to study.	3.101	1.099
4th Factor Managing physical environment	25	I have places where I can study efficiently for my distance education lessons.	2.989	.919
	26	I choose places where nothing distracts me from studying my distance education lessons.	2.861	.911
	27	I study my lessons in places where I can focus.	2.887	.913
	28	I have a regular place to study.	2.981	.932
5th Factor -Effort regulation	29	I study the course subjects until finishing them even though I find the course materials boring.	3.103	.945
	30	I make an effort to understand the subjects in my distance education lessons.	3.100	.981

Table 2. "Independent Groups t-Test" scores by gender variable

	Gender	N		SS	Sd	t	P
Group	Female	197	2,81	,41	597	5.354	0,915
	Male	130	2,93	,46			

3.3. Findings Regarding whether the Self-Regulated Learning Levels of the Pre-Service Teachers Differ with Regard to their Class

Within the scope of the second research question, "one-way ANOVA test" was conducted to reveal whether the self-regulated learning levels of students changed with regard to their class. The results are presented in Table 3.

Table 3. One-Way Analysis of Variance (ANOVA) scores by class variable

Source of Variance	Sum of the square	df	Mean of the squares	F	P	Comparison (post hoc Scheffe test)
Between Groups	97.185	3	31.824	137.9	.000	1-3 1-4
Within Groups	78.489	324	.283			2-3 2-4
Total	175.674	327				3-1 3-2 3-4
						4-1 4-2 4-3

In the Department of Educational Sciences, which was included in the research, the scale was applied to all four grade levels. According to the "Scheffe test" results, the scores of the 1st Year (N=111, X =2.41) and 2nd Year (N=78, X =2.58) students were calculated as lower than the scores of the 3rd Year (N=83, X =3.33) and 4th Year (N=55, X = 3.82) students. The difference between the groups is in favor of the 3rd and 4th Grades. In particular, the score of the 4th grade is considerably higher than the average of all grades. In this case, it was revealed that the self-regulated learning levels of the 3rd and 4th grade students were higher than the others.

4. CONCLUSION AND DISCUSSION

The first result of the study revealed that the self-regulated learning levels of the participants were close to medium. This finding of the study is also supported by similar studies (Baldan, 2017; Baldan Babayiğit & Güven, 2020; Tümen Akyıldız, 2020). On the other hand, Aybek and Aslan (2017) and Güler (2015) revealed in their research that the self-regulated learning levels of pre-service teachers are close to high. Based on these findings, more comprehensive qualitative and quantitative studies can be conducted together to examine the effects of different variables on self-regulated learning skills.

According to the research findings, the self-regulation scores of male students receiving online education at university were found to be significantly higher than the scores of female students. This finding of the study is also supported by similar studies (Tümen Akyıldız, 2020; Zhao, Chen, & Panda 2014). On the other hand, Artsın, Koçdar and Bozkurt (2020), Kaplan (2014), Kaplan and Certel (2018), and Güler (2015) found in their research that female students' self-regulation skills were higher than male students. Karaoğlu and Pepe (2020) and Wolters and Pintrich (1998) revealed that self-regulation skills do not differ according to gender. Contradictory findings regarding whether pre-service teachers' self-regulation skills differ according to gender draw attention. The contradictory appearance of these findings shows that different factors may have an effect on the findings regarding the difference in self-regulation according to gender, apart from the factors examined. Therefore, there is a need to elucidate these possible factors with new studies. In addition, it is thought that this discrepancy in the findings may be effective in terms of learning environments, universities and departments.

The final result obtained from the research is the existence of a significant difference between grade level and self-regulated learning skills. Within the scope of the current research, it has been determined that as the grade increases, the self-regulated learning skills of the students also increase. It has been revealed that especially senior students have the highest scores. This result also overlaps with some research results (Artsın, Koçdar & Bozkurt, 2020; Güler, 2015; Sağırlı, Çiltaş, Azapağası & Zehir, 2010; Tümen Akyıldız, 2020). On the other hand, Şahin (2015), Karaoğlu and Pepe (2020), and Baldan Babayiğit and Güven (2020) stated in their study that self-regulation skills did not differ at the grade level at the higher education level. Considering the findings, it is seen that self-regulation scores reveal conflicting results in different studies. These results, which seem different and contradictory in the literature, can be determined by investigating other factors that have an effect on whether self-regulation differs significantly according to grade level.

4.1. Suggestions

- Guidance activities for students on self-regulation on online education platforms of universities can contribute to the efficiency of online education.
- Instructors' adopting approaches that improve students' self-regulation skills in their course presentations can contribute to the efficiency of online education.
- Students participating in the research participated from various departments of a single university. Comparative new studies to be made in terms of different universities, faculties and departments can make important contributions.

REFERENCES

Artsın, M., Koçdar, S., & Bozkurt, A. (2020). Öğrenenlerin Öz-Yönetimli Öğrenme Becerilerinin Kitlesel Açık Çevrimiçi Dersler Bağlamında İncelenmesi [An Investigation of Learners' Self-Managed Learning Skills in the Context of Massive Open Online Courses]. *Anadolu Üniversitesi Eğitim Bilimleri Enstitüsü Dergisi*, *10*(1), 1–30.

Aybek, B., & Aslan, S. (2017). Öğretmen adaylarının öz-düzenleme düzeylerinin çeşitli değişkenler açısından incelenmesi [Examination of pre-service teachers' self-regulation levels in terms of various variables]. *Eğitimde Kuram ve Uygulama*, *13*(3), 455–470. doi:10.17244/eku.331938

Aydın, S., & Atalay, T. D. (2015). *Öz Düzenlemeli Öğrenme* [Self-Regulated Learning]. Pegem Akademi.

Baldan, B. (2017). *Lisans* öğrencilerinin öz düzenlemeli *öğrenme becerisi düzeyleri ve yükseköğretim programlarının öz düzenlemeli öğrenme becerisini geliştirmedeki rolü* [Self-regulated learning skill levels of undergraduate students and the role of higher education programs in developing self-regulated learning skills] [Master dissertation]. Anadolu University, Turkey.

Baldan Babayiğit, B., & Güven, M. (2020). Self-regulated learning skills of undergraduate students and the role of higher education in promoting self-regulation. *Euroasian Journal of Educational Research*, *20*(89), 47–70. doi:10.14689/ejer.2020.89.3

Bandura, A. (1986). *Social foundations of thought and action: A social cognitive theory*. Prentice-Hall.

Bandura, A. (1997). *Self-efficacy: The exercise of control.* W. H. Freeman.

Bandura, A., & Schunk, D. H. (1981). Cultivating competence, self-efficacy, and intrinsic interest through proximal self-motivation. *Journal of Personality and Social Psychology, 41*(3), 586–598. doi:10.1037/0022-3514.41.3.586

Barnard, L., Lan, W. Y., To, Y. M., Paton, V. O., & Lai, S. L. (2009). Measuring self-regulation in online and blended learning environments. *The internet and higher education, 12*(1), 1–6. doi:10.1016/j.iheduc.2008.10.005

Baysal, A., & Özgenel, M. (2019). Ortaokul öğrencilerinin bağlanma stilleri ve öz-düzenleme düzeyleri arasındaki ilişkinin incelenmesi [Examining the relationship between secondary school students' attachment styles and self-regulation levels]. *Eğitimde Kuram ve Uygulama, 15*(2), 142–152.

Büyüköztürk, Ş., Kılıç Çakmak, E., Akgün, Ö. E., Karadeniz, Ş., & Demirel, F. (2016). *Bilimsel Araştırma Yöntemleri* [Scientific Research Methods]. PEGEM.

Cabı, E. (2015). Öğretmen adaylarının öz-düzenleme stratejileri ve akademik başarısı: Boylamsal bir araştırma [Teacher candidates' self-regulation strategies and academic achievement: A longitudinal study]. *Gazi Üniversitesi Gazi Eğitim Fakültesi Dergisi, 35*(3), 489–506.

Çiltaş, A. (2011). Eğitimde öz-düzenleme öğretiminin önemi üzerine bir çalışma [A study on the importance of self-regulation teaching in education]. *Mehmet Akif Ersoy Üniversitesi Sosyal Bilimler Enstitüsü Dergisi, 3*(5), 1–11.

Dabbagh, N., & Kitsantas, A. (2004). Supporting self-regulation in student-centered web-based learning environments. *International Journal on E-Learning, 3*, 40–47.

Eccles, J. (1983). Expectancies, values and academic behaviors. In J. T. Spence (Ed.), Achievement and achievement motives (pp. 75-146). Freeman.

Ergül, H. (2006). Çevrimiçi eğitimde akademik başarıyı etkileyen güdülenme yapıları [Motivational structures affecting academic success in online education]. *The Turkish Online Journal of Educational Technology, 5*(1), 124–128.

Güler, M. (2015). Öğretmen *adaylarının öz düzenleme becerilerinin; duygusal zekâları, epistemolojik inançları ve bazı değişkenler açısından incelenmesi* [Self-regulation skills of teacher candidates; their emotional intelligence, epistemological beliefs and some variables] [Doctoral dissertation]. Necmettin Erbakan University, Turkey.

Hartley, K., & Bendixen, L. D. (2001). Educational research in the Internet age: Examining the role of individual characteristics. *Educational Researcher, 30*(9), 22–26. doi:10.3102/0013189X030009022

Hrbackova, K., & Safrankova, A. P. (2016). Self-Regulation of Behaviour in Children and Adolescents in the Natural and Institutional Environment. *Procedia: Social and Behavioral Sciences, 217*, 679–687. doi:10.1016/j.sbspro.2016.02.119

Kalaycı, Ş. (2009). *SPSS uygulamalı çok değişkenli istatistik teknikleri* [SPSS applied multivariate statistical techniques]. Asil Yayın.

Kaplan, E. (2014*). Beden eğitimi ve spor öğretmenliği öğrencilerinde özdüzenleme: ölçek uyarlama çalışması* [Self-regulation in physical education and sports teaching students: A scale adaptation study] [Unpublished master dissertation]. Akdeniz University, Turkey.

Kaplan, E., & Certel, Z. (2018). Beden eğitimi ve spor öğretmenliği öğrencilerinin akademik öz-düzenlemelerinin incelenmesi [Examining the academic self-regulation of physical education and sports teacher students]. *Mediterranean Journal of Humanities, 8*(1), 237–246. doi:10.13114/MJH.2018.394

Karagöz, S. (2021). Evaluation of distance education: The sample of guidance and counseling students (Example of Aksaray University). *The Universal Academic Research Journal, 3*(1), 18–25.

Karagöz, S., & Rüzgar, M. E. (2021). An investigation of the prospective teachers' viewpoints about distance education during the COVID-19 pandemic. *International Journal of Curriculum and Instruction, 13*(3), 2611–2634.

Karaoğlu, B., & Pepe, O. (2020). Beden eğitimi öğretmen adaylarının akademik öz düzenleme becerilerinin bazı değişkenlere göre incelenmesi [Examination of academic self-regulation skills of physical education teacher candidates according to some variables]. *Beden Eğitimi ve Spor Bilimleri Dergisi, 14*(2), 214–224.

Kocdar, S., Karadeniz, A., Bozkurt, A., & Buyuk, K. (2018). Measuring self-regulation in selfpaced open and distance learning environments. *The International Review of Research in Open and Distributed Learning, 19*(1), 25–43. doi:10.19173/irrodl.v19i1.3255

McClelland, M. M., & Cameron, C. E. (2011). Self-regulation and academic achievement in elementary school children. *New Directions for Child and Adolescent Development, 2011*(133), 29–44. doi:10.1002/cd.302 PMID:21898897

Mischel, W. (1961). Preference for delayed reinforcement and social responsibility. *Journal of Abnormal and Social Psychology, 62*(1), 1–7. doi:10.1037/h0048263 PMID:13771261

Pekrun, R., Goetz, T., Titz, W., & Perry, R. P. (2002). Academic emotions in students' self-regulated learning and achievement: A program of qualitative and quantitative research. *Educational Psychologist, 37*(2), 91–105. doi:10.1207/S15326985EP3702_4

Pintrich, P. R. (1989). The dynamic interplay of student motivation and cognition in the college classroom. In Advances in motivation and achievement: Motivation enhancing environments (pp. 117-160). Greenwich, CT: JAI Press

Pintrich, P. R. (1999). The role of motivation in promoting and sustaining self-regulated learning. *International Journal of Educational Research, 31*(6), 459–470. doi:10.1016/S0883-0355(99)00015-4

Pintrich, P. R. (2000). The role of goal orientation in self-regulated learning. In Handbook of self-regulation (pp. 451-502). Academic Press.

Pintrich, P. R., & De Groot, E. V. (1990). Motivational and self-regulated learning components of classroom academic performance. *Journal of Educational Psychology, 82*(1), 33–40. doi:10.1037/0022-0663.82.1.33

Pintrich, P. R., & Garcia, T. (1991). Student goal orientation and self-regulation in the college classroom. In Advances in motivation and achievement: Goals and self-regulatory processes. Greenwich, CT: JAI Press.

Pintrich, P. R., Smith, D. A. F., Garcia, T., & McKeachie, W. J. (1993). Reliability and predictive validity of the Motivated Strategies for Learning Questionnaire (MSLQ). *Educational and Psychological Measurement, 53*(3), 801–813. doi:10.1177/0013164493053003024

Pressley, M., & McCormick, C. (1995). *Advanced educational psychology for educators, researchers, and policymakers.* Harpercollins College Division.

Sağırlı, M. Ö., Çiltaş, A., Azapağası, E., & Zehir, K. (2010). Yükseköğretimin öz-düzenlemeyi öğrenme becerilerine etkisi [The effect of higher education on self-regulation learning skills]. *Kastamonu Eğitim Dergisi, 18*(2), 587–596.

Şahin, F. T. (2015). Beden eğitimi ve spor yüksekokulunda öğrenim gören öğrencilerin öz düzenleme yeterliliklerinin incelenmesi [Examination of self-regulation competencies of students studying at physical education and sports school]. *International Journal of Science Culture and Sport, 4*, 425–438.

Schunk, D. H. (2001). Social cognitive theory and selfregulated learning. In Self-regulated learning and academic achievement: Theoretical perspectives (pp. 125-152). Mahwah, NJ: Erlbaum.

Schunk, D. H. (2012). Social cognitive theory. In APA educational psychology handbook. Vol. 1: Theories constructs, and critical Issues (pp. 101–123). Washington, DC: American Psychological Association.

Schunk, D. H., & Rice, J. M. (1987). Enhancing comprehension skill and self-efficacy with strategy value information. *Journal of Reading Behavior*, *19*(3), 285–302. doi:10.1080/10862968709547605

Schunk, D. H., & Zimmerman, B. J. (Eds.). (2012). *Motivation and self-regulated learning: Theory, research, and applications.* Routledge. doi:10.4324/9780203831076

Thoresen, C. E., & Mahoney, M. J. (1974). *Behavioral self-control.* Holt, Rinehart & Winston.

Tümen Akyıldız, S. (2020). Covid-19 sürecinde uygulanan çevrimiçi derslerde üniversite öğrencilerinin öz-düzenlemeli öğrenme düzeyinin incelenmesi [Examining the self-regulated learning level of university students in online courses applied during the Covid-19 process]. In E. Yeşilyurt (Ed.), Eğitim Sosyal ve Beşeri Bilimlerine Multidisipliner Bakış [Multidisiplinary Perspective on Education, Social Sciences and Humanities] (pp. 135 -156). İstanbul: Güven Plus Grup Danışmanlık Yayınları.

Vygotsky, L. (1962). *Thought and language.* MIT Press. doi:10.1037/11193-000

Wolters, C., Yu, S., & Pintrich, P. R. (1996). The relation between goal orientation and students' motivational beliefs and self-regulated learning. *Learning and Individual Differences*, *8*(3), 211–238. doi:10.1016/S1041-6080(96)90015-1

Yamamoto G. T & Altun, D. (2020). Coronavirüs ve Çevrimiçi (Online) Eğitimin Önlenemeyen Yükselişi. *Üniversite Araştırmaları Dergisi, 3*(1), 25-34.

Zhao, H., Chen, L., & Panda, S. (2014). Self-regulated learning ability of Chinese distance learners. *British Journal of Educational Technology*, *45*(5), 941–958. doi:10.1111/bjet.12118

Zimmerman, B. J. (2000). Attaining self-regulation: A social cognitive perspective. In Handbook of self-regulation (pp. 13–39). Academic Press.

Zimmerman, B. J. (2002). Becoming a self-regulated learner: An overview. *Theory into Practice, 41*(2), 64–70. doi:10.120715430421tip4102_2

Zimmerman, B. J., & Kitsantas, A. (1997). Developmental phases in self-regulation: Shifting from process to outcome goals. *Journal of Educational Psychology*, *89*(1), 29–36. doi:10.1037/0022-0663.89.1.29

Zimmerman, B. J., & Martinez-Pons, M. (1988). Construct validation of a strategy model of student self-regulated learning. *Journal of Educational Psychology*, *80*(3), 284–290. doi:10.1037/0022-0663.80.3.284

Zimmerman, B. J., & Martinez-Pons, M. (1992). Perceptions of efficacy and strategy use in the self-regulation of learning. In Student perceptions in the classroom: Causes and consequences (pp. 185-207). Hillsdale, NJ: Erlbaum.

Zimmerman, B. J. & Schunk, D. H. (2001). Reflections on theories of self-regulated learning and academic achievement. *Self-regulated learning and academic achievement: Theoretical perspectives, 2*, 289-307.

Zimmerman, B. J., & Schunk, D. H. (2001). *Self-regulated learning and academic achievement: Theoretical perspectives.* Routledge.

KEY TERMS AND DEFINITIONS

Online Self-Regulation: Self-regulation skills used in online environments.

Self-Regulated: An active and constructive process in which students set their own learning goals, try to regulate their cognition, motivation, and behavior, are guided and constrained by their goals and the contextual features in their environment.

Self-Regulated Learning: A self-directed process by which students transform their mental abilities into academic ability.

Chapter 9

Business and Culture:
A Virtual Exchange Across Four Countries

Marina Apaydin
iD https://orcid.org/0000-0002-0492-4951
American University of Cairo, Egypt

John D. Branch
University of Michigan, USA

Amy Gillett
University of Michigan, USA

ABSTRACT

Virtual exchanges are an emerging form of learning in which students from different countries are connected via technology. The authors created a virtual exchange, Business & Culture, to connect students at institutions in the USA, Egypt, Lebanon, and Libya. The focus of the Business & Culture virtual exchange was on teaching cultural competence, a key skill in today's increasingly globalized workplace. In this chapter, they explore the design and implementation of Business & Culture. They enumerate the challenges of incorporating the needs and resources of four different institutions. They discuss the benefits of the Business & Cultural virtual exchange to both students and instructors. And they outline the evaluation of the Business & Cultural virtual exchange, which allowed them to both gauge its effectiveness and improve its design and implementation.

DOI: 10.4018/978-1-7998-8077-6.ch009

1. INTRODUCTION

Educational exchanges are nothing new. Indeed, the University of Oxford welcomed its first international student, Emo of Friesland, in 1190 (University of Oxford, 2014). But recent decades have witnessed a boom in student mobility. According to the Institute of International Education, for example, the 2018/2019 academic year set a record year for both international students studying in the USA, and Americans studying abroad—1,095,299 and 347,0997 students respectively. On the other side of the Atlantic Ocean, the European Commission has been promoting student mobility since 1987 with its Erasmus program, which has to date seen participation from more than 9 million people and some 4,000 institutions across 31 countries (Erasmus, n.d.).

In the context of business education, globalization and the rise of China, India, and other fast-growing economies, have spurred many business schools to incorporate educational exchanges into their curricula (Loh et al., 2011). The logic is simple. To succeed in the global workplace means having a global mindset—the cultural awareness and cultural consciousness which a global economy demands. And educational exchanges are an effective method to facilitate its development (Finley et al., 2007). Educational exchanges also help to grow other related skills, including emotional resiliency, flexibility, personal autonomy, and openness (Kitsantas & Meyers, 2001).

The COVID-19 pandemic, however, has revealed a significant limitation of traditional educational exchanges: geography. The pandemic caused great disruption to existing educational exchanges, and the uncertainty of when travel would resume made it difficult for most students to plan their future schedules. But even before the pandemic, traveling across borders to seek a cross-cultural experience was infeasible for many students. In the USA, for example, only one in ten undergraduate students studies abroad before graduating (Institute of International Education, 2020). Common reasons for not pursuing a student exchange include scheduling challenges, financial constraints, and onerous degree requirements.

Voilà virtual exchanges, which connect students across two or more countries via technology, to learn together and to collaborate on a project in cross-cultural teams. Such virtual exchanges can be extracurricular or structured within a for-credit course. Virtual exchanges use a variety of communication methods and forms of delivery. According to a 2021 report by the Stevens Initiative, however, most virtual exchanges (38%) feature a blend of asynchronous activities (in which participants share information and engage at different times) and synchronous activities (in which participants engage in real-time) (Stevens Initiative, 2021).

Virtual exchanges have focused on a wide variety of topics—seemingly anything which would benefit from two or more different cultural groups coming together to explore a given topic would be an appropriate choice. According to the Stevens Initiative report, the top three content areas on which virtual exchanges focus are: intercultural dialogue and peace-building (67%); science, technology, engineering, and mathematics (25%); and global or international affairs (24%). Of course, virtual exchanges can focus on multiple content areas, so the total does not sum to 100%. Other content areas which were cited in the report include language learning, education, and entrepreneurship or business.

Virtual exchanges can be effective and low-cost alternatives to traditional educational exchanges, conferring many of the same benefits without the travel requirement. They also offer a unique pedagogical opportunity. The conventional wisdom is that students who study abroad will 'naturally' come to understand and appreciate cultural differences. With virtual exchanges, however, instructors have a more controlled environment in which to facilitate cross-culture learning. Indeed, they can ensure that culture is not simply a passive backdrop, but instead is a topic for student analysis, reflection, and action.

In this chapter, we explore the design and implementation of Business & Culture, a virtual exchange which connects students at institutions in the USA, Egypt, Lebanon, and Libya, and whose focus is cultural competence. The chapter begins by situating virtual exchanges within the broader context of the internationalization of higher education. It then details the Business & Culture virtual exchange, including its rationale, design, and assessment. The chapter continues by describing how the Business & Culture virtual exchange was evaluated. Finally, it discusses the virtual exchange, especially in terms of value for students and instructors.

2. THE INTERNATIONALIZATION OF HIGHER EDUCATION

The internationalization of higher education as a whole might be considered as old as the university itself. In medieval Europe, scholars often spent their sabbaticals abroad, enjoying time in "Oxford, Tübingen or the Sorbonne to pursue their scholarly activities and access the vast resources of the university libraries" (Harris, 2008, p. 352). Latin, which was the *lingua franca* of higher education until the Renaissance, facilitated the itinerant scholar's rambling from *studium* to *studium* (de Ridder-Symeons, 1992). It is not surprising, therefore, that the European Union chose the name ERASMUS (European Community Action Scheme for the Mobility of University Students) for its student exchange program, a nod to one of the most famous academic wandering minstrels.

At the end of the Middle Ages, however, the university lost its academic universalism, becoming an instrument of the state. Indeed, its newfound purpose was to serve the ideological and professional needs of the emerging nation-states of Europe (Scott, 2000). Kerr (1994) characterized this period as the 'convergence model', in which "education, and higher education, not only came to serve the administrative and economic interests of the nation-state but became an essential aspect of the development of national identity" (p. 27). It was during this period that the university also gained its new identification with science and technology.

As these emerging nation-states gained power, national systems of higher education also began to emerge, and these systems were subsequently exported. Johns Hopkins University in Baltimore, for example, adopted the German discovery-oriented approach to higher education, and became the model for the modern American research university (Johns Hopkins University, 2014). The export of national systems of higher education, however, was more often another facet of the European colonization of Africa, Asia, and Latin America (Knight & de Wit, 1995). Although primarily in service of national interests, it also led to the sharing of scientific ideas, and reignited academic exchanges.

The years immediately following World War II triggered an explosion in higher education (Seidel, 1991). Indeed, half of the world's universities have been established since 1945. In the USA in particular, higher education was linked to a broader social equity agenda which aimed to expand educational opportunity and access. Spurred by the GI Bill and the civil rights movement (Newfield, 2011), this agenda led to the massification of higher education and, correspondingly, an almost Fordist assembly-line approach to teaching and research (Scott, 1995). But as highlighted by Scott (2000), the golden age of universities also coincided with the height of the Cold War, and accordingly a kind of nationalism, which, he argued, resulted in (using Kerr's language) a re-convergence.

The 1960s and 1970s, however, saw a rekindling of the internationalization of higher education, despite—or perhaps because of—the Cold War. Both the USA and the USSR began to support international exchange for economic and political motives, resulting in a new form of educational imperialism. The Chicago School of Economics, for example, had a profound impact on the macro-economic policies of Chile, the effects of which can still be felt today. Or consider the legions of African engineers, doctors, and scientists who were educated in universities and institutes across the USSR. The People's Friendship University (now of Russia), for example, was founded in 1960, with the express purpose of educating citizens of (friendly) developing nations.

The internationalization of higher education in the 1960s and 1970s was also spurred by the de-colonization of the developing world, the rapid expansion of higher education globally, and the changing role of the university from a center of intellectual pursuit to a training facility for human resources (Knight & de Wit, 1995). This internationalization took on a decidedly north-south geographical axis, with students moving (usually one-way) from south to north, and staff and technical assistance in the opposite direction. The consequences were both positive (the spread of scientific developments to the south, for example) and negative (brain drain from the south, for example).

The forces of globalization which erupted in the 1980s prompted a new urgency for the internationalization of higher education. This urgency was captured concisely in *A Nation at Risk*, the landmark federal evaluation of American public elementary and secondary education which was commissioned by then-President Ronald Reagan: "Our unchallenged preeminence in commerce, industry, science, and technological innovation is being overtaken by competitors throughout the world" (National Commission on Excellence in Education, 1983, p. 1). In higher education more specifically, the concern over America's global competitiveness led directly to the Centers for International Business Education (CIBE) program, "created under the Omnibus Trade and Competitiveness Act of 1988 to increase and promote the nation's capacity for international understanding and economic enterprise" (U.S. Department of Education, 2016).

The sense of urgency which was prompted by the forces of globalization, however, resulted in a new twist on the internationalization of higher education—a focus on internally-oriented institutional internationalization (cross-cultural training and new area studies programs, for example), and externally-oriented institutional internationalization (educational exchanges and alliances, for example), which were intended to nurture the 'international-ness' of the institution and its stakeholders (See Gacel-Ávila, 2005, for example.). With respect to students specifically, Knight and de Wit (1995) argued that this institutional internationalization of higher education had both economic and cultural drivers. Indeed, institutional internationalization was necessary to equip students for a global labor market. Similarly, institutional internationalization was necessary in order for students to learn about themselves… by confronting alternative world-views.

It was during this era of institutional internationalization that educational exchanges really 'took off' (Lee, 2012). To be fair, Knight and de Wit (1995) noted that four different approaches characterised this institutional internationalization:

1. activity—the addition of curricular and extra-curricular offerings such as international exchanges and joint research,
2. ethos—the creation of an international culture in an institution,
3. competency—the development of international skills and attitudes among students and staff, and
4. process—the integration of an international dimension in all university programs, policies, and procedures.

Similarly, Hamrick (1999) suggested that this institutional internationalization focused on:

1. international studies—the establishment of internationalization as an academic subject (area studies or cultural studies, for example),
2. facilitation of interaction—the furnishing of opportunities for shared experiences (study abroad and foreign student recruitment, for example),
3. international assistance—the provision of foreign aid (instructor exchanges, for example), and
4. preparation of students—the promotion of the 'global citizen' (internationally-themed dormitories, for example).

But it is the growth of educational exchanges during this era of institutional internationalization which is most germane to this chapter.

3. THE BUSINESS & CULTURE VIRTUAL EXCHANGE

3.1. Background

The Business & Culture virtual exchange was triggered by a call for proposals from the Stevens Initiative, an international leader in virtual exchange which advocates for and invests in its growth and diversification. The Stevens Initiative supports virtual exchanges which connect universities in the USA with counterparts in the Middle East North Africa region.

Amy Gillett leads the Education team at the William Davidson Institute (WDI), a nonprofit unit which based at the University of Michigan, whose mission is to advance economic development in low-income and middle-income countries. When Amy saw the call for proposals, she contacted John Branch, a professor of marketing and international business at the University's Ross School of Business who also teaches in many of WDI's management education programs. Together, they drafted a proposal to connect students in multiple campuses to learn about cross-cultural business concepts via virtual exchange.

Tapping WDI's broad international network, Amy and her team contacted the American University of Beirut (AUB) and the American University in Cairo (AUC), to see if there might be interest in joining the proposal. And indeed, there was interest at both universities. From AUB, Marina Apaydin, a professor of strategic management and international business, joined the teaching team. Professor Maha Mourad, a professor of marketing, joined from AUC. Amy and John, along with WDI program manager Meghan Neuhaus, traveled to Beirut and Cairo to flesh out the details of the proposal—including content, scheduling, and pedagogical methods—with Marina and Maha. Together, they agreed to incorporate two case studies into the virtual exchange: one case of an Egyptian jewelry company, and another case which is focused on a Lebanese winery.

Due to the Stevens Initiative's interest in Libya, WDI also invited the Benghazi Youth for Technology and Entrepreneurship in Libya (BYTE) youth incubator in Libya to join the virtual exchange. In contrast to the students from the other three partner schools, the BYTE students participated in the virtual exchange as an extracurricular activity outside their formal university studies.

3.2. Rationale

Educators need creative ways to prepare students for the globalized, interconnected economy which they will soon be entering. A virtual exchange provides an ideal mechanism for connecting students across countries to not only learn together but also to work together. Through a virtual exchange, students come to understand what it means to work across cultures. Time differences, language barriers, miscommunications, and so on, all come into play in a very real way, as students work on projects in cross-cultural teams. On the flip side, students also discover the rewards of working across cultures—the exciting discoveries of what they share with peers who live halfway around the world, and the richness of other country's culinary traditions, music, art, and ways of communicating. By coming 'face-to-face' with another society, students gain a deeper understanding of their own cultures, and realize that there are alternative and equally valid worldviews. A virtual exchange can truly open their eyes and minds to the world. For a student heading into a career in international business, such benefits are enormous.

While several international elective courses are offered to undergraduates at the Ross School of Business, students do not have an international business requirement for graduation. This is surprising given the fact that one of the broader goals of the school is to 'internationalize students'. Bachelor of Business Administration students can opt to participate in a traditional educational exchange, but a mere 17.5% do so. Consequently, a virtual exchange can fill an important role for students, conferring many of the same benefits of traditional educational exchanges.

As for the theme of our virtual exchange, this was also designed to fill a gap, as none of the international elective courses at Ross School had a cultural theme. The business and culture theme of the virtual exchange was premised on the notion that managing in the global economy requires not only knowledge of international business—macroeconomics, exchange rates, global logistics, etc.—but also knowledge of culture. Indeed, human beings are social beasts who organize themselves into groups. These groups, however, differ with respect to their worldviews, their acceptable behaviours, and so on. In other words, social groups (or societies) have cultural differences. These differences create strategic challenges for today's companies, and suggest that managers must develop competencies in cross-cultural business.

The course narrative is that despite globalization, perhaps even because of globalization, culture still matters. The course then explores the conceptualization and operationalization of culture, primarily from anthropological and sociological perspectives. It then argues for the need to develop cultural competence, underlining, ironically, that human culture hinders it. The course continues with a survey of tools for improving cultural competence, including the Hofstede and Trompenaars models—two of the most widespread frameworks in cross-culture studies—which provide frameworks for understanding cultural differences. It concludes by examining how culture impacts international business.

3.3. Modular Design

We designed the Business & Culture virtual exchange to be modular. It is used for different purposes by the four institutions and serves as only one component of their wider pedagogical programming. At AUB, the students study international business, with a focus on cross-cultural management. At AUC, the students follow a course in international marketing, and the emphasis of the Business & Culture virtual exchange is on the consulting project, which the students extend after the virtual exchange has concluded. At BYTE, the virtual exchange is a supplementary activity for high-performing students, most of whom are not pursuing business degrees.

This modular view is one key to the success of the Business & Culture virtual exchange. Indeed, it was very apparent during initial planning for the three partner institutions that trying to create a single 'universal' course would have been folly. Different institutions have different academic calendars, different curricular needs, and so on. And consequently, it was much easier to get buy-in by creating the Business & Culture virtual exchange as a module which each institution could use *in situ*.

At AUB, the virtual exchange was a radical innovation. Indeed, the business school had to retrofit the largest of its auditorium-shaped classrooms, equipping it with the necessary video and audio technology to enable real-time views of the instructor and the students, and facilitate interaction with their virtual partners. In terms of curriculum, the international business course which Marina was teaching was already an elective on offer, and consequently the Business & Culture virtual exchange was designed to be complementary—an opportunity for students to delve into the intricacies of cross-cultural management.

At the University of Michigan's Ross School of Business, the Business & Culture virtual exchange was adopted in concert with a new course entitled Cross-Cultural Business, which John proposed for the Bachelor of Business Administration degree.

Nested within the Cross-Cultural Business course is the Business & Culture virtual exchange, a program of eight connected sessions of two hours each.

During these connected sessions, students across the four countries participate in various experiential activities. In the *My Culture* presentation, for example, students present their individual cultures in teams (in part to debunk common stereotypes), using a specific cultural framework, such as the Hofstede model or Trompenaars model. Students in other countries comment on these presentations and have an opportunity to ask questions of the presenting team. Not only does it help other classrooms to discover a new culture, it also increases the local students' awareness about the roots of their own culture. Other sessions focus on case studies which reveal the challenges and opportunities of operating internationally, including an Egyptian jewelry manufacturer and a Lebanese winery, both of which are contemplating international expansion. Additionally, professors from the four institutions provide hands-on experiential activities and short lectures to the students. In the opening connected session, for example, John presents *My Suit* wherein students learn that his suit represents the contributions of companies from fourteen countries—a perfect illustration of the interconnected global economy.

3.4. Global connections

The Business & Culture virtual exchange facilitates connections among students across countries in a variety of ways. In a traditional in-person classroom, these connections would form naturally as students see each other in class, sit together, and talk during the breaks. In the virtual environment, however, it requires intentional design to forge these connections. For this reason, each connected session has a minimum of one breakout group activity, in which participants are teamed across countries.

We have also created more informal mechanisms for students to become acquainted. By using the cloud-based sharing board Padlet, for example, we enable students, instructors, and program administrators to introduce each other, and incorporate personal photos and videos. We also have a Facebook page to share articles which are related to cross-cultural business. Additionally, we have a blog, in which recent participants are invited to reflect on, and share highlights of, the virtual exchange.

Finally, the Business & Culture virtual exchange involves a simulated internationalization consulting project in which students, working in a geographically-dispersed team, consider a specific country as a possible destination market for a company. They conduct research on the destination market according to the 4Cs of a market (consumers, competitors, context, and channel partners), and analyze the results of this market research, from the company's perspective. In doing so, students put into practice the cross-cultural business concepts and skills of the virtual exchange.

3.5. Assessment

The Business & Culture virtual exchange also incorporates an online assessment—the Business Cultural Intelligence Quotient (BCIQ)—which measures extant student knowledge, and self-reports on motivation, listening and communicative adaptation, and cognitive preparation. The BCIQ is administered before the virtual exchange begins. Marina builds this BCIQ into a broader assignment, which requires students to construct and follow an 'Individual Development Plan'. John re-administers the BCIQ at the conclusion of his course; students can then use results from both assessments for the assignment, the *Cross-Cultural Journal*, in which students reflect on their personal and professional growth throughout the semester. Karim Itani, an AUB student, noted: "Scoring high in my BCIQ on motivation, listening skills, cognitive behavior preparation, and learning behavior are great indicators of my adoption of a *tabula rasa* on which I can base my learning and increase my global knowledge."

4. EVALUATION

4.1. Impact of the Virtual Exchange on Knowledge and Skills

WDI's Performance Measurement and Improvement (PMI) and program teams co-developed a rigorous monitoring, evaluation, and learning (MEL) plan to measure the impact of the virtual exchange on students, and to inform improvements following each offering. The MEL leveraged both quantitative and qualitative data on key constructs such as cross-cultural communication, collaboration, problem-solving, empathy, perspective-taking, cultural intelligence, and knowledge of the differing cultures.

The PMI and program teams held two theory of change workshops to ensure that each team had a deep understanding of the impact pathway. The theory of change was also shared with the Stevens Initiative and its independent evaluator, RTI International. The PMI and program teams co-developed the research questions and indicators of success, using the theory of change model as the foundation. Based on these indicators, the PMI team constructed an electronic questionnaire. The questionnaire captured indicators which were aligned with the outcomes in the theory of change, and also included indicators which were required by RTI (RTI provided the questions for its required indicators.).

The questionnaire was administered electronically (via a platform called Alchemer) to students at the start and end of the semester (the baseline and endline, respectively). Students who were enrolled in the virtual exchange, and a comparison group of undergraduate students who were recruited from the participating institutions, were involved. At baseline, students first provided their email addresses to the PMI team via a Google Form. The Google Form also included the informed consent. An e-mail campaign was auto-scheduled via Alchemer to distribute the questionnaires directly to students' inboxes. The program team requested the instructors to hold time in class both at the baseline and endline points, to ensure high response rates.

The Business & Culture virtual exchange has run three times to-date from September 2019 to May 2021. Across the three semesters, statistically significant improvements were found in students' reported scores on empathy, cross-cultural communication skills, cultural quotients and knowledge on culture. No significant results were found on the remaining key variables of cross-cultural collaboration and problem-solving, and perspective-taking.

The sustainability of the virtual exchange was also explored through interviews with seven alumni, representing all four countries. The lead researcher on the PMI team reached out to 26 alumni across the first two semesters, in April 2021; seven students responded to the request for an interview. The lead researcher asked the students questions in and around the following areas:

· How often did they use the skills and knowledge taught in the class in their day-to-day lives?
· Which areas of their lives did they use these skills?
· Why did they choose the class and were their goals met?
· What unique value did they gain from the class?
· Examples of how they used the key constructs and knowledge gained in the class in their lives.
· How did the experience change them?
· What was their team experience like and what value did it provide?
· Should their institutions continue to offer the class and why?

The interviews sought to understand the students' continued use of the intercultural skills and knowledge of the Business & Culture virtual exchange, at their workplace or in other courses, and with friends and family. Most importantly, they aimed to learn if the virtual exchange had changed students, with regard to their biases and assumptions about people from different cultures.

More than half the students who were interviewed shared that they used the skills and knowledge which they attained in Business & Culture, three to four times per week. All students noted that they used the skills and knowledge in their workplace or university. Even more notably, all students said that the virtual exchange had helped them become more empathetic, perceptive, and less self-absorbed. In summary, the findings indicate that the course was effective in delivering on its objectives.

4.2. Student Response to Virtual Exchange

The findings also suggest that students valued the virtual exchange. Students were asked if they would recommend their course, using a scale of 1 (strongly disagree) to 5 (strongly agree). The vast majority of students (90%) 'strongly agreed' or 'agreed' that they would recommend the course.

Many students described how the course opened their eyes to other cultures. AUB student Victor M. said, "This course has furthered my belief that we should have an open-minded attitude and never let our thoughts become universal facts, especially when it comes to cross-cultural interactions. To illustrate, there is more than one way of looking at something, and we should try to learn from each of those perspectives as we encounter them, especially when we interact with people from different cultures."

Students also cited the program's value in giving them a deeper understanding of their own culture. According to Rami S. from American University in Beirut: "Prior to embarking on this course, I had not thought of evaluating and reflecting upon my own culture. With several of our projects centered around elaborating on our culture and presenting it to a foreign eye, I was able to gain a third-person point of view on my culture – deeply understanding how it shapes me. This was truly an eye-opening experience since I was able to understand how our collective experiences as Lebanese people have allowed us to share several identical traits."

Some students found value in getting a glimpse inside classrooms in other countries. Consider this comment from Zeinab A. from the University of Michigan: "Hearing lessons from professors in different countries and witnessing the way class was conducted in these countries provided valuable insight into the educational systems in these countries. I was able to compare and contrast learning environments and curriculums in a way that gave me a better understanding of higher education in the Middle East."

Another aspect of the virtual exchange which students valued was the opportunity to meet peers in other countries, to build their international networks. Kareem B. of BYTE in Libya said, "This program has been so beneficial for me. It gave me a great opportunity to meet new people from other cultures and other perspectives with whom I could share my thoughts. I had never worked with students from other countries before. It was a pleasure to work with my multinational team from Egypt, United States of America, and Lebanon."

Many students specifically praised the global teamwork aspect of the program. Although they found it challenging to coordinate across time zones, and to navigate cultural differences, they found value in meeting and overcoming these hurdles. Elizabeth R. from the University of Michigan said, "I thought that I had working in a group down to a science, but I had never worked in a group full of students from across the globe. My cross-cultural group had to work much harder at communicating and following up with one another because of the vast time difference between our countries. I discovered that different cultures and students approach tasks differently, and we must be willing to work differently to be successful in diverse groups."

Justin B. of the University of Michigan was able to put the virtual teamwork skills he acquired in Business & Culture to use right after the course in his remote internship at a U.S. Congressional office. He said, "I am thankful for the critical telework skills I obtained through working on a substantial consulting project with students from the MENA region in this course. In navigating obstacles unique to this type of group work, such as having to reconcile time zone differences, I have found the virtual assignments and group projects I am engaged in now to be straightforward in comparison."

Like Justin B., several other students cited the program's value for career development. "I hope this experience will diversify my future job opportunities and help me develop new techniques to keep up with the fast-changing world. Expanding my knowledge and skill base in the program helped me develop into a better version of myself," said Asma E. from BYTE in Libya.

Alexa P., a participant in the first cohort of Business & Culture, has now graduated from the University of Michigan, and has had an opportunity to field test the skills she acquired in the program. She says that she is now thriving at her new company, Veeva Systems, in part due to Business & Culture. She works with colleagues from around the world, and reports that she can effectively and confidently communicate with them regardless of background. She also says that she is more conscious about non-verbal communication because of her experience and is more attuned to subtleties. "Business & Culture has prepared me well for my future," Alexa said, "Regardless of where you are, you don't just work with one culture. Here in the US, we're a mixture of cultures and most people have to learn how to operate among those. Taking a class like Business & Culture really prepares you for this — it puts you in the right mindset. It's a great way to learn how to operate in a more globalized work environment and more internationally connected world."

4.3. Improvements

The evaluation was also conducted in service of making improvements to subsequent offerings, in a kind of double-loop learning as coined by Argyris (1991), in which goals of a particular activity are modified through experience. The evaluation uncovered several issues which we have since addressed to facilitate more meaningful exchanges among the students:

- Students ought to be placed in their teams early in the semester so that they can interact with their teammates. These initial interactions can be focused on socializing and getting acquainted, rather than a higher stakes assessment activity.
- Instructors ought to establish norms and expectations of engagement, so that students have clarity on how to behave in the connected sessions and their teams. These norms and expectations ought to be formalized in a 'code of conduct' which is shared with all students, and to which students commit.
- Students ought to be given the opportunity to evaluate their teammates so that they engage in their teams, and contribute equally to team assignments. Indeed, most students had positive experiences in their teams, but some students found that not all teammates contributed equally, especially to the internationalization consulting project. Consequently, they suggested that instructors facilitate the engagement, and intervene when teammates do not engage fully.
- Students want more opportunities to interact with instructors from other universities. We are now experimenting with virtual coffee chats, during which an instructor will lead an open discussion on topics which are driven by students. These informal sessions will begin with an icebreaker to make students feel comfortable in the virtual setting. The WDI will provide prompts to the instructors to kickstart and guide the conversation. For example, "What attracted you to international business?"
- The course ought to make use of virtual breakout rooms, polls, and other interactive activities to increase student engagement during sessions.

5. DISCUSSION

5.1 The Value of Virtual Exchanges for Students

From our initial three offerings, we have drawn several conclusions about the value of virtual exchanges. First, we have found virtual exchanges to be an effective way to sensitive students to other cultures. They are also cost-effective, because they do not require any travel. Further, they can be conducted at scale. When students connect through their individual devices, there is not even the constraint of seats in a classroom. As long as there are roughly equal numbers of students across the countries, we can easily foresee accommodating 50 students per country each semester.

Internationalization is a strategic goal of many universities these days. But what internationalization is, and how it is implemented, can vary dramatically from university to university. Indeed, as Knight and DeWit (2018) explain: "Internationalization has become a very broad and varied concept, including many new rationales, approaches, and strategies in different and constantly changing contexts." Virtual exchanges are one more mode of internationalization for higher education institutions to understand and consider.

Students in business degree programs tend to be very pragmatic. Through their undergraduate education, they are seeking preparation for the working world. We have seen how the Business & Culture virtual exchange equips them with many in-demand skills for the global workplace, with our impact study showing statistically significant improvements in perspective-taking, cross-cultural communication skills, cultural intelligence, and cultural knowledge. Further, our students have blogged about how the virtual exchange has prepared them for the workplace.

5.2. The Value of Virtual Exchange for Instructors

Virtual exchanges are also enriching not just for students, but also for instructors. They are a wonderful way to nurture new connections and collaboration among instructors who teach in other regions of the world. John, for example, by working together on the curriculum and co-teaching aspects of the virtual exchange, has forged a relationship with Marina Apaydin, professor of international business at the American University of Beirut. They are now collaborating on a co-edited book about the internationalization of higher education. Marina added, "Being a naturalized Canadian who had lived in the United States for six years, I was happy to join this important program to share my understanding and appreciation of the Middle Eastern cultures with the North American students. As is true of the Egyptian jewelry designer from one of the business cases I selected to incorporate into this program, I, too, aspire to change the image of the Middle East in the world through cultural education."

Virtual exchanges might also have unexpected positive externalities. When the Lebanese Revolution erupted, for example, and access to the university became difficult and dangerous, the AUB course shifted seamlessly from in-class to online. This shift subsequently paved the way for a continuous virtual format in 2020, in response to a complete country lockdown as a result of the COVID-19 pandemic.

5.3. Next Steps with the Business & Culture Virtual Exchange

After three semesters as an experimental course, Cross-Cultural Business was accepted as a permanent offering at the Ross School of Business. This means that the course can continue to run every winter semester, assuming student demand. Because the course is based not on the analysis of any one country's culture, but rather on cross-cultural frameworks and tools, we could partner with universities anywhere in the world for the Business & Cultural virtual exchange component.

It would indeed be interesting to add a partner from a different part of the world, one in which the culture is very different than the American or Middle Eastern cultures. While it would be great to include Japan, for example, the fourteen-hour time difference between Tokyo and Ann Arbor would be impractical. Countries in Europe or South America are better candidates, and would certainly introduce other cultural lenses into the Business & Culture virtual exchange.

The grant funding provided by the Stevens Initiative will end after the fourth offering, enabling the Ross School of Business to partner with different universities overseas, including those outside of the Steven-stipulated MENA region. Without the grant funding and accompanying institutional support of WDI helping to facilitate the relationships with the partner universities, will the Ross School be able to maintain the program? That remains an open question, as the Ross School has never run a virtual exchange on its own. Further, if AUB and/or AUC no longer desire to be part of the virtual exchange, will the Ross School be able to identify suitable new partners and onboard them effectively into the program? Another factor that is likely to impact future success of the program is the instructor involvement. Instructors might be reassigned to different courses, or might move to different universities. Will new instructors who are brought on board the program be as committed as the founding team?

Whatever direction Business & Culture ultimately takes, the experience of creating and offering the virtual exchange has been transformative for all three of us. We have seen the power of this mode of learning, and we shall continue to utilize it for years to come. Indeed, we are great believers in the power of educational exchanges. And we are convinced that virtual exchanges are a powerful, and perhaps more importantly, scalable solution to equip our future business leaders with a global mindset.

Business & Culture is supported by the Stevens Initiative, which is sponsored by the U.S. Department of State, with funding provided by the U.S. Government, and is administered by the Aspen Institute. The Stevens Initiative is also supported by the Bezos Family Foundation and the governments of Morocco and the United Arab Emirates.

REFERENCES

Argyris, C. (1991). Teaching Smart People How to Learn. *Harvard Business Review*, *69*(3), 99–109.

de Ridder-Symoens, H. (1992). Mobility. In H. de Ridder-Symoens (Ed.), *A history of the university in Europe* (Vol. 1, pp. 280–304). Cambridge University Press.

Finley, J., Taylor, S., & Warren, L. (2007). Investigating graduate business student's perceptions of the educational value provided by an international travel course experience. *Journal of Teaching in International Business*, *19*(1), 51–82. doi:10.1300/J066v19n01_04

Gacel-Avila, J. (2005). The internationalisation of higher education: A paradigm for global citizenry. *Journal of Studies in International Education*, *9*(2), 121–136. doi:10.1177/1028315304263795

Hamrick, J. (1999). *Internationalizing higher educational institutions: Broadening the approach to institutional exchange.* Paper presented at Managing Institutional Change and Transformation Project, Center for the Study of Higher and Postsecondary Education, University of Michigan, Ann Arbor, MI. Retrieved from http://www.personal.umich.edu/~marvp/facultynetwork/ whitepapers/jimhamrick.html

Harris, S. (2008). Internationalising the university. *Educational Philosophy and Theory*, *40*(2), 346–357. doi:10.1111/j.1469-5812.2007.00336.x

In the Spotlight. (n.d.). *Erasmus+ Brings People Together.* Retrieved from https://ec.europa.eu/programmes/erasmus-plus/anniversary/spotlight-erasmus-brings-people-together_en

Institute of International Education. (2020). *Open Doors Report.* Retrieved from https://opendoorsdata.org/annual-release/

Johns Hopkins University. (2014). *A Brief History of JHU.* Retrieved from https://webapps.jhu.edu/jhuniverse/information_about_hopkins/about_jhu/a_brief_history_of_jhu/

Kerr, C. (1994). *Higher education cannot escape history: Issues for the twenty-first century.* SUNY Press.

Kitsantas, A., & Judith, M. (2001). *Studying abroad: Does it enhance college student cross-cultural awareness?* Paper presented at the combined annual meeting of the San Diego State University and the US Department of Education Centers for International Business Education and Research, San Diego, CA.

Knight, J., & de Wit, H. (1995). Strategies for internationalization of higher education: historical and conceptual perspectives. In H. de Wit (Ed.), *Strategies for Internationalization of Higher education: a comparative study of Australia, Canada, Europe and the United States of America* (pp. 5–33). European Association for International Education.

Knight, J., & de Wit, H. (2018). Internationalization of Higher Education: Past and Future. *International Higher Education, 95*.

Loh, C.-P. A., Steagall, J. W., Gallo, A., & Michelman, J. E. (2011). Valuing Short-Term Study Abroad in Business. *Journal of Teaching in International Business, 22*(2), 73–90. doi:10.1080/08975930.2011.615669

National Commission on Excellence in Education. (1983). *A nation at risk*. Retrieved from https://www2.ed.gov/pubs/NatAtRisk/risk.html

Newfield, C. (2011). *Unmaking the public university: The forty-year assault on the middle class*. Harvard University Press. doi:10.2307/j.ctv1cbn3np

Scott, P. (1995). *The meanings of mass higher education*. The Society for Research into Higher Education & Open University Press.

Scott, P. (2000). Globalisation and higher education: Challenges for the 21st century. *Journal of Studies in International Education, 4*(1), 3–10. doi:10.1177/102831530000400102

Stevens Initiative. (2021). *2021 Survey of the Virtual Exchange Field Report*. Retrieved from https://www.stevensinitiative.org/wp-content/uploads/2021/11/2021-Survey-of-Virtual-Exchange-Field-Report.pdf

University of Oxford. (2014). *International applicants*. Retrieved from https://www.ox.ac.uk/

U.S. Department of Education. (2016). *Programs: Centers for international business education*. Retrieved from https://www2.ed.gov/programs/iegpscibe/index.html

KEY TERMS AND DEFINITIONS

Educational Exchange: A program in which students from a secondary school or university study abroad and earn credit from their home university.

Global Mindset: An awareness and receptivity to other cultures and other people, including the recognition that there is no one 'correct' way of doing things.

Globalization: THE growing interdependence of the world's economies, cultures, and people due to increased trade across borders in goods and services, technology, and flows of people, investment, and information.

Hofstede Model: Also known as the 'Six Dimensions of Culture', this is a well-known model for comparing differences across cultures. Psychologist Geert Hofsteded identified six dimensions on which cultures vary: Power Distance; Individualism Versus Collectivism; Masculinity Versus Femininity; Uncertainty Avoidance; Long-Versus Short-Term Orientation; Indulgence Versus Restraint.

Student Mobility: Students participating in study abroad experiences.

Theory of Change: A description of how and why a given program or intervention is expected to lead to a desired change. Theory of Change starts by defining long-term goals and then works backward to identify necessary preconditions.

Trompenaars Model: Like the Hofstede Model, this is a well-known model for comparing differences across cultures. This model differentiates cultures based on their preferences in seven dimensions: universalism vs. particularism; individualism vs. communitarianism; specific vs. diffuse; neutral vs. affective; achievement vs. ascription; sequential time vs. synchronous time; internal direction vs. external direction.

Virtual Exchange: A program which connect students across two or more countries via technology, to learn together and to collaborate on a project in cross-cultural teams. Virtual exchanges can be embedded within a for-credit course, or structured as an independent extracurricular activity.

Chapter 10

Principal Leadership in an Online Environment:
Lessons From Hybrid and Fully Virtual Learning

Aaron M. Perez
GOAL Academy, USA

ABSTRACT

Principal leadership is a role that revolves around quickly changing tasks. In a broad sense, the ability of a principal leader to communicate clearly, build culture, and empower others has positive benefits that lead to school progress. Along with these skills, another skill to consider mastering is plan development and follow-through. Besides skill-related tasks, taking time to meet with staff to connect on a personal level and empowering staff to continue their professional development is a great method for building work culture, just as the leader would expect staff to connect with students. This is one technique for modeling how one would like his or her staff to interact with students. Lastly, this chapter will focus on some lessons learned from the pandemic, specifically revolved around leading through unknown territory, being comfortable with being uncomfortable, and focusing on the fundamentals of the organization.

INTRODUCTION

Educational challenges are common. However, there has been no bigger challenge in recent educational history than the worldwide pandemic that began in 2018.

DOI: 10.4018/978-1-7998-8077-6.ch010

At that time, brick-and-mortar and hybrid school educators were forced to a fully virtual learning environment (VLE). While educators and leaders in these learning environments have strived their best, the notion of "survival mode" was not completely off the table. While the pandemic has forced schools to move to remote learning, the principles contained in this chapter can benefit school principals that were hybrid or online prior to the pandemic, not only those that have come online since the pandemic started.

The primary roles and responsibilities of a principal in a hybrid or VLE vary from how a principal conducts his or her work in a face-to-face environment. In general, there are three primary responsibilities of a principal: leading culture, empowering staff, and communication with various internal and external stakeholders. The intent of this chapter is to provide best practice solutions for principals in a face-to-face learning environment that have been forced into a VLE or for educational leaders that currently work in a hybrid or VLE.

The purpose of this chapter is to provide lessons learned and strategies to implement for educational leaders (administrators) to consider for leading their staff in a VLE. Moreover, three lessons learned, seven tips, and professional development for principals and Assistant Principals will be discussed in the following sections. The seven tips are tips that include both examples from the recent pandemic and examples from outside the pandemic. The three lessons learned from the pandemic are examples that occur not only within the scope of the pandemic but may have been exacerbated by it. Lastly, a section on professional development and how professional development and professional learning communities operate in a VLE.

SELF-DIRECTED LEADING

Prior to a discussion on how principals lead and conduct their work in a VLE is a discussion on self-directed leading. This construct of self-directed leading is derived from Confessore and Confessore (1994). In this notion of self-directed learning are three key factors: initiative (Ponton,1999), persistence (Derrick, 2001), and resourcefulness (Carr, 1999). In the context of learning, initiative is defined as self-starting. Persistence is sustained initiative. Resourcefulness is not only figuring out how to solve problems, but it also means that the learning prioritizes learning over other tasks.

In a new environment, such as changing from a face-to-face or a hybrid learning environment to a VLE, it is imperative to persist through changes or challenges. In addition, rather than react to situations that arise, it is efficient to anticipate problems and lead the solutions for one's team. Resourcefulness is a key attribute for learners and educators. How can an educator teach something they know little about? Resourcefulness has two components: critical thinking and time management. With respect to critical thinking, resourcefulness is using one's own mental and research resources to solve problems. The other aspect of resourcefulness is utilizing the time that one must prioritize their own learning of working in a new learning environment to help staff and students navigate their new learning environment.

THREE LESSONS LEARNED

This section contains information about the three lessons learned from a high school principal. The lessons in this section are provided from the perspective of a high school principal that leads a multi-district charter school in a large metropolitan.

Lesson 1: Comfortability with Un-Comfortability

The first lesson learned was exacerbated (not arose) from the pandemic. This lesson was how to maintain comfortability with un-comfortability. It is an understatement to say that the pandemic was difficult to lead and manage for many professions, not only education. In the school realm, it is my belief that district leaders, school leaders, staff, and students were all doing their best to lead change while ensuring that student learning was still paramount, despite the uncertainty and chaos of the world-wide pandemic.

The capability to contend with uncertainty is an impactful skill. An impactful skill is the skill for a person to mitigate stress caused by a stressor coupled with a timely situation. It is known that stress is a cause of concern for individuals in many roles in many organizations, however, un-comfortability and stress are common in leadership roles, such as a school principal. Despite the type of learning environment that one is involved with, school Principals and Assistant Principals contend with situations that require the need for impactful skills.

One example from a hybrid multi-district high school with multiple school sites in one metropolitan city, was staff scheduling and ensuring that school sites were appropriately staffed. To provide context, the curriculum for the school is housed online and students can access it at any time. At the school sites, students can get one-on-one tutoring for their teacher. Prior to the pandemic, staff worked at the school site five days a week. When staff transitioned to a virtual schedule, there were two types of schedules, those schedules will be described below.

In the first step of the transition to fully virtual, staff at school sites worked either Monday and Wednesday or Tuesday and Thursday, and every other Friday. Once the pandemic spread and thousands of cases were reported on a daily basis, staff transitioned to working one day a week with limited staff (2-3 staff) on site every day. When staff worked the one-day-a-week schedule, students were only permitted on site for computer technical help or food resources. Instruction was completed completely online. Thus, the curriculum and instruction were provided solely online.

In both instances of the schedule, if a staff member tested positive for the virus or had symptoms, the entire staff that worked with that staff member were required to quarantine. Staff groups that worked on each day were on-call if another staff member group was on quarantine. In other words, during the quarantine period, the staff team that was not on quarantine worked every day at the site until the quarantine period for the other team was over. Behind-the-scenes, the principal communicated with district staff, Assistant Principals and Dean's at the sites, and ensured that sites were deep cleaned before the next day when the next staff group came into the site.

Lesson 2: Leading the Unknown, Unknown

The second lesson learned was how to lead the unknown, unknown (Furr and Dyer, 2014). The unknown, unknown is a concept in which a person is experiencing a circumstance and others involved do not have the knowledge or experience to maneuver the situation. Thus, the unknown, unknown.

How to navigate education during a pandemic was the unknown, unknown. While educators and leaders have expertise in teaching, learning, pedagogy, andragogy, and even online education, the transition from face-to-face instruction or hybrid instruction came with unforeseeable challenges as the shift to fully online learning. However, there are challenges that fully online learning has that are not apparent in face-to-face or hybrid learning.

One challenge for GOAL Academy (a multi-district blended-online high school in the state of Colorado) was the transition to fully virtual tutoring. At GOAL Academy, the curriculum is provided online via Schoology. Students access the curriculum online, work at their own pace, and can schedule face-to-face time with their teacher for tutoring.

While teaching staff were used to virtual interactions with students and staff, many students preferred meeting face-to-face with their teachers for tutoring. Teachers adjusted to student needs by calling engaged students weekly to check-in with students and offer tutoring support. This was an adjustment for students that were used to attending school regularly for tutoring support. As a result, the school embarked upon its highest pass rate in the school's history and a newfound understanding of virtual learning. As a result of the increase in pass rates, the school is now piloting a program in which teachers and support staff are permitted work time from home. While the pandemic has caused turmoil in education, there have also been lessons resulting in better educational practices.

Lesson 3: Focus on Fundamentals

The lesson from focusing on fundamentals involves focusing on the specifics of one's own work and ensuring attention to those details. The role of a school principal in an online or hybrid school differs from a school principal role in brick-and-mortar. Some of the scope of the differences in work will be discussed in the section below, *seven tips for principals*. Examples from hybrid and virtual learning will be discussed in parallel to brick-and-mortar.

Leading oneself and others to focus on details and results had aided in increased efficiency and effectiveness (Grev, 2015). Unforeseen setbacks have been part of the current worldwide pandemic. However, a pandemic is not the only potential setback that motivates one to lead his or herself and their team to focus on the fundamentals of their own work.

The core responsibilities of a principal are communicating well, building school culture, and empowering staff to accomplish their goals (Sheninger, 2014). While these will be discussed in more detail in the next section, the intent is not to be an exhaustive list of every duty or responsibility of a principal, but rather the high-level tasks that the principal is responsible for.

Next, is a discussion on seven tips for principals. In this section, the following topics such as task switching, communication, and culture will be discussed.

SEVEN TIPS FOR PRINCIPALS

This section contains information about the seven tips for principals that lead or have been forced to lead a VLE. These lessons learned are from the perspective of a high school principal.

Task-switching and Time Management

Simply put, task-switching is the ability of a person to change from one task to another (American Psychological Association, 2006). In one day, a principal in brick-and-mortar may switch from a phone conference with a parent to evaluating a teacher's lesson plans to responding to a fight in a classroom to a scheduled fire drill. In some cases, these events can all occur before 10 o'clock in the morning. The ability to move between tasks quickly is essential. It is for this reason and the critical nature of these decisions that the last portion of this section is vital to avoid burnout and fatigue. So, while the ability to switch tasks is imperative, so is the need for self-care.

In a virtual learning environment, task switching is very different. Because students are not in the same physical space as staff, student issues that arise may have already happened several hours in the past and the leader must determine the level of urgency of the situation. Learning a sense of urgency in an online environment is essential. The unpredictable nature of issues that happen when students are in a VLE are sometimes critical. In other words, when students are learning from home, unforeseen issue can arise and the ability of a staff member to decipher if a situation is urgent and act quickly can be vital to the success of the situation.

In one example, a student may be doing well and passing all their classes. In addition, this student also checks in for attendance regularly and there are no know issues of family abuse, drug abuse, or the like. Suddenly, the student stops turning in work and even stops communicating altogether. It is difficult to know why a student is not communicating or turning in work when the student is working in a VLE. At this point it is at the team's responsibility to communicate with parents to figure out why a student is not working or turning in work. Once the phone call or email or test message is completed, it is imperative to document the communications with the family. Once communication with the family has been established, the staff member may return to the previous task.

Tangent to task-switching, it is important to discuss daily planning and time management in a novel environment. In a VLE, schools do not always conduct live lessons. However, in a school that conducts live lessons, provide a schedule for students that utilizes their school calendar and set reminders for students to attend courses and stick to this schedule. Ensure that teachers place planning time on their calendar and notify students that they are not available at that time due to planning. In virtual or hybrid environments, students sometime reach out for help whenever they are working on your class, but students may not always work on a course every day or at the same time every day.

For schools that do not conduct live lessons, ensure that teachers place planning time on their calendars and have teachers stick to this schedule. It is advised that teachers host one hour of virtual office hours twice weekly. This is like how college professors host their office hours.

Communicate well

Effective communication is key to the success of any school (Sheninger, 2014). However, when face-to-face interactions are limited, as they are in a VLE, frequent positive communications are a necessity. Moreover, communication is one of the most important aspects in all of leadership. Once an idea forms and it is time for dissemination of that idea, the leader must make some important decisions about the information that needs distribution. The questions the leader must answer are:

Whom in the organization needs to hear the information, what is the best method for delivery of the information, how does one ensure that all involved have heard and know the information with the level of expected detail and performance of those details.

While there are many methods of communication in an organization, all require a level of understanding of how to communicate and know when one method of communication is better than another. The responsibility of any leader is to model how to communicate in any medium, even to the extent of developing a communication plan for the organization.

One method of communication is to utilize the EXCEL Model (The Flippen Group, 2006). The EXCEL model is a five-step method for clearly communicating with others in any communication format from face-to-face to chat to email. The five steps are: Engage, x-plore, communicate, empower, and launch.

Engage is a welcome or a greeting in one's communication. For example, in a face-to-face setting one would approach someone and say hello, see how the person is doing and then communicate the information needed to convey. In a VLE (via email or chat, i.e., Microsoft Team, Google Chat), one may or may not say hello and get right to communicating their message or asking their question. In other words, one may ask their question and *get to the point* but may not begin the message with a standard greeting that one would do in a face-to-face setting. This can occur by either the sender asking the receiver something about their personal life and/or the sender telling the receiver something about their own personal. In a face-to-face conversation, people generally ask others how they are doing. This step in this communication model is x-plore. Next, is to communicate the message or ask the questions. After the message has been communicated, empower is the method by which those on the email understand "who is doing what by when" (The Flippen Group, 2006). Finally, the launch is a meaningful salutation that directly relates to the person or people that the sender is communicating with.

As an email example:

Engage*: Hi Mr. Martinez,*

X-plore*: I hope you are doing well today and that you had a nice three-day weekend with your family. We decided not to go to the lake this weekend, but we did manage to get some rest and try out a new Brazilian steakhouse on Saturday.*

Communicate*: I am reaching out because I received an update on the Air Force Grant. I have confirmation that the funding will begin next month, November 1, 2021. Until then, we have been authorized to buy the materials needed for the project* *and start working to meet the March 31, 2022 deadline. I know that the deadline is close, so let me know if additional staffing is required at this time.*

Empower*: In closing, let's start the project right away.* **Launch***: I am confident in you and the ability of you and your team to meet the March deadline. I am here to support you.*

Please let me know if you need ANYTHING for this project.

Thank you,

Dr. Perez

In this example, note each section and how the information is communicated. There are times when one may need to write the communicate section first, and then go back to write the x-plore section, etc. (R. McGinnis personal communication, February 2019). However, each section is crucial to following clear communication with all stakeholders.

Nurture your culture

Culture is fundamental to learning (Bruner, 1996). Building a positive culture is crucial for the success of students (Pierson, 2013). The late Rita Pierson stated that "kids don't learn from people they don't like" (2013). After developing a culture that develops trust with students, all staff must continuously honor the culture that has been developed. One method for building and nurturing culture is to develop a Social Contract by which all stakeholders abide.

A Social Contract is a set of norms that embraces the needs of the people in an organization (The Flippen Group, 2016). There are four over-arching questions that drive the lexicon of the Social Contract. The four questions are: (1) How do you like to be treated, (2) How do you think others like to be treated, (3) How do you think your leaders like to be treated, and (4) How do we treat each other in times of conflict (The Flippen Group, 2006). The Social Contract is a tool by which all internal stakeholders communicate with one another and no person, despite position, is treated differently in the organization over another. All team members agree to the Social Contract by signing it. All staff members are accountable to uphold the Social Contract.

Once the Social Contract is developed it is paramount to discuss the contents of it on a monthly basis. On a yearly basis, it is advised to review the Social Contract to ensure that it still fits within the scope of needs of the region. At that time, the

Social Contract can be amended at the discretion of the team. Throughout the year, new team members are trained on the contents of the Social Contract and feedback is accepted from new staff members.

Empower staff

Many tasks require the work of a team. Teamwork, in this context, is defined as every person on the team trusting that the rest of the team to complete their tasks and achieve their goals. At some point, staff may fall short of their goals. When this happens, it is appropriate for supervisors to hold staff accountable to those metrics. However, it is not advised that the employee is met with shame or discouragement. As a leader, it is key to remember that at one point everyone has fallen short of a goal or not me a quota. This is an opportunity for leaders to share their expertise by leading out of a place of difficulty.

When the leader meets with the staff member, this is the opportunity to ask questions about the root causes of the issue. Though not quite this simple, once the root cause is realized, an action plan can be developed, one that supports the staff member, to improve the performance over a specified amount of time. Goals are important to set clear expectations for all involved. It is recommended that goals are measurable, achievable and time-bound. An example of a goal is: To increase the level of passer rate by 4 percent in 9th grade students in the second quarter of school. During the time of the goal, it is advised that the leader periodically check-in with the staff member for ongoing support and development. Once the time of the goal has elapsed, the leader and staff member meet to discuss the next steps. When this goal is met, other goals may surface, and other goals likely surface as a result of the discussion. This process continues with this staff member. Note that there are other methods for empowering staff, this is one example of how to empower staff through growth opportunities for the staff.

Every leader has been placed in a position to lead their staff and manage the processes in their realm of influence. Those that have hired and placed those in the position to lead have identified specific reasons for leadership placement. However, one may not always receive the recognition for the work they are doing, and it is in that times that one must trust in their own abilities to lead their organization. As an aside, it may be apparent that you may have staff that *need* positive feedback about their job performance. It is encouraged that you provide it to them.

Schedule Regular Virtual "Face" Time with your Staff

In a school year not shrouded in a global pandemic, Principals and Assistant Principals at brick-and-mortar schedule time for observation and may also walk-through a teacher's class to observe a teacher teaching. After the observation, the school leader generally schedules time to meet with the teacher to review the feedback and work with the teacher to develop goals and promote teacher growth. In a VLE, the principal cannot accomplish either a walk-through or an observation without some type of modification.

Though schools were forced to close their doors, staff observation and evaluation remained a critical part to the effectiveness of a school and teaching staff. While staff observations and evaluations are different in a VLE than hybrid or brick-and-mortar, many of the topics are similar as in a brick-and-mortar, adapted for an asynchronous VLE. In a VLE, for example, teachers are still responsible for learning and tutoring or building curriculum and lesson planning, to name a few. The observation of these teaching tasks is also different in a VLE and still the responsibility of school leader.

To observe online or hybrid teaching and student learning (virtual teacher observation), the school leader has the option to observe a virtual one-on-one tutoring session, a virtual live lesson, a face-to-face tutoring session, or a face-to-face lesson. A face-to-face lesson is a traditional teaching classroom observation. A face-to-face tutoring session is a session in which a student has requested additional support of the teacher and is meeting with the teacher in a one-on-one setting. A virtual live lesson is a lesson that is conducted in real-time and online with a small or large group of students. A virtual one-on-one tutoring session is a tutoring session with a student that has either been planned or done spontaneously at the request of a student before during or after office hours if the teacher is available. The student may reach out to the Teacher via phone, text, chat, or other school-approved method.

To observe lesson plans and curriculum, two options will be provided, although others may be sufficient for submitting lesson plans. The teacher can submit lesson plans or curriculum to the school leader in either a file format or in an online learning platform or website.

Because most teachers and school leaders have not been trained to develop and observe course materials in a VLE, both teachers and school leaders have an opportunity to build the capacity of one another. Thus, the school leader ought to consider their observation and evaluation of their teachers from the point-of-view that the learning environment is unfamiliar to the teacher, and to themselves. Thus, one may expect a learning curve for teachers to develop understanding of how to develop and teach in a VLE. Conversely, the school leader will have a learning curve in their ability to observe, evaluate, and provide relevant feedback for online content and virtual instruction as well. It should be clear from the leader to the teacher that teaching in a novel environment takes time to master.

In a face-to-face school environment, the school leader often passes by his or her staff in the hallways or schedules times to meet in the office or classroom. In a VLE, the school leader should consider scheduling regular virtual time with staff on a weekly or bi-weekly basis. The purpose of these meetings can vary. The discussion focus of some of the meetings will be on improvement of education and learning, while others may be utilized to check in on staff to see how they are doing, or to simply catch up.

Develop a Plan and Stick to It

School systems are inherently driven by "chaos" because of the uncertainty when dealing with people (Trygestad, 1997; Perez, 2021). And, with the amount of looming uncertainty, the educational leader should consider developing structure in their school and sticking to it as much as possible. In any school structure, just as in most work structures, people are unpredictable, the chaos if you will. Chaos is simply defined as unpredictability. Schools may implement student scheduling to move students from one class to another or keep students in the same class and shift teachers from one class to another to potentially limit unpredictability. However, in a VLE, the chaos is more complex.

In a VLE, the chaos is more complex because each student is working in their own home environment – every student's home is their school environment. The rationale is that in some homes there may be barriers to learning. For example, some cultures do not place a high value on education (Perez, 2012). Some home environments may not have food to feed their students every day, for three meals or more a day. In fact, many schools around the nation were delivering food or had meals for pick up at the school. Moreover, some families may not have the capability to provide internet service for their students. Some internet service providers were offering lower prices on their internet service for low-income families. This is not an exhaustive list of educational barriers, but if a student does not have internet, the student would not be able to attend live lessons. If a school is forced to move from face-to-face learning to virtual learning, it may be unpredictable if the student is able to attend virtual lessons. Educational leaders should consider other barriers and how to assist staff to serve students with barriers to education.

Once these considerations are made, the next step is to develop a plan. Some plans are driven from the top-down and other plans require asking others for their feedback. An example of a top-down plan is to have teachers develop a virtual learning schedule for students to attend live lessons. Thus, students know when their teachers are hosting live lessons. This includes teachers notifying students and parents of the online schedule and providing easy-to-follow links to the virtual classroom in their online learning platform.

When asking for feedback to develop a plan, it is important to ask for the feedback from various staff in various departments, without interjecting one's own ideas into the feedback. Simply put, the leader's role is to ask questions and take notes.

Once the feedback is gathered, the data analyzed in whole, and themes (consistent observations within and between departments) are evaluated for potential solutions. While one may begin with a self-evaluation of the data, it is fitting that the leader evaluate the data with other leaders to gain additional perspective. Next, it is the leader's responsibility to develop, implement, and stick with the developed plan.

Take Time for Yourself (To Rest)

The sum of repeated decision-making, high stress work environments and excessive work hours can be harmful to oneself (Broughton, 2010). In fact, stress has been shown to negatively alter decision-making (Potts, 2021) long-term (Soares, Sampaio, Ferreira, Santos, Marques, Palha, Cerqueria, & Sousa, 2012). Stress can either be personal or work-related (Mental Health Foundation, 2018).

Despite stress and overworking as a known and well-researched topic, job burnout and fatigue of principals remain prevalent (Maxwell, 2020). There are times when so many decisions are made in one day that when asked what one wants for dinner at the end of the day, the answer may be "I don't care" (K. Ouweneel, personal communication, October 6, 2021). Circling back to section 3.1 on quick and accurate decision-making skills, because so many critical decisions are made in a single day, the need for self-care is literally vital.

Every principal is needed in the line of work they are undertaking, especially with principals leaving their jobs every year due to various reasons (Washington, 2020). It is because of these reasons that self-care is important to maintain a healthy balance.

PROFESSIONAL LEARNING

In the realm of education, there are generally two types of professional learning that occur: professional development and professional learning community (PLC). Professional development is learning that is conducted by a leader, trainer or outside agency and there is generally one focus area. A PLC is learning that occurs by a specific group (i.e., Teachers) and there can be multiple topics within the scope of a single meeting in the learning environment.

The information contained here are ideas to consider for a conducting a PLC in a VLE.

Professional learning communities

PLC's provide an opportunity for Teachers to learn from other teachers, or perhaps administrators to learn from other administrators. What is unique about PLC's is that topics can vary between meetings and within a single meeting. Additionally, the learning that takes place is from the perspective of another Teacher teaching the same (or different) courses in the school.

There are two methods for setting the agenda for a PLC. First, the school leader can set the agenda and facilitate the discussion, and the teachers provide the feedback for the teacher agenda topics. Second, the leader facilitates the meeting and fields questions from teachers that have questions, and the feedback is provided by the teachers. In both cases, the feedback is generated primarily by the teacher.

Developing a Culture for PLC's

Because staff are learning from other staff in a professional learning community, there is a level of trust that staff have with one another. While staff are not mandated to trust one another, it is important to the success of the team that there is cohesion and trust to help ensure that the team functions professionally when sharing their expertise. Additionally, the school leader's responsibility lies with empowering staff that they are capable to influence others teaching ability.

When staff are apprehensive to bring up topics in a PLC, the leader can offer suggestions so that the meeting continues to progress and does not become stagnant. So that the staff can focus on discussing their topics during the PLC, a member of the administrative team ought to take notes and disseminate the notes at the end of the PLC. It is appropriate to mention topics that are *consistent issues* for the teaching staff without judgement. While it may be uncomfortable to surface these issues, it should be noted (and reiterated) that *these issues* are common issues, and that the PLC is designed to promote growth in teaching staff. Once the staff have provided guidance, it is a good idea to thank the staff for their contribution to the learning community.

When designing a PLC in which an agenda is developed ahead of time, the school leader may utilize email, chat, survey, or some other method for gathering data. Next, the leader evaluates the data to determine the common themes as talking points for the PLC. The leader can also ask his or her Assistant Principals or Deans for common issues with staff. Again, when discussing these topics during the PLC, it is professional to discuss them as long as the leader indicates that these are common issues, and that the PLC is an opportunity for growth and development of the staff within the group.

Staff culture generally develops over time (Bruner, 1994). While the leader can promote the culture and norms with which the school or team operates, ultimately, it is within the team where the culture and norms are developed. It is critical to care for the culture while it is being developed to ensure that staff are supported and have been provided a learning community that is professional and one that promotes staff development.

Ongoing PLC chats

Another method for a PLC is to develop a "chat" with a staff group (i.e., Teachers) and encourage and promote the chat for staff to help others on a day-to-day basis. It is a great opportunity for administrators to "see" what teachers need help with and to interject solutions as needed. This type of chat can be utilized for any group in an organization. Thus, a chat may be a positive solution to an ongoing PLC for staff. However, because people may be more willing to discuss via chat, cultural care for the discussions is the responsibility of all those involved.

DISCUSSION

The role of a school leader is a complicated role that requires the ability to task shift, sometimes very quickly. The leader has an obligation to the students enrolled at the school, their parents, and the staff he or she leads to respond quickly and accurately. Very literally, someone's life may be at risk with any decision that is made (or not made). Principal leaders are instrumental in communication of information that is relevant to the success of the school. Additionally, because interactions with staff may be limited, especially in online or hybrid school environments, staff empowerment is vital to the team and the school culture (A. VanNorman, personal communication, October 20, 2021). Often, a principal may have a few moments to have a conversation with a staff member. The question is: how does he or she have a meaningful conversation with a staff member that conveys empowerment and growth opportunity? One option is to utilize the following EXCEL model.

- Engage: First, greet the staff member and offer a handshake. During these unprecedented times, some may not have a high level of comfort with handshakes. They may want a fist or elbow bump. That's fine! (This takes about 5-10 seconds).
- X-plore: Next, ask how the staff member is doing. If you know something about the staff member, explore that topic with the staff member. (This takes no more than 1 minute).
- Communicate: You may have topics to discuss with the staff or vice versa. This is the time to do that. If have data, for the staff this is a great time to discuss it. (This can take 2-3 minutes, depending on the topic).

- Empower: First, review your communication with the staff member. Next, let the staff member know that he or she is doing well in one or two areas and that you would like to see them improve in one area as well. (This takes about one minute).
- Launch: The launch should be something meaningful to the staff member, that relates to his or her life, and that is relevant to the current conversation. (This takes about a few seconds).

The EXCEL model is a practical tool that provides a clear path to communicate with others – not only verbally, but also in writing. The model is not intended as a checklist, but as a method for clearly organizing thoughts and communicating with others.

Tangent to communicating clearly with others is communication to the larger team and developing a clear plan and sticking to the developed plan is a strong consideration. Changes that occur in an organization mid-year can cause confusion and frustration with staff. After the start of a school year staff expect that once a plan is in place, it is the responsibility of the leadership to adhere to the plan.

During the pandemic, schools were forced to alter or abandon their normal school schedules. This affected teaching and learning. Some brick-and-mortar schools provided meals to their students that were available for pick-up at the school. Brick-and-mortar and hybrid schools were also learning to lead and manage their staff to a completely virtual status. Though difficult to lead, nurturing one's culture is still fundamental to learning in any school environment. Providing consistency is a starting point to developing culture when chaos arises.

A few methods for modeling positive school culture as a leadership team is to schedule regular one-on-one virtual visits with each staff. Each leader can meet with those that he or she evaluates. Another method is to empower staff: this can be to remind staff how important they are to the mission and vision of the school or to encourage them by providing data and setting new goals. Lastly, providing a clear plan and sticking to the plan and sticking to it is not always easy to do, but the plan should allow for some flexibility for teaching professionals and, when necessary, the Teacher update the school leader when the need for change arises.

The last point is to take time for oneself. Despite the abundance of research, school leaders still leave their positions at an alarming rate due to various reasons, the chief of which is stress. Principals, remember that you are the heartbeat of your school. Take care of yourself.

REFERENCES

American Psychological Association. (2006). *Multitasking: Switching costs*. Retrieved from: https://www.apa.org/research/action/multitask

Broughton, A. (2010). *Work-related stress*. Retrieved from: https://www.eurofound.europa.eu/sites/default/files/ef_files/docs/ewco/tn1004059s/tn1004059s.pdf

Bruner, J. (1996). *The culture of education*. Harvard University Press. doi:10.4159/9780674251083

Carr, P. B. (1999). *The measurement of resourcefulness intentions in the adult autonomous learner* (Doctoral dissertation). Available from ProQuest Dissertations and Theses Global database. (UMI No. 304520149)

Confessore, S. J., & Confessore, G. J. (1994). Learner profiles: A cross-sectional study of selected factors associated with self-directed learning. In H. B. Long (Ed.), *New ideas about self-directed learning* (pp. 201–227). Oklahoma Research for Continuing Professional and Higher Education.

Derrick, M. G. (2001). *The measurement of an adult's intention to exhibit persistence in autonomous learning* (Doctoral dissertation). Available from ProQuest Dissertations and Theses Global database. (UMI No. 276280161)

Furr, N., & Dyer, J. H. (2014). *Leading your team into the unknown: How great managers empower their organizations to innovate*. Retrieved from: https://hbr.org/2014/12/leading-your-team-into-the-unknown

Grev, I. (2015). *5 ways to focus on results instead of the process*. Retrieved from: https://www.bizjournals.com/bizjournals/how-to/growth-strategies/2015/04/5-ways-to-focus-on-results-instead-of-process.html

Maxwell, L. A. (2020). *The pandemic may drive principals to quit*. Retrieved from: https://www.edweek.org/leadership/the-pandemic-may-drive-principals-to-quit/2020/08

Mental Health Foundation. (2018). *Mental Health statistics: Stress*. Retrieved from: https://www.mentalhealth.org.uk/statistics/mental-health-statistics-stress

Perez, A. M. (2020). *An investigation of student and staff perceptions of standardized testing participation as a blended/online high school that serves at-risk students* (Publication No. 28151905) [Doctoral dissertation, Regent University]. ProQuest Dissertations Publishing.

Pierson, R. (2003). *Every kid needs a champion*. Retrieved from: https://www.ted.com/talks/rita_pierson_every_kid_needs_a_champion?language=en

Ponton, M. K. (1999). *The measurement of an adult's intention to exhibit personal initiative in autonomous learning* (Doctoral dissertation). Available from ProQuest Dissertations and Theses Global database. (UMI No. 304520327)

Potts, H. (2021). *A brain-changer: How stress redesigns our decision-making*. Retrieved from: https://thedecisionlab.com/insights/health/stress-redesigns-decision-making/

Sheninger, E. (2014). *Digital leadership: Changing paradigms for changing times. Corwin*. Ontario Principals Council.

Soares, J. M., Sampaio, A., Ferreira, L. M., Santos, N. C., Marques, F., Palha, J. A., Cerqueira, J. J., & Sousa, N. (2012). Stress-induced changes in human decision-making are reversible. *Translational Psychiatry*, 2(7), e131. Advance online publication. doi:10.1038/tp.2012.59 PMID:22760555

The Flippen Group. (2006). *The Flippen Group capturing kids' hearts: Case studies for the Texas Education Agency*. Downloaded from https://www.flippengroup.com/pdf/funding/TEA8CaseStudies.pdf

The Flippen Group. (2016). *Social contract samples: Inspiration for creating a powerful social contract*. Author.

Trygestad, J. (1997). *Chaos in the classroom: An application of chaos theory*. Presented at the Annual Meeting of the American Educational Research Association, Chicago, Il.

Washington. (2020). *I save myself: Five reasons why principals leave their schools*. Retrieved from: https://theeducatorsroom.com/i-saved-myself-five-reasons-why-principals-leave-their-schools/

KEY TERMS AND DEFINITIONS

Brick-and-Mortar: A traditional school environment in which students attend classes and hear lectures from teachers face-to-face in a school building.

EXCEL Model: Is a practical tool that provides a clear path to communicate with others – not only verbally, but also in writing. The model is not intended as a checklist, but as a method for clearly organizing thoughts and communicating with others.

Hybrid Learning: A learning environment in which there are components of virtual learning and brick-and-mortar learning.

Impactful Skill: An impactful skill is the skill for a person to mitigate stress caused by a stressor coupled with a timely situation.

Live Lessons: A live lesson is a lesson that is presented in real time. The lesson may be face-ot-face or in a virtual medium (e.g., video conference).

Unknown, Unknown: A phenomenon in which those involved and those not involved do not have a clear path to solve a problem.

Virtual Learning Environment: A learning environment in which there is no face-to-face contact with students and learning lessons and curriculum are completed online.

Chapter 11
Multi-Tiered Systems of Support in the Virtual Environment:
Similar, yet Different

Faylyn R. Emma
University of Florida, USA

ABSTRACT

The purpose of this chapter is to explain multi-tiered systems of support (MTSS), the process required to implement school change efforts, and how MTSS differs in the virtual environment. The chapter includes a history of legislation leading to the development of MTSS framework and recent legislative changes surrounding school improvement. The components and responsibilities within each level of education related to MTSS are examined through a hierarchy with a discussion of barriers and aspects specific to virtual schools. The chapter also incorporates necessary actions within each stage of implementation and examples of programs that have been used to improve student outcomes at each school level.

INTRODUCTION

The term Multi-tiered Systems of Support (MTSS) often invokes overwhelming feelings of hope, anxiety, and confusion. The concept of a multi-faceted and overarching framework for supporting all the diverse, substantial, and ever-changing needs of every single student can be extensive and ominous. The challenges with implementing a vague and comprehensive system of student supports are further

DOI: 10.4018/978-1-7998-8077-6.ch011

amplified by the physical distance of the virtual learning environment. It can be a true struggle to not only identify the needs of students when they are not physically present, but to also bring together all the services they need to be successful in a functional way with minimal interaction between team members. However, the virtual environment does provide some advantages when implementing a MTSS. For example, the flexibility and increased reliance on technology in the online world can actually enhance the data-driven and student-centered expectations of an MTSS and provide staff with rich data and resources with minimal effort. In order to be successful, MTSS in the virtual environment needs a structure embedded in the regular routines within the school, a consistent commitment from all staff members, and accountability and monitoring.

HISTORY OF MULTI-TIERED SYSTEMS OF SUPPORT

One cannot begin to unpack MTSS without understanding its evolution. Identifying and supporting struggling students is not just educational best practice, but also the federal law. The emphasis on supporting struggling students goes back to the Elementary and Secondary Act (ESEA) of 1965 that was created to ensure that all children in the United States had access to an equal educational opportunity and to address the achievement gap for low-income students. The goal of this legislation was to provide additional funding for educational resources to districts with high populations of low-income students. In 1968, the law was expanded to include at-risk students and create the label of Title I to identify schools with student populations in need of additional funding and support. Unfortunately, the funds were not always directed to the students that needed them, so Congress worked to tighten controls on Title I funds in an effort to ensure they were directed towards the neediest students. In an even more unfortunate series of events, the 1980s led to a sharp decline in educational funding and Congress added the expectation of standardized tests to measure performance and the requirement for schools to create a plan to improve in order to receive funding. Due to variation among states and continued limited federal investment in education, the 1994 renewal of the ESEA added the expectations of state standards and state standardized tests to measure students' performance on these standards as well as required states and districts to identify students not making adequate yearly progress and develop plans for their academic improvement. Then, in 2002, ESEA was transformed into the No Child Left Behind Act (NCLB). The most notable change caused by this legislation was removing control of the federal resources from states and increasing the decision-making power of the federal government. Testing requirements increased to require annual math and reading assessments in lower grades and a high school exam. In addition, adequate yearly progress was no longer a goal, but an expectation, and NCLB set the bar at 100% proficiency in math and reading for all students by 2014. NCLB lapsed in 2007, and Congress was undecided about how to proceed. Congress had authorized additional funding and alternative programs through the American Recovery and Reinvestment Act (ARRA) of 2009, but many federal educational goals came through the form of competitive grants that required schools to adopt national standards, improve their data around student achievement and establish standardized teacher evaluation methods. Due to the continued stall in Congress, in 2011, Congress allowed states to apply for waivers on NCLB expectations as long as they set their own similar goals and established interventions for underperforming schools. Students still had to be tested annually and states had to establish "college and career ready standards," which were mostly up to their interpretation (Wardlow, 2016). Both ESEA and NCLB were finally renewed in 2015 with the new title Every Student Succeeds Act (ESSA) which now dictates expectations for state standards, standardized testing, teacher evaluations, allocation of resources and how states and districts are expected to respond to struggling schools and students. However, the ESSA also transferred control of these items to states and reduced bureaucratic control by the federal government.

Shifting Power to States

A major change from ESEA and NCLB to ESSA is the balance of power. ESSA allows states to determine their own state standards and create their own systems for teacher evaluation as well as to assess school performance, although they must still publish school report cards. Furthermore, states are now responsible for penalizing schools that underperform and determining how to support their lowest performing schools (Wardlow, 2016; Plans, 2015). ESSA provides many funding opportunities for innovation that encourages states to develop plans and accountability systems that result in higher rates of student success. Overall, the ESSA stresses the importance of state and district decision making in education by providing many opportunities for states to focus on areas specific to their student population.

Assessments

While ESSA maintains annual testing in mathematics and reading in grades 3-8 and an annual high school exam, states are given greater flexibility in what these assessments look like. States can create their own tests for grades 3-8, but they must use a nationally recognized test for high school and test data needs to be broken down by school and subgroups (Aragon et al., 2016; Klein, 2016). States are also expected to have at least 95% participation for all students and subgroups in state standardized tests, but they can develop their own opt-out laws (Aragon et al., 2016; Klein, 2016). However, states must implement improvement plans for schools with low participation rates (Aragon et al., 2016). ESSA does grant the freedom to use some computer based adaptive tests. The most impressive change for assessments under ESSA is for "states to pilot an innovative assessment system" where they can "design their assessment system by providing a broad, open-ended list of possible innovative assessments" that include "performance-based or competency-based assessments, portfolios or several interim tests rather than a single summative test" (Aragon et al., 2106, p. 7). ESSA requires states to assess their students annually, but the process for that is largely up to each state.

Indicators

Under ESSA, the indicators required on state accountability plans are expanded to include ELL proficiency and an "other" indicator that states can determine themselves. In addition to graduation rates, proficiency on state assessments, and an academic indicator, states need to include an indicator of student success or school quality (SQSS) that is "valid, reliable and comparable" (Aragon et al., 2016, p. 10). The suggestions for SQSS include "student engagement (e.g., chronic absenteeism), educator engagement, student access to and completion of advanced coursework..., postsecondary readiness...[and] school climate and safety" (Aragon et al., 2016, p. 10). While given less weight, the SQSS must be part of report cards for the districts and state, measured every year for all students and aggregated by subgroup, provide some method to differentiate between schools, and be based on the state plan's long-term goals (Aragon et al., 2016). While the "other" indicator cannot be significant enough to change a school's overall rating, the ESSA gives states the freedom to identify an indicator to target their specific student needs.

Subgroups

One of the largest changes from NCLB to ESSA is the treatment of English Language Learners (ELL). Not only does ESSA change terminology, but it also changes the expectations for assessment of and accountability for ELL students. States do have options for assessing ELL students and reporting their progress, but ESSA expects that ELL students are tested annually, and their assessment scores are included in report cards and accountability plan goals (Plans, 2015). State indicators must also include ELL progress toward proficiency in the English language, but students can remain in the EL subgroup for up to four years rather than the two years allowed under NCLB (Aragon et al., 2016). This is a marked change from NCLB that prioritizes

English proficiency while also returning control of the methods used to serve this subgroup back to the state.

Supporting struggling schools

A common thread between the ESEA, NCLB and ESSA is the focus on improving the performance of students in low performing schools. While states continue to be accountable for all schools failing to meet adequate yearly progress, they are no longer expected to use a prescribed technical assistance program. This is a key change to ESSA from NCLB and where MTSS comes in. States are in sole control of their plan to provide support for and improve low performing schools and "the U.S. Secretary of Education is explicitly prohibited from prescribing any specific strategies or activities a state or district may use" (Aragon et al., 2016, p. 15). In addition, states are required to "reserve up to 7 percent of Title I funds to support low-performing schools…[with] not less than 95 percent" of the reserved grants going to Local Education Agencies (LEAs) "on a formula or competitive basis" (Aragon et al., 2016, p. 15). States are expected to give priority to LEAs that are active in school improvement, demonstrate higher need and are committed to using the funds for improving student achievement. This means that schools actively implementing an MTSS and showing growth are given priority for Title I funds. One interesting item from ESSA is that "a pilot project will let 50 districts try out a weighted student-funding formula, combining state, local, and federal funds to better serve low-income students and those with special needs" (Klein, 2016). ESSA describes levels of support for low performing schools as comprehensive or targeted (Plans, 2015). Comprehensive support is reserved for "the lowest-performing 5 percent of all Title I schools…schools that graduate less than two-thirds of their students… [and] all public schools with a subgroup(s) that is performing at a level equal to student performance at the lowest 5 percent of schools" that are not responding to targeted support (Aragon et al., 2016, p. 16). Rather than districts being expected to intervene in low performing schools, "LEAs are expected to develop and implement, with stakeholder engagement, improvement plans for schools" needing both comprehensive and targeted support (Aragon et al., 2016, p. 16). In other words, they are expected to create a school improvement plan and implement a MTSS framework. Several areas within ESSA provide opportunities for local, state, and federal innovation in education. ESSA places greater emphasis on the opportunities for states to encourage local ownership of struggles and relevant change that meets the needs of the local population.

School engagement

Under ESSA, Title IV evolves to center on student and family engagement, and maintains, but scales back the emphasis on community engagement from previous legislation. New programs include Title IV-A which replaces the former Drug-Free Schools Program and focuses on student support and academic enrichment. This grant program centers on "well-rounded educational opportunities, safe and healthy students, [and] effective use of technology" (Aragon et al., 2016, p. 23). Title IV-E is the Family Engagement in Education Program and offers state grants for developing family engagement centers around the state. The programs that existed under Title IV-F in NCLB are consolidated under ESSA into the National Activities Program. This program "has four subsections: 1) education innovation and research; 2) community support for schools; 3) school safety and 4) academic enrichment" (Aragon et al., 2016, p. 24). Programs that continue from NCLB to ESSA are "21st Century Community Centers, charter school graphs and magnet school assistance," but funding is significantly cut for these programs (Aragon et al., 2016, p. 24). Changes in this section from the original ESEA identify a clear shift in focus that puts more emphasis on the local school and community highlighting the need for local control of programs that serve students and their families within a community. The changes also stress the importance of involving students and their families in academic decision making.

Teacher Quality and Evaluation

In addition to encouraging states to change the focus of curriculum, ESSA redirects the focus of teacher quality and evaluation. ESSA does away with NCLB's highly qualified expectations as well as tying teacher evaluations to student test scores (Klein, 2016). ESSA changes the expectations of a highly qualified teacher to be "that Title I program teachers meet applicable state certification and licensure requirements" (Aragon et al., 2016, p. 18). ESSA does expect states to add teacher quality to the school accountability report cards and the data should include the number and percentage of inexperienced school staff, emergency or temporary licenses, and teachers teaching out of field (Aragon et al., 2016). Additionally, ESSA requires that school accountability data be broken down further to compare high-poverty and low-poverty schools (Aragon et al., 2016; Plans, 2015). In terms of teacher evaluation, ESSA moves away from state-based evaluation systems and permits districts to develop them while also prohibiting the U.S. Secretary of Education from prescribing any specific evaluation systems of measures of effectiveness (Aragon et al., 2016). This gives schools an opportunity to evaluate their teachers based on initiatives they are implementing, such as a MTSS. ESSA uses Title II-A to provide grants to states to assist in obtaining and retaining effective teachers and school leaders in schools with prevalent poverty, minority populations as well as allows states to use Title II funds for competition-based grants that encourage districts to create, implement, and improve their evaluation systems (Aragon et al., 2016). ESSA pushes school districts to take control of their evaluation and recruitment of teachers and school leaders and encourages states to give districts the authority to do so.

State plans

While state accountability plans were also required under NCLB, ESSA makes some key changes to the requirements of these plans. Under ESSA, the Secretary of Education is not allowed to mandate items that states are responsible for such as curriculum standards, progress monitoring tools, state assessments, and indicators used for accountability. States are now free to develop their own state standards, but they must show that those standards align with the requirements of the next level of learning within the state (Aragon et al., 2016). One key change from NCLB to ESSA, is that state plans must have specific goals around the testing, proficiency, and graduation rates of ELL (Klein, 2016). High schools must include graduation rates in addition to the other indicators. Furthermore, states are expected to "identify and intervene in the bottom 5% of performers, and high schools where the graduation rate is 67% or less" (Klein, 2016, p. 6). In other words, states are required to implement a MTSS. ESSA maintains many of the accountability plan requirements from NCLB but provides states with greater flexibility on how they meet those requirements. Essentially, states can develop their own MTSS accountability procedures and action plan and use them to meet the ESSA accountability plan requirement. Much of the ESSA expectations are around data reporting rather than procedures and action steps.

Funding

A key change to funding under ESSA is the accountability for Title I funds. Due to the misappropriation of funds following the ESEA, schools have to limit the use of Title I funds to supplemental items and thoroughly account for every dollar spent (Aragon et al., 2016). Under ESSA, districts are only required to explain their methods for allocating Title I funds but must show that Title I funds are in addition to the state and local money the schools would receive even without the Title I designation (Aragon et al., 2016). The goal is that this will prevent districts from continuing ineffective programs and allow them to be more innovative with the funds. Also, states and districts need to identify schools with struggling subgroups and invest up to 7% of Title I funds in school improvement (Klein, 2016). The ESSA allocated funding specifically for the U.S. Department of Education to determine the "barriers and challenges students face in accessing digital educational content from home" as well as provide recommendations for states, districts, and schools to address these barriers (Wardlow, 2016). In addition, ESSA provides funding under Title IV for addressing 21st Century skills that include "School Climate and Discipline, Educational Technology, Family Engagement, Charter Schools, Accelerated and Blending Learning" (Wardlow, 2016). Title IV-E funds are now available for programs around family engagement in education. ESSA also takes the seven programs under ESEA's Title IV-F and consolidates them into "National Activities" that include "1) education innovation and research; 2) community support for schools; 3) school safety and 4) academic enrichment" (Aragon et al., 2016). While the funding is reduced for programs in these areas, states now have greater flexibility with how the funds are used. Funding has been redirected to focus on the key components of school improvement and the MTSS framework. A final key continuation from NCLB to ESSA is that states must maintain their own level of educational funding to access any federal funds. While federal funding is reduced in many areas, control of several areas is also returned to the states with the expectation that they will fund their own initiatives. Grants are available that encourage local control of key decisions in education. ESSA acknowledges the shortcomings of previous legislation and seeks to provide more opportunities for local innovation and problem solving.

School climate

A major change from NCLB to ESSA is the focus on school climate. The legislation revamps areas of Title-IV to emphasize safe and healthy students and family engagement (Aragon et al., 2016). Not only does school climate impact students' wellbeing and teacher and administrator retention, but researchers suggest that it is closely related to academic performance and graduation rates. High schools with higher school climate scores had significantly higher graduation rates (Buckman et al., 2021) and "a positive school climate can reduce the negative effects of poverty on academic achievement" (Darling-Hammond & Cook-Harvey, 2018, p. 13).

Furthermore, DePaoli et al. (2018) explains that high quality social and emotional learning (SEL) programs result in "an 11-percentage-point gain in achievement scores," a "decreased likelihood of dropping out of school," and "having high social and emotional competency is positively associated with increased high school graduation rates'' (p. 22). Darling-Hammond and Cook-Harvey (2018) suggest that a combination of an effective SEL program and a positive school climate can help close the achievement gap between Black, Latinx, and Native American students and their white peers by reducing the rates of punitive discipline, suspensions and expulsions that keep more minority students out of the classroom than their white counterparts. Hough et al. (2017) found that SEL and school culture and climate measures were accurate predictors of math scores. Under Title-IV, ESSA encourages states to focus efforts in the areas of SEL and school climate and even requires a certain percentage of funding to be dedicated to these areas. Research suggests that emphasis in this area can have a positive impact on student achievement and graduation rates, and both SEL and school climate are part of an effective MTSS framework.

According to a press release from the Office of the Press Secretary (2015), ESSA "rejects the overuse of standardized tests and one-size-fits-all mandates on our schools, ensures that our education system will prepare every child to graduate from high school ready for college and careers, and provides more children access to high-quality state preschool programs." The new bill includes requirements such as high academic standards, support for struggling students and schools, decentralization efforts to empower state and local leaders to develop systems for improvement, reduction in standardized testing requirements, and creation of research-based strategies to drive instruction (U.S. Office of the Press Secretary, 2015). A key component of the new legislation is the requirement for states and schools to develop a framework for supporting struggling schools and students. Both the legislation, and the national initiative resulting from it, focus on developing a MTSS for schools and students.

WHAT IS MTSS?

The goal of a MTSS framework is to combine previously disjoint student services under a single umbrella to address the various needs and barriers students have to learning. MTSS brings previous educational reforms such as Response to Intervention (RTI), Positive Behavioral Interventions and Supports (PBIS) and Social Emotional Learning (SEL) together to better utilize resources and more comprehensively address the educational needs of each student. Previously, these interventions were often provided in disconnected silos, and "given the strong alignment of several key features of RTI and PBIS, increasing attention has been placed on the need for an integrated model that braids initiatives for academic, behavioral and social-emotional needs into a single [MTSS]" (Eagle et. al, 2015, p. 161). RTI, PBIS, and SEL will not be discussed in detail in this chapter as they have already been thoroughly described in other chapters and readers can find additional texts on each of these intervention frameworks to learn more. Rather, it is important to highlight the shared elements between RTI and PBIS which form the foundation for all MTSS frameworks:

- Universal screening of all students, usually in reading and mathematics

Tier 1	Universal core instruction provided to all students, ideally effective for at least 80%
Tier 2	Targeted, supplemental, small group skill remediation for at-risk students (10-15%)
Tier 3	Intensive, individual interventions, for high-risk students (2-5%)

- Professional development in effective instructional practices
- Evidence-based interventions provided on a continuum
- Ongoing progress monitoring
- A team approach that uses data to drive decision making
- The use of implementation science

In addition to these common features, MTSS frameworks use tiered instruction and interventions to provide increasing levels of support as show in Table 1.

Rather than view the various student services provided by a school as independent, MTSS seeks to bring each child the combination of supports they need to thrive. The best way to think of MTSS is as a mind map – use data and observations to generate ideas that might help the student and simply connect and organize those ideas in a meaningful way. The connections and intersections are determined by the schedule of the student, parent input, and professional expertise of school staff as well as existing school structures and procedures. MTSS does not require a reinvention of the wheel, but instead a step back to analyze the whole child and bigger picture.

Moving beyond the concept of a mind map and into the idea of overarching schema, MTSS is founded in a growth mindset. Each school and student's plan can change and grow as necessary for them to be successful. It is important to define the initial plan, incorporating the essential support for the school or student's greatest areas of need – academic, social emotional, and/or behavioral - and implement the plan with fidelity for a period long enough to determine if it is working. Then, the team will meet again and determine the student's progress. If they are progressing, wonderful – keep going! If they are not progressing, then the team should make some changes to the plan and try again. In many cases, students will need more than one system of support. Rather than simply increasing support in a solitary area, MTSS pushes school staff to look at all the issues children face that may cause them to struggle and develop a plan to address them from all sides. Like wearing a mask, washing hands, and social distancing to prevent the spread of coronavirus – while each action is not highly effective alone, they are largely effective when used in combination.

It is important to note that each state and district are responsible for submitting their own framework for MTSS, and schools are required to submit an action plan to fulfill the district's framework. The best resources for understanding and implementing MTSS are the state Department of Education and the district's MTSS framework. However, the research indicates that there is a common structure to MTSS framework that results in successful implementation which ideally leads to increasing student performance. Bohanon et al. (2016) explains that MTSS is often most effective when implemented along with "a school improvement-by-design approach" and "a hallmark of improvement by design is collaboration between local education agencies and outside organisations (sic)" (p. 102). Therefore, it is useful to understand the structures necessary at each level within education to support the effective implementation of MTSS. Additionally, the implementation procedures of any one of the components of MTSS are similar to the implementation of an entire MTSS, so practices and procedures related to both RTI and PBIS will be included, with a focus on the expectations of ESSA: action plans, assessments, struggling schools, subgroup performance, school engagement, school climate, funding, and teacher quality.

BARRIERS TO IMPLEMENTING A MTSS

The struggle with a framework is that it is open to interpretation and does not provide actionable procedures. ESSA simply requires states, districts, and schools to create and submit their own framework and plans for supporting struggling schools and students and provides funding for research and technical assistance to support them in their efforts. Implementation of MTSS is largely left up to districts and individual schools, causing vast inconsistencies and highlighting a variety of barriers. The most consistent barrier to implementation of MTSS emphasized in the research is time (Mason at al., 2019, Arden & Benz, 2018). MTSS requires time for training, time to practice the skills learned in professional development, time to collaborate, time to create additional instructional resources, time to document student progress, time to review data, and time to meet with teams to discuss student progress. Especially when first learning the components of a MTSS, it is very time intensive. This does get better as staff perfect their process and reduce the number of students needing support, and technology can help, but it can initially be quite taxing. Additional barriers to successful MTSS implementation can include a lack of staff understanding, school culture and climate issues, leadership styles, organizational structure, policies, and procedures, staffing and funding (Arden & Benz, 2018; Mason et al., 2019; Duffy, 2018). The best method to combat barriers is to create a structure with clear procedures for implementation and follow the implementation science.

MTSS IN THE VIRTUAL ENVIRONMENT

Implementing MTSS in the virtual environment is similar to implementing MTSS in the brick-and-mortar environment. However, given the distant nature of the online environment, virtual schools are more prone to operating in silos and virtual teachers must make an explicit effort to connect with various departments within the school, colleagues, students, and families. On the contrary, the virtual environment can help overcome many barriers to implementing a MTSS. For example, providing interventions as well as collaborating with teachers and parents are far more flexible in the virtual environment. There are no bell schedules to determine when students need to move onto the next class and no scheduling limitations. Students and teachers can work on tasks at any given time throughout the day. This has both advantages and disadvantages. Teachers can quickly collaborate with other staff members through an instant message or email but may have a harder time reaching a family that has extracurricular activities throughout the day or parents working full time. Many families attend virtual school for its flexibility, so it may also be difficult to get students to attend targeted intervention lessons and be available for calls during school hours. The good news is that lessons can be recorded and viewed later, which allows teachers to create a bank of resources they can use right when students need them rather than having to keep pace with a prescribed program. Unfortunately, recorded lessons still prevent the teacher from directly observing students' performance and teachers must be intentional about gathering evidence that the student viewed the instruction. The ability to record lessons also allows teachers to save items from year to year and build upon their instructional toolkit. The lessons are also available for administrators to observe instruction at any time for evaluation or coaching purposes.

Another benefit to the virtual environment is that many virtual programs have a robust system for documentation. No more digging through file cabinets and spending hours reviewing cumulative folders. All communication and documentation regarding each student are usually readily accessible to pertinent stakeholders and no direct communication is required for a summary of interactions. Teachers can also build time for documentation into their daily schedules. If it is not available in a virtual program, it should be a school priority to establish a secure and comprehensive method for documentation.

It is much easier to individualize instruction in the virtual environment. Courses can be customized based on proficiency and the interventions students are working in. Additionally, there are excellent online intervention programs that are diagnostic and prescriptive. These programs are research-based, provide robust data, and create a completely customized instructional program for each student that should come with potential growth metrics. Teachers mainly have to ensure that students are engaging in the program and regularly monitor their progress. Most established online intervention programs also come with training and quality resources for grouping students and providing targeted interventions. The flexibility of the virtual environment means that students and teachers can spend as much or as little time as they need on particular topics to work to mastery, within the confines of the semester start and end dates.

Behavior issues are quite different in the virtual environment. Rather than being concerned with classroom conduct, virtual teachers are more concerned with successful academic behaviors that they cannot directly observe and general engagement in course work. This is not to say that there are no conduct issues; they are just not as prevalent in virtual school or there are pretty simple procedures for dealing with them. Truancy is a major concern as it is easy for students to simply not login and complete schoolwork, especially if they are not closely monitored by a guardian at home. Processes and procedures for monitoring student's completion of work, alerting staff to students that are not working, and addressing non-engaged students should be a priority for all virtual programs. Some states, like Florida, even fund virtual schools based on course completion.

The second side of behavioral concerns in the virtual environment are successful academic behaviors like time management, note taking, completing practice activities, study skills, and test taking strategies. Data can be gathered in these areas, but it takes more effort from both the student and teacher to collect and document. In the virtual environment, teachers do not have the opportunity to observe students for significant lengths of time and must use snapshots and conversations to ascertain students' needs. Guardians can be a valuable resource in this process, but the older students are, the more likely they are to be completing their schoolwork without supervision. Not only do teachers need to rely on families for information about what is happening at home, but also to communicate when they need help. While there are obvious red flags for serious concerns, small misconceptions can go unnoticed. It is also important to keep track of students that struggle intermittently, are at risk for low performance, or have needed support in the past so staff can intervene quickly. It can be helpful to have at least a few years of brick-and-mortar teaching experience before becoming a virtual teacher, so teachers have experience with recognizing and addressing common areas that students struggle with.

Finally, many virtual schools are free standing or fairly disconnected from the districts that authorize them. Virtual schools may not have access to the same resources as brick-and-mortar schools or they may need to put in more effort to get them. If a virtual school is authorized by a district, the school leader should work with the district liaison to gather all materials related to MTSS as well as ensure staff members are included in district training and collaboration opportunities. Even if the school has access to district resources like the framework, professional development, and manuals, they may be very tailored to the brick-and-mortar environment and need to be adjusted to the virtual world. Virtual school leaders and staff should have a thorough understanding of all available resources to be able to request them if they are working with a district or create them if they are not.

MTSS HIERARCHY

The ESSA, research on effective implementation of an MTSS, and research on the successful implementation of MTSS emphasize the need for different actions within each level of leadership in education to provide the resources necessary to enact school reform, implement MTSS and ultimately, successfully support improvements in student achievement. Printy and Williams (2015) explain that "RTI programming is top-down" while schools are considered loosely coupled organizations (p. 190). Elmore (2000) explains that loose coupling is the result of an early school structure "based on locally centralized school bureaucracy" which resulted in a technical core of teachers that is often buffered from outside influences by school level administration, which ultimately results in policies failing to create change at the classroom level (p. 6). McCart et al. (2015) describes this as "egg-crate structures" and "data-silos" where school structures "separate and isolate teachers in classrooms, preventing them from taking advantage of variations in individual classroom strategies and other teachers' specialized skill for the benefit of students," and district structures are "built around various federal and state funding streams rather than for making decision that support student academic and social achievement" (p. 253) Thus, it is useful to examine the structures of MTSS from a top-down model while exploring how school leaders can use implementation science to overcome loose coupling and spur collaboration amongst the levels to create tighter coupling of school and classroom practices to arrive at effective MTSS implementation that ultimately leads to greater student achievement. This is of particular importance in the virtual environment as departments can become highly specialized and collaboration requires an explicit effort. The next few sections will explore the resources necessary at each level to ensure an overall successful implementation down to the classroom level.

National and State Level

As legislation around supporting struggling schools and students has evolved, the U.S. Department of Education recognized the need for research and support to develop effective MTSS frameworks. Thus, the Office of Special Education Programs (OSEP) created technical assistance centers to guide school staff in selecting reliable universal screeners, establish procedures for meaningful progress monitoring, and gather research-based instructional strategies and resources for interventions (Balu et al., 2015). Morrison et al. (2014) explains that the role of technical assistance centers include:

- Consultation and coaching
- Collecting and disbursing the latest educational research and theories
- Guiding school leaders through the implementation process
- Professional development
- Creating and maintaining task forces
- Hosting conferences
- Assisting districts and schools with plan development

Researchers found that the use of a federally funded technical assistance center such as the Schoolwide Integrated Framework for Transformation (SWIFT) Center, resulted in greater MTSS implementation fidelity, especially when receiving support in Administrative Leadership (Choi et al., 2019). Especially for new and free-standing virtual schools, technical assistance in Site Leadership could be essential to implementing a MTSS.

In addition to federally funded technical assistance, ESSA also places responsibility on states to develop an MTSS framework and adopt principal elements to support it. First and foremost, states must develop an MTSS framework for use across the state. According to the U.S. Office of the Press Secretary (2015), "states must set ambitious targets to close student achievement gaps among subgroups of students in order to meet their goals" as well as identify indicators for annual yearly progress and provide reporting on school-level expenditures. Additionally, states are responsible for adopting state standards to support college and career readiness and establishing standardized testing for all students in the state. States must also be prepared to implement strategies for school improvement for schools failing to make adequate yearly progress that are not responding to district level interventions (U.S. Office of the Press Secretary, 2015). There are further legal requirements at the state level, but these reflect the structures most closely related to MTSS implementation of schools.

District Level

In addition to utilizing the frameworks and standards adopted by the state, school districts have their own set of responsibilities to serve the schools within their district. The ESSA "includes provisions that would require districts to use evidence-based models to support whole-school interventions in [low performing schools] and includes dedicated funding to support interventions in schools" (U.S. Office of the Press Secretary, 2015). Additionally, in consistently underperforming schools, "districts must mount targeted interventions and supports to narrow gaps and improve student achievement" (U.S. Office of the Press Secretary, 2015). School districts are also required to develop resources to directly support schools with MTSS implementation.

District leadership and involvement is essential to MTSS implementation and districts should form a leadership team to guide MTSS efforts (Freeman, 2015). In particular, these teams should focus on assessing schools' readiness for and commitment to MTSS, creating, scheduling, and facilitating training in academic and behavioral interventions, ensuring all district process, procedures and policies align with the essentials of MTSS, and evaluating the success of their endeavors (Freeman, 2015). Additionally, districts should be prepared to provide schools with procedures for implementing school reform, materials to build competency, organizational and leadership drivers, direct resources like curriculum, interventions and universal screeners, and funding and personnel to implement change. Choi (2019) and Bohanon et al. (2016) identify key leadership strategies for successful MTSS implementation as:

- Establishing a collaborative and innovative culture with a mutual mission and vision
- Facilitating professional development based on teacher needs
- Utilizing data to drive decision making
- Empowering schools to develop effective procedures and improve practices
- Working with school leaders to revise policies to support change

The views of district leadership are important to supporting schools in moving into a fully integrated MTSS framework. Superintendent involvement and the consistent message from all district consultants that MTSS is the vehicle for improving school performance is essential to breaking down any negative attitudes about MTSS and encouraging full implementation (Printy & Williams, 2015). Furthermore, providing schools with instructional coaches is vital to working effective MTSS practices into loosely coupled classrooms and establishing interventions as part of teachers' instructional routines. More simply, districts should operate as technical assistance centers for the schools they serve. Districts facilitate MTSS implementation by creating a training and consultation regimen, supporting the use of data to drive decision making by providing technology and robust systems for data collection and analysis, establishing networks of educators to elicit feedback and collaboration, and championing a shared mission and vision around MTSS (Freeman et al., 2015). It is vital for school districts to create an organizational structure that includes a MTSS leadership team with various stakeholders that focuses on organizing resources, reviewing data, and developing drivers essential for implementation while also building and maintaining connections to the individual schools using district personnel such as academic, behavioral, and MTSS coaches.

In addition to leadership, training, and collaboration, a vital piece to a successful MTSS action plan is quality core instruction. While states are responsible for establishing rigorous standards that align with college and career readiness, districts are accountable for making sure that schools have access to curriculum that aligns to the state standards and latest educational research as well as professional development in evidence based instructional practices (Printy & Williams, 2015). This could even be expanded a step further to include a concise curriculum with social emotional learning opportunities to support positive behaviors and real-life examples that students may encounter later in life (Mason et al., 2019). An effective curriculum implemented district wide can bypass some barriers to MTSS such as teacher competence, efficacy, and buy-in. Thus, allowing districts more time to focus on building content specific strategies, effective teaching practices, transformational leadership skills, and implementation drivers.

A significant role of school districts is to provide effective, ongoing professional development to schools and school leaders. Primarily, MTSS professional development should focus on conceptualizing the framework for MTSS, facilitating data fluency, building leadership skills, and effective MTSS implementation strategies. Specifically, "effective professional development opportunities should include a content focus, incorporate active learning, support collaboration, use models of effective practice, provide coaching and expert support, and offer feedback and reflection" (Mason, 2019, p. 209). Training regarding MTSS should also be tiered to support the unique needs of different stakeholders within the process and spiral annually based on the needs of the particular team. For example, first year training for a new school may only include school leadership and instructional staff that will be involved in a pilot. That training might focus on understanding MTSS, implementation drivers, data fluency, and effective Tier 1 instructional practices. The training for the same group the second year might focus more on Tier 2 and 3 interventions while a new group receives the first-year training.

Overall, districts need to gather national and state resources and conduct a needs assessment to determine which resources are necessary and important for their district and the schools they serve. Once needs have been identified, districts should be prepared to create and implement a leadership team with members operating directly in schools and offer and facilitate training and collaboration for district level coaches, school administrators, school leadership teams, MTSS coordinators, and classroom teachers.

School based leadership

Principals. Another common aspect of the research on MTSS implementation is the importance of effective school leadership. Printy and Williams (2015) found that "Integrated Leadership, which is positively related to high quality instruction and high student performance, occurs when the principal is a transformational leader who shares instructional leadership with teachers" (p. 201). Moreover, Choi et al. (2019) found that "to install, implement, and sustain a complex system like MTSS, [their findings on TA] suggest that even when TA is targeted to MTSS, meaningful change might not occur without the mediation of high-quality school leadership" (p. 24). Researchers suggest transformational leaders that implement strategies of effective instructional leadership, improve student's experiences and learning in the classroom (Choi et al., 2019). Principals at higher performing schools establish a vision with high expectations and promote a collaborative and respectful culture that emphasizes shared leadership, continuous learning, and ongoing improvement and innovation (Duffy, 2018). Furthermore, school leaders with high MTSS implementation fidelity use student data to create a sense of urgency and directly engage with building data fluency amongst school staff (Printy & Williams, 2015).

According to Choi et al. (2019):

Common elements of a school leadership role on these fidelity instruments are (a) administrator support with clear vision to drive implementation forward; (b) team members representing grade levels, school sub teams, and multidisciplinary educators including special education; (c) consistent regular meeting with agenda and minutes; (d) set clear action plans and monitor its progress; (e) decisions about resource allocation including staff responsibilities and professional development; and (f) ongoing monitoring and overall MTSS effectiveness with data. (p.16)

Regardless of the services provided at the state or district level, MTSS can only be fully implemented with effective school leadership. Principals must work to build their technical and adaptive skills as well as establish the vision, structure, culture, supports, and procedures to implement change. Principals are the gatekeepers to MTSS implementation.

School Leadership Team (SBLT). Researchers have found that schools with effective MTSS implementation share leadership amongst the staff and work together to achieve the shared vision (Printy & Williams, 2015; Arden & Benz, 2018). School leaders cannot implement a MTSS alone and it is essential for them to facilitate leadership amongst school staff, especially school-based coaches, intervention specialists, and MTSS coordinators. Specifically, Castillo et al. (2016) utilized three groups of stakeholders to implement school reform: "(a) project staff who developed and delivered professional development modules on RtI, (b) RtI coaches responsible for ongoing technical assistance and support to SBLTs and instructional staff, and (c) SBLT members responsible for facilitating RtI implementation in their schools" (p. 40). Minimally, schools should have a SBLT that includes the school leader, a school based instructional coach, and staff providing intensive Tier 2 and 3 interventions in both academics and behavior. Hollingsworth (2019) explains that a leadership team "alleviates the burden voluntary MTSS committees or lone ranger MTSS coordinators may feel by instead promoting the expectation that all staff members are part of the MTSS process, all staff members have a shared responsibility… and all staff members should build evolving toolboxes of interventions" (p. 37). In addition to a transformational leader, schools can improve the fidelity of MTSS implementation by utilizing a data-driven, collaborative, school-based team that includes a coordinator, data facilitator, and instructional leaders such as general education teachers, interventionists, counselors, and special education teachers.

MTSS Coordinator. Another consistency across the research is the utilization of a school based MTSS Coordinator. As discussed in the district roles, tiered professional development that includes coaching and feedback is the most efficient method for changing teacher attitudes and facilitating effective MTSS implementation (Mason et al., 2019). Having a school-based coordinator allows for training to be adapted to the school's needs and purposefully targeted for distinct groups of stakeholders supporting MTSS within the school. Depending on the size of the school and the number of students receiving interventions, this could be a full time or part time position. One school district in Minnesota makes use of existing positions by utilizing the expertise of school psychologists. In this district, school psychologists are responsible for making intervention recommendations, facilitating student success meetings, and monitoring the fidelity of interventions which includes observing and coaching interventionists (Duffy, 2018). In a study of schools in Colorado, Hollingsworth (2019) found that MTSS coordinators were also responsible for creating student profiles, facilitating data chats, and building collective teacher efficacy by providing regular staff development. To ensure that MTSS is identified and supported as necessary to school change, schools should designate an MTSS coordinator at least half time to support data review, implementation fidelity, and school-based training.

IMPLEMENTATION SCIENCE

As discussed early, MTSS is most effectively implemented along with school reform and districts and schools can use implementation science to overcome loose coupling and impact change at the school and classroom level. Thus, it is important to examine the common research-based stages of implementation prior to detailing the classroom practices related to MTSS. The structures put in place at the school and district level must align with evidence-based practices to create change and school reform.

Implementation drivers

In conjunction with the National Implementation Research Network (NIRN), Fixen et al. (2015) conducted research related to implementation and identified key implementation drivers. These drivers summarize the skills and structures that support successful framework implementation. Implementation Drivers include:

- Competency - skills and resources related to learning effective instructional practices, engaging in professional growth, and implementing interventions successfully
- Organization - components related to supporting and maintaining a collaborative and productive culture, allocating resources, and improving the efficiency and use of structures, process, procedures, and systems within an organization
- Leadership - technical skills such as management and accountability, and adaptive skills such as innovation, team building, and conflict resolution

There are entire texts on implementation science that go into much greater detail regarding implementation drivers, and technical assistance centers dedicated to helping schools build these skills, so they will not be discussed at length here. Readers should refer to these resources for more detailed information.

To effectively implement MTSS, both district and school leaders should seek to improve drivers of change while following the stages of implementation. While similar, the roles of the district and school leaderships differ within the actual framework of implementation due to the top-down structure of bureaucratic control. They must develop skills, collaborate above and below, and work within their level to create change and reach full implementation. As previously mentioned, implementation efforts are only as successful as the leaders driving them.

The Stages of Implementation

Successfully implementing a MTSS framework does not miraculously happen overnight. It can take years to reach full implementation and various parts of the district or school can be at different steps in the process. Since implementing a MTSS is such a massive undertaking, it is important to lean into the research and follow the tried-and-true stages that lead to successful implementation. Fixen et al. (2015) define the implementation stages as:

- Exploration: when an organization is assessing readiness to move forward with an implementation effort, analyzing data to determine needs, and is reviewing programs and resources to support interventions.
- Installation: the active selection of a new program, development of performance assessment processes, initial training efforts, and securing of resources.
- Initial Implementation: the early steps taken to introduce new processes, procedures, and programs around MTSS, which often involves feedback and adjustment as staff learn and integrate new changes into daily work.
- Full Implementation: when at least half of the staff working to implement a MTSS have improved their skills and are implementing interventions with elevated levels of success and fidelity

Exploration Stage. The initial stage of implementation is marked by the recognition that change is necessary and begins by collecting baseline data to better understand the needs of the school. School leaders should also take time to honestly reflect on their own knowledge and skills and take ownership and action to improve their professional capacity and skills related to implementation drivers. It is a promising idea to seek out mentorship from a school leader that has already developed those skills or has experience in implementation. Direct reports and other professionals with a direct working relationship can provide feedback on their observations of the school leader's professional capacity in action. To encourage and facilitate candid and supportive responses, it would be wise to collect the feedback anonymously. School leaders can prepare to support effective implementation by learning more about themselves, their state and district MTSS frameworks, their unique school needs (of both the staff and the student population), and the resources available to support them through the process.

At this point, schools are not yet working with a technical assistance provider or receiving explicit training (Freeman et al., 2015). The exploration stage is more about data collection and analysis. To determine what training is necessary, school leaders should focus on assessing the current status of implementation drivers within the school. This can be as simplistic as identifying what is going well and what needs to be improved within the school, or as thorough as itemized analysis of each skill within each category of implementation drivers. Data collection can be done through staff surveys as well as classroom and meeting observations. Fixen et al. (2015) recommend the use of an expert in Active Implementation Framework to conduct the assessments. It would be difficult for anyone to assess skills they do not understand or have not seen in practice. Even if a school leader can use existing resources to collect data, they may not be able to interpret them without support. Valid use of a rubric to analyze observations and assess needs as well as analyzing data as a team require training and experience.

Additionally, a deep dive into student data is vital for identifying and prioritizing the needs of the current student population. Use of the state department of education and school district's evaluation framework can help highlight key areas for improvement. A low school rating is like an alarm bell, signaling distress. However, school leaders still need to assess the situation and identify what sounded the alarm before they can begin addressing the problem. Once the priority populations are determined, school leaders need to dig even deeper to thoroughly comprehend what specifically needs to be addressed and collect information that will help them prioritize future actions to maximize growth with the fewest resources. State testing results may show that subgroups are underperforming, but more detailed information is required to identify the appropriate interventions.

Is a particular subgroup performing lower than another? What specific skills are they struggling with? Are there trends among all students at the school such as low reading comprehension or low data analysis skills? What are possible contributing factors to these issues? Which factors are within the school's control and what does the research say about the effectiveness of addressing those factors?

School leaders should question the data until they are out of ideas. Then, gather a team to ask more questions and generate more ideas. Solicit feedback from all stakeholders in a child's education: administrators, teachers, counselors, support staff, and parents. Part of this process should include identifying high fliers, the students and teachers of the students in the target populations with the greatest growth and achievement. Observing the traits and activities that are related to growth can help identify the skills and behaviors to foster through training and interventions. The teachers facilitating the greatest growth amongst their students will also be essential when seeking input and future school-based leadership. By the end of the exploration stage, school leaders should have identified the greatest areas of need within the school, the priority of addressing those needs, and the staff members that can help address them.

While data collection and analysis are taxing work, this is not to say that direct actions cannot also be taken within the exploration stage to build the foundation for the next steps of the implementation process. This stage is an excellent time for transparency. School leaders cannot singlehandedly transform a school and the obligation of improving performance does not rest solely on their shoulders. This is a prime time to work on building data fluency and foster a spirit of collaboration and innovation within the school culture. Actively working to establish and facilitate professional learning communities is a wonderful way to foster collaboration and the use of data to make decisions. Soliciting feedback and input from the staff not only models the behaviors this process aims to build, but also reveals the needs and views of those on the front lines. Just as MTSS seeks to address the whole child, it also seeks to support the whole school from school leader to classroom assistant, from student to parent, and from support staff to community agency. The exploration stage is the time to recognize what is going well and foster effective strategies throughout all aspects of the school, especially in the areas of instruction and using data to drive decision making. These strengths will become the school's foundation in the next stages.

It is especially important to note that the stages of implementation do not have timelines. A school cannot move from low performing to high performing overnight. It can take years to reach full implementation. Progress takes time and is rarely linear. Furthermore, school leaders cannot hope to accomplish this alone. They will need help from trained professionals and the support of all stakeholders.

Installation. In the second stage of implementation, it is time to detail the action steps to become a high performing school, establish a SBLT to guide the process, select a program to implement, and train school staff in the skills necessary to embrace and support a MTSS. A key element of MTSS is using data to drive decision making. This applies to all aspects of implementing MTSS, from determining which students are in need to evaluating the success of interventions to outlining action steps in each stage of the process. The data gathered during the exploration stage should highlight the greatest area of need. Now, it is time to work with district leadership, a technical assistance provider, and school staff to prioritize those needs in a way that supports the greatest growth with the fewest resources. When considering programs to implement, schools may want to focus on one item at a time, such as Tier 2 or Tier 3 instruction, a reading or math program, or building successful academic behaviors. The goal is to start small to scale up in the future. Ideally, there are now multiple professional learning communities working in both tandem and conjunction to provide feedback on selecting a program. The installation stage is where the work begins to build implementation driver skills to support a successful implementation in the next stage.

Additional steps of the installation stage include reviewing and collecting resources, creating connections and collaboration between different support services, and establishing procedures and routines. School leaders should work with the SBLT to review the budget and prepare to reallocate staff, as necessary. They should also create a plan to provide the instructional blocks necessary for interventions and prepare to adjust the schedule to allow time for students to get additional instructional time in those interventions. In addition to class schedules, school leaders also need to consider the time necessary for training, coaching, collaboration, and documentation. The SBLT should work on processes and procedures that ensure collaboration between services (including community resources), identifying the current instructional practices and routines that are in use, and creating a timeline for MTSS implementation. Processes and procedures might include data collection and review, student referral, staff expectations, task descriptions, instructional practices associated with the program, timelines for student identification, progress monitoring, and review, and collaboration. By the end of the installation stage, schools should have process guides, procedural manuals, collections of resources, a timeline for implementation and training, and the structure to implement a MTSS pilot program. It is particularly important to understand that none of these items will be set in stone. School staff should expect processes and procedures to ebb and flow with their feedback, school needs, and staffing.

During this stage, school leaders can continue to work on building data fluency and effective instructional practices. The stronger the foundation, the more effective implementation will be. School leaders should ensure school staff are collaborating, have the skills and materials they need for effective core instruction, and even consider utilizing a universal, research-based instructional model. Observing and interacting with staff regularly can give school leaders excellent opportunities to help them engage with staff in a positive way and support a professional school culture with a shared vision focused on innovation and collaboration that is essential to MTSS and overall school improvement.

Initial Implementation. While it can feel extremely exciting and rewarding to reach this stage, the work continues. In this stage, the selected program is finally reaching the target population. Many of the actions in this stage will be explicitly defined by the selected program while many of the drivers established in the installation stage will continue. First and foremost, expect resistance. Not only are staff learning and trying to comprehend a new program, but they are also adjusting a new way of doing things. This process is hard. It is important that school leaders continue to facilitate collaboration and empower the members of the SBLT and practitioners while also being open to feedback and change. There will be changes and adjustments. It is particularly important to work with the implementation coaches and experts to determine what changes are reasonable. Effective professional development that includes learning skills, time to practice skills, and coaching based on observations is absolutely vital in this stage. School leaders need to remember to lean into the support system and resources they gathered in previous stages and continue to focus on using the data to drive decision making.

Schools remain in the initial implementation stage until the selected program reaches its full capacity. This may mean that the program expands schoolwide or to Tier 3 within a specific content area. Initial implementation is the longest stage in the process because as one group works to implement or improve a program, the next group is learning the skills to prepare to implement the program. Tiered training that provides specialized instruction to separate groups within the schools can be extremely helpful. Just as tiered interventions work to support the varying needs of students within the school, tiered professional development builds the relative professional capacity of each staff member. To make sound decisions following initial implementation, it is important to track progress as well observe implementation fidelity. These items will be used to inform decisions and can change the future path of a selected program. In this stage, the SBLT will determine if the initial pilot program was successful and work to identify the next group for the program or decide that it was not and choose to change course. Regardless, the goal is to improve and expand each year. The SBLT should work with coaches and implementers to improve processes, refine procedures, and build on routines until the new program feels comfortable.

Full Implementation. At this point, the program is fully embedded into all structures within the school. Veteran staff are fully trained, new teachers are instructed and mentored when they are hired (and screened to be sure they will support the program), and the program is effectively improving student outcomes. In full implementation, it becomes difficult to separate the program from the school culture. Schools are considered to be in this stage when at least 50% of those selected to implement the program are doing so with significant fidelity (Freeman et al., 2015). Now, the processes and procedures are built into all staff training and expectations, and there is accountability for implementing the program.

Even in full implementation, school staff should still continue to improve processes and procedures as well as adjust to changes. The SBLT should expect and anticipate changes and prepare to adapt as necessary. At any given time, schools can experience changes in legislation, funding, structure, staffing, technology, leadership, curriculum, and the needs of the student population. When a person chooses to be an educator, they make a commitment to lifelong learning. Education is an ever-evolving field, and the work is never done.

TEACHERS AND INTERVENTION SPECIALISTS

Classroom practices

Much of MTSS is administrative, but the real work happens with the actions of teachers and those working directly with students to implement interventions. There are skills teachers should have to ensure they are prepared to implement MTSS. Effective classroom practices for successful MTSS implementation include regularly reviewing student data to make instructional decisions, utilizing evidence-based instructional practices, following the recommended logical structure of tiered interventions, and regular progress monitoring and evaluation of students receiving tiered support. Essentially, the final steps of MTSS implementation come down to the choices, skills, and practices of classroom teachers. It is on teachers to actively learn, practice, and improve the skills shared in MTSS professional development.

Researchers have highlighted two important classroom practices for effective MTSS implementation: effective interventions and collaboration. In schools with successful MTSS implementation, general education teachers, interventionists, and special education teachers work seamlessly together to serve all students (Duffy, 2018; Freeman et al., 2015; Harn et al., 2015; Printy & Williams, 2015). As many teachers do not feel confident in their ability to identify and use evidence-based instructional practices or identify and implement Tier 1 interventions, instructional coaches, special education teachers, and intervention specialists can support general education teachers in the development of effective Tier 1 practices (Bouck & Cosby, 2019, p. 37). Many schools, especially those with large student populations, utilize an interventionist for academic support at Tier 2 and Tier 3. As an effective Tier 1 curriculum will serve approximately 80% of students, most schools will need the support of an interventionist to provide Tier 2 and 3 interventions to 20% of students outside of the core Tier 1 curriculum. In addition, the regular progress monitoring, individualization, and implementation fidelity associated with more rigorous interventions, and that are essential for effective implementation, require a significant amount of time. Staff providing interventions will not be able to support the same student load as those providing only core curriculum. Thus, the use of a trained specialist to provide interventions can overcome many barriers and has shown to be effective for both MTSS implementation and growth in student achievement, academically and behaviorally.

PROGRAMS

The ultimate goal of implementing an MTSS framework is improving student achievement. It is essential that schools implement programs with documented evidence for accomplishing this goal. While technical research centers and established districts may have a collection of research-based programs to share with schools, free standing virtual schools may not have easy access to these programs. It is important that school leaders and staff have an awareness of the types of programs that result in significant and lasting increases in student performance. Reviews of data for students that were not successful in school identified academic performance and educational engagement as key contributing factors (Jerald, 2006). Thus, these are excellent areas to focus initial intervention efforts to have the greatest impact on student and school success. This section will discuss diverse types of academic and engagement intervention efforts at each instructional level.

Early Childhood

Early childhood education builds the foundation for all future learning. Students that struggle in their earliest years are at greater risk for remaining behind their peers and dropping out of school (Jerald, 2006). However, a meta-analysis of experimental studies conducted over more than a 50-year period found that participating in early childhood education can reduce special education placements, increase grade level promotion rates, and improve high school graduation rates (McCoy et al., 2017). Examples of successful programs include, but are not limited to, the Child-Parent Center Education program in Chicago and the nationwide Head Start program (Murnane, 2013). In a study to identify the early academic skills that lead to later success, Ribner et al. (2017) found that pre-kindergarten math performance and executive functioning skills were associated with later mathematics and reading ability. Whether implementing a full program or focusing on mathematics through RTI or executive functioning skills through PBIS, intervention efforts in early childhood education can create results that last into adulthood.

Elementary school

Ribner et al. (2017) explains that almost 75% of students who are below proficient on state standardized tests in 3rd grade will remain below proficient into high school and are significantly more likely to drop out of high school. Jerald (2006) also found that students that dropped out had substantially lower grades in fourth grade than their peers that graduated from high school. While there are many years from third to twelfth grade, early student performance is a strong predictor of eventual graduation, especially in the area of mathematics. If working within a k-12 school, elementary should be an initial focus of MTSS efforts. In an analysis of the Tennessee Student/Teacher Achievement Ratio initiative, Murnane (2013) found that students with smaller, high-quality kindergarten classrooms were more likely to attend college and placement in these classes led to higher graduation rates for black males and students with low socioeconomic backgrounds. For elementary schools, an initial step in the school improvement process could be to focus on building kindergarten teacher quality through hiring practices and training and reducing kindergarten class sizes by adjusting resource allocations.

Middle grades

Research suggests that transition years, from fifth grade to sixth grade and eight grade to ninth grade, are pivotal to eventual graduation (Jerald, 2006). A cohort study from Massachusetts that compared all students, dropouts, and graduates, found that "most dropouts never made up the ground they lost during 6th and 9th grade," and "later dropouts experienced a dip in attendance during 6th grade that continued to accelerate until the end of middle school and into high school" (Jerald, 2006, p. 10). Furthermore, in a cohort study in Philadelphia, researchers found that students with low attendance, poor classroom behavior, or a failing grade in math or English in sixth grade had incredibly low chances of graduating from high school. When comparing middle school (grades 6-8) to junior high (grades 7-9), researchers discovered that changing schools in grades 5 and 8 had negative impacts on high school graduation rates. Since enrollment in virtual school programs are not as limited by physical addresses and many virtual schools are k-8 or k-12, implementing efforts to retain students from 5th to 6th grade and 8th to 9th grade can have positive impacts on student performance and engagement. In addition, Sarasota County Schools created criteria to more purposely select eighth grade students for Algebra 1 placement and achieved nearly 100% proficiency among eighth grade students on the state test (Schacter, 2013). The district also created their own computer-based benchmark and offers a two-week summer program to students that do not assess proficient on the Algebra 1 test to help them prepare for a retake (Schacter, 2013). Schools in California found increased Algebra 1 performance amongst students using the Houghton Mifflin Harcourt Fuse online textbook and improved success amongst Hispanic students using the Explicit Direct Instruction program from DataWorks (Schacter, 2013). MTSS efforts at middle school should begin in sixth grade and focus on academic interventions in math and English and building school engagement through family involvement, teaching effective classroom behaviors, and supporting school attendance.

High school

It is especially important for high school student performance and graduation rates that interventions begin long before high school, but some schools have found success with high school intervention programs, especially those targeted at ninth grade success and mathematics performance. Additionally, many virtual schools have an advantage because they are schools of choice. Researchers have found that providing students with choices for high school can lead to increased graduation rates, especially for low income and minority students (Carnoy, 2017; Murane, 2013).

School leaders can capitalize on this advantage by focusing on student success in ninth grade and academic interventions to increase Algebra 1 pass rates.

Freshman Success. Student success in ninth grade is pivotal to eventual graduation. First, ninth grade students tend to struggle the most, academically and behaviorally (McCallumore & Sparapani, 2010). Second, researchers have found that students that fall behind in ninth grade are significantly less likely to graduate from high school than their peers with strong academic success in their first year of high school (Easton et al., 2017; Heppen et al., 2017; Jerald, 2006). There are several intervention models that have effectively improved academic performance and graduation rates. The Talent Development High School Model where ninth grade students are placed in cohorts of students taught by the same set of teachers and enrolled in a "Freshman Seminar" course, found that this intervention "increases the graduation rate of on-time graduation by 8 percentage points" (Murnane, 2013, p. 412). Herlihy & Quint (2006) add that Talent Development Model schools have block scheduling that allow students to take eight credits per year rather than the traditional six to seven, giving students more opportunities to earn credits for graduation. Adding additional courses is even easier to do in the virtual environment.

A similar model, the Ninth Grade Success Academy offers intensive "catch-up" courses for elective credit that support students in building their math and reading skills before taking required courses for graduation like English I and Algebra 1 (Herlihy & Quint, 2006). These courses resulted in a 25-percentage point increase in Algebra 1 pass rates (Herlihy & Quint, 2006, p. 4). The freshman transition courses in Georgia and the first-year academies in Kentucky result in similar improvements in Algebra 1 pass rates and graduation rates (Buckman et al., 2021; McCallumore & Sparapani, 2011). Another program, First Things First, found that theme-based, small learning communities that students remain a part of through high school lead to increased attendance rates and 6 fewer dropouts for every 100 students (Herlihy & Quint, 2006). Mac Iver (2011) found that a dropout prevention program that provides students with an adult advocate and a smaller and more holistic and personalized learning environment led to more positive feelings about school, improved attendance, and improved graduation rates when compared to peers not in a similar program. Ninth grade interventions that create a community within a school and focus on the transition from middle school to high school by increasing engagement and building foundational academic and behavioral skills can be an excellent initial focus area for all high schools.

Mathematics and Credit Recovery. Researchers in a study conducted by the U.S. Department of Education "found that 80 percent of high school dropouts cited their inability to pass Algebra 1 as the primary reason for leaving school" (Schacter, 2013, p. 43). While there are effective strategies for improving mathematics pass rates, there are also effective interventions for students that are not successful on their first attempt. Credit recovery courses are perfect for helping students make up credits and increasing pass rates in the virtual environment. Many online credit recovery programs are diagnostic and prescriptive, allowing students to focus only on the skills they have not yet mastered when repeating a course. DePaoli et al. (2018) found that high schools with higher graduation rates were more likely to offer credit recovery courses than high schools with lower graduation rates. In a study focused on mathematics credit recovery and comparing online instruction to face-to-face instruction in Florida, Hart et al. (2019) explained that students repeating a math course by taking a credit recovery mathematics course virtually "are 4.7 percentage points more likely to pass their remedial course, 1.7 percentage points more likely to jointly take and pass future same-subject courses, and 6.5 percentage points more likely to be observed in a projected final term in senior year, as compared with peers who retake coursework in face-to-face settings" (p. 8). Adding credit recovery courses is an efficient, low resource option for high schools seeking to improve pass and graduation rates.

CONCLUSION

The concept of MTSS is embedded in legislation, the principles of school improvement, and the very tenements of education. While the concept of an open-ended framework that can support innovation in a wide variety of areas can seem overwhelming, it is actually an attempt to pull the gears of student success together into a single, efficient machine. No single program or intervention is going to meet the needs of all stakeholders, so it is important to rely on the data, collaboration, and continuous problem solving and improvement to fully embrace a MTSS. Following the stages of implementation science and improving implementation drivers can guide educational organizations and leaders through the process of putting MTSS into practice and, ultimately, improving school performance and student outcomes. There is an array of evidence-based programs and experts that can guide school leaders through identifying and addressing the needs of their students and schools, but it is important that all educators are aware of the key components of MTSS, the processes through which a MTSS framework is implemented, and why utilizing a MTSS is so vital for school and student performance. The concepts of a MTSS remain consistent regardless of the school setting, but there are unique needs, advantages, and challenges within each type of program. Virtual schools can leverage technology to simplify many processes and procedures within a MTSS framework; however, there are many routines that are vastly different in the online world. It requires dedication and innovation to take concepts written for brick-and-mortar schools and adapt them to the virtual environment. The bright side of both the ESSA and a MTSS framework is that they are designed to be adapted to the environment in which they operate. Regardless of where a school is in the process, start somewhere and keep going.

REFERENCES

Aragon, S., Griffith, M., Wixom, M. A., Woods, J., & Workman, E. (2016). *ESSA: Quick guides on top issues.* Education Commission of the States. Retrieved from https://eric.ed.gov/?id=ED567801

Arden, S. V., & Benz, S. (2018, Fall). The science of RTI implementation: The how and what of building multi-tiered systems of support. *Perspectives on Language and Literacy*, 21–25.

Balu, R., Zhu, P., Doolittle, F., Schiller, E., Jenkins, J., & Gersten, R. (2015). Evaluation of response to intervention practices for elementary school reading. National Center for Education Evaluation and Regional Assistance, Institute of Education Sciences, U.S. Department of Education. NCEE 2016-4000.

Bohanon, H., Gilman, C., Parker, B., Amell, C., & Sortino, G. (2016). Using school improvement and implementation science to integrate multi-tiered systems of support in secondary schools. *Australasian Journal of Special Education*, *40*(2), 99–116. doi:10.1017/jse.2016.8

Bouck, E. C., & Cosby, M. D. (2019). Response to intervention in high school mathematics: One school's implementation. *Preventing School Failure*, *63*(1), 32–42. doi:10.1080/1045988X.2018.1469463

Buckman, D. G., Hand, N. W., & Johnson, A. (2021). Improving high school graduation through school climate. *NASSP Bulletin*, 5–24. doi:10.1177/0192636521993212

Carnoy, M. (2017). *School vouchers are not a proven strategy for improving student achievement: Studies of US and international voucher programs show that the risks to school systems outweigh insignificant gains in test scores and limited gains in graduation rates.* Economic Policy Institute. Retrieved from https://eric.ed.gov/?id=ED579337

Castillo, J. M., Dorman, C., Gaunt, B., Hardcastle, B., Justice, K., & March, A. L. (2016). Design research as a mechanism for consultants to facilitate and evaluate educational innovations. *Journal of Educational & Psychological Consultation*, *26*(1), 25–48. doi:10.1080/10474412.2015.1039125

Choi, J. H., McCart, A. B., Hicks, T. A., & Sailor, W. (2019). An analysis of mediating effects of school leadership on MTSS implementation. *The Journal of Special Education, 53*(1), 15–27. doi:10.1177/0022466918804815

Darling-Hammond, L., & Cook-Harvey, C. M. (2018). *Educating the whole child: Improving school climate to support student success.* Learning Policy Institute. Retrieved from https://eric.ed.gov/?id=ED606462

DePaoli, J. L., Balfanz, R., Atwell, M. N., & Bridgeland, J. (2018). Building a grad nation: Progress and challenge in raising high school graduation rates. Annual Update 2018. *Civic Enterprises.* Retrieved from https://eric.ed.gov/?id=ED585524

Duffy, J. (2018). Implementation of response to intervention (RTI) and a multi-tiered system of support (MTSS): A case study examination of one school district in Minnesota. *Culminating Projects in Education Administration and Leadership,* 40. Retrieved from https://repository.stcloudstate.edu/edad_etds/40

Eagle, J. W., Dowd-Eagle, S. E., Snyder, A., & Holtzman, E. G. (2015). Implementing a multitiered system of support (MTSS): Collaboration between school psychologists and administrators to promote systems-level change. *Journal of Educational & Psychological Consultation, 25*(2-3), 160–177. doi:10.1080/10474412.2014.929960

Easton, J. Q., Johnson, E., & Sartain, L. (2017). *The predictive power of ninth-grade GPA.* University of Chicago Consortium on School Research. Retrieved from http://www.hsredesign.org/wp-content/uploads/2018/07/Predictive-Power-of-Ninth-Grade-Sept-2017-Consortium.pdf

Elmore, R. F. (2000). *Building a new structure for school leadership.* The Albert Shanker Institute.

Fixsen, D.L., Blase, K. A., Naoom, S. F., & Duda, M. A. (2015). Implementation drivers: Assessing best practices. *NIRN, 5*(2015).

Freeman, R., Miller, D., & Newcomer, L. (2015). Integration of academic and behavioral MTSS at the district level using implementation science. *Learning Disabilities (Weston, Mass.), 13*(1), 59–72.

Harn, B., Basaraba, D., Chard, D., & Fritz, R. (2015). The impact of schoolwide prevention efforts: Lessons learned from implementing independent academic and behavior support systems. *Learning Disabilities (Weston, Mass.), 13*(1), 3–20.

Hart, C. M., Berger, D., Jacob, B., Loeb, S., & Hill, M. (2019). Online learning, offline outcomes: Online course taking and high school student performance. *AERA Open, 5*(1). Advance online publication. doi:10.1177/2332858419832852

Herlihy, C. M., & Quint, J. (2006). *Emerging evidence on improving high school student achievement and graduation rates: The effects of four popular improvement programs. Issue Brief.* National High School Center. Retrieved from https://eric.ed.gov/?id=ED501076

Hollingsworth, S. M. (2019). Multi-tiered system of supports as collective work: A (re)structuring option for middle schools. *Current Issues in Middle Level Education, 24*(2). Advance online publication. doi:10.20429/cimle.2019.240204

Jerald, C. D. (2006). *Identifying potential dropouts: Key lessons for building an early warning data system. A dual agenda of high Standards and high graduation rates.* Achieve, Inc. Retrieved from https://eric.ed.gov/?id=ED499838

Klein, A. (2016). States, districts will share more power under ESSA. *Education Digest, 81*(8), 4. https://search.proquest.com/openview/dc7a395e4f446ec3c5b07b91d380a298/1.pdf?pq-origsite=gscholar&cbl=25066

Mac Iver, M. A. (2011). The challenge of improving urban high school graduation outcomes: Findings from a randomized study of dropout prevention efforts. *Journal of Education for Students Placed at Risk, 16*(3), 167–184. doi:10.1080/10824669.2011.584497

Mason, E. N., Benz, S. A., Lembke, E. S., Burns, M. K., & Powell, S. R. (2019). From professional development to implementation: A district's experience implementing mathematics tiered systems of support. *Learning Disabilities Research & Practice, 34*(4), 207–214. doi:10.1111/ldrp.12206

McCallumore, K. M., & Sparapani, E. F. (2010). The importance of the ninth grade on high school graduation rates and student success. *Education Digest, 76*(2), 60.

McCart, A. B., Sailor, W. S., Bezdek, J. M., & Satter, A. L. (2014). A framework for inclusive educational delivery systems. *Inclusion, 2*(4), 252–264. doi:10.1352/2326-6988-2.4.252

McCoy, D. C., Yoshikawa, H., Ziol-Guest, K. M., Duncan, G. J., Schindler, H. S., Magnuson, K., Yang, R., Koepp, A., & Shonkoff, J. P. (2017). Impacts of early childhood education on medium-and long-term educational outcomes. *Educational Researcher, 46*(8), 474–487. doi:10.3102/0013189X17737739 PMID:30147124

Morrison, J. Q., Russell, C., Dyer, S., Metcalf, T., & Rahschulte, R. L. (2014). Organizational structures and processes to support and sustain effective technical assistance in a state-wide multi-tiered system of support initiative. *Journal of Education and Training Studies, 2*(3), 129–137. doi:10.11114/jets.v2i3.415

Murnane, R. J. (2013). US high school graduation rates: Patterns and explanations. *Journal of Economic Literature, 51*(2), 370–422. doi:10.1257/jel.51.2.370

Plans, A. (2015). The every student succeeds act: Explained. *Education Week*. Retrieved from https://www.ride.ri.gov/Portals/0/Uploads/Documents/Information-and-Accountability-User-Friendly-Data/ESSA/CoP/Education_Week_Every_Student_Succeeds_Act_Explained.pdf

Printy, S. M., & Williams, S. M. (2015). Principals' decisions: Implementing response to intervention. *Educational Policy, 29*(1), 179–205. doi:10.1177/0895904814556757

Ribner, A. D., Willoughby, M. T., & Blair, C. B. Family Life Project Key Investigators. (2017). Executive function buffers the association between early math and later academic skills. *Frontiers in Psychology, 8*, 869. doi:10.3389/fpsyg.2017.00869 PMID:28611712

Schachter, R. (2013). Solving our algebra problem: Getting all students through algebra I to improve graduation rates. *District Administration, 49*(5), 43–46. https://eric.ed.gov/?id=EJ1013968&source=post_page-----------------------

U. S. Office of the Press Secretary. (2015, Dec. 2). *Fact sheet: Congress acts to fix no child left behind.* Retrieved from https://obamawhitehouse.archives.gov/the-press-office/2015/12/03/fact-sheet-congress-acts-fix-no-child-left-behind

U.S. Dept. of Education. (2020). *Every Student Succeeds Act.* Retrieved from https://www2.ed.gov/policy/elsec/leg/essa/index.html

Wardlow, L. (2016). *The every student succeeds act in historical context.* Pearson. Retrieved from www.pearsoned.com/every-student-succeeds-act-historical/

Chapter 12
Perceptions of Faculty of Sport Sciences Students on Distance Education During the COVID–19 Period:
Perceptions of University Students on Distance Education

Bijen Filiz
ⓘD https://orcid.org/0000-0001-5863-3861
Afyon Kocatepe University, Turkey

Ferman Konukman
ⓘD https://orcid.org/0000-0002-9508-8874
Qatar University, Qatar

Ertan Tüfekçioğlu
ⓘD https://orcid.org/0000-0002-9660-5009
King Fahd University of Petroleum and Minerals, Saudi Arabia

Neslihan Arıkan Fidan
ⓘD https://orcid.org/0000-0003-2579-7418
Gazi University, Turkey

ABSTRACT

The purpose of this study was to determine the perceptions of the sport sciences students on distance education in terms of the advantages, disadvantages, difficulties, concerns, and suggestions during the COVID-19 period. The mixed method was used in the study. Participants were 312 volunteer university students. A questionnaire and an open-ended question were used. Results indicated that male students considered the advantages of distance education more important. In addition, students studying in the departments of Coaching Education and Physical Education and Sport Teaching considered the disadvantages of distance education

DOI: 10.4018/978-1-7998-8077-6.ch012

more important. Female students considered the difficulties of distance education less important, and students who prefer distance education had more concerns about distance education. In conclusion, students suggested extending the duration of the lesson, strengthening the technology and internet infrastructure, conducting the lessons interactively, teaching the lessons more efficiently by the teachers, and standardizing the lesson practices.

INTRODUCTION

Technology in the information age has provided many important benefits to educational programs. Technology can be assessed as an effective tool in the distribution of information (Orakcı & Gelişli, 2021; Orakcı, 2020). Technology in the information age has provided many important benefits to educational programs. Although traditional ways of instruction are commonly accepted in teaching and learning environments, many higher education institutions have started to implement distance education and technology as an instructional tool. The introduction of computers into the business world in the mid-1950s made essential changes for future perspectives of the education because the purpose of the first generation of computers had been mainly scientific. Historically, the early 1960s saw the integration of computers into both business and scientific life. However, this was only related to limited applications and functions. Later, microprocessors were used to build microcomputers in the mid-1970s and the first personal computers (PCs) were introduced for individual use in business and in education. As a result, plenty of educational and business software was also developed. In this period, the computer attracted the imagination and attention of educators to see how it could improve learning and thinking. (Bull et al., 1989; Bull, Sigmon & Shidisky, 1991; Harris & Anderson, 1991; McKethan, Everhart & Sanders, 2001; Wagonner, 1992; Wilkinson et al., 1999).

The history of computer-based instruction indicated that this type of technology existed for more than 70 years. The first one was a flight simulator for pilots at the Massachusetts Institute of Technology (MIT) in 1950 (Lockard, Abrams & Many, 1997). One of the first interventions for educational technology called as PLATO (Programmed Logic for Automatic Teaching), was developed in the 1960s at the University of Illinois (Hammond, 1972). This program aimed to teach different educational subjects such as nursing, geometry, and pharmacology. In addition to this, The National Science Foundation provided $10 million grant for PLATO and TICCIT (Time-Shared Interactive Computer-Controlled Information Television System) in 1970. TICCIT was invented at Brigham Young University and MITHE Corporation. The major purpose of this intervention was to develop a quality teaching and learning using computers and television for community colleges courses in mathematics and English (Merril, Schneider & Fletcher, 1980). Consequently, the results of research conducted by the Educational Testing Service indicated that PLATO provided significant academic performance in chemistry, biology, and English, Moreover, TICCIT also improved significant results for community college students in English and Mathematics. Finally, research indicated that both PLATO and TICCIT students had positive attitudes toward computer-based education (Steinberg, 1991).

Due to the COVID-19 outbreak, majority of the countries around the world have forced serious restrictions on social life and educational practice to tackle the issue of COVID-19. Such as social isolation and restrictions on travel, sports, leisure activities, work, and school attendance. As a result, schools in all countries were suspended. The teaching and learning process was provided by using distance learning education. The infrastructure and resources of all schools in the countries were mandated to prevent the epidemic, to minimize the learning issues while the epidemic continues, and to ensure the continuity of learning. (Filiz & Konukman, 2020). Therefore, COVID-19 has changed the face of education in many different ways. Before the mandatory change to virtual rather than convenience traditional instruction, researchers argued that online programs were inadequate in terms of quality delivery (Montelongo, 2019; Morris, 2018).

The current COVID-19 pandemic has mandated not only K-12 schools but also higher education to consider how to apply quality and equitable education using distance education programs. Supporters of distance education indicated several strengths of online education such as flexibility for traditional and non-traditional students, low tuition costs for those in higher education, promoting the diversity of the student body with accessible education for students (Deming et al., 2015). In addition, supporters emphasized that more classes can be provided in the online setting while others believed student enrollment could be improved in distance education compared to traditional ones (Montelongo, 2019). However, regardless of the instructional method, quality teaching skills must be applied for student involvement, retention, and academic success.

Up to date, several distance education platforms provided prerecorded lectures and webinars such as Coursera, edX, Khan Academy, and Udemy. Recently, several institutions started to create online teaching modules that physical education teachers can use for distance learning in their schools. These modules provided sport specific content related videos, assessment techniques, and teaching solutions compared to the traditional school environment. For example, Virginia Tech founded a virtual university campus in 1993 and one of the first online-distance education master degree started in Physical Education Pedagogy. This was a problem based learning program and called "electronic" master in Physical Education. Recently, there are many graduate online programs in Physical Education Pedagogy. Besides, Massive Open Online Courses (MOOC) became very common in this century and these online courses provided free distance education in higher education institutions (Beard & Konukman, 2020).

The distance education process can be thought of as a process that affects institutions, teachers, students, parents and other learning partners. The need for a technological infrastructure, organization of learning environments, students' taking responsibility for learning, lesson preparations of teachers and technology level of use, the level of parents to follow the process will affect the efficiency of distance education (Durnalı, Orakcı, & Özkan, 2018; Durnalı, Orakcı, & Aktan, 2019). In Turkey, distance education programs in Physical Education Pedagogy in universities came to the forward with the pandemic process. This was a first in formal education in this field. Initially, there was no scientific data on the effects of distance education in Turkey. However, recently, studies have been carried out for university students regarding distance education (Akgün, 2020; Aktaş et al., 2020; Altuntaş et al., 2020; Bingöl, 2020; Buluk & Equalti, 2020; Genç, Zengin & Yönetim, 2020; Gürler, Uslu & Daştan, 2020; Orçanlı & Bekmezci, 2020; Saltürk & Güngör, 2020; Yakar & Yakar, 2021). However, it has been observed that there are very few studies on the students of the Faculty of Sport Sciences (Aktaş et al., 2020). The pandemic process still continues. It is thought that it is important to determine the effects of distance education, which suddenly appears with the pandemic process, on sport science students, and the data obtained from this study will contribute to updates for distance education.

Research objective

The purpose of this research was to determine the perceptions of the sport science students studying at the Faculty of Sports Sciences about distance education during the COVID-19 period. In this context, the research questions are as follows:

1. What are the students' opinions on the advantages of distance education by gender?
2. What are the students' opinions on the disadvantages of distance education according to the department?
3. What are the students' opinions on the difficulties of distance education by gender?
4. What are the students' concerns about distance education according to their education preferences?
5. What are the students' suggestions regarding distance education?

METHOD

This section provides information about the research design, participants, procedure, measures and data analysis.

Research design

In this study, mixed method was used to determine the opinions of the students studying at the Faculty of Sports Sciences about distance education during the COVID-19 period. Mixed methods research is a method in which the researcher integrates two sets of data collecting both quantitative and qualitative data to understand the research problem and then draws conclusions using the advantages of integrating these two sets (Creswell, 2017). Parallel method, one of the mixed method models, was used in the research. The purpose of parallel mixed methods research is to collect both qualitative and quantitative data simultaneously, combine these data and use the results to understand a research problem (Fırat, Yurdakul, & Ersoy, 2014). The quantitative part of the research is based on the answers given by the students to the questions regarding their opinions on distance education during the COVID-19 period. The qualitative part of the research consists of students' opinions on their suggestions regarding distance education.

Participants

The research group consisted of students studying at Afyon Kocatepe University Faculty of Sport Sciences in the 2020-2021 academic spring term. Participants were 312 volunteer university students. In this study, easily accessible (random) sampling method was preferred. A detailed study is not carried out in the random sample selection. Therefore, there is no planned sampling process. The size of the sample mostly depends on the preference of the researcher (Baştürk ve Taştepe, 2013).

Of the students in the research group, 174 (54.2%) were female and 147 (45.8%) were male. 125 (38.9%) of the students study in the Department of Physical Education and Sports Teaching (PEST), 114 (35.5%) in the Department of Coaching Education, and 82 (25.5%) in the Department of Recreation. 205 (63.9%) of students own a computer or laptop, 116 (36.1%) do not; 239 (74.5%) have their own study room, 82 (25.5%) do not. 53 (16.5%) of the students think that the distance education provided is sufficient, 265 (83.5%) think that it is not enough; 210 (65.4%) think that it is appropriate to have distance education during the pandemic process, 111 (34.6%) think that it is not appropriate; 74 (23.1%) think that there should be face-to-face education during the pandemic process, 169 (52.6%) think that there should be distance education, 78 (24.3%) think that there should be hybrid education.

Procedure

Ethics committee approval was obtained before the study. Afterwards, students were reached through social media groups and personal media accounts, and an electronic questionnaire was administered. Before starting the survey, a consent form was presented. The form included the purpose of the study, the criteria for inclusion in the study and the right of withdrawal of the participants. Finally, the obtained data were transferred to the SPSS program.

Measures

For quantitative data in the research, "The Questionnaire of Opinions on Distance Education in the COVID-19 Process" was used. The questionnaire prepared by the researchers consists of four items. The items consist of three answers: Less important (1), Important (2), Very important (3). The Cronbach Alpha reliability coefficient of the items was calculated as .88 in total, .80 for advantage, .81 for disadvantage, .78 for difficulty and .82 for anxiety. For qualitative data, an open-ended question was asked to get information about students' suggestions for distance education.

Data analysis

In the quantitative dimension of the study, data analysis began with standard procedures for data cleaning and screening (Tabachnick & Fidell, 2013). No data were extracted from the dataset because of the lack of extreme values that would affect the data analysis. Frequency and percentage analyses were used to determine the demographic variables, while chi-square analysis was used to determine the opinions of students on distance education by gender, department, and educational preference. In the qualitative dimension of the study, content analysis was used for studensts' responses to open-ended questions about suggestions on distance education. For the content analysis, coding of data, theme identification, organization of the data according to the theme codes, and interpretation of the findings were followed. The qualitative data set was coded as "S 1, S 2, and S 3..." As a result, three-page long answers were obtained from the open-ended questions, along with 68 coded units. Finally, for an internal measure of reliability, the agreement between the two researchers was calculated by "consensus," as suggested by Miles et al. (1994). A consensus of 87% was attained from the data obtained from open-ended questions.

Table 1. Students' opinions on the advantages of distance education by gender

	Gender	Less important n (%)	Important n (%)	Very important n (%)	df	$\chi 2$	p
I can listen to the lessons over and over again.	Female	75 (23.4%)	49 (15.3%)	50 (15.6%)	2	7.190	.027*
	Male	48 (15.0%)	36 (11.2%)	63 (19.6%)			
I do not have transportation problems	Female	27 (15.5%)	94 (54.0%)	53 (30.5%)	2	7.904	.019*
	Male	26 (17.7%)	57 (38.8%)	64 (43.5%)			
My financial expenses have decreased.	Female	27 (8.4%)	93 (29.0%)	54 (16.8%)	2	.188	.910
	Male	24 (7.5%)	75 (23.4%)	48 (15.0%)			
I can spend more time with my family	Female	17 (5.3%)	101 (31.5%)	56 (17.4%)	2	6.183	.045*
	Male	26 (8.1%)	68 (21,2%)	53 (16.5%)			
I can devote more time to myself	Female	43 (13.4%)	95 (29.6%)	36 (11.2%)	2	5.993	.050
	Male	42 (13.1%)	61 (19.0%)	44 (13.7%)			
I think the spread of the virus is prevented	Female	36 (11.2%)	100 (31.2%)	38 (11.8%)	2	12.740	.002*
	Male	29 (9.0%)	60 (18.7%)	58 (18.1%)			

*p <.001

FINDINGS

In this section, students' findings regarding the advantages, disadvantages, difficulties, concerns and suggestions of distance education provided. In Table 1, the students' opinions on the advantages of distance education by gender are displayed with the chi-square test.

In Table 1, a significant difference was found in the answers given by the students to the questions "I can listen to the lessons over and over again, I do not have transportation problems, I can spend more time with my family, I think the spread of the virus is prevented" regarding the advantages of distance education by gender. As an advantage, most of the female (15.6%) and male students (19.6%) stated that it was very important to be able to listen to the lessons over and over again. Most of the female (15.3%) and male (43.5%) students stated that it was important and very important that they did not have transportation problems. In addition, most of the female (31.5%) and male (21.2%) students stated that it was important to spend more time with their families. Finally, most of the female (31.2%) and male (18.7%) students stated that it was important in preventing the spread of the virus. According to the results, it can be stated that male students considered the advantages of distance education more important. There was no significant difference according to gender

Table 2. Students' opinions on the disadvantages of distance education according to the department

	Department	Less important n (%)	Important n (%)	Very important n (%)	df	χ2	P
I cannot immediately ask the teacher about the subject that I do not understand	PEST	31 (9.7%)	47 (14.6%)	47 (14.6%)	4	15.019	.005*
	Coaching Ed.	12 (3.7%)	38 (11.8%)	64 (19.9%)			
	Recreation	15 (4.7%)	20 (6.2%)	47 (14.6%)			
I cannot quite grasp the subject	PEST	19 (5.9%)	44 (13.7%)	62 (19.3%)	4	14.233	.007*
	Coaching Ed.	10 (3.1%)	38 (11.8%)	66 (20.6%)			
	Recreation	7 (2.2%)	14 (4.4%)	61 (19.0%)			
I cannot take the applied lessons in practice	PEST	19 (5.9%)	29 (9.0%)	77 (29.0%)	4	11.010	.026*
	Coaching Ed.	10 (3.1%)	36 (11.2%)	68 (21.2%)			
	Recreation	6 (1.9%)	13 (4.0%)	63 (19.6%)			
I cannot exchange enough information with my friends	PEST	16 (5.0%)	40 (12.5%)	69 (21.5%)	4	4.076	.396
	Coaching Ed.	8 (2.5%)	35 (10.9%)	71 (22.1%)			
	Recreation	8 (2.5%)	20 (6.2%)	54 (16.8%)			
I cannot benefit enough from the knowledge and experience of teachers	PEST	17 (5.3%)	40 (12.5%)	68 (21.2%)	4	11.061	.026*
	Coaching Ed.	10 (3.1%)	37 (11.5%)	67 (20.9%)			
	Recreation	6 (1.9%)	14 (4.4%)	62 (19.3%)			

*p <.001

in other variables (p>.001). In Table 1, the students' opinions on the disadvantages of distance education according to the department are given with the chi-square test.

In Table 2, a significant difference was found in the answers given by the students to the questions regarding the disadvantages of distance education according to the department: "I cannot immediately ask the teacher about the subject that I do not understand, I cannot quite grasp the subject fully, I cannot take the applied lessons in practice, I cannot benefit enough from the knowledge and experience of the teachers." As a disadvantage, most of the students studying in the departments of PEST (14.6%), Coaching Ed. (19.9%) and Recreation (14.6%) stated that it was very important that they could not immediately ask the teacher about the subject they did not understand. Most of the students studying in the departments of PEST (19.3%), Coaching Ed. (20.6%) and Recreation (19.0%) stated that it was very important that they could not fully grasp the subject they did not understand. In addition, most of the students studying in the department of PEST (29.0%), Coaching Ed. (21.2%) and Recreation (19.6%) stated that it was very important that they could not take the applied lessons in practice. Finally, most of the students studying in the department of

Table 3. Students' opinions on the difficulties of distance education by gender

	Gender	Less important n (%)	Important n (%)	Very important n (%)	df	χ2	P
There is no internet where I live	Female	90 (28.0%)	59 (18.4%)	25 (7.8%)	2	9.779	.008*
	Male	62 (19.3%)	43 (13.4%)	42 (13.1%)			
I don't have a computer	Female	97 (30.2%)	42 (13.1%)	35 (10.9%)	2	3.371	.185
	Male	83 (25.9%)	25 (7.8%)	39 (12.1%)			
I don't have a study room of my own.	Female	107 (33.3%)	35 (10.9%)	32 (10.0%)	2	6.730	.025*
	Male	71 (22.1%)	33 (10.3%)	43 (13.4%)			
I can't concentrate in the lessons	Female	22 (6.9%)	59 (18.4%)	93 (29.0%)	2	7.224	.027*
	Male	31 (16.5%)	33 (21.8%)	83 (54.8%)			

*p <.05

PEST (21.2%), Coaching Ed. (20.9%) and Recreation (19.3%) stated that it was very important that they could not benefit enough from the knowledge and experience of teachers. According to the results, it can be stated that the students studying in the departments of Coaching Ed. and PEST considered the disadvantages of distance education more important. There was no significant difference in the other variable according to the department (p>.001). In Table 3, the students' opinions on the difficulties of distance education by gender are given with the chi-square test.

In Table 3, a significant difference was found in the answers given by the students to the questions "There is no internet where I live, I don't have a study room of my own, I can't concentrate in the lessons" regarding the disadvantages of distance education according to the department. As a difficulty, most of the female (28.0%) and male students (19.3%) stated that there is no internet in their place of residence was less important. In addition, most of the female (33.3%) and male (22.1%) students stated that not having a room of their own was less important. Finally, most of the female (29.0%) and male (54.8%) students stated that it was very important that they could not concentrate in the lessons. According to the results, it can be stated that female students considered the difficulties of distance education less important. In the other variable, no significant difference was found according to gender (p>.001). In Table 4, the students' opinions on their concerns about distance education according to the educational preference are given with the chi-square test.

In Table 4, a significant difference was found in the answers given by the students to the questions "not learning the subject well, not having enough experience for my professional life, not being able to develop myself enough, not having enough information" according to their education preferences. As concerned, most of the students who preferred face-to-face (15.0%), distance (42.4%) and hybrid (13.1%)

Table 4. Students' opinions on their concerns about distance education according to the educational preference

	Educational preference	Less important n (%)	Important n (%)	Very important n (%)	df	χ^2	p
Not learning the subject well	Face to face	9 (2.8%)	17 (5.3%)	48 (15.0%)	4	19.975	.001*
	Distance	9 (2.8%)	24 (7.5%)	136 (42.4%)			
	Hybrid	12 (3.7%)	24 (7.5%)	42 (13.1%)			
Not having enough experience for my professional life	Face to face	14 (4.4%)	14 (4.4%)	46 (14.3%)	4	19.511	.001*
	Distance	5 (1.6%)	35 (10.9%)	129 (40.2%)			
	Hybrid	11 (3.4%)	19 (5.9%)	48 (15.0%)			
not being able to develop myself enough	Face to face	12 (3.7%)	19 (5.9%)	43 (13.4%)	4	11.486	.022*
	Distance	9 (2.8%)	36 (11.2%)	124 (38.6%)			
	Hybrid	12 (3.7%)	19 (5.9%)	47 (14.6%)			
Not having enough information	Face to face	11 (3.4%)	23 (7.2%)	40 (12.5%)	4	12.454	.012*
	Distance	7 (2.2%)	44 (13.7%)	118 (36.8%)			
	Hybrid	11 (3.4%)	18 (5.6%)	49 (15.3%)			
Getting low grades in exams	Face to face	10 (3.1%)	27 (8.4%)	37 (11.5%)	4	6.369	.173
	Distance	12 (3.7%)	47 (14.6%)	110 (34.3%)			
	Hybrid	10 (3.1%)	24 (7.5%)	44 (13.7%)			

*p < .001

education stated that not being able to learn the subject was very important. Most of the students who preferred face-to-face (14.3%), distance (40.2%) and hybrid (15.0%) education stated that it was very important that they did not have enough experience for their professional life. In addition, most of the students who preferred face-to-face (13.4%), distance (38.6%) and hybrid (14.6%) education stated that it was very important not to develop themselves sufficiently. Finally, most of the students who prefer face-to-face (12.5%), distance (36.8%) and hybrid (15.3%) education stated

Table 5. Suggestions of students about distance education

Theme	Theme codes	Frequency (f)	Percent (%)
Suggestions	Extending the duration of the lesson	44	13.7
	Improvement of technological and internet infrastructure	68	21.2
	Interactive conduct of the lesson	37	11.5
	More efficient teaching by the teacher	30	9.3
	Standardization of lesson practices by the teacher	29	9.0

that it was very important that they did not have enough information. According to the results, it can be stated that students who preferred distance education had more concerns about distance education. In the other variable, there was no significant difference according to education preference (p>.001).

The students were asked about their suggestions for distance education could be during the pandemic process, and the answers received are presented below:

When asked whether they had suggestions about the distance education, the students suggested that the lesson duration be extended (n = 44, 13.7%). For example, S 18, 41, 189, and 277 stated, *"The duration of the lesson should be extended, we do not understand the subjects well enough."* S 121 stated *"The time is limited to 50 minutes, the teachers briefly explain the topics."* Further, S 213 stated, *""I think students are not given enough time to learn."*

As a suggestion, students stated that technology and internet infrastructure should be developed (n = 68, 21.2%). For example, S 75, S 183 and S 311 stated, *"Internet connection drops, system crashes when busy."* S 44 and S 165 stated *"The image freezes when the video is opened from the system."* S 189 and S 312 stated *"Sound and image quality can be improved, infrastructure should be strengthened."*

As a suggestion, students stated that the lesson be conducted interactively (n = 37, 11.5%). For example, S 7, S 147 and S 263 stated, "It is good for students to attend lessons." S 28 and S 147 stated *"Only the teacher teaches the lessons, it sounds like a lullaby, we should attend the lessons as well."* S 59 and S 260 stated *"We cannot attend the lessons, microphones and cameras must be turned on in the lessons."* Further S 116 and S 291 stated *"Some teachers do not turn on their cameras, our microphones are also turned off, we only listen to the teacher's voice, we cannot focus on the lesson."*

As a suggestion, students suggested that it would be good for teachers to teach more efficiently (n = 30, 9.3%). For example, S 24 and S 134 stated, *"I would like teachers to pay attention to the way they teach."* S 78 and S 306 stated *"Lesson times are short, we don't understand every lesson very well anyway, I think that teachers should explain the lesson in a more understandable and efficient way."*

As a suggestion, students suggested standardization of lesson practices by teachers (n = 29, 9.0%). For example, S 49 and S 150 stated, *"Some teachers ask difficult questions in the exam, some shorten the exam time, some give homework, it should be standard practice."* Further S 284 and S 219 stated *"Some teachers want to be required to attend classes, some do not. I think there should be an obligation to attend classes and grades should be given accordingly."*

This study is one the first attempts to determine the perceptions of the sport sciences students about distance education during the COVID-19 period. However, the study has the following limitations, which should be carefully considered:

- The study is limited by the subjects' characteristics such as gender, age, previous experiences.
- The study is limited by the measurement methods and procedures applied within the measurement process.

DISCUSSION AND CONCLUSION

Covid-19 affected student lives in many ways and students were obligated to attend online classes via distance learning tools such as television and internet. Institutions adjusted themselves to this new normal and majority of the students attended to distance education for two years. The purpose of this research was to determine the perceptions of the sport science students studying at the Faculty of Sports Sciences about distance education during the COVID-19 period. Results showed that male students considered the advantages of distance education more important than females. Also, students studying in the departments of Coaching Education and Physical Education and Sport Teaching considered the disadvantages of distance education more important. Besides, female students considered the difficulties of distance education less important than males; Moreover, students who prefer distance education had more concerns about the quality of distance education. In addition, The results indicated that majority of the students had tehnology issues because of the infrastructure problem in their region.

In brief, students proposed extending the duration of the lesson, strengthening the technological and internet infrastructure, conducting the lessons interactively, teaching the lessons more efficiently by the teachers and standardizing the lesson practices. Instructor quality plays an essential role in affecting the students' satisfaction in distance education (Gopal, R., Singh, V. & Aggarwal 2021). Most faculty members are new to the using new technologies and skills in distance learning. The features of different online platforms provide effective interactive learnign environment, which might seem complicated to the faculty members. Therefore, the universities should consider practical workshops for their faculty members before starting the semesters. These workshops increase instructors quality and help improve unique teaching skills. Moreover, even the students can adapt better with orientations and seminars that can increase students's readiness (Herguner et al 2021).

In the final analysis, Chickering and Gamson (1991) indicated seven key principles to the teaching and learning in distance education practices. These involve student-teacher contact, cooperation between students, using active learning scenarios, giving prompt feedback, producing time-on-task, mandating high teacher expectations and respect for diverse individuals and styles of learning. In conclusion, research indicated that educators following these seven key principles reported empowered, successful and competent (Crews, Wilkinson & Neill, 2015).

In conclusion, similar to the findings of Aktaş et. al (2020) this study find that there are gender differences toward attitues to distance education. Also Bingöl (2020), Gürler, Uslu and Daştan (2020) replicated same restuls and found that gender was an important factor on perception of students in terms of participation and attendance to distance education courses in general. Definitely, there are differences in terms of scientific disciplines. It seems that students emhasize more stress if their expertise rely on clinical fields or more practical applications are required compared to theoritical fields. The lack of physical contact with peers limits the experience of physical performance through distance education. It seems that there are many advantages and disadvantages of distance education in general. Advancements in technology provided many unique benefits to higher education programs and institutions are trying to receive benefits of this. Non traditional working class students have limited time to attend college classes compared to non traditional students. Therefore, distance education provides many unique benefits with online instructional modules and student can complete their higher education via distance learning. However, practical part is very difficult in distance learning and students need more hands on education. In this case blended instruction is highly recommended. In a recent study, (Ismaili, 2021) majority of the college students had positive attitudes toward the distance learning experience. This may be related to the characteristics of this new generation. Because they are highly technology- oriented and skillful in this area. However, it should be careful in this comment because the teaching and learning environment is related to human interaction and teachers are key components. Students may get many benefits as long as lectures are synchronous.

FUTURE RESEARCH DIRECTIONS

Future studies should focus on the effects of distance education in different subject matters and nationalities. This may provide an universal approach to understand the reality of distance learning in terms of teaching effectiveness and student performance.

Effect of the lack of physical contact with peers in distance learning, physical and mental health issues may be investigated in future research.

RECOMMENDATIONS

According to the results, it has been determined that male students consider the advantages of distance education more important in terms of listening to the lesson over and over, not having transportation problems, reducing financial expenses, spending more time with themselves and their families. The reasons why female students see these issues as an advantage in distance education at a lower level can be investigated. Moreover, it has been determined that the students of the recreation department have a lower level of situations such as not being able to immediately ask the teacher about the subject they do not understand, not being able to grasp the subject fully, and not being able to benefit from the teachers' knowledge sufficiently. It can be investigated why these situations, which are the disadvantages of distance education, are at a lower level in the students of the Recreation department. In addition, it is seen that the difficulties of distance education are more important than male students. The reason for this can be examined.

According to the results, it has been determined that the students who prefer distance education have more concerns about distance education. The reasons for this must be examined and necessary precautions must be taken. In line with the suggestions of the students, it can be ensured that the internet infrastructure is strengthened, that the instructors teach the lesson more efficiently and standardize their practices, that they turn on the cameras during the lesson and teach interactively.

REFERENCES

Akgün, A. İ. (2020). COVID-19 sürecinde acil durum uzaktan eğitimi yoluyla verilen muhasebe eğitimine yönelik öğrenci görüşleri. *Açıköğretim Uygulamaları ve Araştırmaları Dergisi, 6*(4), 208–236.

Aktaş, Ö., Büyüktaş, B., Gülle, M., & Yıldız, M. (2020). COVID-19 virüsünden kaynaklanan izolasyon günlerinde spor bilimleri öğrencilerinin uzaktan eğitime karşı tutumları. *Sivas Cumhuriyet Üniversitesi Spor Bilimleri Dergisi, 1*(1), 1–9.

Altuntaş, E. Y., Başaran, M., Özeke, B., & Yılmaz, H. (2020). COVID–19 pandemisi sürecinde üniversite öğrencilerinin yükseköğretim kurumlarının uzaktan eğitime yönelik stratejilerine ve öğrenme deneyimlerine ilişkin algı düzeyleri. *Halkla İlişkiler ve Reklam Çalışmaları E-Dergisi, 3*(2), 8–23.

Baştürk, S., & Taştepe, M. (2013). *Evren ve örneklem: Bilimsel araştırma yöntemleri.* Vize Yayıncılık.

Beard, J., & Konukman, F. (2020). Teaching online physical education: The art of connection in the digital classroom. *Journal of Physical Education, Recreation & Dance, 91*(7), 49–51. doi:10.1080/07303084.2020.1785772

Bingöl, B. (2020). Peyzaj mimarlığı öğrencilerinin COVID-19 sürecinde acil uzaktan öğretim üzerine görüşleri: Burdur Mehmet Akif Ersoy Üniversitesi örneği. *Avrupa Bilim ve Teknoloji Dergisi*, (20), 890–897.

Bull, G., Harris, J., Loyd, J., & Short, J. (1989). The electronic academical village. *Journal of Teacher Education*, *40*(4), 27–31. doi:10.1177/002248718904000405

Bull, G., Sigmon, T., & Shidisky, C. (1991). Specifications for computer networks for support of cooperative ventures between universities and public schools. *Computers in Schools, 8*(1/2/3), 183-185.

Buluk, B., & Eşitti, B. (2020). Koronavirüs (COVID-19) sürecinde uzaktan eğitimin turizm lisans öğrencileri tarafından değerlendirilmesi. *Journal of Awareness*, *5*(3), 285–298. doi:10.26809/joa.5.021

Chickering, A. W., & Gamson, Z. F. (1991). *Applying the seven principles for good practice in undergraduate education. New directions in teaching and learning.* Jossey-Boss.

Creswell, J. W. (2017). A concise introduction to mixed methods research. Ankara: Pegem.

Crews, T. B., Wilkinson, K., & Neill, J. (2015). Principles for good practice in undergraduate education: Effective online course design to assist students' success. *Journal of Online Learning and Teaching*, *11*(1), 87–103.

Deming, D. J., Goldin, C., Katz, L. F., & Yuchtman, N. (2015). Can online learning bend the higher education cost curve? *The American Economic Review*, *105*(5), 496–501. doi:10.1257/aer.p20151024

Durnalı, M., Orakcı, Ş., & Aktan, O. (2019). The smart learning potential of Turkey's education system in the context of FATIH project. In A. Darshan Singh, S. Raghunathan, E. Robeck, & B. Sharma (Eds.), *Cases on Smart Learning Environments* (pp. 227–243). IGI Global. doi:10.4018/978-1-5225-6136-1.ch013

Durnalı, M., Orakcı, Ş., & Özkan, O. (2018). Turkey's higher education potential for human capital of eurasian region. In O. Karnaukhova, A. Udovikina, & B. Christiansen (Eds.), *Economic and Geopolitical Perspectives of the Commonwealth of Independent States and Eurasia* (pp. 201–224). IGI Global. doi:10.4018/978-1-5225-3264-4.ch009

Filiz, B., & Konukman, F. (2020). Teaching strategies for physical education during 16 the COVID-19 Pandemic. *Journal of Physical Education, Recreation & Dance*, *91*(9), 49–51. doi:10.1080/07303084.2020.1816099

Fırat, M., Yurdakul, I. K., & Ersoy, A. (2014). Bir eğitim teknolojisi araştırmasına dayalı olarak karma yöntem araştırması deneyimi. *Eğitimde Nitel Araştırmalar Dergisi*, 2(1), 64–85. doi:10.14689/issn.2148-2624.1.2s3m

Genç, S. Z., Engin, G., & Yardım, T. (2020). Pandemi (COVID-19) sürecindeki uzaktan eğitim uygulamalarına ilişkin lisansüstü öğrenci görüşleri. *Atatürk Üniversitesi Kazım Karabekir Eğitim Fakültesi Dergisi*, (41), 134–158.

Gopal, R., Singh, V., & Aggarwal, A. (2021). Impact of online classes on the satisfaction and performance of students during the pandemic period of COVID 19. *Education and Information Technologies*, 26(6), 6923–6947. doi:10.100710639-021-10523-1 PMID:33903795

Gürler, C., Uslu, T., & Daştan, İ. (2020). Evaluation of distance learning from student perspective in COVID-19 pandemic. *Atatürk Üniversitesi Sosyal Bilimler Enstitüsü Dergisi*, 24(4), 1895–1904.

Hammond, A. L. (1972). Plato & ticcit: CAI in action. *College and University Business*, 66, 39–42.

Harris, J., & Anderson, S. (1991). Cultivating teacher telecommunications networks from the grass roots up: The electronic academical village at Virginia. *Computers in Schools*, 8(1/2/3), 191-202.

Hergüner, G., Yaman, Ç., Sarı, S. C., Yaman, M. S., & Dönmez, A. (2021). The effect of online learning attitudes of sports sciences students on their learning readiness to learn online in the era of the new coronavirus pandemic (COVID-19). *The Turkish Online Journal of Educational Technology*, 20(1), 68–77.

Ismaili, Y. (2021). Evaluation of students' attitude toward distance learning during the pandemic (COVID-19): A case study of ELTE university. *On the Horizon*, 29(1), 17–30. doi:10.1108/OTH-09-2020-0032

Lockard, J., Abrams, D. P., & Many, W. A. (1997). *Microcomputers for twenty-first century educators* (4th ed.). Longman.

McKethan, R., Everhart, B., & Sanders, R. (2001). The effects of multimedia software instruction and lecture-based instruction on learning and teaching cues of manipulative skills on preservice physical education teachers. *Physical Educator*, 58(1), 2–13.

Merrill, M. D., Schneider, E. W., & Fletcher, K. A. (1980). *TICCIT*. Educational Technology Publications.

Miles, M. B., Huberman, M. A., & Saldana, J. (1994). *Qualitative data analysis: An expanded sourcebook*. Sage.

Montelongo, R. (2019). Less than/more than: Issues associated with high-impact online teaching and learning. *Administrative Issues Journal: Connecting Education, Practice and Research, 9*(1), 68–79.

Morris, S. M. (2018). Online learning shouldn't be "less than". *Inside Higher Ed.* Retrieved from https://www.insidehighered.com/digital-learning/views/2018/04/04/are-we-giving-online-students-education-all-nuance-and-complexity

Orakcı, Ş. (2020). The future of online learning and teaching in higher education. In Global Approaches to Sustainability Through Learning and Education. Hershey, PA: IGI Global. doi:10.4018/978-1-7998-0062-0.ch003

Orakcı, Ş., & Gelişli, Y. (2021). Educational policy actions in the times of Covid-19 and suggestions for future applications in Turkey. In L. Kyei-Blankson, J. Blankson, & E. Ntuli (Eds.), *Handbook of Research on Inequities in Online Education During Global Crises* (pp. 475–493). IGI Global. doi:10.4018/978-1-7998-6533-9.ch024

Orçanlı, K., & Bekmezci, M. (2020). Üniversite öğrencilerinin COVID-19 pandemisinde uzaktan eğitim algısının belirlenmesi ve bazı demografik değişkenlerle ilişkisi. *Uluslararası İktisadi ve İdari Bilimler Dergisi, 6*(2), 88–108. doi:10.29131/uiibd.836277

Saltürk, A., & Güngör, C. (2020). Üniversite öğrencilerinin gözünden COVID-19 pandemisinde uzaktan eğitime geçiş deneyimi. *Adıyaman Üniversitesi Sosyal Bilimler Enstitüsü Dergisi,* (36), 137–174. doi:10.14520/adyusbd.788716

Steinberg, E. R. (1991). *Computer-assisted instruction: A synthesis of theory, practice and technology*. Lawrence Erlbaum.

Tabachnick, B., & Fidell, L. (2013). *Using multivariate statistics, 6th international edition (cover) edn*. Sage Publications.

Waggoner, M. (1992). Planning for the use of computer conferencing in collaborative learning. In D. Carey, R. Carey, D. Willis, & J. Willis (Eds.), *Technology and teacher education annual-1992* (pp. 556–561). Association for the Advancement of Computing in Education.

Wilkinson, C., Hillier, R., Padfield, G., & Harrison, J. (1999). The effects of volleyball software on female junior high school students' volleyball Performance. *Physical Educator, 4*, 202–209.

Yakar, L. Y., & Yakar, Z. Y. (2021). Eğitim fakültesi öğrencilerinin uzaktan eğitime karşı tutumlarının ve e-öğrenmeye hazır bulunuşluklarının incelenmesi. *Mersin Üniversitesi Eğitim Fakültesi Dergisi, 17*(1), 1–21.

KEY TERMS AND DEFINITIONS

Advantage: Any state, circumstance, opportunity, or means specially favorable to success, interest, or any desired.

Concern: Concern means to deal or be involved with or to cause an anxious feeling.

COVID-19: Coronavirus disease (COVID-19) is an infectious disease caused by the SARS-CoV-2 virus.

Difficulty: The quality or state of being hard to do, deal with, or understand.

Disadvantage: An unfavourable circumstance or condition that reduces the chances of success or effectiveness.

Distance Education: Distance Education is a field of education that focuses on the pedagogy, technology, and instructional. system designs that aim to deliver education to students who are not physically "on site" in a traditional classroom or campus.

Education: Education is both the act of teaching knowledge to others and the act of receiving knowledge from someone else. Education also refers to the knowledge received through schooling or instruction and to the institution of teaching as a whole.

Suggestion: The process by which one thought leads to another especially through association of ideas

Compilation of References

Aaronson, D., Barrow, L., & Sander, W. (2002). *Teachers and student achievement in the Chicago public high schools.* Working Paper Series WP-02-28, Federal Reserve Bank of Chicago. doi:10.1086/508733

Abamu, J. (2017). *Students Say They Are Not as Tech Savvy as Educators Assume.* EdSurge Inc. https://www.edsurge.com/news/2017-06-20-students-say-they-are-not-as-tech-savvy-as-educators-assume

Abdel-Basset, M., Manogaran, G., & Mohamed, M. (2018). Internet of Things (IoT) and its impact on supply chain: A framework for building smart, secure and efficient systems. *Future Generation Computer Systems, 86*, 614–628. doi:10.1016/j.future.2018.04.051

Abrahamson, A. L. (1998, June 3–6). *An Overview of Teaching and Learning Research with Classroom Communication Systems.* Paper presented at the International Conference of the Teaching of Mathematics, Village of Pythagorion, Samos, Greece.

Adanır, H., & Ilgaz, G. A. (2020). Providing online exams for online learners: Does it really matter for them? *Education and Information Technologies, 25*(2), 1255–1269. doi:10.100710639-019-10020-6

Akgün, A. İ. (2020). COVID-19 sürecinde acil durum uzaktan eğitimi yoluyla verilen muhasebe eğitimine yönelik öğrenci görüşleri. *Açıköğretim Uygulamaları ve Araştırmaları Dergisi, 6*(4), 208–236.

Akkoyunlu, B. (2002). Educational technology in Turkey: Past, present and future. *Educational Media International, 39*(2), 165–174. doi:10.1080/09523980210155352

Aktaş, Ö., Büyüktaş, B., Gülle, M., & Yıldız, M. (2020). COVID-19 virüsünden kaynaklanan izolasyon günlerinde spor bilimleri öğrencilerinin uzaktan eğitime karşı tutumları. *Sivas Cumhuriyet Üniversitesi Spor Bilimleri Dergisi, 1*(1), 1–9.

Ally, M. (2004). *Foundations of educational theory for online learning.* AU Press.

Ally, M. (2008). Foundations of educational theory for online learning. In *The Theory and Practice of Online Learning* (2nd ed., pp. 15–44). Athabasca University Press.

Ally, M., Grimus, M., & Ebner, M. (2014). Preparing teachers for a mobile world, to improve access to education. *Prospects*, *44*(1), 1–17. doi:10.100711125-014-9293-2

Alrasheedi, M., & Capretz, L. F. (2015). Determination of Critical Success Factors Affecting Mobile Learning: A Meta-Analysis Approach. *The Turkish Online Journal of Educational Technology*, *14*(2), 41–51.

Altun, A. (2008, May). Yapılandırmacı öğretim sürecinde viki kullanımı. *International Educational Technology Conference (IETC)'da sunulan bildiri.*

Altuntaş, E. Y., Başaran, M., Özeke, B., & Yılmaz, H. (2020). COVID–19 pandemisi sürecinde üniversite öğrencilerinin yükseköğretim kurumlarının uzaktan eğitime yönelik stratejilerine ve öğrenme deneyimlerine ilişkin algı düzeyleri. *Halkla İlişkiler ve Reklam Çalışmaları E-Dergisi*, *3*(2), 8–23.

Aly, İ. (2013). Performance in an online introductory course in a hybrid classroom setting. *Canadian Journal of Higher Education*, *43*(2), 85–99. doi:10.47678/cjhe.v43i2.2474

American Psychological Association. (2006). *Multitasking: Switching costs.* Retrieved from: https://www.apa.org/research/action/multitask

Andersen, J. F., Norton, R. W., & Nussbaum, J. F. (1981). Three Investigations Exploring Relationships Between Perceived Teacher Communication Behaviors and Student Learning. *Communication Education*, *30*(4), 377–392. doi:10.1080/03634528109378493

Anderson, J. (2020). *Brave New World The coronavirus pandemic is reshaping education.* Retrieved from https://qz.com/1826369/how-coronavirus-is-changing-education/

Anderson, T. (2003). Getting the Mix Right Again: An updated and theoretical rationale for interaction. *International Review of Research in Open and Distance Learning*, *4*(2), 1–14.

Aragon, S., Griffith, M., Wixom, M. A., Woods, J., & Workman, E. (2016). *ESSA: Quick guides on top issues.* Education Commission of the States. Retrieved from https://eric.ed.gov/?id=ED567801

Arden, S. V., & Benz, S. (2018, Fall). The science of RTI implementation: The how and what of building multi-tiered systems of support. *Perspectives on Language and Literacy*, 21–25.

Ardid, M., Gómez-Tejedor, J. A., Meseguer-Dueñas, J. M., Riera, J., & Vidaurre, A. (2015). Online exams for blended assessment. Study of different application methodologies. *Computers & Education*, *81*, 296–303. doi:10.1016/j.compedu.2014.10.010

Argyris, C. (1991). Teaching Smart People How to Learn. *Harvard Business Review*, *69*(3), 99–109.

Artsın, M., Koçdar, S., & Bozkurt, A. (2020). Öğrenenlerin Öz-Yönetimli Öğrenme Becerilerinin Kitlesel Açık Çevrimiçi Dersler Bağlamında İncelenmesi [An Investigation of Learners' Self-Managed Learning Skills in the Context of Massive Open Online Courses]. *Anadolu Üniversitesi Eğitim Bilimleri Enstitüsü Dergisi*, *10*(1), 1–30.

Ateş, A., & Altun, E. (2008). Bilgisayar öğretmeni adaylarının uzaktan eğitime yönelik tutumlarının çeşitli değişkenler açısından incelenmesi. *Gazi Eğitim Fakültesi Dergisi, 28*(3), 125–145.

Atıcı, B., & Özmen, B. (2011). *Blog kullanımının sınıf topluluğu duygusuna etkisi*. Uluslararası Eğitim Teknolojileri Sempozyumu'nda sunulan bildiri.

Aybek, B., & Aslan, S. (2017). Öğretmen adaylarının öz-düzenleme düzeylerinin çeşitli değişkenler açısından incelenmesi [Examination of pre-service teachers' self-regulation levels in terms of various variables]. *Eğitimde Kuram ve Uygulama, 13*(3), 455–470. doi:10.17244/eku.331938

Aydın, S., & Atalay, T. D. (2015). *Öz Düzenlemeli Öğrenme* [Self-Regulated Learning]. Pegem Akademi.

Aytekin, Ç. (2011). Wiki uygulamalarına iletişimsel yaklaşım ile bir model önerisi. *Online Academic Journal of Information Technology, 2*(5), 7–17.

Bakerson, M., Trottier, T., & Mansfield, M. (2015). The value of embedded formative assessment: An integral process in online learning environments implemented through advances in technology. In S. Koç, X. Liu, & P. Wachira (Eds.), *Assessment in Online and Blended Learning Environments*. Information Age Publishing, Inc.

Balakrishnan, K. (2021). Empowering Emerging India through Excellence in Education-Reflections On NEP 2020. *Elementary Education Online, 20*(1), 3596–3602.

Baldan Babayiğit, B., & Güven, M. (2020). Self-regulated learning skills of undergraduate students and the role of higher education in promoting self-regulation. *Euroasian Journal of Educational Research, 20*(89), 47–70. doi:10.14689/ejer.2020.89.3

Baldan, B. (2017). *Lisans öğrencilerinin öz düzenlemeli öğrenme becerisi düzeyleri ve yükseköğretim programlarının öz düzenlemeli öğrenme becerisini geliştirmedeki rolü* [Self-regulated learning skill levels of undergraduate students and the role of higher education programs in developing self-regulated learning skills] [Master dissertation]. Anadolu University, Turkey.

Ball, S. J. (2021). *The education debate*. Policy Press. doi:10.2307/j.ctv201xhz5

Balu, R., Zhu, P., Doolittle, F., Schiller, E., Jenkins, J., & Gersten, R. (2015). Evaluation of response to intervention practices for elementary school reading. National Center for Education Evaluation and Regional Assistance, Institute of Education Sciences, U.S. Department of Education. NCEE 2016-4000.

Banathy, B. H., & Jenlink, P. M. (2004). Systems inquiry and its application in education. In D. Jonassen (Ed.), *Handbook of research for educational communications and technology* (2nd ed., pp. 37–58). Lawrence Erlbaum Associates.

Bandura, A. (1986). *Social foundations of thought and action: A social cognitive theory*. Prentice-Hall.

Bandura, A. (1997). *Self-efficacy: The exercise of control*. W. H. Freeman.

Bandura, A., & Schunk, D. H. (1981). Cultivating competence, self-efficacy, and intrinsic interest through proximal self-motivation. *Journal of Personality and Social Psychology, 41*(3), 586–598. doi:10.1037/0022-3514.41.3.586

Barbosa, H., & Garcia, F. (2005). Importance of Online Assessment in the E-learning Process. *6th International Conference on Information Technology Based Higher Education and Training*, F3B/1-F3B/6. 10.1109/ITHET.2005.1560287

Barnard, L., Lan, W. Y., To, Y. M., Paton, V. O., & Lai, S. L. (2009). Measuring self-regulation in online and blended learning environments. *The internet and higher education, 12*(1), 1–6. doi:10.1016/j.iheduc.2008.10.005

Baştürk, S., & Taştepe, M. (2013). *Evren ve örneklem: Bilimsel araştırma yöntemleri*. Vize Yayıncılık.

Baturay, M. H., & Daloğlu, A. (2010). E-portfolio assessment in an online English language course. *Computer Assisted Language Learning, 23*(5), 413–428. doi:10.1080/09588221.2010.520671

Bayram, S. (1999). *Bilgisayar destekli öğretim teknolojileri*. Marmara Üniversitesi Yayınevi Kitap Koleksiyonu.

Baysal, A., & Özgenel, M. (2019). Ortaokul öğrencilerinin bağlanma stilleri ve öz-düzenleme düzeyleri arasındaki ilişkinin incelenmesi [Examining the relationship between secondary school students' attachment styles and self-regulation levels]. *Eğitimde Kuram ve Uygulama, 15*(2), 142–152.

Beard, J., & Konukman, F. (2020). Teaching online physical education: The art of connection in the digital classroom. *Journal of Physical Education, Recreation & Dance, 91*(7), 49–51. doi:10.1080/07303084.2020.1785772

Beatty, I. D. (2004, February 3). *Transforming Student Learning with Classroom Communication Systems*. Retrieved October 1, 2021, from http://www.utexas.edu/academic /cit/services/cps/ECARCRS.pdf

Benson, R., & Brack, C. (2010). *Online Learning and Assessment in Higher Education: A Planning Guide*. Chandos Publishing. doi:10.1533/9781780631653

Benson, R., & Samarawickrema, G. (2009). Addressing the context of e-learning: Using transactional distance theory to inform design. *Distance Education, 30*(1), 5–21. doi:10.1080/01587910902845972

Berge, Z. L. (2000). Components of the online classroom. *New Directions for Teaching and Learning, 84*(84), 23–28. doi:10.1002/tl.843

Betts, K. (2009). Lost in Translation: Importance of Effective Communication in Online Education. *Online Journal of Distance Learning Administration, 12*(2). https://www.westga.edu/~distance/ojdla/summer122/betts122.html

Beyth-Marom, R., Saporta, K., & Caspi, A. (2005). Synchronous vs. asynchronous tutorials: Factors affecting students' preferences and choices. *Journal of Research on Technology in Education*, *37*(3), 245–262. doi:10.1080/15391523.2005.10782436

Bingöl, B. (2020). Peyzaj mimarlığı öğrencilerinin COVID-19 sürecinde acil uzaktan öğretim üzerine görüşleri: Burdur Mehmet Akif Ersoy Üniversitesi örneği. *Avrupa Bilim ve Teknoloji Dergisi*, (20), 890–897.

Bohanon, H., Gilman, C., Parker, B., Amell, C., & Sortino, G. (2016). Using school improvement and implementation science to integrate multi-tiered systems of support in secondary schools. *Australasian Journal of Special Education*, *40*(2), 99–116. doi:10.1017/jse.2016.8

Bonanno, P. (2015). Assessing Technology-Enhanced Learning: A Process-Oriented Approach. In S. Koç, X. Liu, & P. Wachira (Eds.), *Assessment in Online and Blended Learning Environments*. Information Age Publıshıng, Inc.

Booth, R., & Berwyn, C. (2003). The development of quality online assessment in vocational education and training. *Australian Flexible Learning Framework*, *1*, 17–32.

Boston, C. (2002). The Concept of Formative Assessment. *Practical Assessment, Research & Evaluation*, *8*(9), 1–4.

Bouck, E. C., & Cosby, M. D. (2019). Response to intervention in high school mathematics: One school's implementation. *Preventing School Failure*, *63*(1), 32–42. doi:10.1080/1045988X.2018.1469463

Bouhnik, D., Giat, Y., & Sanderovitch, Y. (2009). Asynchronous learning sources in a high-tech organization. *Journal of Workplace Learning*, *21*(5), 416–430. doi:10.1108/13665620910966811

Bozkurt, A. (2014). *Ağ toplumu ve öğrenme: Bağlantıcılık. In Akademik Bilişim 2014 (pp. 601-606)*. Mersin Üniversitesi.

Breault, R. (2016). Emerging issues in duoethnography. *International Journal of Qualitative Studies in Education: QSE*, *29*(6), 777–794. doi:10.1080/09518398.2016.1162866

Brindley, J. E., Blaschke, L. M., & Walti, C. (2009). Creating effective collaborative learning groups in an online environment. *International Review of Research in Open and Distributed Learning*, *10*(3). Advance online publication. doi:10.19173/irrodl.v10i3.675

Britain, S., & Liber, O. (1999). A Framework for Pedagogical Evaluation of Virtual Learning Environments. Academic Press.

Britain, S., & Liber, O. (2004). *A framework for pedagogical evaluation of virtual learning environments*. Academic Press.

Brody, J. E. (2017). Social Interaction Is Critical for Mental and Behavioral Health. *New York Times*. https://www.nytimes.com/2017/06/12/well/live/having-friends-is-good-for-you.html

Broughton, A. (2010). *Work-related stress*. Retrieved from: https://www.eurofound.europa.eu/sites/default/files/ef_files/docs/ewco/tn1004059s/tn1004059s.pdf

Bruner, J. (1996). *The culture of education*. Harvard University Press. doi:10.4159/9780674251083

Buckman, D. G., Hand, N. W., & Johnson, A. (2021). Improving high school graduation through school climate. *NASSP Bulletin*, 5–24. doi:10.1177/0192636521993212

Bull, G., Sigmon, T., & Shidisky, C. (1991). Specifications for computer networks for support of cooperative ventures between universities and public schools. *Computers in Schools, 8*(1/2/3), 183-185.

Bull, G., Harris, J., Loyd, J., & Short, J. (1989). The electronic academical village. *Journal of Teacher Education, 40*(4), 27–31. doi:10.1177/002248718904000405

Buluk, B., & Eşitti, B. (2020). Koronavirüs (COVID-19) sürecinde uzaktan eğitimin turizm lisans öğrencileri tarafindan değerlendirilmesi. *Journal of Awareness, 5*(3), 285–298. doi:10.26809/joa.5.021

Burbank, J., & Cooper, F. (2010). *Empires in World History: Power and the Politics of Difference*. Princeton University Press.

Büyüköztürk, Ş., Kılıç Çakmak, E., Akgün, Ö. E., Karadeniz, Ş., & Demirel, F. (2016). *Bilimsel Araştırma Yöntemleri* [Scientific Research Methods]. PEGEM.

Cabı, E. (2015). Öğretmen adaylarının öz-düzenleme stratejileri ve akademik başarısı: Boylamsal bir araştırma [Teacher candidates' self-regulation strategies and academic achievement: A longitudinal study]. *Gazi Üniversitesi Gazi Eğitim Fakültesi Dergisi, 35*(3), 489–506.

Capon, N., & Kuhn, D. (2004). What's so good about problem-based learning? *Cognition and Instruction, 22*(1), 61–79. doi:10.12071532690Xci2201_3

Carlson, K. (2021). Supporting Students Through Online Learning. In Handbook of Research on Inequities in Online Education During Global Crises (pp. 148-162). IGI Global. doi:10.4018/978-1-7998-6533-9.ch008

Carminucci, J., Hodgman, S., Rickles, J. & Garet, M. (2021). *Student attendance and enrollment loss in 2020-21*. American Institutes for Research. https://www.air.org/sites/default/files/2021-07/research-brief-covid-survey-student-attendance-june-2021_0.pdf

Carnoy, M. (2017). *School vouchers are not a proven strategy for improving student achievement: Studies of US and international voucher programs show that the risks to school systems outweigh insignificant gains in test scores and limited gains in graduation rates*. Economic Policy Institute. Retrieved from https://eric.ed.gov/?id=ED579337

Carr, P. B. (1999). *The measurement of resourcefulness intentions in the adult autonomous learner* (Doctoral dissertation). Available from ProQuest Dissertations and Theses Global database. (UMI No. 304520149)

Castillo, J. M., Dorman, C., Gaunt, B., Hardcastle, B., Justice, K., & March, A. L. (2016). Design research as a mechanism for consultants to facilitate and evaluate educational innovations. *Journal of Educational & Psychological Consultation*, *26*(1), 25–48. doi:10.1080/10474412.2015.1039125

Centre for Teaching Excellence. (2021). *Gamification and game-based learning.* University of Waterloo. https://uwaterloo.ca/centre-for-teaching-excellence/teaching-resources/teaching-tips/educational-technologies/all/gamification-and-game-based-learning

Chambers, D., Scala, J., & English, D. (2020). *Promising practices brief: Improving student engagement and attendance during COVID-19 school closures.* U.S. Department of Education. https://insightpolicyresearch.com/wp-content/uploads/2020/08/NSAES_COVID19_Whitepaper_Final_508.pdf

Chang, N. & Petersen, N. (2005). Cybercoaching: An Emerging Model of Personalized Online Assessment. *Online Assessment, Measurement and Evaluation: Emerging Practices*, 110-130. . doi:10.4018/978-1-59140-747-8.ch008

Chanpet, P., Chomsuwan, K., & Murphy, E. (2020). Online project-based learning and formative assessment. Technology. *Knowledge and Learning*, *25*(1), 685–705. doi:10.100710758-018-9363-2

Chickering, A. W., & Ehrmann, S. (1996). Implementing the seven principles: Technology as a lever. *AAHE Bulletin*.

Chickering, A. W., & Gamson, Z. F. (1991). *Applying the seven principles for good practice in undergraduate education. New directions in teaching and learning.* Jossey-Boss.

Choi, J. H., McCart, A. B., Hicks, T. A., & Sailor, W. (2019). An analysis of mediating effects of school leadership on MTSS implementation. *The Journal of Special Education*, *53*(1), 15–27. doi:10.1177/0022466918804815

Çiltaş, A. (2011). Eğitimde öz-düzenleme öğretiminin önemi üzerine bir çalışma [A study on the importance of self-regulation teaching in education]. *Mehmet Akif Ersoy Üniversitesi Sosyal Bilimler Enstitüsü Dergisi*, *3*(5), 1–11.

Clark, D. (2014). Robert Gagné's Nine Steps of Instruction. *Big Dog & Little Dog's Performance Juxtaposition.* http://www.nwlink.com/~donclark/hrd/learning/id/nine_step_id.html

Clotfelter, C., Ladd, H., & Vigdor, J. (2007). *How and why do teacher credentials matter for student achievement?* NBER Working Paper. doi:10.3386/w12828

Clouse, S. F., & Evans, G. E. (2003). Graduate business students performance with synchronous and asynchronous interaction e-learning methods. *Decision Sciences Journal of Innovative Education*, *1*(2), 181–202. doi:10.1111/j.1540-4609.2003.00017.x

Coates, H., James, R., & Baldwin, G. (2005). A critical examination of the effects of learning management systems on university teaching and learning. *Tertiary Education and Management*, *11*(1), 19–36. doi:10.1080/13583883.2005.9967137

Coker, F. H., & Scarboro, A. (1990). Writing to Learn in Upper-Division Sociology Courses: Two Case Studies. *Teaching Sociology*, *18*(2), 218–222. doi:10.2307/1318494

Confessore, S. J., & Confessore, G. J. (1994). Learner profiles: A cross-sectional study of selected factors associated with self-directed learning. In H. B. Long (Ed.), *New ideas about self-directed learning* (pp. 201–227). Oklahoma Research for Continuing Professional and Higher Education.

Creswell, J. W. (2017). A concise introduction to mixed methods research. Ankara: Pegem.

Crews, T. B., Wilkinson, K., & Neill, J. (2015). Principles for good practice in undergraduate education: Effective online course design to assist students' success. *Journal of Online Learning and Teaching*, *11*(1), 87–103.

Croitoru, C. N. (2016). A Critical Analysis of Learning Management Systems in Higher Education. DINU. *Ecological Informatics*, *16*(1), 5–18.

Crompton, H. (2013). The Benefits and Challenges of Mobile Learning. *Learning and Leading with Technology*, 38–39.

D'Angelo, C. (2018). The impact of technology: Student engagement and success. *Technology and the Curriculum*. https://techandcurriculum.pressbooks.com/chapter/engagement-and-success/

Dabbagh, N. H., Jonassen, D. H., Yueh, H.-P., & Sanouiloua, M. (2000). Assessing a problem-based learning approach to an introductory instructional design course: A case study. *Performance Improvement Quarterly*, *13*(3), 60–83. doi:10.1111/j.1937-8327.2000.tb00176.x

Dabbagh, N., & Kitsantas, A. (2004). Supporting self-regulation in student-centered web-based learning environments. *International Journal on E-Learning*, *3*, 40–47.

Darling-Hammond, L., & Cook-Harvey, C. M. (2018). *Educating the whole child: Improving school climate to support student success*. Learning Policy Institute. Retrieved from https://eric.ed.gov/?id=ED606462

Davis, F. (1989). Perceived Usefulness, Perceived Ease of Use, and User Acceptance of Information Technology. *Management Information Systems Quarterly*, *13*(3), 319–340. doi:10.2307/249008

Davis, F. D., Bogozzi, R., & Warshaw, P. R. (1989). User acceptance of computer technology: A comparison of two theoretical models. *Management Science*, *35*(8), 982–1003. doi:10.1287/mnsc.35.8.982

de Ridder-Symoens, H. (1992). Mobility. In H. de Ridder-Symoens (Ed.), *A history of the university in Europe* (Vol. 1, pp. 280–304). Cambridge University Press.

Dede, C., & Kremer, A. (1999). Increasing students' participation via multiple interactive media. *Invention: Creative Thinking About Learning and Teaching*, *1*(1), 7.

Deming, D. J., Goldin, C., Katz, L. F., & Yuchtman, N. (2015). Can online learning bend the higher education cost curve? *The American Economic Review*, *105*(5), 496–501. doi:10.1257/aer.p20151024

Demirel, Ö. (Ed.). (2010). *Eğitimde Yeni Yönelimler*. Apegem Akademi.

DePaoli, J. L., Balfanz, R., Atwell, M. N., & Bridgeland, J. (2018). Building a grad nation: Progress and challenge in raising high school graduation rates. Annual Update 2018. *Civic Enterprises.* Retrieved from https://eric.ed.gov/?id=ED585524

Deperlioğlu, Ö., & Köse, U. (2010). *Web 2.0 Teknolojilerinin eğitim üzerindeki etkileri ve örnek bir öğrenme yaşantısı. In XII. Akademik Bilişim Konferans Bildirileri.* Muğla Üniversitesi.

Derrick, M. G. (2001). *The measurement of an adult's intention to exhibit persistence in autonomous learning* (Doctoral dissertation). Available from ProQuest Dissertations and Theses Global database. (UMI No. 276280161)

Distance Learning. (n.d.). *National Center for Education Statistics.* Retrieved from https://nces.ed.gov/fastfacts/display.asp?id=79

Doğan, D., Duman, D., & Seferoğlu, S. S. (2011). E-öğrenme ortamlarında toplumsal buradalığın arttırılması için kullanılabilecek iletişim araçları. *Akademik Bilişim*, 2-4.

Downes, S. (2005). *An Introduction to Connective Knowledge.* https://www.downes.ca/post/33034

Downes, S. (2011). *"Connectivism" and connective knowledge.* https://www.huffingtonpost.com/stephendownes/connectivismandconnecti_b_804653.html

Ducate, L. C. I, & Lomicka, L. (2008). Adventures in the blogosphere: From blog readers to blog writers. *Computer Assisted Language Learning*, *21*(1), 9–28. doi:10.1080/09588220701865474

Duffy, J. (2018). Implementation of response to intervention (RTI) and a multi-tiered system of support (MTSS): A case study examination of one school district in Minnesota. *Culminating Projects in Education Administration and Leadership*, 40. Retrieved from https://repository.stcloudstate.edu/edad_etds/40

Durnalı, M., Orakcı, Ş., & Aktan, O. (2019). The smart learning potential of Turkey's education system in the context of FATIH project. In A. Darshan Singh, S. Raghunathan, E. Robeck, & B. Sharma (Eds.), *Cases on Smart Learning Environments* (pp. 227–243). IGI Global. doi:10.4018/978-1-5225-6136-1.ch013

Durnalı, M., Orakcı, Ş., & Özkan, O. (2018). Turkey's higher education potential for human capital of eurasian region. In O. Karnaukhova, A. Udovikina, & B. Christiansen (Eds.), *Economic and Geopolitical Perspectives of the Commonwealth of Independent States and Eurasia* (pp. 201–224). IGI Global. doi:10.4018/978-1-5225-3264-4.ch009

Du, S., & Lin, J. (2012). Research on System Design and Security Management for Campus Mobile Learning. *IEEE International Conference on Computer Science and Automation Engineering (CSAE).* 10.1109/CSAE.2012.6273001

Eagle, J. W., Dowd-Eagle, S. E., Snyder, A., & Holtzman, E. G. (2015). Implementing a multitiered system of support (MTSS): Collaboration between school psychologists and administrators to promote systems-level change. *Journal of Educational & Psychological Consultation, 25*(2-3), 160–177. doi:10.1080/10474412.2014.929960

Easton, J. Q., Johnson, E., & Sartain, L. (2017). *The predictive power of ninth-grade GPA.* University of Chicago Consortium on School Research. Retrieved from http://www.hsredesign. org/wp-content/uploads/2018/07/Predictive-Power-of-Ninth-Grade-Sept-2017-Consortium.pdf

Eccles, J. (1983). Expectancies, values and academic behaviors. In J. T. Spence (Ed.), Achievement and achievement motives (pp. 75-146). Freeman.

Edmondson, A. (2018, June 14). *How to turn a group of strangers into a team.* YouTube. https:// youtu.be/3boKz0Exros

Edmondson, A. C. (2012). *Teaming: How organizations learn, innovate, and compete in the knowledge economy.* Jossey-Bass.

Elmas, Ç., Doğan, N., Biroğul, S., & Mehmet, K. O. Ç. (2008). Moodle eğitim yönetim sistemi ile örnek bir dersin uzaktan eğitim uygulaması. *Bilişim Teknolojileri Dergisi, 1*(2).

Elmore, R. F. (2000). *Building a new structure for school leadership.* The Albert Shanker Institute.

Erdoğan, Y., Bayram, S., & Deniz, L. (2007). Web tabanlı öğretim tutum ölçeği: Açıklayıcı ve doğrulayıcı faktör analizi çalışması. *Uluslararası İnsan Bilimleri Dergisi, 4*(2), 1–14.

Ergül, H. (2006). Çevrimiçi eğitimde akademik başarıyı etkileyen güdülenme yapıları [Motivational structures affecting academic success in online education]. *The Turkish Online Journal of Educational Technology, 5*(1), 124–128.

Ertmer, P., & Koehler, A. A. (2014). Online case-based discussions: Examining coverage of The afforded problem space. *Educational Technology Research and Development, 62*(5), 617–636. doi:10.100711423-014-9350-9

Evans-Cowley, J. (2010). Planning in the Real-Time City: The Future of Mobile Technology. *Journal of Planning Literature, 25*(2), 136–149. doi:10.1177/0885412210394100

Fabre, P. (2019, June 3). A duoethnography study: How people's life histories shape their current academic beliefs. *Espacios, 40*(8), http://www.revistaespacios.com/a19v40n08/a19v40n08p29.pdf

Fies, C., & Marshall, J. (2006). Classroom Response Systems: A Review of the Literature. *Journal of Science Education and Technology, 15*(1), 101–109. doi:10.100710956-006-0360-1

Filiz, B., & Konukman, F. (2020). Teaching strategies for physical education during 16 the COVID-19 Pandemic. *Journal of Physical Education, Recreation & Dance, 91*(9), 49–51. doi: 10.1080/07303084.2020.1816099

Finley, T. (2014). *Dipsticks: Efficient ways to check for understanding.* Edutopia. https://www. edutopia.org/blog/dipsticks-to-check-for-understanding-todd-finley

Finley, J., Taylor, S., & Warren, L. (2007). Investigating graduate business student's perceptions of the educational value provided by an international travel course experience. *Journal of Teaching in International Business, 19*(1), 51–82. doi:10.1300/J066v19n01_04

Fırat, M., Yurdakul, I. K., & Ersoy, A. (2014). Bir eğitim teknolojisi araştırmasına dayalı olarak karma yöntem araştırması deneyimi. *Eğitimde Nitel Araştırmalar Dergisi, 2*(1), 64–85. doi:10.14689/issn.2148-2624.1.2s3m

Fixsen, D.L., Blase, K. A., Naoom, S. F., & Duda, M. A. (2015). Implementation drivers: Assessing best practices. *NIRN, 5*(2015).

Flowers, N., Mertens, S. B., & Mulhall, P. F. (2000). How teaming influences classroom practices. *Middle School Journal, 32*(2), 52–59. doi:10.1080/00940771.2000.11495267

Freeman, R. (1997). *Managing open systems.* Kogan Page.

Freeman, R., Miller, D., & Newcomer, L. (2015). Integration of academic and behavioral MTSS at the district level using implementation science. *Learning Disabilities (Weston, Mass.), 13*(1), 59–72.

Furr, N., & Dyer, J. H. (2014). *Leading your team into the unknown: How great managers empower their organizations to innovate.* Retrieved from: https://hbr.org/2014/12/leading-your-team-into-the-unknown

Gacel-Avila, J. (2005). The internationalisation of higher education: A paradigm for global citizenry. *Journal of Studies in International Education, 9*(2), 121–136. doi:10.1177/1028315304263795

Gagné, R. (1985). *The Conditions of Learning and the Theory of Instruction* (4th ed.). Holt, Rinehart, and Winston.

Garrison, D. R. (2003). Self-directed Learning and Distance Education. In M. G. Moore & W. G. Anderson (Eds.), *Handbook of Distance Education.* Lawrence Erlbaum Associates.

Genç, S. Z., Engin, G., & Yardım, T. (2020). Pandemi (COVID-19) sürecindeki uzaktan eğitim uygulamalarına ilişkin lisansüstü öğrenci görüşleri. *Atatürk Üniversitesi Kazım Karabekir Eğitim Fakültesi Dergisi*, (41), 134–158.

Gikandi, J. W., Morrow, D., & Davis, N. E. (2011). Online formative assessment in higher education: A review of the literature. *Computers & Education, 57*(4), 2333–2351. doi:10.1016/j.compedu.2011.06.004

Gladwell, M. (2002). *The tipping point.* Back Bay Books.

Godwin-Jones, R. (2008). Emerging technologies. Web-writing 2.0: Enabling, documenting, and assessing writing online. *Language Learning & Technology, 12*(2), 7–13.

Gopal, R., Singh, V., & Aggarwal, A. (2021). Impact of online classes on the satisfaction and performance of students during the pandemic period of COVID 19. *Education and Information Technologies, 26*(6), 6923–6947. doi:10.100710639-021-10523-1 PMID:33903795

Gottfried, M. A. (2009). Excused Versus Unexcused: How Student Absences in Elementary School Affect Academic Achievement. *Educational Evaluation and Policy Analysis, 31*(4), 392–415. doi:10.3102/0162373709342467

Goyal, J. K., Daipuria, P., & Jain, S. (2021). An alternative structure of delivering management education in India. *Journal of Educational Technology Systems, 49*(3), 325–340. doi:10.1177/0047239520958612

Graff, M. (2003). Cognitive Style and Attitudes Towards Using Online Learning and Assessment Methods. *Electronic Journal of e-Learning, 1*(1), 21-28.

Gray, K., Thompson, C., Sheard, J., Clerehan, R., & Hamilton, M. (2010). Students as Web 2.0 authors: Implications for assessment design and conduct. *Australasian Journal of Educational Technology, 26*(1), 105–122. doi:10.14742/ajet.1105

Grev, I. (2015). *5 ways to focus on results instead of the process.* Retrieved from: https://www.bizjournals.com/bizjournals/how-to/growth-strategies/2015/04/5-ways-to-focus-on-results-instead-of-process.html

Gülbahar, Y., Kalelioğlu, F., & Madran, O. (2010). Sosyal ağların eğitim amaçlı kullanımı. In XV. Türkiye'de İnternet Konferansı. İstanbul Teknik Üniversitesi.

Güler, M. (2015). Öğretmen *adaylarının öz düzenleme becerilerinin; duygusal zekâları, epistemolojik inançları ve bazı değişkenler açısından incelenmesi* [Self-regulation skills of teacher candidates; their emotional intelligence, epistemological beliefs and some variables] [Doctoral dissertation]. Necmettin Erbakan University, Turkey.

Gupta, A. (2021). Teacher-entrepreneurialism: A case of teacher identity formation in neoliberalizing education space in contemporary India. *Critical Studies in Education, 62*(4), 422–438. doi:10.1080/17508487.2019.1708765

Gürler, C., Uslu, T., & Daştan, İ. (2020). Evaluation of distance learning from student perspective in COVID-19 pandemic. *Atatürk Üniversitesi Sosyal Bilimler Enstitüsü Dergisi, 24*(4), 1895–1904.

Guskey, T. R. (1988). Teacher efficacy, self-concept, and attitudes toward the implementation of instructional innovation. *Teaching and Teacher Education, 4*(1), 63–69. doi:10.1016/0742-051X(88)90025-X

HaddadPajouh, H., Dehghantanha, A., Parizi, R. M., Aledhari, M., & Karimipour, H. (2021). A survey on internet of things security: Requirements, challenges, and solutions. *Internet of Things, 14*, 100129. doi:10.1016/j.iot.2019.100129

Hadullo, K., Oboko, R., & Omwenga, E. (2018). Factors affecting asynchronous e-learning quality in developing countries university settings. *International Journal of Education and Development Using ICT, 14*(1), 152-163.

Hammond, A. L. (1972). Plato & ticcit: CAI in action. *College and University Business, 66*, 39–42.

Hammoud, R. I. (2006). *Interactive Video Algorithm and Technologies*. Springer. doi:10.1007/978-3-540-33215-2

Hamrick, J. (1999). *Internationalizing higher educational institutions: Broadening the approach to institutional exchange.* Paper presented at Managing Institutional Change and Transformation Project, Center for the Study of Higher and Postsecondary Education, University of Michigan, Ann Arbor, MI. Retrieved from http://www.personal.umich.edu/~marvp/facultynetwork/whitepapers/jimhamrick.html

Handal, B., Ritter, R., & Marcovitz. (2014). *Implementing Large Scale Mobile Learning School Programs: To BYOD or not to BYOD.* In EdMedia, Tampere, Finland.

Harmon, O. R., & Lambrinos, J. (2008). Are Online Exams an Invitation to Cheat? *The Journal of Economic Education*, *39*(2), 116–125. doi:10.3200/JECE.39.2.116-125

Harn, B., Basaraba, D., Chard, D., & Fritz, R. (2015). The impact of schoolwide prevention efforts: Lessons learned from implementing independent academic and behavior support systems. *Learning Disabilities (Weston, Mass.)*, *13*(1), 3–20.

Harrington, A. M. (2010). Problematizing the hybrid classroom for ESL/EFL students. *TESL-EJ*, *14*(3), 1–13.

Harris, J., & Anderson, S. (1991). Cultivating teacher telecommunications networks from the grass roots up: The electronic academical village at Virginia. *Computers in Schools, 8*(1/2/3), 191-202.

Harris, S. (2008). Internationalising the university. *Educational Philosophy and Theory*, *40*(2), 346–357. doi:10.1111/j.1469-5812.2007.00336.x

Hart, C. M., Berger, D., Jacob, B., Loeb, S., & Hill, M. (2019). Online learning, offline outcomes: Online course taking and high school student performance. *AERA Open*, *5*(1). Advance online publication. doi:10.1177/2332858419832852

Hartley, K., & Bendixen, L. D. (2001). Educational research in the Internet age: Examining the role of individual characteristics. *Educational Researcher, 30*(9), 22–26. doi:10.3102/0013189X030009022

Haşlaman, T., Demiraslan, Y., Mumcu, F. K., Dönmez, O., & Aşkar, P. (2008). Çevrimiçi ortamda yapılan grup tartışmasındaki iletişim örüntülerinin söylem çözümlemesi yoluyla incelenmesi. *Hacettepe Üniversitesi Eğitim Fakültesi Dergisi*, *35*(35), 162–174.

Hergüner, G., Yaman, Ç., Sarı, S. C., Yaman, M. S., & Dönmez, A. (2021). The effect of online learning attitudes of sports sciences students on their learning readiness to learn online in the era of the new coronavirus pandemic (COVID-19). *The Turkish Online Journal of Educational Technology*, *20*(1), 68–77.

Herlihy, C. M., & Quint, J. (2006). *Emerging evidence on improving high school student achievement and graduation rates: The effects of four popular improvement programs. Issue Brief.* National High School Center. Retrieved from https://eric.ed.gov/?id=ED501076

Hew, K. F., & Brush, T. (2007). Integrating Technology into K–12 Teaching and Learning: Current knowledge gaps and recommendations for future research. *Educational Technology Research and Development*, *55*(3), 223–252. doi:10.100711423-006-9022-5

Hiltz, S. R. (1997). Impacts of college-level courses via asynchronous Learning Networks: Some Preliminary Results. *Journal of Asynchronous Learning Networks*, *1*(2), 1–19.

Hodges, C., Moore, S., Lockee, B., Trust, T., & Bond, A. (2020, March 27). The difference between emergency remote teaching and online learning. *EduCause Review*. https://er.educause.edu/articles/2020/3/the-difference-between-emergency-remote-teaching-and-online-learning

Hollingsworth, S. M. (2019). Multi-tiered system of supports as collective work: A (re)structuring option for middle schools. *Current Issues in Middle Level Education*, *24*(2). Advance online publication. doi:10.20429/cimle.2019.240204

Hopperton, L. G. (1998). Computer conferencing and college education. *The College Quarterly*, *5*(2).

How Many Students are Actually Reading Below Grade Level?! (2021). *ASCEND Learning Center*. https://www.ascendlearningcenter.com/blog-highlights/howmanystudents

Hrastinski, S. (2007). The Potential of Synchronous Communication to Enhance Participation in Online Discussions, *International Conference on Information Systems*, 9–12.

Hrastinski, S. (2008). A study of asynchronous and synchronous e-learning methods discovered that each supports different purposes. *EDUCAUSE Quarterly*, *4*, 51–55.

Hrbackova, K., & Safrankova, A. P. (2016). Self-Regulation of Behaviour in Children and Adolescents in the Natural and Institutional Environment. *Procedia: Social and Behavioral Sciences*, *217*, 679–687. doi:10.1016/j.sbspro.2016.02.119

Hung, S. T. A., & Huang, H. T. D. (2016). Blogs as a learning and assessment instrument for English-speaking performance. *Interactive Learning Environments*, *24*(8), 1881–1894. doi:10.1080/10494820.2015.1057746

Hwang, W. Y., & Wang, C. Y. (2004). A study of learning time patterns in asynchronous learning environments. *Journal of Computer Assisted Learning*, *20*(4), 292–304. doi:10.1111/j.1365-2729.2004.00088.x

In the Spotlight. (n.d.). *Erasmus+ Brings People Together*. Retrieved from https://ec.europa.eu/programmes/erasmus-plus/anniversary/spotlight-erasmus-brings-people-together_en

Institute of International Education. (2020). *Open Doors Report*. Retrieved from https://opendoorsdata.org/annual-release/

Ismail, I., Azizan, S. N., & Azman, N. (2013). Mobile Phone as Pedagogical Tools: Are Teachers Ready? *International Education Studies*, *6*(3), 36–47. doi:10.5539/ies.v6n3p36

Ismaili, Y. (2021). Evaluation of students' attitude toward distance learning during the pandemic (COVID-19): A case study of ELTE university. *On the Horizon, 29*(1), 17–30. doi:10.1108/OTH-09-2020-0032

İşman, A. (2011). *Uzaktan Eğitim*. Pegem Akademi.

Jacobo, J. (2019). *Teens spend more than 7 hours on screens for entertainment a day: Report.* ABC News. https://abcnews.go.com/US/teens-spend-hours-screens-entertainment-day-report/story?id=66607555#:~:text=Teens%20spend%20an%20average%20of,technology%20and%20media%20for%20children

Jaffee, D. (1997). Asynchronous learning: Technology and pedagogical strategy in a distance learning course. *Teaching Sociology, 25*(4), 262–277. doi:10.2307/1319295

Jerald, C. D. (2006). *Identifying potential dropouts: Key lessons for building an early warning data system. A dual agenda of high Standards and high graduation rates.* Achieve, Inc. Retrieved from https://eric.ed.gov/?id=ED499838

Johns Hopkins University. (2014). *A Brief History of JHU*. Retrieved from https://webapps.jhu.edu/jhuniverse/information_about_hopkins/about_jhu/a_brief_history_of_jhu/

Johnson, G. M. (2006). Synchronous and asynchronous text-based CMC in educational contexts: A review of recent research. *TechTrends, 50*(4), 46–53. doi:10.100711528-006-0046-9

Jonassen, D. H. (1994). Technology as cognitive tools: Students as designers. *IT Forum Paper, 1*, 67-80.

Joshi, A., Virk, A., Saiyad, S., Mahajan, R., & Singh, T. (2020). Online assessment: Concept and applications. *Journal of Research in Medical Education & Ethics, 10*(2), 49–59. doi:10.5958/2231-6728.2020.00015.3

Joy, S. (2021, July 13). Students lag in learning as Covid-19 pandemic widens digital gap. *Deccan Herald*. https://www.deccanherald.com/national/students-lag-in-learning-as-covid-19-pandemic-widens-digital-gap-1008227.html

Kağızmanlı, T. B., Tatar, E., & Zengin, Y. (2014). Öğretmen adaylarının matematik öğretiminde teknoloji kullanımına ilişkin algılarının incelenmesi. *Ahi Evran Üniversitesi Kırşehir Eğitim Fakültesi Dergisi, 14*(2), 349–370.

Kalaycı, Ş. (2009). *SPSS uygulamalı çok değişkenli istatistik teknikleri* [SPSS applied multivariate statistical techniques]. Asil Yayın.

Kamenetz, A. (2019). *It's A Smartphone Life: More Than Half of U.S. Children Now Have One.* NPR. https://www.npr.org/2019/10/31/774838891/its-a-smartphone-life-more-than-half-of-u-s-children-now-have-one

Kaplan, E. (2014*). Beden eğitimi ve spor öğretmenliği öğrencilerinde özdüzenleme: ölçek uyarlama çalışması* [Self-regulation in physical education and sports teaching students: A scale adaptation study] [Unpublished master dissertation]. Akdeniz University, Turkey.

Kaplan, E., & Certel, Z. (2018). Beden eğitimi ve spor öğretmenliği öğrencilerinin akademik öz-düzenlemelerinin incelenmesi [Examining the academic self-regulation of physical education and sports teacher students]. *Mediterranean Journal of Humanities, 8*(1), 237–246. doi:10.13114/MJH.2018.394

Karadağ, A., & Şen, Y. A. (2014). *Uzaktan Eğitimde Rol Alan Kişiler ve Öğretmen Öğrenci Rolleri*. Anadolu Üniversitesi.

Karagöz, S. (2021). Evaluation of distance education: The sample of guidance and counseling students (Example of Aksaray University). *The Universal Academic Research Journal, 3*(1), 18–25.

Karagöz, S., & Rüzgar, M. E. (2021). An investigation of the prospective teachers' viewpoints about distance education during the COVID-19 pandemic. *International Journal of Curriculum and Instruction, 13*(3), 2611–2634.

Karaman, S., Özen, Ü., Yıldırım, S., & Kaban, A. (2009). Açık kaynak kodlu öğretim yönetim sistemi üzerinden internet destekli (harmanlanmış) öğrenim deneyimi. *Akademik Bilişim Konferansı*, 11-13.

Karaman, S., Kaban, A., & Yıldırım, S. (2010). Sınıf blogu ile grup bloglarının öğrenci katılımı ve görüşleri açısından karşılaştırılması. *Eğitim Teknolojileri Araştırmaları Dergisi, 1*(2), 1–12.

Karaoğlu, B., & Pepe, O. (2020). Beden eğitimi öğretmen adaylarının akademik öz düzenleme becerilerinin bazı değişkenlere göre incelenmesi [Examination of academic self-regulation skills of physical education teacher candidates according to some variables]. *Beden Eğitimi ve Spor Bilimleri Dergisi, 14*(2), 214–224.

Karataş, S. (2005). *Deneyim Eşitliğine Dayalı İnternet Temelli ve Yüz yüze Öğrenme Sistemlerinin Öğrenci Başarı ve Deneyimi Açısından Karşılaştırılması*. Doktora Tezi, Ankara Üniversitesi, Eğitim Bilimleri Enstitüsü.

Karppinen, P. (2005). Meaningful learning with digital and online videos: Theoretical perspectives. *Association for the Advancement of Computing In Education Journal, 13*(3), 233–250.

Kayler, M., & Weller, K. (2007). Pedagogy, Self-Assessment, and Online Discussion Groups. *Journal of Educational Technology & Society, 10*(1), 136–147.

Kearns, L. R. (2012). Student Assessment in Online Learning: Challenges and Effective Practices. *Journal of Online Learning and Teaching, 8*(3), 198–208.

Kearsley, G., & Blomeyer, R. (2004). Preparing K—12 Teachers to Teach Online. *Educational Technology, 44*(1), 49–52.

Keegan, D. (1986). *The foundations of distance education*. Croom Helm.

Keegan, D. (1996). *Foundations of Distance Education*. Routledge.

Kerr, C. (1994). *Higher education cannot escape history: Issues for the twenty-first century*. SUNY Press.

Khine, M. S., & Lourdusamy, A. (2003). Blended learning approach in teacher education: Combining face-to-face instruction, multimedia viewing and online discussion. *British Journal of Educational Technology*, *34*(5), 671–675. doi:10.1046/j.0007-1013.2003.00360.x

Khlaif, Z. N., Salha, S., & Kouraichi, B. (2021). Emergency remote learning during COVID-19 crisis: Students' engagement. *Education and Information Technologies*, *26*(6), 7033–7055. Advance online publication. doi:10.100710639-021-10566-4 PMID:33935578

Kim, S., & Kim, J. N. (2016). Bridge or buffer: Two ideas of effective corporate governance and public engagement. *Journal of Public Affairs*, *16*(2), 118–127. doi:10.1002/pa.1555

King, A. (1994). Guiding knowledge construction in the classroom: Effects of teaching children how to question and how to explain. *American Educational Research Journal*, *31*(2), 338–368. doi:10.3102/00028312031002338

King, A., Staffieri, A., & Adelgais, A. (1998). Mutual peer tutoring: Effects of structuring tutorial interaction to scaffold peer learning. *Journal of Educational Psychology*, *90*(1), 134–152. doi:10.1037/0022-0663.90.1.134

King, C., Guyette, R., & Piotrowski, C. (2009). Online exams and cheating: An empirical analysis of business students' views. *The Journal of Educators Online*, *6*(1), 1–11. doi:10.9743/JEO.2009.1.5

Kitsantas, A., & Judith, M. (2001). *Studying abroad: Does it enhance college student cross-cultural awareness?* Paper presented at the combined annual meeting of the San Diego State University and the US Department of Education Centers for International Business Education and Research, San Diego, CA.

Klann, G. (2003). *Crisis leadership: Using military lessons, organizational experiences, and the power of influence to lessen the impact of chaos on the people you lead.* Center for Creative Leadership.

Klecker, B. M. (2007). The impact of formative feedback on student learning in an online classroom. *Journal of Instructional Psychology*, *34*(3), 161–165.

Klein, A. (2016). States, districts will share more power under ESSA. *Education Digest*, *81*(8), 4. https://search.proquest.com/openview/dc7a395e4f446ec3c5b07b91d380a298/1.pdf?pq-origsite=gscholar&cbl=25066

Knight, J., & de Wit, H. (2018). Internationalization of Higher Education: Past and Future. *International Higher Education, 95*.

Knight, J., & de Wit, H. (1995). Strategies for internationalization of higher education: historical and conceptual perspectives. In H. de Wit (Ed.), *Strategies for Internationalization of Higher education: a comparative study of Australia, Canada, Europe and the United States of America* (pp. 5–33). European Association for International Education.

Knowles, M. (1996). Adult learning. In R. L. Craig (Ed.), *ASTD training & development handbook: A guide to human resource development* (4th ed., pp. 253–265). McGraw Hill.

Knowles, M. S. (1990). *The Adult Learner: A Neglected Species*. Gulf Publishing Co.

Kocdar, S., Karadeniz, A., Bozkurt, A., & Buyuk, K. (2018). Measuring self-regulation in selfpaced open and distance learning environments. *The International Review of Research in Open and Distributed Learning, 19*(1), 25–43. doi:10.19173/irrodl.v19i1.3255

Kochtanek, T. R., & Hein, K. K. (2000). Creating and nurturing distributed asynchronous learning environments. *Online Information Review, 24*(4), 280–293. doi:10.1108/14684520010350632

Korman, H. T. N., O'Keefe, B., & Repka, F. (2020). *Missing in the margins: Estimating the scale of the COVID-19 attendance crisis*. Bellwether Education Partners. https://bellwethereducation. org/publication/missing-margins-estimating-scale-covid-19-attendance-crisis#How%20did%20 you%20estimate%201-3%20million%20missing%20students?

Kurt, G., Atay, D., & Ozturk, H. A. (2020, June 16). Student engagement in K12 online education during the pandemic: The case of Turkey. *Journal of Research on Technology in Education*. Advance online publication. doi:10.1080/15391523.2021.1920518

Kurubacak, G. (2000). *Online learning: A study of students' attitudes towards Web-based instruction* (WBI) (Doctoral dissertation). University of Cincinnati.

Lampe, C., Wohn, D. Y., Vitak, J., Ellison, N. B., & Wash, R. (2011). Student use of Facebook for organizing collaborative classroom activities. *International Journal of Computer-Supported Collaborative Learning, 6*(3), 329–347. doi:10.100711412-011-9115-y

Lam, S., Cheng, R. W., & Choy, H. C. (2010). School support and teacher motivation to implement project-based learning. *Learning and Instruction, 20*(6), 487–497. doi:10.1016/j. learninstruc.2009.07.003

Leibold, N., & Schwarz, L. M. (2015). The Art of Giving Online Feedback. *The Journal of Effective Teaching, 15*(1), 34–46. https://uncw.edu/jet/articles/vol15_1/leibold.html

Lei, H. (2004). Contextual collaboration: Platform and applications. IEEE International Conference on Services Computing. (SCC 2004). *Proceedings., 2004*(2004), 197–206. doi:10.1109/ SCC.2004.1358007

Liberman, M. (2020, Nov 11). How hybrid learning is (and is not) working during COVID-19: 6 case studies. *Education Week*. https://www.edweek.org/leadership/how-hybrid-learning-is-and-is-not-working-during-covid-19-6-case-studies/2020/11

Lickerman, A. (2010). The Effect of Technology on Relationships. *Psychology Today*. https://www. psychologytoday.com/us/blog/happiness-in-world/201006/the-effect-technology-relationships

Linnenbrink, E. A., & Pintrich, P. R. (2003). The role of self-efficacy beliefs in student engagement and learning in the classroom. *Reading & Writing Quarterly, 19*(2), 119–137. doi:10.1080/10573560308223

Liyanagunawardena, T. R., Adams, A. A., & Williams, S. A. (2013). MOOCs: A systematic study of the published literature 2008-2012. *International Review of Research in Open and Distance Learning*, *14*(3), 202–227. doi:10.19173/irrodl.v14i3.1455

Lockard, J., Abrams, D. P., & Many, W. A. (1997). *Microcomputers for twenty-first century educators* (4th ed.). Longman.

Lock, J. V., & Redmond, P. (2015). Empowering Learners to Engage in Authentic Online Assessment. In S. Koç, X. Liu, & P. Wachira (Eds.), *Assessment in Online and Blended Learning Environments*. Information Age Publishing, Inc.

Loder, M. (2020). *The Fingerprints of your Classroom*. Arizona State University. https://teachonline.asu.edu/2020/05/universal-design-and-your-allyies-pedagogical-strategies/

Loey, M., Manogaran, G., Taha, M. H. N., & Khalifa, N. E. M. (2021). A hybrid deep transfer learning model with machine learning methods for face mask detection in the era of the COVID-19 pandemic. *Measurement*, *167*, 108288. doi:10.1016/j.measurement.2020.108288 PMID:32834324

Loh, C.-P. A., Steagall, J. W., Gallo, A., & Michelman, J. E. (2011). Valuing Short-Term Study Abroad in Business. *Journal of Teaching in International Business*, *22*(2), 73–90. doi:10.1080/08975930.2011.615669

Loyalka, P., Liu, O. L., Li, G., Kardanova, E., Chirikov, I., Hu, S., Yu, N., Ma, L., Guo, F., Beteille, T., Tognatta, N., Gu, L., Ling, G., Federiakin, D., Wang, H., Khanna, S., Bhuradia, A., Shi, Z., & Li, Y. (2021). Skill levels and gains in university STEM education in China, India, Russia and the United States. *Nature Human Behaviour*, *5*(7), 892–904. doi:10.103841562-021-01062-3 PMID:33649462

Mac Iver, M. A. (2011). The challenge of improving urban high school graduation outcomes: Findings from a randomized study of dropout prevention efforts. *Journal of Education for Students Placed at Risk*, *16*(3), 167–184. doi:10.1080/10824669.2011.584497

Mann, B. L. (2006). Testing the Validity of the Post and Vote Model of Web-Based Peer Assessment. In Online Assessment, Measurement, and Evaluation: Emerging Practices. Hricko Science Publishing. doi:10.4018/978-1-59140-747-8.ch009

Markel, S. L., & Ecl, E. E. (2001). Technology and education online discussion forums. *Online Journal of Distance Learning Administration*, 4.

Marley, C., Faye, A. D., Hurst, E., Moeller, J., & Pinkerton, A. (2021). Moving Beyond 'You Said, We Did': Extending an Ethic of Hospitality to The Student Feedback Process. In *Online Postgraduate Education in a Postdigital World* (pp. 1–19). Springer. doi:10.1007/978-3-030-77673-2_1

Maslow, A. (1943). A theory of human motivation. *Psychological Review*, *50*(4), 370–396. doi:10.1037/h0054346

Mason, E. N., Benz, S. A., Lembke, E. S., Burns, M. K., & Powell, S. R. (2019). From professional development to implementation: A district's experience implementing mathematics tiered systems of support. *Learning Disabilities Research & Practice*, *34*(4), 207–214. doi:10.1111/ldrp.12206

Maxwell, L. A. (2020). *The pandemic may drive principals to quit*. Retrieved from: https://www.edweek.org/leadership/the-pandemic-may-drive-principals-to-quit/2020/08

Mayer, R. (2021). *Multimedia Learning* (3rd ed.). Cambridge University Press., doi:10.1017/9781316941355

McCallumore, K. M., & Sparapani, E. F. (2010). The importance of the ninth grade on high school graduation rates and student success. *Education Digest*, *76*(2), 60.

McCart, A. B., Sailor, W. S., Bezdek, J. M., & Satter, A. L. (2014). A framework for inclusive educational delivery systems. *Inclusion*, *2*(4), 252–264. doi:10.1352/2326-6988-2.4.252

McClelland, M. M., & Cameron, C. E. (2011). Self-regulation and academic achievement in elementary school children. *New Directions for Child and Adolescent Development*, *2011*(133), 29–44. doi:10.1002/cd.302 PMID:21898897

McCombs, B. L. (2001). What do we know about students and learning? The student centered framework: Bringing the educational system into balance. *Educational Horizons*, (Spring), 182–193.

McCoy, D. C., Yoshikawa, H., Ziol-Guest, K. M., Duncan, G. J., Schindler, H. S., Magnuson, K., Yang, R., Koepp, A., & Shonkoff, J. P. (2017). Impacts of early childhood education on medium-and long-term educational outcomes. *Educational Researcher*, *46*(8), 474–487. doi:10.3102/0013189X17737739 PMID:30147124

McKethan, R., Everhart, B., & Sanders, R. (2001). The effects of multimedia software instruction and lecture-based instruction on learning and teaching cues of manipulative skills on preservice physical education teachers. *Physical Educator*, *58*(1), 2–13.

McMullan, M., Endacott, R., Gray, M., Jasper, M. A., Miller, C. M., Scholes, J., & Webb, J. (2003). Portfolios and assessment of competence: A review of the literature. *Journal of Advanced Nursing*, *41*(3), 283–294. doi:10.1046/j.1365-2648.2003.02528.x PMID:12581116

Mehrabian, A. (1971). *Silent Messages*. Wadsworth Publishing.

Mental Health Foundation. (2018). *Mental Health statistics: Stress*. Retrieved from: https://www.mentalhealth.org.uk/statistics/mental-health-statistics-stress

Merrill, M. D., Schneider, E. W., & Fletcher, K. A. (1980). *TICCIT*. Educational Technology Publications.

Michael, A., Armando, F., Rean, G., Anthony, D. J., Randy, K., Andy, K., ... Matei, Z. (2010). Bulut bilişimin görüntüsü. *ACM'nin İletişimi*, *53*(4), 50–58.

Miles, M. B., Huberman, M. A., & Saldana, J. (1994). *Qualitative data analysis: An expanded sourcebook*. Sage.

Milone, A. S., Cortese, A. M., Balestrieri, R. L., & Pittenger, A. L. (2017). The impact of proctored online exams on the educational experience. *Currents in Pharmacy Teaching & Learning, 9*(1), 108–114. doi:10.1016/j.cptl.2016.08.037 PMID:29180142

Mischel, W. (1961). Preference for delayed reinforcement and social responsibility. *Journal of Abnormal and Social Psychology, 62*(1), 1–7. doi:10.1037/h0048263 PMID:13771261

Mohan, G. V. M. (2021). Higher Education in India-Issues and Challenges. Assessment, Accreditation and Ranking Methods for Higher Education Institutes in India. *Current Findings and Future Challenges*, 134.

Montelongo, R. (2019). Less than/more than: Issues associated with high-impact online teaching and learning. *Administrative Issues Journal: Connecting Education, Practice and Research, 9*(1), 68–79.

Moore. M. (1973). Toward a theory of independent learning and teaching. *Journal of Higher Education, 44*, 661-679.

Moore, J. L., & Marra, R. M. (2005). A comparative analysis of online discussion participation protocols. *Journal of Research on Technology in Education, 38*(2), 191–212. doi:10.1080/153 91523.2005.10782456

Moore, M. (1990). *Background and overview of contemporary American distance education.* Pergamon.

Moore, M. G., & Kearsley, I. G. (2012). *Distance education: A systems view of online learning* (3rd ed.). Wadsworth Publishing.

Moore, R. (1992). *Writing to Learn Biology.* Harcourt Brace Jovanovich.

Moran, K. (2016). *How Chunking Helps Processing.* Nielsen Norman Group. https://www.nngroup.com/articles/chunking/

Morris, S. M. (2018). Online learning shouldn't be "less than". *Inside Higher Ed.* Retrieved from https://www.insidehighered.com/digital-learning/views/2018/04/04/are-we-giving-online-students-education-all-nuance-and-complexity

Morrison, J. Q., Russell, C., Dyer, S., Metcalf, T., & Rahschulte, R. L. (2014). Organizational structures and processes to support and sustain effective technical assistance in a state-wide multi-tiered system of support initiative. *Journal of Education and Training Studies, 2*(3), 129–137. doi:10.11114/jets.v2i3.415

Mo, S. (2011). Evidence on instructional technology and student engagement in an auditing course. *Academy of Educational Leadership Journal, 15*(4). http://citeseerx.ist.psu.edu/viewdoc/download?doi=10.1.1.727.5418&rep=rep1&type=pdf#page=157

Murata, R. (2002). What does team teaching mean? A case study of interdisciplinary teaming. *The Journal of Educational Research, 96*(2), 67–77. doi:10.1080/00220670209598794

Murnane, R. J. (2013). US high school graduation rates: Patterns and explanations. *Journal of Economic Literature, 51*(2), 370–422. doi:10.1257/jel.51.2.370

Muthuprasad, T., Aiswarya, S., Aditya, K. S., & Jha, G. K. (2021). Students' perception and preference for online education in India during COVID-19 pandemic. *Social Sciences & Humanities Open, 3*(1), 100101. doi:10.1016/j.ssaho.2020.100101 PMID:34173507

National Commission on Excellence in Education. (1983). *A nation at risk*. Retrieved from https://www2.ed.gov/pubs/NatAtRisk/risk.html

Newfield, C. (2011). *Unmaking the public university: The forty-year assault on the middle class.* Harvard University Press. doi:10.2307/j.ctv1cbn3np

Newman, B. (1994). *The Marketing of the President: Political Marketing as Campaign Strategy.* Sage.

Nimavat, N., Singh, S., Fichadiya, N., Sharma, P., Patel, N., Kumar, M., Chauhan, G., & Pandit, N. (2021). Online Medical Education in India–Different Challenges and Probable Solutions in the Age of COVID-19. *Advances in Medical Education and Practice, 12*, 237–243. doi:10.2147/AMEP.S295728 PMID:33692645

Noe, R. A. (2009). *İnsan Kaynaklarının Eğitimi ve Geliştirilmesi.* Beta Basım A. Ş.

Northouse, P. G. (2019). *Leadership: theory and practice* (8th ed.). SAGE Publications, Inc.

November, A. (2010). Power Down or Power Up? In H. Jacobs Hayes (Ed.), *Curriculum 21: Essential education for a changing world.* ASCD.

Office of Civil Rights. (2021). *Education in a pandemic: The disparate impacts of COVID-19 on America's students.* United States Department of Education. https://www2.ed.gov/about/offices/list/ocr/docs/20210608-impacts-of-covid19.pdf

Orakcı, Ş. (2020). The future of online learning and teaching in higher education. In Global Approaches to Sustainability Through Learning and Education. Hershey, PA: IGI Global. doi:10.4018/978-1-7998-0062-0.ch003

Orakcı, Ş., & Gelişli, Y. (2021). Educational policy actions in the times of Covid-19 and suggestions for future applications in Turkey. In L. Kyei-Blankson, J. Blankson, & E. Ntuli (Eds.), *Handbook of Research on Inequities in Online Education During Global Crises* (pp. 475–493). IGI Global. doi:10.4018/978-1-7998-6533-9.ch024

Orçanlı, K., & Bekmezci, M. (2020). Üniversite öğrencilerinin COVID-19 pandemisinde uzaktan eğitim algısının belirlenmesi ve bazı demografik değişkenlerle ilişkisi. *Uluslararası İktisadi ve İdari Bilimler Dergisi, 6*(2), 88–108. doi:10.29131/uiibd.836277

Özçınar, H., & Öztürk, E. (2008). Student opinions about case discussions in online environments. *Yuzuncu Yıl University Journal of Educational Faculty, 5*(2), 154–178.

Özmen, Z. M. (2010). Bir lisansüstü öğrencisinin telekonferans ve uzaktan eğitim uygulamaları dersindeki deneyimleri. *Turkish Journal of Computer and Mathematics Education (Turcomat)*, *1*(2), 217–232.

Palloff, R. M., & Pratt, K. (2003). *The Virtual Student: A Profile and Guide*. Jossey - Bass.

Palloff, R. M., & Pratt, K. (2009). *Assessing the Online Learner: Resources and Strategies for the Faculty*. Jossey - Bass.

Pandit, D., & Swati, A. (2021). *Exploring challenges of online education in COVID times*. FIIB Business Review. doi:10.1177/2319714520986254

Pappas, C. (2016). *Top 8 eLearning Barriers that Inhibit Online Learners Engagement with eLearning Content*. eLearning Industry. https://elearningindustry.com/top-elearning-barriers-that-inhibit-online-learners-engagement-elearning-content

Park, Y. (2011). A Pedagogical Framework for M-learning: Categorizing Educational Applications of Mobile Technologies into Four Types. *International Review of Research in Open and Distance Learning*, *12*(2), 78–102. doi:10.19173/irrodl.v12i2.791

Paun, G. (2020). Building A Brand: Why A Strong Digital Presence Matters. *Forbes*. https://www.forbes.com/sites/forbesagencycouncil/2020/07/02/building-a-brand-why-a-strong-digital-presence-matters/?sh=306ff1a849f2

Pease, M. A., & Kuhn, D. (2011). Experimental analysis of the effective components of problem-based learning. *Science Education*, *95*(1), 57–86. doi:10.1002ce.20412

Pekrun, R., Goetz, T., Titz, W., & Perry, R. P. (2002). Academic emotions in students' self-regulated learning and achievement: A program of qualitative and quantitative research. *Educational Psychologist*, *37*(2), 91–105. doi:10.1207/S15326985EP3702_4

Perez, A. M. (2020). *An investigation of student and staff perceptions of standardized testing participation as a blended/online high school that serves at-risk students* (Publication No. 28151905) [Doctoral dissertation, Regent University]. ProQuest Dissertations Publishing.

Peters, O. (1988). Distance teaching and industrial production: A comparative interpretation in ouline. In D. Sewart, D. Keegan, & B. Holmberg (Eds.), *Distance education: International perspectives* (pp. 95–113). Routledge.

Peters, O. (2010). *Distance Education in Transition* (5th ed.). BIS-Verlag der Carl von Ossietzky Universität Oldenburg.

Pierson, R. (2003). *Every kid needs a champion*. Retrieved from: https://www.ted.com/talks/rita_pierson_every_kid_needs_a_champion?language=en

Pintrich, P. R. (1989). The dynamic interplay of student motivation and cognition in the college classroom. In Advances in motivation and achievement: Motivation enhancing environments (pp. 117-160). Greenwich, CT: JAI Press

Pintrich, P. R. (2000). The role of goal orientation in self-regulated learning. In Handbook of self-regulation (pp. 451-502). Academic Press.

Pintrich, P. R., & Garcia, T. (1991). Student goal orientation and self-regulation in the college classroom. In Advances in motivation and achievement: Goals and self-regulatory processes. Greenwich, CT: JAI Press.

Pintrich, P. R. (1999). The role of motivation in promoting and sustaining self-regulated learning. *International Journal of Educational Research, 31*(6), 459–470. doi:10.1016/S0883-0355(99)00015-4

Pintrich, P. R., & De Groot, E. V. (1990). Motivational and self-regulated learning components of classroom academic performance. *Journal of Educational Psychology, 82*(1), 33–40. doi:10.1037/0022-0663.82.1.33

Pintrich, P. R., Smith, D. A. F., Garcia, T., & McKeachie, W. J. (1993). Reliability and predictive validity of the Motivated Strategies for Learning Questionnaire (MSLQ). *Educational and Psychological Measurement, 53*(3), 801–813. doi:10.1177/0013164493053003024

Plans, A. (2015). The every student succeeds act: Explained. *Education Week*. Retrieved from https://www.ride.ri.gov/Portals/0/Uploads/Documents/Information-and-Accountability-User-Friendly-Data/ESSA/CoP/Education_Week_Every_Student_Succeeds_Act_Explained.pdf

Ponnamperuma, G. G. (2005). Portfolio assessment. *Journal of Veterinary Medical Education, 32*(3), 279–284. doi:10.3138/jvme.32.3.279 PMID:16261482

Ponton, M. K. (1999). *The measurement of an adult's intention to exhibit personal initiative in autonomous learning* (Doctoral dissertation). Available from ProQuest Dissertations and Theses Global database. (UMI No. 304520327)

Potts, H. (2021). *A brain-changer: How stress redesigns our decision-making*. Retrieved from: https://thedecisionlab.com/insights/health/stress-redesigns-decision-making/

Pressley, M., & McCormick, C. (1995). *Advanced educational psychology for educators, researchers, and policymakers*. Harpercollins College Division.

Printy, S. M., & Williams, S. M. (2015). Principals' decisions: Implementing response to intervention. *Educational Policy, 29*(1), 179–205. doi:10.1177/0895904814556757

Reeves, T.C. (2000). Alternative assessment approaches for online learning environments in higher education. *Educational Computing Research, 23*(1), 101-111.

Reiss, S., & Reips, U. D. (2016). Online-Assessment. In K. Schweizer & C. DiStefano (Eds.), *Principles and Methods of Test Construction*. Hogrefe.

Ribner, A. D., Willoughby, M. T., & Blair, C. B.Family Life Project Key Investigators. (2017). Executive function buffers the association between early math and later academic skills. *Frontiers in Psychology, 8*, 869. doi:10.3389/fpsyg.2017.00869 PMID:28611712

Richards, E. (2020, Dec 12). Students are falling behind in online school. Where's the COVID-19 'disaster plan' to catch them up? *USA Today*. https://www.usatoday.com/in-depth/news/education/2020/12/13/covid-online-school-tutoring-plan/6334907002/

Rodgers, D. (2012). *The social media dilemma in education: Policy design, implementation and effects*. University of Southern California Dissertations and Theses, USC Digital Library. https://digitallibrary.usc.edu/CS.aspx?VP3=DamView&VBID=2A3BXZ88RGS9&SMLS=1&RW=1241&RH=591&FR_=1&W=1736&H=898

Rose, C. (2013). BYOD: An Examination of Bring Your Own Device In Business. *Review of Business Information Systems*, *17*(2), 65–70. doi:10.19030/rbis.v17i2.7846

Sadler, D. R. (1989). Formative assessment and the design of instructional systems. *Instructional Science*, *18*(2), 119–144. doi:10.1007/BF00117714

Sağırlı, M. Ö., Çiltaş, A., Azapağası, E., & Zehir, K. (2010). Yükseköğretimin öz-düzenlemeyi öğrenme becerilerine etkisi [The effect of higher education on self-regulation learning skills]. *Kastamonu Eğitim Dergisi*, *18*(2), 587–596.

Şahin, F. T. (2015). Beden eğitimi ve spor yüksekokulunda öğrenim gören öğrencilerin öz düzenleme yeterliliklerinin incelenmesi [Examination of self-regulation competencies of students studying at physical education and sports school]. *International Journal of Science Culture and Sport*, *4*, 425–438.

Saltürk, A., & Güngör, C. (2020). Üniversite öğrencilerinin gözünden COVID-19 pandemisinde uzaktan eğitime geçiş deneyimi. *Adıyaman Üniversitesi Sosyal Bilimler Enstitüsü Dergisi*, (36), 137–174. doi:10.14520/adyusbd.788716

Sawchuk, S. (2021, July 14). Extreme chronic absenteeism? Pandemic school attendance data is bleak, but incomplete. *Education Week*. https://www.edweek.org/technology/extreme-chronic-absenteeism-pandemic-school-attendance-data-is-bleak-but-incomplete/2021/07

Sawyer, R. D., & Norris, J. (2012). *Understanding qualitative research: Duoethnography*. Oxford University Press. doi:10.1093/acprof:osobl/9780199757404.001.0001

Sawyer, R., & Norris, J. (2015). Spr). Duoethnography: A retrospective 10 years after. *International Review of Qualitative Research*, *8*(1), 1–4. doi:10.1525/irqr.2015.8.1.1

Schachter, R. (2013). Solving our algebra problem: Getting all students through algebra I to improve graduation rates. *District Administration*, *49*(5), 43–46. https://eric.ed.gov/?id=EJ1013968&source=post_page------------------------

Schindler, L. A., Burkholder, G. J., Morad, O. A., & Marsh, C. (2017). Computer-based technology and student engagement: A critical review of the literature. *International Journal of Education Technology in Higher Education*, *14*(25), 25. Advance online publication. doi:10.118641239-017-0063-0

Schrum, L., & Hong, S. (2002). From the field: Characteristics of successful tertiary online students and strategies of experienced online. *Education and Information Technologies, 7*(1), 5–16. doi:10.1023/A:1015354423055

Schunk, D. H. (2001). Social cognitive theory and selfregulated learning. In Self-regulated learning and academic achievement: Theoretical perspectives (pp. 125-152). Mahwah, NJ: Erlbaum.

Schunk, D. H. (2012). Social cognitive theory. In APA educational psychology handbook. Vol. 1: Theories constructs, and critical Issues (pp. 101–123). Washington, DC: American Psychological Association.

Schunk, D. H., & Rice, J. M. (1987). Enhancing comprehension skill and self-efficacy with strategy value information. *Journal of Reading Behavior, 19*(3), 285–302. doi:10.1080/10862968709547605

Schunk, D. H., & Zimmerman, B. J. (Eds.). (2012). *Motivation and self-regulated learning: Theory, research, and applications.* Routledge. doi:10.4324/9780203831076

Scott, P. (1995). *The meanings of mass higher education.* The Society for Research into Higher Education & Open University Press.

Scott, P. (2000). Globalisation and higher education: Challenges for the 21st century. *Journal of Studies in International Education, 4*(1), 3–10. doi:10.1177/102831530000400102

Seifert, T., & Feliks, O. (2018). Online self-assessment and peerassessment as a tool to enhance student-teachers' assessment skills. *Assessment & Evaluation in Higher Education, 44*(2), 169–185. doi:10.1080/02602938.2018.1487023

Senge, P., Smith, B., Kruschwitz, N., Laur, J., & Schley, S. (2008). *The necessary revolution: How individuals and organizations are working together to create a sustainable world.* Doubleday.

Serneels, P., & Dercon, S. (2021). Aspirations, Poverty, and Education. Evidence from India. *The Journal of Development Studies, 57*(1), 163–183. doi:10.1080/00220388.2020.1806242

Sevli, O. (2011). *Bulut bilişim ve eğitim alanında örnek bir uygulama* (Unpublished master's thesis). Süleyman Demirel Üniversitesi, Isparta.

Shaked, H. (2021, May). Instructional leadership in times of crises and the goal of schooling. In J. Glanz (Ed.), *Crisis and Pandemic Leadership: Implications for Meeting the Needs of Students, Teachers, and Parents* (p. 71). Rowman & Littlefield.

Shank, P., & Sitze, A. (2004). *Making Sense of Online Learning A Guide for Beginners and the Truly Skeptical.* John Wiley & Sons, Inc.

Sharples, M. (2013). Mobile learning: Research, practice and challenges. *Distance Education in China, 3*(5), 5–11.

Sheninger, E. (2014). *Digital leadership: Changing paradigms for changing times. Corwin.* Ontario Principals Council.

Sheskey, T. (2010). Creating Learning Connections with Today's Tech-Savvy Student. In H. Jacobs Hayes (Ed.), *Curriculum 21: Essential education for a changing world*. ASCD.

Siemens, G. (2004). *Connectivism: A learning theory for the digital age*. http://www.elearnspace.org/Articles/connectivism.htm

Siemens, G. (2008). *About: Description of connectivism. Connectivism: A learning theory for today's learner*. http://www.connectivism.ca/about.html

Siemens, G. (2005). Connectivism: A learning theory for the digital age. *International Journal of Instructional Technology & Distance Learning, 2*(1), 1–8.

Simonson, M., Smaldino, S., Albright, M., & Zvacek, S. (2006). *Teaching and learning at a distance: Foundations of distance education* (3rd ed.). Prentice Hall.

Sinclair, P. M., Levett-Jones, T., Morris, A., Carter, B., Bennett, P. N., & Kable, A. (2017). High engagement, high quality: A guiding framework for developing empirically informed asynchronous e-learning programs for health professional educators. *Nursing & Health Sciences, 19*(1), 126–137. doi:10.1111/nhs.12322 PMID:28090732

Skylar, A., Higgins, K., Boone, R., Jones, P., Pierce, T., & Gelfer, J. (2005). Distance education: An exploration of alternative methods and types of instructional media in teacher education. *The Journal of Special Education, 20*(3), 25–33.

Smidt, H., Thornton, M., & Abhari, K. (2017). The future of social learning: A novel approach to connectivism. *Proceedings of the 50th Hawaii International Conference on System Sciences*. 10.24251/HICSS.2017.256

Soares, J. M., Sampaio, A., Ferreira, L. M., Santos, N. C., Marques, F., Palha, J. A., Cerqueira, J. J., & Sousa, N. (2012). Stress-induced changes in human decision-making are reversible. *Translational Psychiatry, 2*(7), e131. Advance online publication. doi:10.1038/tp.2012.59 PMID:22760555

Sparks, S. D. (2019). Why Teacher-Student Relationships Matter. *Education Week*. https://www.edweek.org/teaching-learning/why-teacher-student-relationships-matter/2019/03

Spoelma, J. (2018). *Communication Breakdown: How Misunderstandings Happen and What to Do About Them*. https://careerforesight.co/blog-feed/communication-breakdown-how-misunderstandings-happen-and-what-to-do-about-it

Steinberg, E. R. (1991). *Computer-assisted instruction: A synthesis of theory, practice and technology*. Lawrence Erlbaum.

Stephen, S. A. (2015). Enhancing the learning experience in finance using online video clips. *Journal of Financial Education*, 103-116.

Stevens Initiative. (2021). *2021 Survey of the Virtual Exchange Field Report*. Retrieved from https://www.stevensinitiative.org/wp-content/uploads/2021/11/2021-Survey-of-Virtual-Exchange-Field-Report.pdf

Stone, R. J. (1991). Virtual Reality and Cyberspace: From Science Fiction To Science Fact. *Information Services & Use*, *11*(5-6), 283–300. doi:10.3233/ISU-1991-115-603

Susam, T., Durnalı, M., & Orakcı, Ş. (2020). Administering education and training through a web-based system: E-curriculum. In M. Durnalı (Ed.), *Utilizing Technology, Knowledge, and Smart Systems in Educational Administration and Leadership*. IGI Global. doi:10.4018/978-1-7998-1408-5.ch002

Tabachnick, B., & Fidell, L. (2013). *Using multivariate statistics, 6th international edition (cover) edn*. Sage Publications.

The Flippen Group. (2006). *The Flippen Group capturing kids' hearts: Case studies for the Texas Education Agency*. Downloaded from https://www.flippengroup.com/pdf/funding/TEA8CaseStudies.pdf

The Flippen Group. (2016). *Social contract samples: Inspiration for creating a powerful social contract*. Author.

The UDL Guidelines. (n.d.). *CAST*. https://udlguidelines.cast.org

Thoresen, C. E., & Mahoney, M. J. (1974). *Behavioral self-control*. Holt, Rinehart & Winston.

Thornhill, S., Asensio, M., & Young, C. (2002). *Video Streaming. A guide for educational development*. JISC.

Trygestad, J. (1997). *Chaos in the classroom: An application of chaos theory*. Presented at the Annual Meeting of the American Educational Research Association, Chicago, Il.

Tümen Akyıldız, S. (2020). Covid-19 sürecinde uygulanan çevrimiçi derslerde üniversite öğrencilerinin öz-düzenlemeli öğrenme düzeyinin incelenmesi [Examining the self-regulated learning level of university students in online courses applied during the Covid-19 process]. In E. Yeşilyurt (Ed.), Eğitim Sosyal ve Beşeri Bilimlerine Multidisipliner Bakış [Multidisciplinary Perspective on Education, Social Sciences and Humanities] (pp. 135 -156). İstanbul: Güven Plus Grup Danışmanlık Yayınları.

U. S. Office of the Press Secretary. (2015, Dec. 2). *Fact sheet: Congress acts to fix no child left behind*. Retrieved from https://obamawhitehouse.archives.gov/the-press-office/2015/12/03/fact-sheet-congress-acts-fix-no-child-left-behind

U.S. Department of Education. (2016). *Programs: Centers for international business education*. Retrieved from https://www2.ed.gov/programs/iegpscibe/index.html

U.S. Dept. of Education. (2020). *Every Student Succeeds Act*. Retrieved from https://www2.ed.gov/policy/elsec/leg/essa/index.html

UNESCO. (2002). *Open and Distance Learning. Trends, Policy and Strategy Considerations*. UNESCO.

University of Oxford. (2014). *International applicants*. Retrieved from https://www.ox.ac.uk/

Uşun, S. (2006). Uzaktan Eğitim. Ankara: Nobel Yayınları.

Van der Pol, J., Van den Berg, B. A. M., Admiraal, W. F., & Simons, P. R. J. (2008). The nature, reception, and use of online peer feedback in higher education. *Computers & Education, 51*, 1804–1817. doi: .06.001 doi:10.1016/j.compedu.2008

Venkatesh, V., & Davis, F. D. (2000). A theoretical extension of the technology acceptance model: Four longitudinal field studies. *Management Science, 46*(2), 186–204. doi:10.1287/mnsc.46.2.186.11926

Voice. (n.d.). *Literary Terms.* https://literaryterms.net/voice/

Vygotsky, L. (1962). *Thought and language.* MIT Press. doi:10.1037/11193-000

Waggoner, M. (1992). Planning for the use of computer conferencing in collaborative learning. In D. Carey, R. Carey, D. Willis, & J. Willis (Eds.), *Technology and teacher education annual-1992* (pp. 556–561). Association for the Advancement of Computing in Education.

Wardlow, L. (2016). *The every student succeeds act in historical context.* Pearson. Retrieved from www.pearsoned.com/every-student-succeeds-act-historical/

Washington. (2020). *I save myself: Five reasons why principals leave their schools.* Retrieved from: https://theeducatorsroom.com/i-saved-myself-five-reasons-why-principals-leave-their-schools/

Westhuizen, D. (2016). Guidelines for Online Assessment for Educators. Commonwealth of Learning.

Wiggins, G. (2015). 27 Characteristics of Authentic Assessment. *Teach Thought.* https://www.teachthought.com/pedagogy/27-characteristics-of-authentic-assessment/

Wilkinson, C., Hillier, R., Padfield, G., & Harrison, J. (1999). The effects of volleyball software on female junior high school students' volleyball Performance. *Physical Educator, 4*, 202–209.

William, D., & Scalise, K. (2021). Formative Assessment for Remote Teaching: Evidence and Feedback. *Respond & Reimagine: Academics in Uncertain Times,* (16), 9.

Wolters, C., Yu, S., & Pintrich, P. R. (1996). The relation between goal orientation and students' motivational beliefs and self-regulated learning. *Learning and Individual Differences, 8*(3), 211–238. doi:10.1016/S1041-6080(96)90015-1

Wong, R. M. F., & Hew, K. F. (2010). The Impact of Blogging and Scaffolding on Primary School Pupils' Narrative Writing: A Case Study. *International Journal of Web-Based Learning and Teaching Technologies, 5*(2), 1–17. doi:10.4018/jwltt.2010040101

Yakar, L. Y., & Yakar, Z. Y. (2021). Eğitim fakültesi öğrencilerinin uzaktan eğitime karşı tutumlarının ve e-öğrenmeye hazır bulunuşluklarının incelenmesi. *Mersin Üniversitesi Eğitim Fakültesi Dergisi, 17*(1), 1–21.

Yamamoto G. T & Altun, D. (2020). Coronavirüs ve Çevrimiçi (Online) Eğitimin Önlenemeyen Yükselişi. *Üniversite Araştırmaları Dergisi, 3*(1), 25-34.

Zhao, H., Chen, L., & Panda, S. (2014). Self-regulated learning ability of Chinese distance learners. *British Journal of Educational Technology, 45*(5), 941–958. doi:10.1111/bjet.12118

Zimmerman, B. J. & Schunk, D. H. (2001). Reflections on theories of self-regulated learning and academic achievement. *Self-regulated learning and academic achievement: Theoretical perspectives, 2*, 289-307.

Zimmerman, B. J. (2000). Attaining self-regulation: A social cognitive perspective. In Handbook of self-regulation (pp. 13–39). Academic Press.

Zimmerman, B. J., & Martinez-Pons, M. (1992). Perceptions of efficacy and strategy use in the self-regulation of learning. In Student perceptions in the classroom: Causes and consequences (pp. 185-207). Hillsdale, NJ: Erlbaum.

Zimmerman, B. J., & Schunk, D. H. (2001). *Self-regulated learning and academic achievement: Theoretical perspectives.* Routledge.

Zimmerman, B. J. (2002). Becoming a self-regulated learner: An overview. *Theory into Practice, 41*(2), 64–70. doi:10.120715430421tip4102_2

Zimmerman, B. J., & Kitsantas, A. (1997). Developmental phases in self-regulation: Shifting from process to outcome goals. *Journal of Educational Psychology, 89*(1), 29–36. doi:10.1037/0022-0663.89.1.29

Zimmerman, B. J., & Martinez-Pons, M. (1988). Construct validation of a strategy model of student self-regulated learning. *Journal of Educational Psychology, 80*(3), 284–290. doi:10.1037/0022-0663.80.3.284

About the Contributors

Aaron Michael Perez recently graduated from Regent University and is the Principal for GOAL High School in the Denver Region, an alternative education blended/online high school in Colorado.

Senol Orakci is a lecturer in the Department of Curriculum and Instruction at Aksaray University in Turkey. His work focuses on thinking skills, education technology, teacher education, curriculum studies, and international education.

* * *

Marina Apaydin is an associate professor of management at The American University in Cairo with over a decade of teaching experience in the Middle East and North Africa. Apaydin holds a PhD degree in strategic management and innovation from the Western University (Canada), an MBA in finance and international business and an MA in Islamic studies, both from the University of California at Los Angeles (UCLA), and a MS in Unmanned Aerial Vehicles (UAV) from the Leningrad Electrical Engineering University (LETI). Before moving to academia, Apaydin held a position of the deputy director for management at UNESCO's World Heritage Center in Paris, which had culminated two decades of her prior professional experience in finance, business consulting, and marketing in several industries across Europe, the Middle East, and the USA. Apaydin developed and published the 3A framework for critical thinking, which later served as a basis for Contemporary Management textbook by McGraw-Hill. It also became a way of life for hundreds of her students who adopted this acronym for their alumni association. She taught strategic and cross-cultural management, innovation, international business, decision-making, change management, team-building, and business communications and delivered workshops on case writing, teaching, and learning to professors and students at several universities in Canada, Turkey, China, Egypt, and Lebanon, both, in situ and virtually. She also has published impact-factor academic and practitioner articles on this subject. Apaydin works and teaches in English, French, Italian, Russian, and Arabic.

Neslihan Arikan Fidan works as an academic in the Department of the Physical Education and Sport Teaching at the Faculty of Sport Sciences, Gazi University, Turkey since 11 years. Academic interests are sports sociology, sports philosophy, sports education, and sports history. She takes part in two projects that are still being carried out at the university.

Jennifer Bowens has a Masters in Education from Ashford University. She is currently serving as an Assistant Principal at GOAL High School, which is an online/blended high school in Colorado that primarily serves at-risk students. She has spent nearly 10 years in this setting, helping students find success in a caring, supportive, and personalized hybrid environment.

John D. Branch currently teaches a variety of marketing and international business courses at the undergraduate, MBA, and executive levels at the Stephen M. Ross School of Business at the University of Michigan (USA), and serves as Co-Director of the Yaffe Digital Media Initiative. Previously, he was Academic Director of the School's weekend and evening MBA programmes; earlier, he was also Director of Educational Outreach at the University's William Davidson Institute. John also holds an appointment at the University's Center for Russian, East European, & Eurasian Studies.

Alvaro Brito is an educator with a Master's Degree in Teaching from the University of Southern California and a Master's Degree in Educational Technology from California State University, Fullerton. A fully credentialed teacher and currently serving teachers as a 21st Century Learning Specialist at Compton Unified School District. Alvaro is currently enrolled in the Ed.D Educational Technology Program at Boise State University.

Kristen Carlson is an Assistant Professor of Curriculum & Instruction with research interests in learning design, online learning, authentic assessment, and teacher effectiveness. Experience in teaching science education grades 5 through 12, teacher education pedagogy and foundation courses, field experience supervision, coordinator of the teacher education unit performance assessment, program director of graduate level technology integration, instructional design, and educational leadership & technology.

Mehmet Durnali, Ph.D., received his doctorate in Education Administration in 2018 from the Institute of Educational Science at Hacettepe University, Turkey. He is an associate professor of educational sciences at the Faculty of Education, Zonguldak Bülent Ecevit University. He has published several books, book chapters, articles and conference papers in the field of educational administration, school effectiveness, school leadership, educational supervision, psychological assessment, teacher training, organizational goals, organizational behaviors, psychological assessment, the use of ICT in education, knowledge management, technological leadership, lifelong learning and project management.

Faylyn Emma is currently a MTSS Coordinator for a full-time, public, virtual school and pursuing a doctorate in Education Leadership and Policy Administration from the University of Florida. She has a masters degree in Mathematics Education from Georgia State University and a bachelors of arts in English Literature from the University of Central Florida. She has 16 years of experience supporting struggling students across all academic levels in a variety of settings.

Prasad G. is Assistant Professor (Sr.Gr.), Aerospace Engineering, Dayananda Sagar University, Bangalore, India. Prof. Prasad G, received his Masters degree and Bachelors degree in Aeronautical Engineering from Anna University. He has 7 years of teaching experience. He is SPOC for SWAYAM NPTEL Local chapter and Indian Space Research Organisation IIRS coordinator at Dayananda Sagar University, Bangalore, India. Prior to joining Dayananda Sagar University, he worked at Anna University. He has published 20 articles in reputed Scopus Indexed International Journals with good Impact Factor. 10 Journals related to Unmanned Aerial Vehicle and Industry 5.0. He has completed two funded project sponsored by The Institution of Engineers (India) and Tamilnadu State Council for Science and Technology. Awarded Indian National Science Academy (INSA) Visiting Scientist Programme 2019 and Awarded Science Academies' Summer Research Fellowship Programme (SRPF) 2019. He is a Professional Membership of American Institute of Aeronautics and Astronautics, Institution of Engineers, Life Member in Indian Cryogenic Council and Life Member in Shock Wave Society. Reviewer in Aircraft Engineering and Aerospace Technology, International Journal of Engine Research and Journal of The Institution of Engineers (India): Series C.

Amy Gillett is the vice president of the Education sector and specializes in designing and delivering executive education programs in emerging markets. Prior to joining WDI, Gillett served in the foreign service in Prague, Czech Republic as a Masaryk Fellow responsible for political and economic research. She also worked as a marketing executive for Hewlett-Packard and The Clorox Company. She has a

Master of Business Administration degree from Cornell University where she attended as a Park Leadership Fellow, a master's degree in Russian and Eastern European studies from Stanford University and a bachelor's degree in Slavic languages and literature from Stanford University. Additionally, Gillett holds certificates from the Pushkin Institute in Moscow and St. Petersburg State University in Russia. She is fluent in Russian and speaks some Czech, French, and Spanish.

Ferman Konukman, Ph.D., is an Assistant Professor of Physical Education in the Department of Physical Education at Qatar University, Doha in QATAR. Dr. Konukman's education includes a PhD in the Health & Physical Education Program at Virginia Polytechnic Institute and State University (Virginia Tech); an M. Ed degree from the University of Nebraska Lincoln, Department of Health & Human Performance with an emphasis in Physical Education and Sport Studies; an M. Sc. degree from Virginia Polytechnic Institute, Health Promotion Program; and an undergraduate degree in Physical Education & Sports from Middle East Technical University in Ankara, Turkey. He was a faculty member at Central Washington University Ellensburg and State University of New York (SUNY) The College at Brockport. His research interests are children's physical activity and health, teaching and coaching effectiveness in PE and teaching sport skills to children with autism.

Juliana M. Namada is an Assistant Professor of Strategic Management at United States International University- Africa, School of Business. She holds a PhD and master's in business administration specializing in Strategic Management from the University of Nairobi, School of Business. She teaches and supervises students in Business Administration at undergraduate, Masters and Doctoral levels in the university. She has published in refereed journals both locally and internationally. She has published four book chapters. Her research interests are in strategic management with a bias in strategic planning. Dr. Juliana is a member of the Academy of Management and Africa Academy of Management. In terms of service to the profession, she is an editorial member of two peer reviewed journals and reviews for several refereed journals.

Devery J. Rodgers has been impacting education for over 25 years as a K12 teacher, administrator, and university professor. During her tenure, Dr. Rodgers has led three education technology departments, and her primary research interest is Education Technology Leadership. Having received her doctorate in Education Leadership from the University of Southern California, she is currently an Education Leadership Professor at the California State University, Long Beach. Dr. Rodgers is engaged in a deep and long-term exploration of the application of the tenets, tools, and methods towards performance improvement in education, expanding on her research interests of Education Technology Leadership (Tech Equity with African-American girls, digital technologies in teaching and learning, and instructional technology professional development). Her experiences build on her goal to promote a quality education for all students.

Ertan Tufekcioglu is a lecturer in the physical education department at King Fahd University of Petroleum and Minerals. He completed his doctorate at Marmara University, Department of Sports and Health. His research focuses on WATSU® therapy, in-water performance improvement and rehabilitation practices and body-based life coaching.

Index

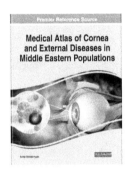
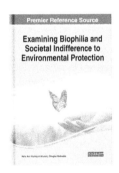
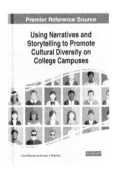

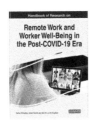

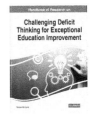

Milton Keynes UK
Ingram Content Group UK Ltd.
UKHW051342121124
2786UKWH00032B/140